TEACHER'S GUIDE

Succeeding in Mathematics

LEVEL 4

WORKTEXT

Revised

Otto C. Bassler

Professor of Mathematics Education
George Peabody College for Teachers of Vanderbilt University
Nashville, Tennessee

John R. Kolb

Professor of Mathematics and Mathematics Education
North Carolina State University
Raleigh, North Carolina

Mary S. Craighead

Primary Teacher, St. Vincent School
Nashville, Tennessee

William L. Gray

Associate Professor of Education
University of Maryland Baltimore County
Baltimore, Maryland

Illustrated by Ellen Goins

Steck-Vaughn Company   Austin, Texas

GRADE LEVEL DESIGNATIONS

The books in the K-6 *Succeeding in Mathematics* series are ungraded to provide teachers flexibility in meeting individual needs of their pupils. To determine the suggested grade level of books, refer to the ISBN number which is printed above the copyright notices and on the back of each cover. These numbers are coded to indicate grade levels. The next-to-last digit specifies the suggested level, beginning with 0 for Level K. Thus, the 3 in 0973-2 indicates a Level 3 book.

Level	Pupil's Edition	Teacher's Edition
K	0970-8	0990-2
1	0971-6	0991-0
2	0972-4	0992-9
3	0973-2	0993-7
4	0974-0	0994-5
5	0975-9	0995-3
6	0976-7	0996-1

T.E. ISBN 0-8114-0994-5

Copyright © 1981 by Steck-Vaughn Company, Austin, Texas
Also copyright 1977

6 7 8 9 0 HG 92

Contents

Introduction

Succeeding in Mathematics is a K-6 series designed and organized for average and below average students in mathematics. Prerequisite concepts and procedures are thoroughly reviewed before proceeding gradually into unfamiliar material. The program is organized in a manner which allows pupils to be taught in groups according to differences in their abilities and their particular mathematical needs. Teachers may use the varied activities suggested in the Teacher's Edition progressively with the class or individually with small groups. Thus, a wide range of needs can be met simultaneously. By varying the instructional activities presented, the teacher can work with several groups of children on the same material, but at a different stage of complexity and at a different pace. The Worktext® are organized to enable students to work with varying levels of independence—either individually, in pairs, in small groups, or as a class.

In the *Succeeding in Mathematics* program, fundamental skills and concepts are emphasized. A basic strand of mathematical content is stressed—that which focuses upon operations and problem solving with whole numbers and fractional numbers. Geometric content concentrates upon metric geometry and measurement rather than nonmetric geometry. This reflects the philosophy that it is better for students to master the essential core of basic mathematics rather than skim over a wide span of mathematical topics.

PHILOSOPHY OF THE PROGRAM

Children learn by acting on their environment. The child's actions come first. Only after the action can experiences be represented in thought and expressed in language. The foundation of each mathematical idea must be the child's active manipulation of concrete objects.

Since mathematical concepts and processes are abstract, they must go through several stages before they become formed in the child's mind. Mathematical ideas develop from actions to finished ideas in thought through the following stages.

Stage 1—Physical Manipulation of Objects. In this stage the child actually manipulates physical objects. He or she performs actions, such as putting two sets together, folding paper to form geometric shapes, and filling containers with water to determine which one holds more.

Stage 2—Mental Manipulation of Objects. After gaining experience in manipulating physical objects, the child begins to think about moving or changing the objects without actually performing these actions. In this stage the child may be dealing with pictures or representing objects in his or her thoughts and performing actions on them mentally. It is important to note that the objects and actions must be familiar ones.

Stage 3—Mental Manipulation of Ideas. Most mathematical ideas and processes require mental manipulation (actions carried out in thought) of abstract ideas. When the child can think of the numbers 15 and 19 abstractly and perform the operation addition on them without any physical referent, he or she is operating in Stage 3.

Lower level books in the *Succeeding in Mathematics* program deal exclusively with Stage 1 and Stage 2 behaviors. As children mature, more Stage 3 behaviors are expected of them, and by Levels 5 and 6 they should be working extensively with Stage 3 behaviors. Because students progress through these stages at varying rates, it is essential that instruction be somewhat individualized so that students who need instruction on an idea at a lower stage of development may get the help they need. If students are expected to perform in Stage 3 before they have developed through the other stages, they will probably be unsuccessful. The students may learn the new idea rotely, but it will not become a part of their operational thought. Many times when students are experiencing difficulty in learning a new mathematical idea, they need to return to an earlier stage to get a foundation for understanding. It is quite likely that much more time and more frequent returns to earlier stages will be necessary for slow learners.

Another feature of *Succeeding in Mathematics* is that it is success oriented. Students must be convinced that they can do mathematics before they will be willing to attempt it. By progressing gradually through the stages mentioned above, each student will have ample opportunity for successfully completing many mathematical tasks. All students should achieve success in Stages 1 and 2. There may, however, be some students who will have only limited success in Stage 3. These students should be able to perform all of the mathematical tasks when they are provided with a framework from the physical world which makes the task meaningful to them.

Succeeding in Mathematics presents a strong program for developing computational skills. A large percentage of the instructional program is devoted to developmental activities intended to build skill in computational routines. Previously learned skills are reviewed carefully. New material is encountered and mastered in small bits. Initial exercises for a new concept provide students with guidance and offer opportunities for them to check their progress. Later exercises gradually reduce the students' dependence upon outside guidance. Only after a new concept is fully developed and assimilated by students, are they required to perform the entire procedure without guidance. Thus, new material is actually taught, not just presented to students to learn themselves.

There is a substantial amount of drill and practice material in each Worktext®. Drill and practice material are only valuable after a sufficient amount of developmental teaching. It is only after students have had considerable exposure to a concept or skill that practice will be effective. It is the teacher's obligation to insure that sufficient developmental activities for understanding have been presented prior to having students practice the concept on a Worktext® page. Drill given too soon may cause students to attempt to rotely memorize the procedure to follow without first acquiring an understanding of the mathematics involved.

An integral part of this program is the wide variety of lessons which are designed to develop problem-solving skills and mathematical reasoning. Word problems have been carefully woven into the *Succeeding in Mathematics* program. Entire lessons are devoted to specific aspects of problem solving and mathematical reasoning, in addition to the many word problems which are scattered throughout each chapter. Students are taught to determine the correct operation to use in word problems, to translate verbal symbols into mathematical sentences, to solve the problems, to distinguish answers from solutions, and to check the reasonableness of answers. In building these skills, students learn how, when, and where the mathematics that they are learning can be applied. This makes the instructional program more meaningful to the students and provides additional motivation for learning mathematics. Problem solving is begun gradually with simple one-step problems in Levels K-4 and is extended to two-step problems in Levels 5-6.

One of the conditions that sometimes limits a student's learning of mathematics is the vocabulary used to describe and explain particular concepts. For this reason, the reading level and vocabulary of each Worktext® has been carefully controlled. The reading level has been kept well below the grade level of the mathematical content. Mathematics is the primary goal of *Succeeding in Mathematics*. Reading has been kept to a minimum. In this way students can more easily focus their attention on the mathematics involved rather than expending time and effort on attempting to read and translate verbal descriptions.

After students have completed each Worktext® page, their work should be checked. Students' attention should be directed to each incorrectly worked exercise, and care should be taken to insure that the students correct their work. Correcting errors provides a sense of accomplishment for students and helps to instill a feeling of succeeding in mathematics.

In Level K each Worktext® page should be used only as a check on how well students understood the activities which were used to explain or introduce a concept. In each subsequent level the amount of teaching done in the Worktext® increases. Thus, each page becomes less a checking device and more a teaching instrument. The number of activities used to teach concepts decreases with each level.

TEACHER'S EDITIONS

Each *Succeeding in Mathematics* Worktext® is accompanied by a Teacher's Edition which provides a guide for using the pupil's pages. The Teacher's Edition for each level consists of a detailed teaching guide which is bound in front of full-sized pupil's pages that have been annotated with answers to all exercises. At Levels 4-6 pupil pages have also been annotated with suggestions for teaching the lessons presented in the Worktext®.

The organization of each lesson in Levels K-6 is complete and easy to follow. Included is the Objective of the lesson, Background for the teacher, suggested Materials, Procedure to follow in teaching the lesson and using the Worktext® page, and Additional Activities for students who need further instruction.

The Objective is a precise statement or statements which indicate the purpose of the exercises on each Worktext® page. The Background section provides useful information, usually of a mathematical nature. It may summarize the mathematics involved in the lesson or provide the teacher with a deeper understanding of the mathematical foundation upon which the lesson is based. Other types of information found in this section include where the skills and concepts developed in one lesson are used in subsequent lessons, information that should be recalled by students prior to beginning the lesson, and places in the lesson where students may have difficulty achieving the specified objective. It is recommended that each Background section be read carefully before beginning to present the lesson to the students.

The materials necessary to teach a lesson are listed in the Materials section. Reference to this section provides the busy teacher with a list of suggested materials to be gathered before beginning to teach the lesson. Most of the suggested materials are readily available in the classroom. Of course, teachers may substitute other items for any of the materials whenever they wish. Sometimes, directions are given for students to make some materials. These materials should be kept for use in later lessons.

The Procedure section specifies activities that should be completed prior to having the students work in their Worktext®. These activities are described in detail and many times include statements and questions (printed in color) that the teacher might use in teaching the lesson. Generally, only one illustration of an activity is provided. Teachers should provide variations and repeat the activity several times before moving on to the next activity. As an activity progresses, the teacher should evaluate the success that students are having with the concept. The teacher should continue each activity until students have acquired the mathematical behavior embodied in the activity. Only after all the activities have been completed should students be required to work the Worktext® exercises.

Complete directions for using each Worktext® page are also provided under Procedure. To reduce the problems that are caused by reading deficiencies in students, the teacher should read the explanations on the Worktext® page with the class. When examples are provided in the student's book, it is important for the teacher to discuss them with the students to determine if the students understand the procedure to follow in completing exercises similar to the example.

The Additional Activities section includes suggestions for reinforcing concepts with those students who need further developmental work as indicated by their responses on the Worktext® page. Teachers are urged to use these and other activities as needed to help students achieve success with one concept before moving on to another one.

DIAGNOSTIC AND PRESCRIPTIVE FEATURES

Several features of the *Succeeding in Mathematics* program allow the teacher to continually assess student progress and prescribe appropriate correctives. The exercises on each Worktext® page in the lower level books are designed to assess whether or not students have achieved the objective set forth in the Teacher's Edition. These exercises should not be graded for the purpose of evaluating pupils. Rather, they should be used to determine if additional instructional activities are needed. If students cannot complete the exercises correctly, the instructional procedure used has not done an effective job. It then becomes necessary to reteach the material.

The developmental exercises are constructed to focus on just one step in a process or one particular aspect of a concept. Thus, when it is observed that a student is unable to complete a particular set of exercises, the teacher knows the particular obstacle the student has encountered and can act to eliminate it.

Students sometimes make errors that fall into patterns. By carefully observing the pattern, the difficulty the student has encountered can be pinpointed. Where such patterns can be identified, they are noted in the Teacher's Edition. The teacher is advised to look for these error patterns in each student's work.

Each chapter in the Level 1-6 Worktext® contains a Chapter Review and a Check-Up. The Chapter Review summarizes and synthesizes the concepts and skills developed within the chapter. The review pages should be used to determine if pupils need additional instruction on a particular concept. Page references for each exercise are given in the Teacher's Edition. This allows the teacher to direct the pupil to the Worktext® page where each type of exercise was presented in detail. The reviews enable students to see what concepts they have mastered before they complete the Check-Up. In doing so, they can get the additional work they need on the concepts they do not understand before they go on to the Check-Up. Thus, they should have mastered all the concepts and skills necessary to succeed on the Check-Up before they begin to work that page. The Check-Up should serve as a practice exercise. Students should complete the Check-Up independently. It, too, can be used to determine if the students have acquired all the behaviors taught in the chapter. If they have not, it will be necessary to go back and reteach the concepts again. Students who do well on the Chapter Review should also do well on the Check-Up—thus reinforcing their success in mathematics.

When students have mastered the material in a chapter, there is a booklet of Mastery Reviews for Levels 1-6 which can be used for the purpose of grading their work. Each of these Mastery Reviews is similar in nature to the Check-Ups in the Worktext®. The items are modified from the Check-Ups to prevent direct recall or recognition.

Assessment and evaluation of the students' work

is a continuous process. The students' work should be observed and assessed each day. The purpose of this assessment (with the exception of the Mastery Reviews) is not to grade students. Rather, the purpose is to provide them with knowledge of results and direction for improvement and to provide the teacher with feedback that can be used to design the most effective learning activities.

Scope and Sequence

for

Succeeding in Mathematics

The following pages illustrate the sequential development of the mathematical concepts and skills presented for Kindergarten through Level 6 in the *Succeeding in Mathematics* program. Each of the five major content strands is presented in its entirety on facing pages—Numbers and Numeration on pages x and xi, Addition and Subtraction on pages xii and xiii, Multiplication and Division on pages xiv and xv, Geometry and Measurement on pages xvi and xvii, and Problem Solving on pages xviii and xix.

Designed for easy reference from level to level within each content strand, the chart enables you to quickly determine what topics are presented within a particular content strand at each level.

NUMBERS AND NUMERATION

	KINDERGARTEN	LEVEL ONE	LEVEL TWO	LEVEL THREE
SETS	Identify sets of objects Identify and specify parts of sets Compare sets, using "more," "fewer," and "same as" Form one-to-one correspondence Join and separate sets	Identify sets Form one-to-one correspondence Recognize subsets Recognize equivalent sets Associate cardinal numbers with sets of objects Join sets as readiness for addition Separate sets as readiness for subtraction Recognize empty sets Compare sets, using "equal," "less than," and "greater than"	Join and separate sets Form sets with members to 100 Form arrays as readiness for multiplication	
WHOLE NUMBERS	Count to 20 Recognize zero as the name for empty set Identify number of objects in sets to 20 Write numerals through 9 Read and identify numerals to 20 Recognize order of numbers to 20	Count to 100 Read and write numerals through 99 Group objects in tens and ones Recognize zero as name for empty set Write expanded names to 99 Read and identify ordinal numbers and word names to 9th Read and write word names one through ten Recognize order of numbers to 99	Count to 500 Read and write numerals to 500 Identify place value—ones, tens, and hundreds Write expanded names for numbers to 500 Order numbers to 100 Recognize order of numbers to 500 • Use >, <, and = Read and identify ordinal numbers and word names to 20th	Count to 1000 Read and write numerals to 1000 Recognize place value—ones, tens, and hundreds Write expanded names to 1000 Order numbers to 1000 Read word names for numbers to 1000 Complete number sentences using >, <, and = Read and write Roman numerals less than 40
FRACTIONAL NUMBERS—FRACTIONS	Recognize one-half of a whole	Identify ½ of objects and sets Read and write ½ Identify ½ of even numbers 2 through 10	Identify fractional parts of a set or a whole—½, ⅓, ⅔, ¼, 2/4, ¾ Read and write ½, ⅓, ⅔, ¼, 2/4, ¾	Review halves, thirds, and fourths Identify fractional parts of a set or a whole—sixths, eighths, tenths, and hundredths Read and write fractions less than one Recognize fractions that name one whole Order fractions with like denominators, using pictures or number lines
FRACTIONAL NUMBERS—DECIMALS				Read and write names for money—dollars and cents
FRACTIONAL NUMBERS—RATIOS AND PERCENTS				

x

LEVEL FOUR	LEVEL FIVE	LEVEL SIX

Count to 10,000
Read and write numerals
   to 10,000
Recognize place value—
   ones, tens, hundreds,
   and thousands
Round numbers to
   nearest ten
Write expanded names
   to 10,000
Order numbers to 10,000
Read word names for
   numbers to 10,000
Read and write Roman
   numerals less than 400
	Identify periods and place value
	   to 999,999
	Write expanded names to 999,999
	Write word names for numbers
	   to 999,999
	Order numbers to 999,999
	Round numbers to nearest ten,
	   hundred, and thousand
		Identify periods and place value
		   to 999,999,999
		Write word names for numbers
		   to 999,999,999
		Round to any specified place value

Interpret parts of fractions—
   numerators and denomi-
   nators
Read and write mixed
   numerals
Relate improper fractions and
   mixed numerals, using
   pictures
Identify equivalent fractions,
   using pictures
Order fractions, using pictures
   or number lines
	Identify parts of fractions and mixed
	   numerals
	Distinguish among proper fractions, im-
	   proper fractions, and mixed numerals
	Name fractions and mixed numerals on
	   number lines
	Write word names for fractions with
	   denominators to twelfths
	Interpret a fraction as the answer to the
	   division of the numerator by the
	   denominator
	Write equivalent fractions in higher and
	   lower terms
	Find like denominators for fractions by
	   writing sets of equivalent fractions
	Order fractions and mixed numerals—like
	   and unlike denominators
	Identify and write fractions and mixed
	   numerals in lowest terms
	Rename improper fractions as mixed
	   numerals by division
	Write remainders in division as fractions
		Write equivalent fractions in higher and
		   lower terms by a short method
		Find like denominators for fractions and
		   mixed numerals by a short method
		Order mixed numerals and fractions by a
		   short method
		Rename improper fractions as mixed
		   numerals in lowest terms
		Rename mixed numerals as improper
		   fractions in lowest terms

Read and write names for
   money to $100
	Rename fractions and mixed numerals
	   (denominators of 10 or 100) as decimals
	Identify place value in decimals to
	   hundredths
	Read and write decimals to hundredths
	Rename decimals as fractions or mixed
	   numerals
	Identify and write equivalent decimals
	Order decimals to hundredths
	Round to the nearest one and tenth
		Identify place value in decimals to ten-
		   thousandths
		Read and write decimals to
		   ten-thousandths
		Rename decimals as fractions and mixed
		   numerals in lowest terms
		Round quotients to a specified place value
		   when renaming fractions as decimals by
		   division
		Order decimals to ten-thousandths
		Round to the nearest one, tenth, hundredth,
		   and thousandth

		Interpret the meaning of percent Interpret the meaning of ratio Relate percents to fractions and decimals

ADDITION AND SUBTRACTION

	KINDERGARTEN	LEVEL ONE	LEVEL TWO	LEVEL THREE
WHOLE NUMBERS	Find one more than a specified number to 10 Find one less than a specified number to 10 Complete addition facts with sums to 10 by counting Complete subtraction facts with minuends to 10 by counting Recognize the concept of addition as putting things together Recognize the concept of subtraction as taking things away	Add facts with sums to 10 Subtract facts with minuends to 10 Add 2-digit numbers (no renaming; restricted facts) Subtract 2-digit numbers (no renaming; restricted facts) Relate addition and subtraction Add and subtract facts on number lines	Add 100 basic facts Subtract 100 basic facts Identify related addition and subtraction facts Add 2-digit numbers (renaming ones as tens) Add 3-digit numbers with sums to 500 (no renaming) Subtract 2- and 3-digit numbers (no renaming)	Review 100 basic addition facts . Review 100 basic subtraction facts Identify parts of addition sentences Add 2- and 3-digit numbers (with renaming) Add columns of 1-digit numbers (four addends) Subtract 2- and 3-digit numbers (with renaming) Check subtraction by addition
FRACTIONAL NUMBERS—FRACTIONS				
FRACTIONAL NUMBERS—DECIMALS				Add and subtract with decimals as money (three digits)

LEVEL FOUR	LEVEL FIVE	LEVEL SIX
Identify parts of addition and subtraction sentences Add 4-digit numbers (with renaming) Add columns of 2-digit numbers (three addends) Rename across zeros in subtraction Check subtraction by addition	Add columns of 3-digit numbers (three addends) Review and extend renaming across zeros in subtraction Add and subtract 6-digit numbers Estimate sums and differences by rounding	Add and subtract 9-digit numbers Add columns of 4-digit numbers (four addends) Estimate sums and differences to appropriate place values
Add with fractions having like denominators— sums to 1 Subtract with fractions having like denominators—minuends to 1	Add and subtract with fractions— like and unlike denominators Add and subtract with mixed numerals—like and unlike denominators	Add and subtract with fractions and mixed numerals, using the short form Subtract with mixed numerals where a whole must be renamed—unlike denominators
Add and subtract with decimals as money (four digits)	Add and subtract with decimals to hundredths Estimate sums and differences rounding to specified place values	Add and subtract with decimals to ten-thousandths Place decimal points in sums and differences by estimating Annex zeros for renaming in subtraction

MULTIPLICATION AND DIVISION

	KINDERGARTEN	LEVEL ONE	LEVEL TWO	LEVEL THREE
WHOLE NUMBERS		Count by fives and tens to 100 Perform repeated addition on number lines as readiness for multiplication	Count by twos to 100 Count by fives and tens to 500 Find products by counting objects in arrays Perform multiplication as repeated addition Perform repeated subtraction with objects and on number lines as readiness for division	Skip count by any interval to 1000 Form arrays and partition sets of objects Show multiplication and division on number lines Multiply basic multiplication facts (restricted to 6 or less as a factor, including zero) Relate division facts to given multiplication facts Relate multiplication as repeated addition Relate division as repeated subtraction Relate multiplication and division as opposite operations Divide basic division facts (restricted to 6 or less as the divisor) Multiply a 1-digit number times a 2-digit number by writing partial products and adding Divide with 1-digit divisors and 1-digit quotients with remainders by using a subtractive algorithm Use a subtractive algorithm to divide with 1-digit divisors and 2-digit quotients with no remainders Relate fractions and division Identify parts of multiplication sentences Multiply three 1-digit factors (all factors restricted to 6 or less) Check division by multiplication
FRACTIONAL NUMBERS—FRACTIONS				
FRACTIONAL NUMBERS—DECIMALS				

LEVEL FOUR	LEVEL FIVE	LEVEL SIX
Identify parts of multiplication and division sentences Multiply 100 basic multiplication facts Divide 90 basic division facts Specify division facts from related multiplication facts Multiply three 1-digit factors Multiply a 1-digit number times a 3-digit number by writing partial products and by using the short form Find trial quotients Divide 1-digit divisors and 1- and 2-digit quotients with remainders by using the division algorithm in the long form Divide with multiples of 10 as the divisor and 1-digit quotients with no remainders by using the division algorithm in the long form Check division by multiplication and addition	Multiply mentally by 10, 100, 1000, and their multiples Multiply a 3-digit number times a 3-digit number by using the long and short forms Find trial quotients by using the first digit of the divisor and the first one or two digits of the dividend Correct trial quotients that are too large or too small Determine if a quotient has 1, 2, or 3 digits Use the long division algorithm with 2-digit divisors and 3-digit quotients in the long and short forms Perform long division with zeros in quotients Estimate products by rounding	Multiply by 3- and 4-digit factors with zeros in the multiplier Divide with 2-digit divisors and 4-digit quotients by using the short form
Find number of objects in fractional part of a set as readiness for multiplication with fractions	Multiply with fractions Multiply whole numbers times fractions Interpret multiplication with fractions as "of"	Review multiplying with fractions Multiply with mixed numerals Multiply two fractional numbers— one named by a fraction and the other by a mixed numeral Remove common factors to simplify fractions before multiplying Identify reciprocals of fractions Divide with fractions and mixed numerals
		Multiply and divide mentally with decimals by powers of ten to ten-thousandths Determine the position of the decimal point in quotients and products by estimation Multiply and divide decimals and place the decimal point in the answer by using estimation or the shortcut

GEOMETRY AND MEASUREMENT

	KINDERGARTEN	LEVEL ONE	LEVEL TWO	LEVEL THREE
NONMEASUREMENT	Identify and draw triangles, squares, rectangles, and circles	Identify and draw triangles, squares, rectangles, and circles Identify and draw points and segments Recognize end points and points between end points	Review identification of triangles, squares, rectangles, and circles Draw segments with given points as end points	Identify and draw lines, line segments, curves, and angles Identify right angles Identify plane regions bounded by triangles, squares, rectangles, and circles
MEASUREMENT	Compare lengths, weights, sizes, and temperatures Recognize penny, nickel, dime, and cent symbol (¢)	Recognize amounts of money—1¢, 5¢, 10¢, 25¢, 50¢, $1 Make change for values less than 10¢ Tell time to the hour Compare lengths and liquid capacities Find lengths and liquid capacities in nonstandard units Use a ruler to find lengths in centimeters and inches Find liquid capacities in liters Use the calendar to determine the day, week, month, and year Recognize the relationships between days and weeks	Extend recognization of coins and their values Make change for values less than $1 Tell time to nearest quarter hour Find lengths in meters and yards Read thermometers Compare lengths, weights, and liquid capacities Find weights in nonstandard units Use scales to find weights in grams, kilograms, and pounds Find liquid capacities in liters, quarts, and cups	Tell time to nearest minute Find lengths in millimeters, centimeters, half centimeters, meters, inches, half inches, feet, and yards Draw segments to a specified length Interpret and use kilometer as a measure of distance Find perimeters of triangles, rectangles, and squares by adding lengths Measure weights in grams, kilograms, pounds, and ounces Measure temperatures in degrees Celsius Measure liquid capacities in liters, milliliters, cups, pints, quarts, and gallons Find areas by counting square regions that cover rectangular regions Relate units within systems for length, weight, and liquid capacity

LEVEL FOUR	LEVEL FIVE	LEVEL SIX
Identify and draw lines, line segments, rays, and angles Identify and draw parallel lines and right angles Identify and draw types of quadrilaterals (rectangle, parallelogram, square) Identify diameters and radii of circles Identify planes Identify cubes, boxes, cylinders, spheres, and cones	Distinguish among line figures, plane figures, and space figures Classify angles as right, obtuse, or acute Distinguish among solid regions, plane regions, and their boundaries	Identify and draw perpendicular and parallel lines Draw rectangles, squares, right triangles, and parallelograms, using ruler and protractor Classify special quadrilaterals by their properties (rectangles, parallelograms, squares) Sketch circular cylinders, circular cones, pyramids, and prisms Draw a circle by locating the set of points a given distance from a fixed point Identify centers, radii, and diameters of circles Identify congruent and similar figures
Measure lengths to the nearest millimeter and eighth inch Find perimeters by measuring lengths of sides and adding Relate the sizes of metric units for measuring length Relate the sizes of English units for measuring length Relate units of length, weight, and liquid capacity in metric system Measure temperatures in degrees Celsius and degrees Fahrenheit Find areas of rectangular regions by counting and by multiplication Find volumes by counting number of cubes needed to build boxes	Relate the size of metric units of length, weight, and liquid capacity to the size of familiar objects Specify the relationships between units within systems for measuring length, weight, and liquid capacity Convert from whole units to other whole units within a system of measurement for length, weight, and liquid capacity Identify approximate Celsius readings for familiar temperature situations Compare angles visually and with a model Measure angles to the nearest 10°, using a degree ruler Distinguish between area and perimeter for the same shape Find areas of plane regions by counting standard units of area in the metric and English systems Find areas of rectangular regions by multiplying length times width Identify standard units of volume in the metric and English systems Compute volumes of boxes by multiplying length times width times height Add, subtract, and rename measures in the English system Add measures in the metric system	Measure angles to the nearest degree, using a protractor Use decimals to express metric units Use a formula to find areas of rectangular regions and square regions Use a formula to find perimeters of rectangles Use a formula to find volumes of boxes Interpret scale drawings Relate the measure of diameters to the circumferences of circles Convert whole and fractional units to other units within a system of measurement for length, weight, time, and liquid capacity Add, subtract, and multiply measures in the English system Add and multiply measures in the metric system

PROBLEM SOLVING

	KINDERGARTEN	LEVEL ONE	LEVEL TWO	LEVEL THREE
VERBAL PROBLEMS	Identify actions such as pushing together or taking apart in stories as readiness for addition and subtraction Compare sets in verbal situations, using "more," "fewer," and "same as"	Identify addition or subtraction from a given situation Choose correct number sentences for verbal or picture problems—addition and subtraction Identify answers for situations described verbally—addition and subtraction Write sentences for pictured actions—addition and subtraction	Identify the correct operation in short verbal statements—addition and subtraction Write number sentences to fit action situations or short verbal statements—addition and subtraction Solve problems, using addition and subtraction	Identify the correct operation to solve verbal problems—addition and subtraction Write and solve number sentences for verbal problems—addition, subtraction, multiplication, and division Solve problems when data is presented in charts, pictures, or maps
MATHEMATICAL REASONING				Check reasonableness of answers

LEVEL FOUR	LEVEL FIVE	LEVEL SIX
Identify and translate phrases that mean addition, subtraction, multiplication, and division Solve 1-step verbal problems involving addition, subtraction, multiplication, and division Select the correct data from pictures, charts, maps, and graphs Identify the correct operation and solve verbal problems —addition, subtraction, multiplication, and division Perform 2 consecutive operations as readiness for 2-step problems	Solve 2-step verbal problems Recognize and distinguish situations involving area, perimeter, and volume Convert given information before solving problems, such as one week is seven days Solve problems involving arithmetic averages Solve verbal problems involving fractional numbers—addition and subtraction Distinguish among addition, subtraction, multiplication, and division as the operation for solving verbal problems	Recognize and ignore extraneous data Solve verbal problems involving fractional numbers—addition, subtraction, multiplication, and division
Estimate answers in applied situations—addition and subtraction Identify simple number patterns Interpret data presented in bar graphs and picture graphs	Find exact and approximate solutions involving either addition, subtraction, or multiplication Distinguish between mathematical answers and solutions Utilize patterns to perform mathematical operations Select the best approximation Read and interpret picture graphs, bar graphs, line segment graphs, and circle graphs	Distinguish between mathematical answers and solutions Complete bar graphs and line segment graphs from given data Place decimal points to show reasonable approximations for measures of familiar objects and situations

Numbers and Numeration

Page 1

OBJECTIVES

- Count the objects in specified sets
- Compare the number of objects in different sets

BACKGROUND

Counting is the way we determine how many objects are in a set. When we count, we match the elements of the set to the counting numbers in a one-to-one fashion, that is, we match 1 to the first element, 2 to the second element, and so on. The last counting number that is used tells us the number of objects in the set.

Many different ways can be used to name numbers. We might name numbers by drawing a stick for each object in the set. Showing another person this drawing would convey an idea about the number of objects in a set. We could also use our fingers to indicate the number of objects in the set. For example, a student may hold up three fingers to tell the number of pencils that he has. In this case, three fingers is just another way of naming 3.

MATERIALS

sets of objects, such as
   paper clips
   buttons
   blocks
   sticks

PROCEDURE

Activity 1—Let's see how many students we have in our class. Count off by saying 1, 2, 3, and so on as I point to you. Point to a student for number 1. Continue around the room. How many students do we have in our class? (The last number counted tells the number of students.) Let's check that count by starting with someone else. Recount the students in the same way. Did we get the same number on both counts? (Yes.) Write the numeral which names the number on the chalkboard. Next count the set of boys, and then count the set of girls. Which of the two sets has more children in it?

Activity 2—Show a set of three counting blocks. How could we tell someone how many counting blocks we had if we did not know names for numbers? Help students to see that they could show three blocks by matching a finger to each of the counting blocks, or they could draw three sticks. Continue having students tell the number of objects in sets having less than ten objects. Then show a set of fifteen objects. How could we tell someone how many objects are in this set without using names for numbers? Help students to see that they might flash ten fingers and five more, or they might draw fifteen sticks. When drawing fifteen sticks, it is helpful to draw them in groups of five for easier reference. Show this on the chalkboard. Continue with examples of this type.

Then have students tell which of two sets has more objects in it without using numbers. To do this, students must match the objects in the two sets one-to-one until all of the objects in one set have been used. If all of the objects in the second set also have been used, the two sets have the same number of objects in them. If there are still some objects in the second set, then the second set has more objects in it.

WORKTEXT® PAGE 1—For teaching suggestions, see the annotated pupil's page.

Pages 2-3

OBJECTIVES

- Recognize and write digits
- Recognize and write the names for 2-digit numbers

BACKGROUND

The essential features of the hindu-arabic system of numeration that we use are: (1) there are ten digits —0, 1, 2, 3, 4, 5, 6, 7, 8, and 9—that are used to name numbers less than 10; (2) grouping is done by tens; and (3) numbers larger than 9 are named by using two or more digits placed side by side.

Each position or place in the numeral has a specific value.

Since we use the number 10 as the basic number for grouping and place value, our system is a *base ten* or *decimal* system. We probably use ten digit symbols and regroup 10 ones because we have ten fingers. In fact, the term *digit* is an abbreviation of the Latin word *digitus,* which means finger or toe.

This lesson is a review, and the teacher may decide to have students complete the exercises on Worktext® pages 2–3 without any initial teaching activities. There are, however, some activities included which can be used to develop the competencies necessary for completion of these pages or as additional activities.

MATERIALS

cards numbered 1 through 9 in large numerals on one side with a like number of dots on the other side
9 cards with 10 dots each

PROCEDURE

Activity 1—Show a card with 3 dots on it. How many dots are on this card? (3.) Have a student come to the chalkboard and write the numeral 3. If the student needs help, show the numeral written on the back of the number card. Continue with the cards having less than 10 dots. Each of the symbols that we have written on the chalkboard is called a digit. Each digit names a number less than 10. Digits are also used to name numbers larger than 9. To name a number larger than 9, we use two or more digits.

Activity 2—Show one of the cards which has 10 dots on it. How many dots are on this card? (10.) Have a student come to the chalkboard and write the numeral for 10 on the board. To write the numeral for ten, we use the digit 1 and the digit 0. The position in which these numerals are written is important. The digit on the left tells us the number of tens. Continue by showing several cards with 10 dots on them and writing the numeral that tells the sum of the number of dots on all of the cards.

Now show three cards with 10 dots on them and one card with 4 dots on it. How many dots are on all of these cards? (34.) Have a student write 34 on the chalkboard. Continue with examples of this type having students write the 2-digit numeral on the chalkboard.

Activity 3—Write 43 on the chalkboard. How many tens are shown by this numeral? (4.) How many ones are shown by this numeral? (3.) Have a student come to the chalk tray and show 43 dots by putting up 4 cards with 10 dots each and 1 card with 3 dots. Continue with activities in which students must iden-

tify the meaning of 2-digit numerals and illustrate the number of dots named using the numeral cards.

What is the largest number that can be named with one digit? (9.) What is the smallest number that can be named with two digits? (10.) What is the largest number that can be named with two digits? (99.)

WORKTEXT® PAGES 2–3—For teaching suggestions, see the annotated pupil's pages.

Page 4

OBJECTIVE

■ Write the standard name, expanded name, and word name for numbers less than 100

BACKGROUND

There are many ways to write names for numbers. The form in which we ordinarily write number names will be called the *standard name* for a number. When we write the digits 7 and 3 side by side, we have written a standard name. We read this numeral as "seventy-three." *Seventy-three* is called the *word name* for the number. The standard name, 73, can be translated as 70 + 3 or as 7 tens, 3 ones. These last two names for 73 are called *expanded names,* because they show the place value for each of the digits. These two forms of expanded names will be emphasized in this lesson.

Children looking at a numeral like 36 may see no reason why the 3 has a larger value than the 6. They see only the 3 and the 6 and cannot see the value of the place they occupy in the numeral. That is something that must be understood. For children to understand, they must have some way to see the place value of each digit as concretely as they see the digits 3 and 6. In this lesson, students will be required to show the place values for the 3 and the 6 by selecting bundles of sticks to represent 36. They will also be required to write standard names, expanded names, and word names for numbers between 10 and 100. In this way, they will begin to visualize the value of each place in a numeral and, hence, to gain a better understanding of place value.

MATERIALS

cards with single digits printed on them—2 cards for each digit

99 tongue depressors (or sticks)
9 rubber bands

PROCEDURE

Activity 1—Have 9 bundles of 10 tongue depressors and 9 loose tongue depressors on the desk. Place digit cards 4 and 7 side by side. What number does this name? (47.) Have a student show 4 tens using the tongue depressors. Have a second student show 7. (name of student) and (name of student) have shown the number 47 by showing 4 tens and 7 ones. Change the position of the cards to show 74. Does this represent the same number? (No.) Why not? (It now means 7 tens and 4 ones.) Continue illustrating numbers between 10 and 100 in this way.

Activity 2—Show 3 bundles of 10 tongue depressors and 5 single tongue depressors. Have a student select digit cards to represent the number of tongue depressors. Continue having students identify the standard name for sets of tongue depressors.

Activity 3—Write 55 on the chalkboard. How many tens are represented in this number? (5.) How many ones are represented in this number? (5.) Write 55 = 5 tens, 5 ones on the chalkboard. What is the standard name for 5 tens? (50.) What is the standard name for 5 ones? (5.) We can also write 55 = 50 + 5. Write this on the chalkboard. These are two expanded names for the standard name 55. Write the word name *fifty-five* on the chalkboard and have students read it. Continue with exercises of this type. Have students write standard names, expanded names, and word names for numbers on the chalkboard.

WORKTEXT® PAGE 4—For teaching suggestions, see the annotated pupil's page.

Page 5

OBJECTIVES

- Identify which of two numerals names the larger number
- Use the symbols > and < to complete number sentences

BACKGROUND

When comparing two whole numbers, we can always tell whether one is larger than the other. All we need do is compare the digits place by place.

For example, 72 is larger than 65, since 7 tens is larger than 6 tens; 53 is smaller than 57, since the number of tens are equal and 3 ones is smaller than 7 ones.

When writing sentences that compare numbers, we use the symbols > and <. The symbol < means *is less than,* and the symbol > means *is greater than.* These symbols always point to the smaller number.

MATERIALS

18 bundles of 10 tongue depressors
18 single tongue depressors

PROCEDURE

Activity 1—Write 37 and 39 on the chalkboard. Ask a student to show 37 tongue depressors. Make sure that he shows 3 groups of ten and 7 ones. Ask a second student to show 39. Make sure he shows 3 groups of ten and 9 ones. Which of the two students has the most sticks? (The one with 39.) Why does he have the most? Help students to see that they both have the same number of tens, but that 9 ones is more than 7 ones. Continue with this process, varying the numbers and teaching students to first compare the tens' digits. If the tens' digit in one number is larger than the tens' digit in another number, then the first number is the larger. If the tens' digits are the same, then one must check the ones' digits to determine which of the two numbers is larger.

Activity 2—Write the sentence *thirty-five is less than thirty-nine* on the chalkboard. Directly beneath this write 35 < 39. Point to the symbol for *is less than.* This symbol is read "is less than." This symbol always points to the smaller number. Then write the sentence *forty-five is greater than thirty-seven* on the chalkboard. Directly below it write 45 > 37. Point to the symbol for *is greater than.* This symbol is read "is greater than." Note that it again points to the smaller number. Then write various pairs of 2-digit numbers on the chalkboard and have students put the correct symbol between these to show if the first number is less than or greater than the second number.

Activity 3—Draw a number line on the chalkboard and have students help to name the points on the number line with numerals. Is 15 to the right of 12 or to the left of 12? (To the right of 12.) Is 15 larger than or smaller than 12? (Larger than.) Continue asking such questions. Do larger numbers always appear to the right of smaller numbers on the number line? (Yes.) Continue with the activity, having students identify smaller and larger numbers using the number line.

Page 6

OBJECTIVES

- Identify numbers that tell how many objects are in a set
- Identify numbers that tell the position of an object in a set

BACKGROUND

Cardinal numbers tell how many objects are in a given set. To find the cardinal number of a set, we count the elements in the set. The number name for the last element counted is the cardinal number of the set. Numbers which tell the position of an object in a set, such as first, second, and third, are called *ordinal numbers*.

MATERIALS

calendar for the current month

PROCEDURE

Display the calendar. How many days are in this month? Numbers that tell how many objects are in a set are called cardinal numbers. How many days are in a week? (7.) Does 7 tell us how many members are in a set? (Yes.) For this reason, what is 7 called? (A cardinal number.) Continue asking questions about how many elements are in particular sets. Each of these answers designates a cardinal number.

What is the first day of the week? (Sunday.) Look at the calendar. On what day does the third day of the month fall? Continue asking questions of this type. Numbers that tell us the position of an element in the set, such as the third day of the month or the fourth day of the week, are called ordinal numbers. They tell us the position of an element in the set. Continue asking questions about ordinal numbers until all students in the class can answer them readily.

It is not expected that students will master the definitions of cardinal and ordinal. It *is* important that students know that there are two kinds of numbers: one kind that tells *how many* and one kind that tells *position*.

Pages 7-8

OBJECTIVES

- Regroup 10 ones as 1 ten
- Regroup 10 tens as 1 hundred
- Identify the place values in a 3-digit number

BACKGROUND

When we are naming numbers, each group of 10 objects is "bundled together" to form a new group with a new name. Students have already bundled 10 ones together to form 1 ten. Ten bundles of 10 are grouped together to form 1 hundred, and so on. In this lesson, students will learn to interpret symbols for numbers less than 1,000. They will actually see groups of 1, groups of 10, and groups of 100. In this way, students will begin to understand the meaning of each digit in number names less than 1,000.

MATERIALS

5 bundles of 100 tongue depressors
9 bundles of 10 tongue depressors
9 single tongue depressors
rubber bands

PROCEDURE

Activity 1—Show 1 bundle of 100 tongue depressors. How many sticks do you think are in this bundle? How could we find out for sure how many sticks are in this bundle? (By counting them.) Have groups of students help to count the tongue depressors in each of the large bundles. As they are doing this, ask them to use rubber bands to bundle groups of 10 together. This will help them keep track of how many tongue depressors they have counted. How many sticks do you have? (100.) How many bundles of 10 do you have? (10.) Whenever we have 10 groups of 10, we bundle these together to form 1 group of 100. Each of these sets is 1 bundle of 10 tens, or 100.

Activity 2—Show 3 bundles of 100 sticks, 2 bundles of 10 sticks, and 5 single sticks. How many bundles of 100 sticks do we have? (3.) How many bundles of 10 sticks do we have? (2.) How many ones do we have? (5.) Write 3 hundreds, 2 tens, 5 ones = 325 on the chalkboard. Explain that each digit in the numeral 325 has a particular place value that can be seen using the bundles of sticks. Continue showing numbers named by three digits using the sticks and writing the standard name and an expanded name on the chalkboard.

Then write a standard name such as 179 on the chalkboard and have students select bundles of sticks to represent this number. Make sure that they select 1 bundle of 100, 7 bundles of 10, and 9 single sticks. Continue with this activity until all students can identify the correct bundles of sticks for a given standard name and can write the standard name for a specified number of sticks.

WORKTEXT® PAGES 7–8—For teaching suggestions, see the annotated pupil's pages.

ADDITIONAL ACTIVITIES

Materials: teacher-prepared duplicated sheet with sets of dots on it. Have one set of dots contain 100 dots, have a second set of dots contain 185 dots, and a third set of dots contain 350 dots. Have students draw rings around groups of 10 dots and then rings around groups of 10 tens. After they have done this, have them identify the total number of dots in each set.

Pages 9-10

OBJECTIVE

■ Write the standard name and the expanded name for numbers between 100 and 1,000

BACKGROUND

After students thoroughly understand numbers named by two digits, it is a simple matter to extend these concepts to numbers named by three digits. Standard names and word names should be emphasized in this lesson. Students will be required to show the place values for each of the three digits used to name numbers between 100 and 1,000. In this way, they will form a mental image of the value for each place in a numeral.

MATERIALS

cards with single digits printed on them—3 cards for each digit

9 bundles of 100 tongue depressors
9 bundles of 10 tongue depressors
9 single tongue depressors

PROCEDURE

Activity 1—Show a bundle of 100 tongue depressors. How many sticks are in this bundle? (100.) Now show a bundle of 10. How many sticks are in this bundle? (10.) How many of these bundles does it take to make one of the larger bundles? (10.) When we have 10 bundles of 10 sticks, we put them together to form 1 bundle of how many sticks? (100.) Now show a single stick. This represents 1. How many of these do we need to have a bundle of 10? (10.) When we have 10 single sticks, we put them together to form 1 bundle of 10 sticks.

Show 3 bundles of 100 sticks, 5 bundles of 10 sticks, and 7 single sticks. How many hundreds are there in this number? (3.) Have a student find a card with the numeral 3 and hold it up for the class to see. How many tens are in this number? (5.) Have a second student find a numeral 5 and hold it up for the class to see. Should the tens' digit be on the right or the left of the hundreds' digit? (The right.) Have the students stand so that the student holding the tens' digit is to the right of the student holding the hundreds' digit. How many ones are in this number? (7.) Have a third student find a numeral 7 and stand in the proper place so that the number named by the three digits is 357. Have a fourth student write this numeral on the chalkboard. Explain that the numeral means 3 hundreds, 5 tens, 7 ones. Have the three students change positions. Is the number named by these three digits the same as the first number? (No.) Continue with additional activities of this type.

Activity 2—Draw a number line on the chalkboard with 12 unit spaces on it. Mark one of the middle spaces with the numeral 264. I have named one of the points on the number line. What did I use to name this point? (264.) What number comes just after 264? (265.) Have a student write 265 in the correct place. What number comes just before 264? (263.) Have a student write 263 in the appropriate place. Continue with this activity until all of the points on the number line have been named. Then repeat the activity using different numbers. If students have difficulty with any of these numbers, illustrate them using the bundles of sticks.

Activity 3—Write 284 and 289 on the chalkboard. Which of these names the larger number? (289.) Why does 289 name the larger number? (It has the same number of hundreds and tens, but more ones than 284.) Help students to see that when comparing the size of 3-digit numbers you look first at the hundreds' digit. If the hundreds' digit of one is larger than the other, then that is the larger number. If the hundreds' digits are equal, you look at the tens' digit. If the tens' digit of one number is larger than the other, then that is the larger number. Finally, if the hundreds' and tens' digits of the two numbers are equal, you look at the ones' digits and determine which of the two numbers is larger by comparing the ones' digits. Continue with this activity having the students identify which of two numbers is larger. After several examples, remind students of the symbols for *is less than* and *is greater than*. Have them write these symbols on the chalkboard between the numbers after they have determined which of the two numbers is larger.

WORKTEXT® PAGES 9–10—For teaching suggestions, see the annotated pupil's pages.

Page 11

OBJECTIVE

■ Recognize the number of dollars as the hundreds' digit, the number of dimes as the tens' digit, and the number of pennies as the ones' digit when converting dollars, dimes, and pennies to cents

BACKGROUND

Dollars, dimes, and pennies are a good concrete referent for showing place value. The number of dollars corresponds to the number of hundreds, the number of dimes corresponds to the number of tens, and the number of pennies corresponds to the number of ones. To emphasize this, the money equivalent for sets of dollars, dimes, and pennies should be expressed in cents.

PROCEDURE

WORKTEXT® PAGE 11—For teaching suggestions, see the annotated pupil's page.

ADDITIONAL ACTIVITIES

Materials: flannel board and 9 felt models each of dollars, dimes, and pennies. Put 3 models of dollars, 2 models of dimes, and 4 models of pennies on the flannel board. How many dollars are on the

flannel board? (3.) How many cents are 3 dollars equal to? (300.) How many dimes are on the flannel board? (2.) How many cents are 2 dimes equal to? (20.) How many pennies are on the flannel board? (4.) Altogether, how many cents are represented on the flannel board? (324.) Put a chart on the chalkboard with columns labeled dollars, dimes, pennies, and cents. Complete the entries in the chart for 3 dollars, 2 dimes, and 4 pennies. Continue with examples in which the students identify the number of dollars, the number of dimes, and the number of pennies. Then have the students complete the entries. In these exercises, emphasize that the number of dollars is the hundreds' digit in the amount of money, the number of dimes is the tens' digit in the amount of money, and the number of pennies is the ones' digit in the amount of money.

Pages 12-13

OBJECTIVES

■ Recognize 1 thousand as 10 hundreds

■ Recognize the number of ten dollars as the thousands' digit when converting to cents

■ Identify the place value for the digits in a numeral named by four digits

BACKGROUND

The numbers from 1,000 to 9,999 are introduced for the first time in this lesson. It is important for students to have a wide variety of experiences with these numbers before completing the Worktext® pages. For this reason, the introductory activities may require two instructional days.

MATERIALS

10 bundles of 100 tongue depressors
1 bundle of 10 tongue depressors
1 single tongue depressor
flannel board
9 felt models each of pennies, dimes, dollar bills, and ten-dollar bills

PROCEDURE

Activity 1—Show a single stick. Suppose that I had 4 sticks like this. What numeral would I write to show how many sticks I had? (4.) Have a student come to the chalkboard and write the numeral 4. Now show a bundle of 10 sticks. Suppose I had 6 bundles of sticks like this. How many sticks would

I have? (60.) Have a student come to the chalkboard and write the numeral 60. Show a bundle of 10 sticks and a single stick. Suppose I had 6 bundles of 10 sticks and 4 single sticks. How many sticks would that be? (64.)

Show a bundle of 100 sticks. How many sticks are in this bundle? (100.) Suppose I had 5 bundles like this. How many sticks would I have? (500.) Finally, show 10 bundles of 100 sticks. How many sticks are in 10 of these bundles? (10 hundred, or 1,000.) When we have 10 bundles of 100, we bundle these together into a new, larger bundle which is called 1 thousand. Write the words *one thousand* on the chalkboard, and next to them write the standard name *1,000.* Point to the digits. This is the standard name for 1,000. One thousand means ten hundreds. Show a bundle of 1,000 sticks. How many sticks are in this bundle? (1,000.) If I had 7 of these big bundles, how many sticks would I have? (7,000.) Continue asking questions of this type.

Activity 2—We can also show a thousand by using money. How many pennies are in 1 dollar? (100.) Put a model of a one-dollar bill on the flannel board. How many pennies are in 10 dollars? (1,000.) Put a model of a ten-dollar bill on the flannel board. Whenever we have 10 one-dollar bills, we group them together to form 1 ten-dollar bill, which is the same as 1 thousand cents. Put 2 ten-dollar bills on the flannel board. How many cents are represented now? (2,000 cents.) Continue representing amounts of money using different numbers of ten-dollar bills. In each case, ask how many cents are represented.

Now put 1 ten-dollar bill, 3 one-dollar bills, 4 dimes, and 2 pennies on the flannel board. How many ten-dollar bills are on the flannel board? (1.) How many cents does this represent? (1,000.) Ask similar questions for the number of dollars, dimes, and pennies. When we have one thousand, three hundred, forty-two cents represented, we write the standard name for this as 1,342. The 1 tells us how many thousands, the 3 tells us how many hundreds, the 4 tells us how many tens, and the 2 tells us how many ones are in the number. Continue representing different amounts of money on the flannel board and writing the standard name for the number of cents in the amount.

Activity 3—Write 2,785 on the chalkboard. The 2 in this numeral means 2 what? (Thousands.) Continue asking what each of the digits means in the numeral. Write several additional numerals on the chalkboard and identify the place value for each of the digits within the numeral.

Suppose we had 4 thousands, 1 hundred, 2 tens, and 5 ones. What standard name would we write? (4,125.) Have a student come to the chalkboard and write this standard name. Continue with additional examples in which students must identify the standard name from the expanded name.

WORKTEXT® PAGES 12–13—For teaching suggestions, see the annotated pupil's pages.

Pages 14-15

OBJECTIVES

■ Write the standard name and the expanded name for numbers between 1,000 and 10,000

■ Identify which of two counting numbers between 1,000 and 10,000 is the larger

BACKGROUND

This lesson introduces two different ways to write expanded names for numbers between 1,000 and 10,000. For example, 2,568 may be written as 2,000 + 500 + 60 + 8 or as 2 thousands, 5 hundreds, 6 tens, 8 ones. Students are also provided with a wide range of exercises which permit them to obtain a better understanding of the counting numbers between 1,000 and 10,000. They are asked to write the name for the number that comes just after or just before a given number. They are also asked to complete the following number patterns: ones' patterns, which require counting by ones; tens' patterns, which require counting by tens; and hundreds' patterns, which require counting by hundreds.

MATERIALS

cards with single digits printed on them—4 cards for each digit

PROCEDURE

Activity 1—Place four chairs in front of the classroom side by side. Have four students sit in these chairs. Give each student a set of digit cards. Have each student hold up one of their digit cards. What number is represented by these digits? Help students read the correct number. Which student is holding up the thousands' digit? Which student is holding up the hundreds' digit? Continue the questioning to the ones' digit. These students are going to hold up different cards, and you are to read the number that is represented. Have students hold up different digit cards and have members of the class read the numbers that are named.

Let four other students sit in the chairs. Now we are going to have members of the class tell a number, and the students sitting in the chairs will have to show that number. Remember the number should be between 1,000 and 10,000.

Activity 2—Draw a chart like that in exercise A on the chalkboard. Write 8,472 in the standard name column. We can write one expanded name for this numeral by writing 8,000 + 400 + 70 + 2. This means that we have 8 thousands, 4 hundreds, 7 tens, and 2 ones. Write these digits in the appropriate columns. Have students complete the chart using various numbers.

Activity 3—Draw a number line on the chalkboard with 12 unit spaces on it. Mark one of the middle spaces 2,755. I have named one of the points on the number line. What number names the point? (2,755.) What number comes just after 2,755? (2,756.) Have a student write this numeral in the correct place. What number comes just before 2,755? (2,754.) Have a student write this numeral in the appropriate place. Continue with this activity until all of the points on the number line have been named. Then erase these numbers, name one of the points on the number line with another numeral, and continue as in the above example.

Erase the numerals for the number line. Now let's see if we can count by tens on the number line. Name two consecutive points on the number line 4,640 and 4,650. Have students complete the number line counting by tens. Continue with this activity until students can count easily by tens. Then complete number line patterns where the students are counting by 100 and also by 1,000.

Activity 4—Write 6,285 and 6,295 on the chalkboard. Which of these names the larger number? (6,295.) Why does 6,295 name the larger number? (It has the same number of thousands and hundreds, but more tens than 6,285.) Continue with this activity, having students identify which of two numbers is larger. After several examples, remind students of the symbols < (is less than) and > (is greater than). Have them use these symbols between two numbers to make a true sentence.

WORKTEXT® PAGES 14–15—For teaching suggestions, see the annotated pupil's pages.

Page 16

OBJECTIVES
■ Write the standard name for word names arising in a written passage

■ Solve money problems involving dollars, dimes, and pennies

BACKGROUND
Each chapter will contain verbal problems for the students to solve. In the exercises on page 16, the students must read the problems to identify the numbers and write the standard names. Then these numbers must be compared to determine which is larger. Translation from verbal passages to mathematical numerals and sentences is an important skill and will be continually emphasized throughout *Succeeding in Mathematics*.

PROCEDURE

WORKTEXT® PAGE 16—For teaching suggestions, see the annotated pupil's page.

ADDITIONAL ACTIVITIES
Materials: flannel board, felt models—2 dollars, 20 dimes, and 20 pennies. Have students illustrate various amounts of money on the flannel board. For example, ask a student to place 3 dimes and 7 pennies on the flannel board. How much money is represented? (37 cents.) Have a second student write this numeral on the chalkboard. Continue representing various amounts of money on the flannel board and writing the numeral to represent this amount of money on the chalkboard. Point to the numerals on the chalkboard. Which numeral represents the most money? Which numeral represents the least money?

Have a student put 14 dimes on the flannel board. How many cents does this represent? (140.) Is this enough to buy a toy boat which costs 129 cents? (Yes.) Continue with exercises of this type.

Pages 17-18

OBJECTIVE
■ Round numbers under 1,000 to the nearest ten

MATERIALS
100 counting blocks

PROCEDURE
Activity 1—Put 23 blocks on the desk. Without

counting these blocks, guess how many there are. What is your guess? (Accept all guesses and write them on the board.) Then have a student count the blocks. Whose guess was closest to the number of blocks? Continue with this activity until students have had a chance to guess for several different sets of blocks.

Now I am going to limit the numbers that you can use for guessing. You may only guess a multiple of 10, that is, you may guess 10, 20, 30, 40, 50, 60, and so on. Put 44 blocks on the desk. Which multiple of 10 do you think is closest to the number of blocks on the desk? Have students guess. Have a student count the blocks. Which multiple of 10 is closest to the number of blocks on the desk? (40.) Continue with this activity until students can identify the multiple of 10 closest to different numbers of blocks.

Activity 2—Draw a number line with 11 marks on it on the chalkboard. Name the mark on the left 30. Have students come to the chalkboard and name the remainder of the marks. Which of the numbers that have been named on the number line are closer to 30? (31, 32, 33, 34.) Have a student draw a ring around each of these numbers. Which of the numbers are closer to 40? (36, 37, 38, 39.) Have a student put a box around each of these numbers. Which number is halfway between 30 and 40? (35.) Have a student put a triangle around 35. Sometimes we do not need to know the exact number. We might say that there are about 30 blocks or there are about 50 blocks. When we state a number to the nearest multiple of 10, such as 30 or 50, we have rounded the number to the nearest ten. The numbers that are circled on this number line would be rounded to 30. The numbers that have boxes around them and the number that has a triangle around it are rounded to 40. Continue with this activity by naming different sets of numbers on the number line and asking students which of these would be rounded to the lower multiple of 10 and which to the higher multiple of 10.

Activity 3—Draw the number line shown below on the chalkboard.

Point to the marks halfway between each multiple of 10 and have different students put the numbers represented by these points on the number line. 78 is between which two multiples of 10? (70 and 80.) 78 is closer to which multiple of 10? (80.) How would we round 78 to the nearest ten? (We would round it to 80.) Continue asking these questions for a variety of numbers that could be represented on this number line. Do not include multiples of 5 in these initial activities.

Now look at the numbers such as 85. Which two multiples of 10 is it between? (80 and 90.) Is it closer to one of these? (No.) We will round 85 to the higher multiple of 10. 85 is rounded to 90. Continue discussing the multiples of 5 on the number line.

WORKTEXT® PAGES 17–18—For teaching suggestions, see the annotated pupil's pages.

Page 19

OBJECTIVES

- Identify numbers less than 1,000 named by Egyptian numerals
- Name numbers less than 1,000 using Egyptian numerals

BACKGROUND

Each chapter will contain one or more activities for the more capable students to complete independently. These pages may be used as enrichment for the better students while the less capable students complete additional activities on concepts previously presented in the chapter.

Egyptian numerals provide another method for naming counting numbers. This is an interesting system because it uses pictures to name numbers and also because it is an additive system. In an additive system, each symbol represents a specified value, and to obtain the number the values of the symbols are added. The Egyptian numerals introduced in this lesson are staff (/) for the number 1, heelbone (∩) for the number 10, scroll (9) for the number 100, and lotus flower (ϟ) for the number 1,000.

PROCEDURE

WORKTEXT® PAGE 19—For teaching suggestions, see the annotated pupil's page.

Page 20

OBJECTIVES

- Tell time to the nearest five-minute interval
- Write numerals to show a specified time

MATERIALS

demonstration clockface

PROCEDURE

Activity 1—Show 3:15 on the demonstration clockface. Between which two numbers is the hour hand on the clockface pointing? (3 and 4.) To which number on the clockface is the minute hand pointing? (3.) What time is shown on the clockface? (3:15, fifteen minutes past three, or quarter past three.) Write 3:15 on the chalkboard. This is read as 3:15, or 15 minutes past 3. How did you know that it was 15 minutes past 3? (The space between each pair of numbers on the clockface represents 5 minutes, and when the minute hand points to 3 it is 3 five-minute spaces past the hour.) Continue showing different times on the clockface and having students read these times.

Activity 2—Write 7:35 on the chalkboard. What are the different ways we can read this time? (7:35, 35 minutes past 7, or 25 minutes before 8.) Choose a student to demonstrate 7:35 on the clockface. Make sure that the hour hand is between 7 and 8 and the minute hand is pointing to 7. Continue writing different times on the chalkboard, having students read the times and demonstrate them on the clockface.

WORKTEXT® PAGE 20—For teaching suggestions, see the annotated pupil's page.

ADDITIONAL ACTIVITIES

Students should be encouraged to tell time each day. There should be a clock in the room. Also, a schedule of activities should be written in a prominent place in the room, and the times for each activity should be listed. The teacher can ask questions based on the schedule. What time do we go to recess? What time is lunch? What time do we study mathematics? How many more minutes until we begin spelling? These types of questions interspersed through the day will provide students with valuable activities in learning how to tell time.

Page 21

OBJECTIVE

■ Review the mastery of skills and concepts presented in chapter 1

BACKGROUND

The *Succeeding in Mathematics* series provides two reviews for each chapter: a chapter check-up in the pupil's Worktext®, and a separate mastery review. The check-up is intended for the student to use to help discover any areas he or she may need to work on before taking the mastery review. The mastery review is intended for the teacher to use for grading and evaluation purposes.

The items on the check-up are directly related to specific concepts in particular lessons and can be used diagnostically.

WORKTEXT® PAGE 21—Have students complete the chapter review. Each exercise is diagnostic in nature. If students respond incorrectly to an exercise, it indicates that they have not mastered the necessary skills and concepts. When this occurs, activities from the chapter should be repeated. Students having difficulty with the exercises are referred to the following pages in the Worktext®: exercise A, page 2; exercise B, pages 4, 7, and 12; exercise C, pages 4, 9, and 14; exercise D, pages 5 and 10; exercise E, pages 10 and 15; and exercise F, pages 17 and 18.

Page 22

OBJECTIVE

■ Test for mastery of skills and concepts presented in chapter 1

BACKGROUND

The *Succeeding in Mathematics* series provides two reviews for each chapter: a chapter check-up in the pupil's Worktext®, and a separate mastery review. The check-up is intended for the student to use to help discover any areas he or she may need to work on before taking the mastery review. The mastery review is intended for the teacher to use for grading and evaluation purposes.

The items on the check-up are directly related to specific concepts in particular lessons and can be used diagnostically.

For some chapters the teacher may wish to use the check-up as a pretest. Students who have already mastered certain concepts and skills may be able to omit some of the corresponding lessons. These students could work on enrichment materials, work ahead in the Worktext®, or help the teacher with other students.

The check-up will be most beneficial to students if they view it as an ally instead of an opponent. This can be attained by scoring answers right or wrong, but not assigning the students a grade on the check-up. Always stress that the check-up allows students to show how much they know rather than what they do not know. Of course, being able to perform well on the check-up enhances the students' chances of doing well on the mastery review.

PROCEDURE

WORKTEXT® PAGE 22—Have students complete the page independently.

2 Addition

Page 23

OBJECTIVE

■ Add two numbers using sets of objects

BACKGROUND

The operation of addition is based upon actual physical manipulation. Addition is the process associated with joining sets of objects or putting things together. To find the sum of two numbers such as 5 + 9, we would first find a set of five objects and then a second set of nine different objects. The sum for 5 + 9 is found by joining these two sets and counting the number of elements in the new set. This yields the addition sentence 5 + 9 = 14.

This is not a new concept for students at this level. In fact, they should begin to use this Worktext® with a good conceptual knowledge of addition and knowledge of most of the basic addition facts. These concepts need to be repeated, however, so that the process for addition may be extended and so that students can respond automatically to the basic addition facts.

MATERIALS

10 red blocks
10 blue blocks

PROCEDURE

Activity 1—Show the set of 10 red blocks and the set of 10 blue blocks. Suppose I want to add 4 + 7 using the blocks. Have a student put 4 red blocks on the desk. Have a second student put 7 blue blocks on the desk. How can we use the 4 red blocks and the 7 blue blocks to find the sum 4 + 7? Help students to see that you need to join the two sets and then count the set of blocks. How many blocks are on the desk? (11.) What is the sum of 4 + 7? (11.) Continue using the blocks in this way and practicing simple addition facts.

Emphasize that to add two numbers such as 9 + 5, you first find a set of 9 blocks and a set of 5 different blocks. Then put these two sets together and count the number of blocks in the new set.

Activity 2—We can also show how to add numbers by drawing pictures on the chalkboard. Write 3 + 8 on the chalkboard. Let's draw sticks to show each of these numbers. How many sticks should I draw to show the first number? (3.) Do that. How many sticks should I draw to show the second number? (8.) Do that. How many sticks have I drawn on the board altogether? (11.) How did you find out? (By counting.) Continue illustrating additions by drawing stick pictures on the chalkboard.

WORKTEXT® PAGE 23—For teaching suggestions, see the annotated pupil's page.

Pages 24-25

OBJECTIVES
- Find sums on the number line
- Identify the parts in an addition sentence as addends and sum

BACKGROUND

The number line is a convenient model for adding. To add 8 + 4 on the number line, we start at 8 and count 4 spaces to the right. Care must be taken that students do not count the 8 but rather begin the count at 9. The stopping point is the sum. Students should be encouraged to start at the first addend listed and count the number of spaces indicated by the second addend. Since addition is commutative, however, it is sometimes more convenient to start at the larger addend and count the number of spaces indicated by the smaller addend. This shortens the addition process on the number line.

Students should also learn to identify the parts in an addition sentence. For the addition 8 + 4 = 12, 8 and 4 are called addends and 12 is called the sum. Students should become thoroughly familiar with these terms so that they can follow directions.

PROCEDURE

Activity 1—Draw a number line on the board. Have students help you put the numerals 0 through 18 on this number line. To add 5 + 8 on the number line, we start at 5 and count 8 spaces to the right. Show them that they begin counting at 6, that is, count the 8 spaces after 5. What would be the stopping point if you started at 5 and went 8 spaces to the right? (13.) This stopping point is the sum for the addition. What is the sum of 5 + 8? (13.) Continue with examples of this type. For each of these exercises, have a student show the procedure used to add on the number line. Have a second student complete the addition sentence.

Activity 2—Leave the number line on the chalkboard. Write the addition 1 + 8. What is the answer to this addition? (9.) How could we find it on the number line? (Start at 1 and count 8 spaces to the right or start at 8 and count 1 space to the right.) Which of these two methods is easier? (Starting at 8 and counting 1 space.) In the addition sentence 1 + 8 = 9, we call 1 and 8 the addends and 9 the sum. We could write this addition sentence in a column as +8. Continue writing additions on the chalk-

$$\begin{array}{r} 1 \\ +8 \\ \hline 9 \end{array}$$

board in column form. Have students find the sum, explain how this sum could be found using the number line, identify the addends and the sum, and then write the addition in sentence form on the chalkboard.

WORKTEXT® PAGES 24–25—For detailed teaching suggestions, see the annotated pupil's pages.

Pages 26-27

OBJECTIVE
- Find the sums for the 100 basic addition facts

MATERIALS
15 sets of addition flash cards
10 red counting blocks
10 blue counting blocks

PROCEDURE

Activity 1—Have the sets of blocks on a desk. Have a number line with numerals 0 through 18 drawn on the chalkboard. Today we are going to review addition facts. Each of you take out a clean piece of paper and a pencil. When I hold up an addition flash card, I want you to write the sum on your piece of paper. Hold up a flash card such as 3 + 5. What was the sum? (8.) Check to see that everyone got the correct answer by asking for a show of hands. If there were errors, ask a student to show how to find the sum using the blocks. Have a second student use the number line on the chalkboard to find the sum. Continue drilling on the addition facts in this way.

Activity 2—Form pairs of students and give each pair of students a set of flash cards. As one student shows the additions, the other should give the sum. After going through the cards one time this way, the students' roles should be reversed. Again, you should promote success by encouraging students to use the number line or the blocks to find those sums which they do not know.

WORKTEXT® PAGES 26–27—For detailed teaching suggestions, see the annotated pupil's pages.

Pages 28-29

OBJECTIVES

■ Recognize that changing the order of the addends does not change the sum
■ Recognize that changing the way the addends are grouped does not change the sum

BACKGROUND

For each addition sentence such as $7 + 9 = 16$, there is a second addition sentence which is also true—in this instance, $9 + 7 = 16$. This leads us to conclude that $7 + 9 = 9 + 7$, which is an example of the commutative property of addition. Generally, the commutative property says that for whole number addition, $a + b = b + a$. Students should learn to recognize that changing the order of the addends does not change the sum. Of course, students need not be introduced to the word *commutative* at this level.

In order to add three addends, such as $6 + 3 + 1$, we must first find the sum for two of these addends and then add the third addend to this sum. For example, we might add $6 + 3$ first, obtaining 9, and then add $9 + 1$. We might also choose to add $3 + 1$ first and then add $6 + 4$. In each instance, we find that the sum is 10. This leads us to conclude that $(6 + 3) + 1 = 6 + (3 + 1)$. This is an example of the associative property of addition, which can be more generally written as $(a + b) + c = a + (b + c)$. As with the term *commutative,* students need not be required to learn the term *associative.* Rather, they should learn that the way addends are grouped does not change the sum.

Investigating these two properties provides students with more opportunities to find the sums for basic addition facts as well as to learn general principles of addition.

PROCEDURE

WORKTEXT® PAGES 28–29—For detailed teaching suggestions, see the annotated pupil's pages.

ADDITIONAL ACTIVITIES

Materials: 10 red blocks, 10 blue blocks, and 10 green blocks for each student. Use the blocks to show additions illustrating the commutative property and the associative property.

Page 30

OBJECTIVES

■ Translate from written or oral statements to addition sentences
■ Solve addition word problems

PROCEDURE

WORKTEXT® PAGE 30—For teaching suggestions, see the annotated pupil's page.

Page 31

OBJECTIVES

■ Write expanded names for numbers less than 1,000
■ Complete number patterns for numbers less than 1,000
■ Determine which of two numbers less than 1,000 is larger

PROCEDURE

WORKTEXT® PAGE 31—For teaching suggestions, see the annotated pupil's page.

Page 32

OBJECTIVES

■ Identify amounts of cents from dimes and pennies
■ Add amounts of money using dimes and pennies

BACKGROUND

One of the very convenient models that we can use to develop addition for 2- and 3-digit numbers is our monetary system. Dimes and pennies can be used to develop the notion of addition of 2-digit numbers. If we represent each 2-digit number using dimes and pennies, then the sum can be found by adding the number of pennies and adding the number of dimes. In later lessons this will be extended to addition of 3-digit numbers using dollars, dimes, and pennies.

MATERIALS
flannel board
10 felt models of dimes
10 felt models of pennies

PROCEDURE
Activity 1—Put 3 dimes and 7 pennies on the flannel board. How many dimes are on the flannel board? (3.) How many pennies are on the flannel board? (7.) How much money is on the flannel board? (37 cents.) Write on the chalkboard 37 = 3 tens, 7 ones = 30 + 7. Continue illustrating amounts of money in this manner and have students complete the sentences on the chalkboard.

Activity 2—Put 7 dimes and 4 pennies on the flannel board. Suppose I had this much money and got 1 dime and 2 pennies more. How much money did I have at first? (74 cents.) How much money did I get? (12 cents.) How can we show this on the flannel board? (Put 1 dime and 2 pennies on the flannel board.) Is this an addition situation or a subtraction situation? (Addition.) What do we have to do to add? (Count all the money on the flannel board.) How much money did I have in the end? (86 cents.) Write

$$\begin{array}{r} 74¢ \\ +12¢ \\ \hline 86¢ \end{array}$$

the addition on the chalkboard. No renaming should be included in this lesson.

WORKTEXT® PAGE 32—For teaching suggestions, see the annotated pupil's page.

Page 33

OBJECTIVE
■ Add two 2-digit numbers when no renaming is required

BACKGROUND
When adding two 2-digit numbers, students should be instructed to add the ones' digits first and then the tens' digits. Although this is not essential when no renaming is required, it is essential in later lessons where 10 ones must be renamed as 1 ten. A previous level of *Succeeding in Mathematics* has already introduced adding two 2-digit numbers, both with renaming and without renaming. These lessons, however, will redevelop these concepts in a manner which will reinforce the procedure that we use for adding numbers.

PROCEDURE
Write the exercise shown below on the chalkboard.

3 tens, 4 ones	30 + 4	34
+1 ten, 5 ones	+10 + 5	+15
___ tens,___ones	___ +___	___

Look at this exercise. It shows three ways to add the numbers 34 and 15. Let's look at the first way to write these, 3 tens, 4 ones and 1 ten, 5 ones. To add these numbers, we first add the ones. What is the sum of 4 ones and 5 ones? (9 ones.) Now we add the tens. How much are 3 tens and 1 ten? (4 tens.) What is the sum of 3 tens, 4 ones added to 1 ten, 5 ones? (4 tens, 9 ones.) Complete the other two ways to add 34 and 15 in a similar manner. We have just shown three ways to add 34 + 15. Two of these ways are with expanded names and one is with the standard name. Continue illustrating the short form to add two 2-digit numbers when renaming is not required.

WORKTEXT® PAGE 33—For teaching suggestions, see the annotated pupil's page.

ADDITIONAL ACTIVITIES
Materials: flannel board, felt models of dimes and pennies. Write the addition

$$\begin{array}{r} 22¢ \\ +45¢ \end{array}$$

on the chalkboard. Let's illustrate this on the flannel board using coins. What coins should I use to show 22 cents? (Two dimes and two pennies.) Have a student show this. What coins should I use to show 45 cents? (Four dimes and five pennies.) Have another student show this. To add these two amounts of money, we count how much money is on the flannel board altogether. How many pennies are on the flannel board? (7.) How many dimes are on the flannel board? (6.) What is the amount of money on the flannel board? (67 cents.) Write this sum on the chalkboard. To add 22¢ + 45¢, we first add the pennies and then we add the dimes. What is 5 + 2? (7.) Show students that 7 is written in the sum in the ones' column. Now we move to the tens' column and add the tens. What is 4 tens + 2 tens? (6 tens.) Point to the 6 in the sum. We have written 6 tens in the sum. Continue with examples of this type illustrating each addition of two 2-digit numbers on the flannel board using models of dimes and pennies.

After students understand the procedure for adding two 2-digit numbers using models of dimes and pennies, have them solve additions without illustrating the numbers using the dimes and pennies.

Pages 34-35

OBJECTIVES

- Rename 10 ones as 1 ten
- Rename 10 tens as 1 hundred
- Add two 2-digit numbers when renaming is required

BACKGROUND

The process of renaming is one of the more difficult concepts in addition. Renaming is necessary if the sum in one column is ten or more. When the sum of the ones' digits is 10 or more, it is necessary to rename 10 ones as 1 ten. When the sum of the tens' digits is 10 or more, it is necessary to rename 10 tens as 1 hundred. When renaming is required, it is essential that the student add the ones first.

MATERIALS

9 green counters per student
18 red counters per student
18 white counters per student

PROCEDURE

Activity 1—Ask students to sort their counters and make sure that they have 18 white counters, 18 red counters, and 9 green counters. Today we are going to play some games with counters. Each white counter will be equal to 1, each red counter will be equal to 10, and each green counter will be equal to 100. Write this on the chalkboard. Write 34 on the chalkboard. To show the number 34, using counters, I would use 3 red counters and 4 white counters. Have each student show 34 with the counters. Continue by having students show numbers less than 1,000 using their counters. Check to make sure that each student is using green counters for hundreds, red counters for tens, and white counters for ones.

Activity 2—How many white counters are equal to 1 red counter? (10.) How many white counters are equal to 1 green counter? (100.) Suppose that I have 15 white counters. How could I use red and white

counters to show this same number? (1 red and 5 white counters.) Whenever we have more than 10 white counters, we can regroup 10 white counters as 1 red counter. Suppose we have 3 red counters and 17 white counters. If we regroup 10 white counters as 1 red counter, what counters would we have? (4 reds and 7 whites.) Make a chart similar to the one below and continue with this activity.

Tens	Ones	Tens	Ones
3	17	4	7

Continue with this same activity and extend it to renaming 10 tens as 1 hundred. Ask the same types of questions as indicated above but use red and green counters.

Activity 3—Let's see if we can use the counters to add two numbers. Show 23 with your counters. Check to make sure that each student has 2 red and 3 white counters. Using different counters, show the number 51. Check to make sure that each student has shown 5 red and 1 white counters. If we put these two sets of counters together, how many white counters will we have? (4.) How many red counters will we have? (7.) What number is represented by this set of counters? (74.) Write on the chalkboard in column form the addition $\begin{array}{r}23\\+51\end{array}$. What is the sum for this addition? (74.) Is this the same number that we found with our counters? (Yes.)

Let's see if we can add 35 + 47 using our counters. To show 35, what must we do? (Use 3 red and 5 white counters.) Do that now. How can we show 47? (Use 4 red and 7 white counters.) Use a different set of counters to show that on your desk. How many white counters do you have on your desk altogether? (12.) Is this more than 10 white counters? (Yes.) Can we regroup 10 white counters as 1 red counter? (Yes.) Do that now. What number is represented on your desk? (82.)

Write on the chalkboard in column form $\begin{array}{r}35\\+47\end{array}$. To add these two numbers, we first add the ones. What is the sum of 7 ones + 5 ones? (12 ones.) Since 12 ones is more than 10 ones, we rename 12 ones as 1 ten and 2 ones. We write the 2 in the ones' column in the sum and write the 1 in the tens' column above the 3. Show how this is done in your example on the chalkboard. Now we add 1 ten, 3 tens and 4 tens. What is the sum? (8 tens.) We write 8 in the tens' column in the sum. Show this on the chalkboard. Continue with examples of this type until students recall how to add two 2-digit numbers when renaming is involved. Make sure that some of your examples require the student to rename 10 tens as 1 hundred.

WORKTEXT® PAGES 34–35—For teaching suggestions, see the annotated pupil's pages.

ADDITIONAL ACTIVITIES

Materials: flannel board, models of dimes and pennies. Use these materials as a teaching device in the same way that the counters were used in activity 3 to illustrate additions. Make sure that each addition given to the students has a sum which is less than 100.

Page 36

OBJECTIVES

■ Add columns of four 1-digit numbers
■ Add columns of four 2-digit numbers when renaming may be required

BACKGROUND

In this lesson, students are encouraged to find the sum by adding up the column and then to check their work by adding down the column. This is an example of the commutative property of addition.

MATERIALS

30 white counters per student
20 red counters per student
2 green counters per student

PROCEDURE

Activity 1—Write the addition 5 + 9 + 6 + 4 in column form on the chalkboard. Suppose that we want to add more than two numbers. For example, we may wish to add this column of numbers. How could we use our counters to find this sum? (Form sets of 5 white counters, 9 white counters, 6 white counters, and 4 white counters.) Do that on your desk. How many white counters do you have altogether? (24.) Now let's see if we can add without using the counters. Let's add from the bottom up. What is the sum of 4 + 6? (10.) What is the sum of 10 + 9? (19.) What is the sum of 19 + 5? (24.) Did we get the same sum when we added up the column as when we used our counters? (Yes.) Now

let's see if we can find the sum adding down the column. What is the sum of 5 + 9? (14.) What is the sum of 14 + 6? (20.) What is the sum of 20 + 4? (24.) Did we get the same sum? (Yes.)

Activity 2—Repeat the procedure for activity 1 to find the sum of a column of four 2-digit numbers.

WORKTEXT® PAGE 36—For teaching suggestions, see the annotated pupil's page.

Page 37

OBJECTIVE

■ Estimate answers by rounding each number to the nearest 10 and adding

BACKGROUND

A very important skill for students to learn is how to estimate answers. Estimating the results before performing the operation provides a means of testing whether your answer is reasonable and if it is approximately correct. This skill is especially important when one is using a calculator which gives no printed record.

PROCEDURE

Draw a number line on the chalkboard and label points with the numbers from 50 to 60, inclusive. Review rounding numbers to the nearest ten, using the procedures outlined in the material for Worktext® pages 17 and 18.

WORKTEXT® PAGE 37—For teaching suggestions, see the annotated pupil's page.

Page 38

OBJECTIVES

■ Identify amounts of cents stated as dollars, dimes, and pennies
■ Add amounts of money using dollars, dimes, and pennies

BACKGROUND

Dollars, dimes, and pennies are used to introduce students to addition of 3-digit numbers. In this model, dollars correspond to the number of hundreds, dimes correspond to the number of tens, and pennies correspond to the number of ones. Students should be encouraged to add the pennies first, the dimes second, and then the dollars. This continues and reinforces the pattern of adding the ones first, adding the tens second, and adding the hundreds third that has already been taught in the sections on the addition of 2-digit numbers.

MATERIALS

flannel board
5 felt models of dollar bills
10 felt models of dimes
10 felt models of pennies

PROCEDURE

Adapt the activities for Worktext® page 32 to teach addition of dollars, dimes, and pennies.

WORKTEXT® PAGE 38—For teaching suggestions, see the annotated pupil's page.

Page 39

OBJECTIVES

■ Add two 3-digit numbers when no renaming is required

MATERIALS

9 green counters per student
9 red counters per student
9 white counters per student

PROCEDURE

Adapt the prelesson activities for Worktext® pages 34-35 to teach addition of 3-digit numbers without renaming.

WORKTEXT® PAGE 39—For teaching suggestions, see the annotated pupil's page.

Pages 40-41

OBJECTIVES

■ Rename 10 ones as 1 ten and 10 tens as 1 hundred
■ Add two 3-digit numbers when renaming is required

MATERIALS

9 green counters per student
18 red counters per student
18 white counters per student

PROCEDURE

Adapt the activities for Worktext® pages 34-35 to teach addition of 3-digit numbers with renaming.

WORKTEXT® PAGES 40–41—For teaching suggestions, see the annotated pupil's pages.

ADDITIONAL ACTIVITIES

Materials: flannel board, models of dollars, dimes, and pennies. Use this teaching device in the same way that counters were used to illustrate additions. Make sure that each addition has a sum less than 1,000.

Page 42

OBJECTIVE

■ Solve word problems involving addition

BACKGROUND

Solving verbal problems is a difficult task for young children. It is necessary to provide them with a technique for solving verbal problems and also to provide them with many illustrations of problems to be solved.

To solve verbal problems, teachers should encourage students to perform the following steps: (1) read the problem carefully; (2) determine what is to be found; (3) determine what information is given; (4) determine the operation that can be used to solve the problem; (5) solve the problem; (6) state the answer in a complete sentence; and (7) check the answer.

Sometimes as students are identifying what is to be found and what facts are given, it is helpful to draw pictures of these facts or to represent these facts using models. This is especially true for children who have difficulty in translating from English sentences to mathematical sentences.

PROCEDURE

Have the following problem written on the board: Juan and Rita were saving dimes. Juan had saved 15 dimes, and Rita had saved 18 dimes. How many dimes did they have altogether? Read the problem to the class and then have the class read the problem with you. What are we to find? (The number of dimes Juan and Rita have together.) What facts are we given? (Juan had 15 dimes, and Rita had 18 dimes.) What must we do to find the number of coins altogether? (Add 15 + 18.) Each of you add 15 + 18. How many coins are there? (33.) Have students state the solution in a complete sentence and check this answer by adding again.

Continue with problems of this type specifying in detail the procedures suggested above for solving verbal problems.

WORKTEXT® PAGE 42—For teaching suggestions, see the annotated pupil's page.

Page 43

OBJECTIVE
■ Write roman numerals for numbers less than 300

BACKGROUND

Another system sometimes used to name counting numbers is the system of roman numerals. Roman numerals are used in various ways, such as to denote chapters in books or to give the year of production of films or movies. This is an additive system similar to the Egyptian hieroglyphic system. In an additive system each symbol represents a specified value and the value of the number is obtained by adding the values of each of the symbols. The roman numerals introduced in this lesson are I for the number 1, V for the number 5, X for the number 10, L for the number 50, and C for the number 100. To

write a number such as 168, we write CLXVIII. The value of this number is obtained by adding 100 + 50 + 10 + 5 + 1 + 1 + 1, which equals 168.

The numerals 4 and 9 are usually represented today by a subtractive rather than an additive group of symbols. The symbol for 4 is IV rather than IIII; the symbol for 40 is XL rather than XXXX, and so on. This is not introduced. Students may be aware of the subtractive aspect from its use on clockfaces.

PROCEDURE

WORKTEXT® PAGE 43—For teaching suggestions, see the annotated pupil's page.

Page 44

OBJECTIVE
■ Review the concepts and skills developed in chapter 2

PROCEDURE

WORKTEXT® PAGE 44—Have students complete the chapter review. Worktext® page references for the exercises in this chapter review are: exercise A, pages 24, 25, and 26; exercise B, pages 28 and 29; exercise C, pages 33, 34, 35, 36, 39, 40, and 41; and exercise D, page 42.

As students are completing addition exercises, their work should be carefully checked. Look for error patterns such as these:

Incorrect response to addition facts.	$\begin{array}{r} 33 \\ +48 \\ \hline 82 \end{array}$	$\begin{array}{r} 163 \\ +228 \\ \hline 392 \end{array}$
Adding in place.	$\begin{array}{r} 33 \\ +48 \\ \hline 711 \end{array}$	$\begin{array}{r} 163 \\ +228 \\ \hline 3811 \end{array}$
Forgetting to rename tens or hundreds.	$\begin{array}{r} 33 \\ +48 \\ \hline 71 \end{array}$	$\begin{array}{r} 162 \\ +275 \\ \hline 337 \end{array}$
Adding from left to right.	$\begin{array}{r} 42 \\ +73 \\ \hline 16 \end{array}$	$\begin{array}{r} 378 \\ +160 \\ \hline 439 \end{array}$

If any of these error patterns occur, it is essential that initial teaching activities on the pages referred to above be used as remediation activities.

Remedial instruction which is indicated by a review of error patterns in student work should be conducted before the check-up is administered.

Page 45

The last page of each chapter is a check-up designed to indicate the pupils' understanding of the concepts and skills presented in the chapter. Have students complete Worktext® page 45 independently.

Subtraction

Page 46

OBJECTIVES

- Recognize subtraction as a take-away situation
- Write subtraction sentences illustrated by objects

BACKGROUND

Subtraction is the inverse operation of addition. Both concepts should be developed from physical experiences. Addition is related to joining sets. Subtraction is related to the removal of part of a set. In this lesson students should be encouraged to physically remove elements from a set and to identify the subtraction sentence from this physical action.

MATERIALS

10 red blocks
10 blue blocks

PROCEDURE

Activity 1—Show the set of 10 red blocks. There are 10 red blocks in this set. Have a student remove 3 of these blocks from the set. How many blocks were removed? (3.) How many blocks are left? (7.) We write the subtraction sentence $10 - 3 = 7$. Write this subtraction sentence on the chalkboard. Continue with examples of this type. In each case, ask how many blocks were removed and how many blocks remain. Then write the subtraction sentence that was illustrated by this physical situation on the chalkboard.

Another type of subtraction situation can be illustrated when the numbers of objects in two different sets are compared. Have a student choose 7 red blocks. Have a second student choose 5 blue blocks. Which student has more blocks? How many more blocks does (name of student) have? Write the sentence $7 - 5 = 2$ on the chalkboard. Here we compared the number of blocks in two sets. (name of student) had 7 blocks and (name of student) had 5 blocks. To find how many more blocks are in one set than the other, we subtract. Continue with examples of this type. In each case write the subtraction sentence on the chalkboard.

Activity 2—Draw 8 dots on the chalkboard. How many dots are there? (8.) To show that some of these dots are taken away, I will draw a circle with an arrow around the dots. Draw a circle with an arrow around 5 dots. How many dots have been taken away? (5.) How many dots are left? (3.) What subtraction sentence could we write? ($8 - 5 = 3$.) Write this subtraction sentence on the chalkboard. Continue with examples of this type. Have students help in writing the subtraction sentences on the chalkboard.

Write $8 - 2$ on the chalkboard. How many objects should we start with? (8.) Have a student draw 8 dots. How many objects must we remove from this set? (2.) Have a student show this. How many objects are left? (6.) What is the difference of 8 − 2? (6.) Continue having students draw pictures to illustrate subtraction situations.

WORKTEXT® PAGE 46—For teaching suggestions, see the annotated pupil's page.

Pages 47-48

OBJECTIVES

- Name the subtrahend, the minuend and the difference in a subtraction exercise
- Subtract using the number line

BACKGROUND

In a subtraction sentence such as 11 − 8 = 3, 11 is called the *minuend,* 8 is called the *subtrahend,* and 3 is called the *difference.* Students should not be tested on these terms. They are introduced as labels for parts of subtraction exercises to facilitate communication between teacher and student.

A convenient model for showing subtraction is the number line. To subtract 11 − 5 on the number line, we start at 11 and count 5 spaces to the left. Care must be taken that students do not count 11, but rather begin their count to the left, starting with 10. The stopping point is the difference.

PROCEDURE

Activity 1—Draw a number line on the chalkboard and label points from 0 to 18. Write 5 − 3 on the chalkboard. To show this subtraction, we start at the number 5 and count 3 spaces to the left. The first number that you count is 4. What is the second number that you would count? (3.) What is the third number that you would count? (2.) We have now counted 3 spaces to the left. What is the stopping point? (2.) What is the difference of 5 − 3? (2.) Continue finding differences for subtractions using the number line. Have students write the subtraction sentence for each illustration.

Activity 2—Draw the number line picture shown below on the chalkboard.

At what number did we start? (11.) How many spaces did we travel to the left? (5.) At what number did

we stop? (6.) This number line shows the subtraction sentence 11 − 5 = 6. Continue the activity.

Activity 3—Leave the number line on the chalkboard and write the subtraction 12 − 8. Use the number line to find the difference. What is the difference? (4.) We already know that the answer in a subtraction sentence is called the difference. The other two numbers in a subtraction sentence also have special names. In the subtraction sentence 12 − 8 = 4, we call 12 the minuend, 8 the subtrahend, and 4 the difference. We can also write this subtraction sentence in column form as $\begin{array}{r} 12 \\ -\ 8 \\ \hline 4 \end{array}$. The minuend is the number from which another number is to be subtracted. The subtrahend is the number to be subtracted. The difference is the answer. Continue to write subtractions on the chalkboard. Have the students use the number line to find the differences. Also have them identify the minuend and the subtrahend in each of the completed subtraction sentences.

WORKTEXT® PAGES 47–48—For teaching suggestions, see the annotated pupil's pages.

Pages 49-50

OBJECTIVES

- Recognize that addition and subtraction are opposite operations
- Write related addition or subtraction facts from a given addition or subtraction fact

BACKGROUND

The lesson emphasizes the relationship between addition and subtraction. When we know one addition fact, such as 6 + 4 = 10, we know a second addition fact and two subtraction facts: 4 + 6 = 10, 10 − 4 = 6, and 10 − 6 = 4. These related facts are important, because they emphasize the commutative property for addition and provide us with a method for checking subtraction.

PROCEDURE

WORKTEXT® PAGES 49–50—For teaching suggestions, see the annotated pupil's pages.

ADDITIONAL ACTIVITIES

Materials: 10 red counting blocks and 10 blue counting blocks per student. Form a set of 5 red counting blocks. Now form a set of 7 blue counting blocks. If we put these two sets together, how many blocks will we have? (12.) What addition sentences can we write? (5 + 7 = 12 and 7 + 5 = 12.) Have a chart similar to that shown in exercise C, page 50 on the chalkboard. Have students write the above addition sentences in the table. You have 12 blocks in front of you. If you take away the 5 red blocks, how many blocks will you have left? (7.) What subtraction sentence does this show? (12 − 5 = 7.) Write this subtraction fact on the board. Illustrate the other subtraction fact by reforming the set of 12 blocks and taking the set of 7 blue blocks from the set. Continue with activities of this type. Have the students identify the addition and subtraction sentences using their blocks and then complete the chart by writing the addition and subtraction facts.

Pages 51-52

OBJECTIVE
- Find the differences for the 100 basic subtraction facts

MATERIALS
set of subtraction flash cards

PROCEDURE
Activity 1—Today we are going to play a game using subtraction facts. Take a sheet of paper and number lines from 1 to 10. When I hold up a subtraction flash card, write the difference beside the first number before I tell you the answer. If I tell you the answer before you can write it, leave the space blank.

Adjust the timing according to the ability of the class. After showing 10 cards, ask pupils how many have all 10 answers, how many have 9, and so on. Continue for several games. Then let students take turns showing the cards and giving the answers. Note students who have difficulty with subtraction facts so that they can be given additional drill later.

Activity 2—Form pairs of students and give each pair of students part of a set of flash cards. As one student shows the subtractions, the other should give the differences. After going through the cards one time this way, the students' roles should be reversed. Pairs of students should exchange cards after each game. Encourage students to use a

number line or blocks to find those differences which they do not know.

WORKTEXT® PAGES 51–52—For teaching suggestions, see the annotated pupil's pages.

ADDITIONAL ACTIVITY

Today we are going to learn a new game. We will start with a number, and each player can subtract either 1, 2, or 3 from this number. The player who obtains the difference 0 wins the game. Let's start with the number 14. I want to subtract 3 from 14. What is the difference? (11.) Remember, you can subtract 1, 2, or 3 from the number that we have left. What would you like to subtract from 11? Call on a student and have them give the number that they wish to subtract and the difference. Continue until a student obtains the number 0. That student is the winner. After students understand the rules for the game, group them in pairs and have them play the game together. If abler students are paired, the rules of the game might be expanded to permit them to subtract 1, 2, 3, 4, or 5 from the starting number. Under these circumstances, they would have to start with numbers larger than 20.

Page 53

OBJECTIVES
- Translate from written or oral statements to subtraction sentences
- Solve word problems involving subtraction

BACKGROUND
In this lesson students will learn words that are to be translated as subtraction and how these words can be used in actual problem situations. As with addition, words that mean to subtract are introduced in isolation first so that students can gain facility in translating phrases that mean subtraction before they are required to apply this ability in a problem situation.

PROCEDURE
Activity 1—Write the phrase *seven subtracted from thirteen* on the chalkboard. Have students read this phrase in unison. What do you think this phrase means? Help students to see that the phrase tells

you to subtract. When we say 7 subtracted from 13, should we write 13 − 7 or 7 − 13? (13 − 7.) Why should we write 13 as the minuend and 7 as the subtrahend? (Because the phrase tells us to subtract 7 from 13.) Thirteen is the number from which 7 is to be subtracted. Seven is the number to be subtracted. Continue discussing phrases such as 8 less 2, the difference of 11 and 7, 12 decreased by 9, and 13 subtract 4. Each of these phrases can be translated as subtraction. In each case, emphasize which number is to be the minuend and which number the subtrahend. This is important, since subtraction is not commutative.

Activity 2—Ask a student to draw 7 stars on the chalkboard. Ask a second student to erase 4 of these stars. (name of student) drew 7 stars on the chalkboard and (name of student) took away 4 of these. How many stars are left? (3.) What subtraction sentence could we write to show this? (7 − 4 = 3.) What words did I use when I told you the problem indicated subtraction? (Took away.) Continue having students draw pictures on the chalkboard and illustrating the various words that mean to subtract. In each case, write the subtraction sentence for the problem on the chalkboard.

WORKTEXT® PAGE 53—For teaching suggestions, see the annotated pupil's page.

Page 54

OBJECTIVE

■ Subtract two 2-digit numbers when no renaming is required

BACKGROUND

We may subtract two 2-digit numbers in a variety of ways. We can do this on the number line by starting at the minuend and counting back the number of spaces indicated by the subtrahend. We can subtract numbers written with expanded names. The more conventional way is to subtract the ones first and then to subtract the tens. The first two methods should be used to explain why this last short form works.

PROCEDURE

Write the subtractions shown below on the chalkboard.

7 tens, 4 ones	70 + 4	74
−2 tens, 3 ones	−20 + 3	−23
_ tens, _ ones	_ _ + _	_ _

Look at the three ways to write the number 74 and the three ways to write the number 23. Let's look at the first way to write these numbers, 7 tens, 4 ones and 2 tens, 3 ones. If we want to subtract these numbers, we first subtract the ones. What is the difference of 4 ones minus 3 ones? (1 one.) Write this difference. Now we subtract the tens. What is the difference of 7 tens and 2 tens? (5 tens.) Write this difference. What is the difference of 7 tens, 4 ones minus 2 tens, 3 ones? (5 tens, 1 one.) Complete the other ways to subtract 74 − 23 in a similar fashion. We have just shown three ways to subtract 74 − 23. Two of these ways are with expanded names and one is with the standard name.

Continue with exercises illustrating the short form to subtract two 2-digit numbers when renaming is not required. Have students do more and more of the work on the chalkboard.

WORKTEXT® PAGE 54—For teaching suggestions, see the annotated pupil's page.

ADDITIONAL ACTIVITIES

Materials: flannel board, felt models of dimes and pennies. Write 65¢ −14¢ on the chalkboard. Let's illustrate this subtraction on the flannel board. What coins should I use to show 65¢? (6 dimes and 5 pennies.) Have a student show this. How can I subtract 14¢? (Take away 1 dime and 4 pennies.) Have a student do this. The difference is the amount of money left on the flannel board. How much money is left? (51¢.) Go to the chalkboard. To subtract 65¢ − 14¢, we first subtract the ones, and then we subtract the tens. What is the difference of 5 − 4? (1.) Write 1 in the ones' column in the difference. Now we subtract tens. What is the difference of 6 tens − 1 ten? (5 tens.) Write 5 in the tens' column in the difference. Continue with exercises of this type, illustrating each subtraction of two 2-digit numbers on the flannel board using models of dimes and pennies and then showing how this is written on the chalkboard.

Page 55

OBJECTIVE

■ Rename 1 ten as 10 ones

BACKGROUND

In subtraction, sometimes there are not enough ones, tens, hundreds, etc. to subtract from. When this is the case, it is necessary to rename a larger unit as 10 smaller units. Renaming should be presented so that students recognize that the number remains the same even though its name has been changed.

MATERIALS

flannel board
9 felt models of dimes
18 felt models of pennies
9 red counters per student
18 white counters per student

PROCEDURE

Activity 1—Have students put their red and white counters on their desks. Hold up a red counter. How many white counters can be exchanged for this red counter? (10.) Why? (Because each red counter equals 10 white counters.) Show 32 using your counters. How many red counters did you use? (3.) How many white counters did you use? (2.) Suppose that we needed more than 2 white counters. How could we do this? Help the students to see that 1 red counter could be exchanged for 10 white counters. Exchange 1 red counter for 10 white counters. Now how many red counters do you have? (2.) How many white counters do you have? (12.) Write on the chalkboard 3 tens, 2 ones = 2 tens, 12 ones.

Continue with activities emphasizing the process of renaming 1 ten as 10 ones. In each case, write the expanded name on the chalkboard. Help the students to see that when 1 ten is renamed as 10 ones, the number of tens is decreased by 1 and the number of ones is increased by 10.

Activity 2—Have a student come to the flannel board and show 43¢ using dimes and pennies. Make sure that the student puts 4 dimes and 3 pennies on the flannel board. Suppose we wanted to take 7 pennies from the 43¢. Are there enough pennies to do this? (No.) Could we change 4 dimes and 3 pennies so that we could take 7 pennies from it? (Yes.) How? (Exchange 1 dime for 10 pennies.) Have a student show this. How many dimes do we have now? (3.) How many pennies do we have now? (13.) Could we now take 7 pennies from the amount on the flannel board? (Yes.) Help students to understand that if more pennies are needed, 1 dime can always be exchanged for 10 pennies. Continue with this activity until students can rename tens as ones and specify the number of tens and the number of ones after renaming has taken place.

WORKTEXT® PAGE 55—For teaching suggestions, see the annotated pupil's page.

Page 56

OBJECTIVE

■ Subtract a 2-digit number from a 2-digit number when renaming is required

BACKGROUND

When there are not enough ones to subtract from, it is necessary to rename 1 ten as 10 ones. Adding these ones to the number of ones in the minuend permits subtraction in the ones' column. When renaming of this type is needed to complete the subtraction, it is essential that students subtract in the ones' column first and then go on to subtract in the tens' column.

MATERIALS

9 red counters per student
18 white counters per student

PROCEDURE

Activity 1—Remember that 1 red counter is equal to 10 white counters. Put 2 red and 5 white counters in the middle of your desk. How could we show the same number using only 1 red counter? (Exchange 1 red counter for 10 white counters.) Do this. After exchanging 1 red counter for 10 white counters, how many white counters do you have? (15.) How many red counters do you have? (1.) Check to make sure that each student has done this correctly. Continue with exercises of this type.

Activity 2—Let's use our counters to show how to subtract 31 − 14. Write on the chalkboard $\begin{array}{r} 31 \\ -14 \end{array}$. First, you must use your counters to show 31. How do you do that? (Use 3 red counters and 1 white counter.) Now we want to take away 14 from this. Are there enough ones from which to take 4? (No.) How could we get enough ones? (Exchange 1 red counter for 10 white counters.) Do that. What counters do you have on your desk? (2 red and 11 white.) Are there enough ones from which to take 4 now? (Yes.) Take 4 ones from the 11 ones on your desk. How many ones do you have left? (7.) Can you take 1 ten from the 2 tens that you have left? (Yes.) Do that. How many tens do you have left? (1.) What is the difference of 31 − 14? (17.) Write 17 on the chalkboard. Continue with exercises of this type. In each case make sure that students are renaming 1 ten as 10 ones correctly.

Does anyone know a short way to find differences like these? Help students to see that they subtract the ones' digits first. If there are not enough ones to subtract from, they must rename 1 ten as 10 ones. Show them how to cross out the tens' digit in the minuend and decrease it by 1. After they have done this, they must add 10 ones to the number of ones in the minuend and write this sum above the number of ones. Now have them subtract in the ones' column and write this difference. Then have them subtract in the tens' column and write this difference. Continue with exercises in which a 2-digit number is subtracted from a 2-digit number and renaming is necessary. Write each example on the chalkboard and have students find the difference.

WORKTEXT® PAGE 56—For teaching suggestions, see the annotated pupil's page.

ADDITIONAL ACTIVITIES

Materials: flannel board, 9 felt models of dimes, 18 felt models of pennies. Use the felt models of dimes and pennies in the same way that you used red and white counters to illustrate subtractions which require renaming 1 ten as 10 ones. Provide students with sufficient practice so that they understand the process of subtracting two 2-digit numbers when there are not enough ones to subtract from. After completing each example using the models of dimes and pennies on the flannel board, illustrate the short form of the subtraction on the chalkboard.

Page 57

OBJECTIVE
■ Check subtraction by addition

BACKGROUND

Each subtraction specifies a related addition. For example, 45 − 24 = 21 specifies the related addition 21 + 24 = 45. We can use this relationship to check subtraction. After a difference has been found, we can check by adding the difference to the subtra-

hend. The sum of these two numbers should equal the minuend. If it does not, a mistake has been made and the student should recheck both the subtraction and the related addition.

Checking subtraction is important, and students should always be encouraged to check their work.

PROCEDURE

Write $\frac{62}{-15}$ on the chalkboard. Are there enough ones to subtract from? (No.) What must we do? (Rename 1 ten as 10 ones.) Have a student show this procedure. Now can we subtract in the ones' column? (Yes.) What is 12 ones − 5 ones? (7 ones.) Write 7 in the ones' column. What is 5 tens − 1 ten? (4 tens.) Write 4 in the tens' column. What is the difference when 15 is subtracted from 62? (47.) We can use a related addition to check this subtraction. If we add the subtrahend, 15, to the difference, 47, what number should we get? (62.) Let's do that. Write $\frac{15}{+\ 47}$ on the chalkboard. What do we do first? (Add the ones.) What do we get when we add 7 ones + 5 ones? (12 ones.) We rename 10 of these ones as 1 ten. We write the 2 that is left in the ones' column and then write the 1 in the tens' column. Now add the tens. What is the sum of the tens? (6.) Is this sum equal to the minuend in the subtraction? (Yes.) Continue finding differences for subtractions and checking them by addition. Make sure that each student understands the subtraction check.

WORKTEXT® PAGE 57—For teaching suggestions, see the annotated pupil's page.

Page 58

OBJECTIVES
■ Subtract a 1-digit number from a 2-digit number when renaming is not required
■ Subtract a 1-digit number from a 2-digit number when renaming is required

PROCEDURE

WORKTEXT® PAGE 58—For teaching suggestions, see the annotated pupil's page.

ADDITIONAL ACTIVITIES

1. Materials: 9 red and 18 white counters per student. Write $\begin{array}{r} 22 \\ -\ 9 \\ \hline \end{array}$ on the chalkboard. Let's use our counters to show this subtraction. How can we show 22 with our counters? (Use 2 red and 2 white counters.) Are there enough white counters to take 9 from? (No.) What can we do? (Exchange 1 red for 10 white counters.) Do that. Now do you have enough white counters to take 9 from? (Yes.) Take 9 white counters from the 12 that you have on your desk. How many white counters do you have left? (3.) How many red counters do you have? (1.) What is the difference when 9 is subtracted from 22? (13.) Write this on the chalkboard. Continue with examples in which students are to subtract a 1-digit from a 2-digit number. After the subtraction is performed using the counters, write the subtraction on the chalkboard in column form and show how we write the difference.

2. We are going to play a game similar to one you have played before. Write the number 47 on the chalkboard. To complete this game, players, in turn, select any number from 1 to 9 to be subtracted from 47. The player who finds a difference of 0 first is the winner. I'll start. I want to subtract 5 from 47. The difference that I find is 42. Now have a student select a number from 1 to 9 to subtract from 42. After the number has been selected, it must be subtracted from 42 by the student. Continue in this way until some student gets to 0. Then divide the students into pairs to play. For each game, you should provide the starting number and let the students select which digits they wish to subtract from it. Students must perform their own subtractions and their opponents must check each subtraction to make sure it is correct.

Page 59

OBJECTIVES

- Differentiate between addition and subtraction situations
- Solve word problems involving addition and subtraction

BACKGROUND

Students must practice previously learned behaviors in a wide variety of settings. In this lesson, students will be required first to identify if a problem requires addition or subtraction and then to solve problems. Recognizing which of these two operations to perform is essential if students are to become good problem solvers.

PROCEDURE

Activity 1—Today I am going to try to trick you. I will ask you questions, and you must decide if you should add or subtract to find the answer. After you have decided, find the answer on your paper. Remember, you will have to listen very carefully to the question that I ask. Let's start. What is 7 increased by 9? Repeat the sentence. Do you add or subtract to find the answer? (Add.) What words tell you to add? (Increased by.) What numbers do you add? (7 and 9.) Write $7 + 9$ on your paper and find the sum. What is the sum? (16.) Continue: How much larger is 12 than 8? What is 42 decreased by 11? How much is 14 and 29? What is 32 decreased by 15? What is 32 increased by 15? What is 47 minus 28?

Activity 2—Have a problem like the following written on the chalkboard: Tina and Marie were saving bottle caps. Tina saved 64, and Marie saved 47. How many more bottle caps did Tina save than Marie? Remind students that the first step in solving a problem is to read it carefully. Have a student read the problem aloud. What are we to find? (How many more bottle caps Tina has than Marie.) What information are we given? (Tina saved 64 bottle caps, and Marie saved 47 bottle caps.) Should we add or subtract these numbers? (Subtract.) What words in the problem tell us to subtract? (The first words in the question, how many more.) Have a student write the subtraction at the board while the rest of the students are completing it at their desks. What is the difference? (17.) How could we check this answer? (Add $17 + 47$.) Do that. What is the sum of $17 + 47$? (64.) Now let's state our answer in a complete sentence. What complete sentence tells us the answer to this problem? (Tina had 17 more bottle caps than Marie.)

Continue with problems of this type.

WORKTEXT® PAGE 59—For teaching suggestions, see the annotated pupil's page.

Page 60

OBJECTIVE

- Subtract two 3-digit numbers when no renaming is required

MATERIALS

9 green counters per student
9 red counters per student
9 white counters per student

PROCEDURE

Activity 1—Ask students to sort their counters. What value have we assigned to the white counters? (1.) What value have we assigned to the red counters? (10.) What value have we assigned to the green counters? (100.) How many red counters are equal to 1 green counter? (10.) How many white counters are equal to 1 green counter? (100.)

Use your counters to show the number 329 on your desk. How many green counters did you use? (3.) How many red counters did you use? (2.) How many white counters did you use? (9.) Write on the chalkboard the sentence 329 = 300 + 20 + 9. Continue illustrating numbers less than 1,000 using the counters. Make sure that each student is using the green counters for hundreds, the red counters for tens, and the white counters for ones. Have students write the expanded names for these numbers.

Activity 2—Now let's use our counters to subtract. Write $\begin{array}{r} 284 \\ -152 \\ \hline \end{array}$ on the chalkboard. To find the answer to this subtraction, we first show 284 with our counters. Do that. If we are subtracting 152 from 284, how many white counters must we remove? (2.) How many white counters are left? (2.) Write 2 in the ones' column on the chalkboard. Now how many red counters must we remove? (5.) Do that. How many red counters are left? (3.) Write 3 in the tens' column on the chalkboard. How many green counters must we remove? (1.) Do that. How many green counters are left? (1.) Write 1 in the hundreds' column on the chalkboard. What is the difference when 152 is subtracted from 284? (132.) Emphasize that to subtract two 3-digit numbers, we first subtract the ones, then the tens, and then the hundreds. Continue with exercises of this type until students thoroughly understand.

WORKTEXT® PAGE 60—For teaching suggestions, see the annotated pupil's page.

Page 61

OBJECTIVE

■ Rename 1 hundred as 10 tens

MATERIALS

flannel board
18 felt models of pennies
18 felt models of dimes
9 felt models of dollar bills
9 green counters per student
18 red counters per student
18 white counters per student

PROCEDURE

Activity 1—Have a student come to the flannel board and show 240¢ using dollars and dimes. How many dollars did (name of student) use? (2.) How many dimes did (name of student) use? (4.) Suppose we want to take 8 dimes from the 2 dollars and 4 dimes. Are there enough dimes to do this? (No.) Could we exchange a dollar for 10 dimes? (Yes.) How many dollars would there be after we did this? (1.) How many dimes would there be? (14.) Have a student show this. Now can we take 8 dimes from the dollars and dimes we have on the flannel board? (Yes.) Write on the chalkboard 2 dollars, 4 dimes equals 1 dollar, 14 dimes. Help students to understand that if more dimes are needed, 1 dollar can always be exchanged for 10 dimes. Continue with this activity until students can exchange dollars for dimes.

After several statements are written on the chalkboard, ask students to convert these statements to number sentences. For example, 2 dollars, 4 dimes equals 1 dollar, 14 dimes is translated to the number sentence 200 + 40 = 100 + 140. Explain that 100 has been renamed as 10 tens in each number sentence.

Activity 2—Repeat activity 1, using counters and different examples. Emphasize the process of renaming 1 hundred as 10 tens. In each case, write the expanded name on the chalkboard. Help the students to see that when 1 hundred is renamed as 10 tens, the number of tens is increased by 10 and the number of hundreds is decreased by 1.

After students thoroughly understand how 1 hundred can be renamed as 10 tens, you should review the process of renaming 1 ten as 10 ones. At this time, both processes should not be used in the same example at the same time. However, students should practice renaming 1 hundred as 10 tens in numbers such as 175 and should also practice renaming 1 ten as 10 ones in numbers such as 392.

WORKTEXT® PAGE 61—For teaching suggestions, see the annotated pupil's page.

OBJECTIVES

- Subtract a 3-digit number from a 3-digit number when renaming tens as ones is required
- Subtract a 3-digit number from a 3-digit number when renaming hundreds as tens is required

MATERIALS

9 green counters per pupil
18 red counters per pupil
18 white counters per pupil

PROCEDURE

Activity 1—Put 4 green, 2 red, and 7 white counters in the middle of your desk. What number does this represent? (427.) Are there enough red counters to take 7 red counters from this number? (No.) What would you have to do to get enough? (Exchange 1 green for 10 red counters.) Do that. How many green counters do you have now? (3.) How many red counters do you have now? (12.) Are there enough red counters so that you can subtract 7 red counters? (Yes.) Take away 7 red counters. The counters left represent what number? (357.) What subtraction is illustrated? (427 − 70 = 357.)

Continue with subtractions in which 1 green counter must be exchanged for 10 red counters or in which 1 red counter must be exchanged for 10 white counters. After the counters have been manipulated, write the subtraction that was illustrated in column form on the chalkboard.

$$
\begin{array}{r} 384 \\ \end{array}
$$

Activity 2—Write -127 on the chalkboard. Now let's see if you can use your counters to subtract 384 − 127. First, you must use your counters to show 384. How do you do that? (Use 3 green, 8 red, and 4 white counters.) Are there enough ones from which to take 7? (No.) How could you get enough ones? (Rename 1 ten as 10 ones.) Do that. What counters do you have left? (3 green, 7 red, 14 white.) Are there enough ones from which to take 7 now? (Yes.) Take 7 ones from the 14 ones you have on your desk. How many ones do you have left? (7.) Have a student complete this step of the subtraction at the chalkboard. After this step, the subtraction

should look like this:
$$
\begin{array}{r} {\scriptstyle 7\,14} \\ 3\,\cancel{8}\,\cancel{4} \\ -\ 127 \\ \hline 7 \end{array}
$$
. Are there enough

tens from which to take 2? (Yes.) Use your counters to show this. How many tens are left? (5.) Have another student write 5 in the tens' column on the chalkboard. Are there enough hundreds from which to take 1? (Yes.) Use your counters to show this. How many hundreds do you have left? (2.) Have another student write 2 in the hundreds' column on the chalkboard. The completed subtraction should look like this:

$$
\begin{array}{r} {\scriptstyle 7\,14} \\ 3\,\cancel{8}\,\cancel{4} \\ -\ 127 \\ \hline 257 \end{array}
$$
. What is the difference when 127 is sub-

tracted from 384? (257.) Continue with exercises in which students use their counters to complete subtractions and write the subtraction on the chalkboard. Some of the subtractions should require that students rename 1 hundred as 10 tens. Others should have students rename 1 ten as 10 ones. Both of these processes should not be considered in the same subtraction exercise at this point.

After students thoroughly understand this process using the counters and can write the subtraction on the chalkboard, consider several subtractions without using the counters. Have students subtract in the ones' column first, the tens' column second, and the hundreds' column third.

WORKTEXT® PAGES 62–63—For teaching suggestions, see the annotated pupil's pages.

ADDITIONAL ACTIVITIES

Materials: flannel board, 9 felt models of dollar bills, 18 felt models of dimes, 18 felt models of pennies. Use the felt models of dollars, dimes, and pennies in the same way that you used green, red, and white counters to illustrate subtractions which require renaming 1 hundred as 10 tens or 1 ten as 10 ones. Provide students with sufficient practice so that they understand the process of subtracting two 3-digit numbers when regrouping is required. After completing each example using the models of dollars, dimes, and pennies on the flannel board, illustrate the short form of the subtraction on the chalkboard.

Page 64

OBJECTIVE

- Rename 1 hundred as 10 tens and 1 ten as 10 ones

MATERIALS

flannel board
18 felt models of pennies
18 felt models of dimes
9 felt models of dollar bills
9 green counters per student
18 red counters per student
18 white counters per student

PROCEDURE

Adapt the activities for Worktext® pages 55 and 61 to teach renaming hundreds as tens and tens as ones in the same numbers.

WORKTEXT® PAGE 64—For teaching suggestions, see the annotated pupil's page.

Pages 65-66

OBJECTIVE

■ Subtract a 3-digit number from a 3-digit number when renaming hundreds as tens and tens as ones is required

MATERIALS

9 green counters per pupil
18 red counters per pupil
18 white counters per pupil

PROCEDURE

Adapt the activities for Worktext® pages 62–63 to teach subtraction of 3-digit numbers when renaming hundreds as tens and tens as ones is required.

WORKTEXT® PAGES 65–66—For teaching suggestions, see the annotated pupil's pages.

ADDITIONAL ACTIVITY

Materials: flannel board, 9 felt models of dollar bills, 18 felt models of dimes, 18 felt models of pennies. Use the felt models of dollars, dimes, and pennies in the same way that you used green, red, and white counters to illustrate subtractions which require renaming 1 hundred as 10 tens and 1 ten as

10 ones. Provide sufficient practice so that students are able to subtract two 3-digit numbers when regrouping is required. After each example has been shown on the flannel board, write the indicated subtraction on the chalkboard and find the difference using the short form.

Page 67

OBJECTIVE

■ Complete a cross-number puzzle in which the exercises are additions, subtractions, and number patterns

PROCEDURE

WORKTEXT® PAGE 67—For teaching suggestions, see the annotated pupil's page.

Page 68

OBJECTIVE

■ Review the concepts and skills developed in chapter 3

PROCEDURE

WORKTEXT® PAGE 68—Have students complete the chapter review. Worktext® page references for the exercises in this chapter review are: exercise A, pages 47, 48, and 51; exercise B, pages 51 and 52; exercise C, pages 55, 61, and 64; exercise D, pages 56, 63, and 66; and exercise E, pages 57, 58, and 63.

Page 69

The last page of each chapter is a check-up designed to indicate the pupils' understanding of the concepts and skills that were presented in the chapter. Have the students complete Worktext® page 69.

Multiplication

Pages 70-71

OBJECTIVES
- Show the relationship between a multiplication sentence and an addition sentence with a repeated addend
- Identify the factors and the product in a multiplication sentence

BACKGROUND

Multiplication of whole numbers can be thought of as repeated addition of equal addends. To find the number of objects in four sets, each of which has five objects, we could add $5 + 5 + 5 + 5 = 20$, or we could multiply $4 \times 5 = 20$. The 4 in the multiplication sentence tells the number of times the addend appears. The 5 in the multiplication sentence is the value of each addend. In this lesson students should concentrate on the relationship between multiplication and addition. The concept is developed through pictures, and then students are asked to write multiplication sentences from given addition sentences and addition sentences from given multiplication sentences. In this way, students will learn that multiplication is a fast way of performing addition.

MATERIALS
30 white counters per student
flannel board
40 white flannel dots

PROCEDURE

Activity 1—Distribute the counters. Form 3 sets of 5 counters. How many counters are in each set? (5.) How many counters are in the 3 sets altogether? (15.) What addition sentence can we write to show this? ($5 + 5 + 5 = 15$.) We can also write this as a multiplication sentence. The multiplication sentence that we write is $3 \times 5 = 15$. Write $3 \times 5 = 15$ on the chalkboard. The 3 in the multiplication sentence tells us that there are 3 equal addends. The 5 in the multiplication sentence tells us that each addend is equal to 5. We read the multiplication sentence $3 \times 5 = 15$. Continue using the counters to form sets with equal numbers of counters. Identify the addition sentence and the multiplication sentence for each situation.

Activity 2—Have a student form a row of 3 dots on the flannel board. Have a second student form a row of 3 dots underneath the first row. Continue until there are 6 rows of 3 dots. How many rows of dots are there? (6.) How many dots are in each row? (3.) What is the total number of dots on the flannel board? (18.) What addition sentence could we write to show this? ($3 + 3 + 3 + 3 + 3 + 3 = 18$.) What multiplication sentence could we write to show this? ($6 \times 3 = 18$.) Write these sentences on the chalkboard. Continue illustrating multiplication sentences and addition sentences using rectangular arrays of dots on the flannel board. Have students write the addition sentence and the multiplication sentence illustrated by each array.

Activity 3—Suppose I want to find the answer to the multiplication 4×3. We could read this multiplication as 4 threes. How could I use the dots on the flannel board to find the answer? (Form 4 rows of 3 dots each.) Have a student do this. What is the answer to 4×3? (12.) Write this multiplication sentence on the chalkboard. In this multiplication, 4 and 3 are called factors. The 12 is called the product. Point to each of the numbers in turn and ask the class what each number is called. Now write 3×6 on the chalkboard. What are the numbers 3 and 6 called? (Factors.) What is the answer to this multiplication called? (The product.) How could we find the product? (Form 3 rows of 6 dots.) What is the product? (18.) Continue with activities in which students are given a multiplication or are asked to find the product by forming arrays of dots. Emphasize the relationship between multiplication sentences and addition sentences and the names of the parts of multiplication sentences.

WORKTEXT® PAGES 70-71—For teaching suggestions, see the annotated pupil's pages.

Page 72

OBJECTIVE
- Find products for multiplications using the number line

PROCEDURE

Draw a number line on the board and have students help to label the points from 0 to 36. Today we are going to learn how to multiply using the number line. Suppose that we want to multiply 4 × 6. Write 4 × 6 on the chalkboard. What is the related addition for this multiplication? (6 + 6 + 6 + 6.) Write 6 + 6 + 6 + 6 on the chalkboard. How could we use the number line to add 6 + 6 + 6 + 6? (Start at 0 and take 4 hops of 6 spaces each to the right.) Show this procedure by drawing arrows to indicate the hops. After we have taken 4 hops of 6 spaces each, at what number do we stop? (24.) What is the product of 4 × 6? (24.) Finish writing the sentence 4 × 6 = 24 on the chalkboard. Also complete the sentence 6 + 6 + 6 + 6 = 24. Let's review what we did. To find 4 × 6 on the number line, we started at 0 and took 4 hops of 6 spaces each. We took 4 hops because the first factor in the multiplication was 4. We took hops of 6 spaces each because the second factor in the multiplication was 6. Continue doing multiplications on the number line. Have students begin at 0 and show hops to the right with arrows. For each multiplication ask questions such as: How many hops must we take? How many spaces long is each hop? At what number do we stop? What is the product? Make sure that you write each multiplication sentence and each related addition sentence on the chalkboard. Emphasize that the number of hops is always the first factor named and the spaces in each hop is the second factor named in the multiplication.

> WORKTEXT® PAGE 72—For teaching suggestions, see the annotated pupil's page.

ADDITIONAL ACTIVITIES

Materials: flannel board, dots. Draw a number line on the chalkboard and label points from 0 to 36. Write a multiplication such as 3 × 5 on the chalkboard. Have one student come to the chalkboard and show this on the number line while another student goes to the flannel board and constructs 3 rows of 5 dots. Ask each student what product was found and check to make sure that these products agree. Continue having students complete multiplications using the number line and the flannel board. After each multiplication, emphasize that a multiplication such as 3 × 5 means 3 fives. The student using the number line should show 3 hops of 5 spaces each and the student using the flannel board should make 3 rows of 5 dots. This activity may be repeated daily until students can easily find products using either the flannel board or the number line.

Page 73

OBJECTIVE

■ Show that when the order of the factors is changed, the product is unchanged

BACKGROUND

In this lesson students will be introduced to the idea that 3 × 6 = 6 × 3. This is a specific example of the commutative property of multiplication, which says that if a and b are whole numbers, then $a \times b = b \times a$. Pupils should understand the concept that changing the order of the factors does not change the product. They need not be introduced to the term *commutative* at this time.

There are two reasons for introducing this lesson at this time. First, it provides students with an opportunity to practice multiplication facts. Second, it is a means for generating new multiplication facts. For example, if students know that 2 × 6 = 12, they also know that 6 × 2 = 12.

MATERIALS

20 cards with different dot arrays representing multiplications

PROCEDURE

Activity 1—Hold up a dot card with 4 rows of 6 dots on it. How many rows of dots are on this card? (4.) How many dots are in each row? (6.) What multiplication is shown by this dot picture? (4 × 6.) How many dots are on the card? (24.) What is the product of 4 × 6? (24.) Write the multiplication sentence 4 × 6 = 24 on the chalkboard. Hold the same card up again. Watch very closely as I turn the card. Rotate the card 90 degrees. How many rows of dots are there on this picture? (6.) How many dots are in each row? (4.) What multiplication is shown by this picture? (6 × 4). Are there still 24 dots on the card? (Yes.) What is the product of 6 × 4? (24.) Write this multiplication sentence on the chalkboard. We have used the same card to show two different multiplication facts. This card shows 6 × 4 = 24, and it also shows 4 × 6 = 24. Suppose that I had a card which showed 3 × 7 = 21. What other multiplication would be shown by this card if we turned it? (7 × 3 = 21.) Continue with exercises of this type.

Activity 2—Write the multiplication 2 × 7 on the chalkboard. What dot picture should we draw to show this multiplication? Help the students to see that they should draw a dot picture with 2 rows of

7 dots each. Have a student draw this picture on the chalkboard. What is the product of 2 × 7? (14.) What picture should we draw to show 7 × 2? (A dot picture with 7 rows of 2 dots each.) Have a student draw this picture. Do these two pictures have the same number of dots? (Yes.) What is the product of 7 × 2? (14.) Continue to have students draw dot pictures on the chalkboard to illustrate pairs of multiplications.

WORKTEXT® PAGE 73—For teaching suggestions, see the annotated pupil's page.

Pages 74-75

OBJECTIVES

- Find products for multiplications in which 0 is one of the factors
- Find products for multiplications in which 1 is one of the factors

BACKGROUND

The numbers 0 and 1 play important roles in multiplication. When 0 is a factor in a multiplication, the product is always equal to 0. This is sometimes called the zero property of multiplication and is generally stated $a \times 0 = 0 \times a = 0$. The number 1 as a factor also has a special role in multiplication. It is called the multiplicative identity, which means that any number times 1 is equal to that number. We can state this in a general sense by writing $a \times 1 = 1 \times a = a$. Students need not refer to these properties by name, but they should be familiar with the concepts of multiplication by 0 and 1.

MATERIALS

36 index cards per student

PROCEDURE

Activity 1—Write the multiplication 5 × 0 on the chalkboard. How is this read? (5 × 0 or 5 zeros.) Let's write the addition sentence that we can use to help us find the product. What should we write? (0 + 0 + 0 + 0 + 0 = 0.) What is the product of 5 × 0? (0.) Continue with examples in which a multiplication with one factor 0 is written on the board and students help to find the product by writing the related addition sentence. What is a short way to find the product

when one of the factors is 0? Help the students to see that the product will always be 0.

Continue writing multiplications such as 9 × 0, 5 × 0, 11 × 0, and so on on the chalkboard. Have students complete the sentences. We can also write the multiplication sentence 5 × 0 = 0 in column form. Do that. Have students come to the chalkboard and write each multiplication sentence in column form.

Activity 2—Distribute 19 index cards to each student. Have students complete each card by putting a multiplication fact with 0 as a factor on it. They should write the multiplications in column form and put the multiplication with its product on the back of each card. For example, $\times 0$ with 4 above should be on one side, and $\times 0$ with 4 above and 0 below should be on the other side.

The completion of this activity not only provides students with a set of multiplication flash cards but also requires students to write these multiplication facts two times. The facts that should be completed are 0 × 0 through 9 × 0 and 0 × 1 through 0 × 9. After students have completed their flash cards, use a teacher set of flash cards to provide a short period of drill on the multiplication facts in which 0 is one of the factors.

Activities 3 and 4—Adapt activities 1 and 2 to develop multiplication facts in which 1 is one of the factors.

WORKTEXT® PAGES 74–75—For teaching suggestions, see the annotated pupil's pages.

ADDITIONAL ACTIVITIES

1. Now I am going to try to trick you. Sometimes I will say that you are to find the product of two numbers. When I ask for the *product,* what should you do with the numbers? (Multiply them.) Other times I will ask for the *sum* of the two numbers. What operation should you perform then? (Addition.) Sometimes I will ask you for the *difference* of two numbers. What should you do then? (Subtract.) You will have to listen very carefully to know what operation to perform. Let's begin. What is the product of 0 and 7? (0.) What is the sum of 5 and 0? (5.) What is the product of 5 and 1? (5.) What is the difference of 8 and 0? (8.) Continue asking questions about products, sums, and differences. Make sure that the facts are ones that students know. You may wish to expand on this activity by having students write each multiplication, addition, or subtraction on the chalkboard. If students have difficulty, make sure that they understand which operation to perform.

2. Materials: 36 pupil-made multiplication flash cards for each student. Group students in pairs and have them drill each other using the flash cards they made in activity 2 and activity 4. It may be necessary to provide drill on these multiplication facts for a short period each day. In this way, students will learn to respond automatically to these facts.

3. Materials: spinners made from paper plates, cardboard strips, and paper fasteners. See the model below.

Give a spinner to each pair of students. Have one student spin the pointer and call out 0 or 1. The other student should respond with the product of the number called out times the number the pointer stops on. Have students verify answers and alternate spinning the pointer. If you wish, the game may be made competitive by awarding 1 point for each correct answer and setting a game at so many points.

Pages 76-77

OBJECTIVES

- Find products for multiplication facts in which 2 is one of the factors
- Find products for multiplication facts in which 3 is one of the factors

BACKGROUND

In this lesson students will learn the multiplication facts in which one of the factors is 2 or 3. After students have learned these facts in isolation, it is essential that they practice all of the multiplication facts that have been learned up to this point. This aids retention as well as permits practice of a number of multiplication facts in one drill.

MATERIALS

28 index cards per student

PROCEDURE

Activity 1—Write the multiplication 2×7 on the chalkboard. How could we read this? (2×7 or 2 sevens.) How could we find this product? (Add $7 + 7$.) Have a student draw 2 rows of 7 dots. What is the sum of $7 + 7$? (14.) What is the product of 2×7? (14.) Continue illustrating multiplications in which

one of the factors is 2. After each fact such as $2 \times 7 = 14$ has been developed, ask the following question: What other fact do we know? ($7 \times 2 = 14$.) Develop all of the multiplication facts having at least one factor of 2 in this way.

Activity 2—Distribute 15 index cards to each student. Draw a number line on the chalkboard which has numbers from 0 to 18 marked on it. Have students use the number line to develop the multiplication facts having 2 as one of the factors. Have them complete their cards by writing a multiplication on one side and the multiplication with its answer on the other side.

Activities 3 and 4—Adapt activities 1 and 2 to develop the multiplication facts having 3 as one of the factors.

WORKTEXT® PAGES 76-77—For detailed teaching suggestions, see the annotated pupil's pages.

ADDITIONAL ACTIVITIES

1. Materials: 1 set of pupil-made flash cards with factors of 0, 1, 2, and 3 per pupil. Pair students and have them drill each other using flash cards having multiplication facts with factors of 2 or 3. Then all of the cards that they have constructed so far should be mixed together and the students should drill each other on multiplication facts having factors of 0, 1, 2, or 3.

2. I'm going to try to trick you again. Remember, *find the sum* means add, *find the difference* means subtract, and *find the product* means multiply. Listen very carefully. What is the product of 2 and 4? (8.) What is the sum of 3 and 9? (12.) What is the difference of 7 and 3? (4.) Continue asking questions which require students to identify the sum, difference, or product of two numbers when one of the numbers is 0, 1, 2, or 3.

3. Materials: 1 spinner for each pair of students. Use the spinners that were developed in the last lesson and have students drill on multiplication facts. Students should call out 0, 1, 2, or 3 as one of the factors.

Page 78

OBJECTIVES

- Identify words that mean to multiply
- Solve word problems describing multiplication situations

BACKGROUND

There are many phrases which imply multiplication. The students have already become familiar with phrases such as 4 fives, 2 rows of 6, the product of 2 and 5, and 3 equal sets of 4. In this lesson, phrases that mean multiplication are emphasized, and students are then to look for these phrases in verbal problems. Emphasis on these phrases that mean multiplication helps the student to differentiate between addition situations, multiplication situations, and subtraction situations.

MATERIALS

flannel board
30 flannel dots

PROCEDURE

Activity 1—Have a student come to the flannel board and show 2 sets of 7 dots. (name of student) has shown 2 sets of 7 dots. What multiplication should we write to show this? (2×7.) How many dots are on the flannel board? (14.) Write the phrase *2 sets of 7* on the chalkboard, and next to it write the translation *2×7*. The translation for 2 sets of 7 is 2×7.

Have a student put 4 fives on the flannel board. What is the translation for 4 fives? (4×5.) What is the product of 4×5? (20.) Are there 20 dots on the flannel board? (Yes.) Continue giving students phrases that mean multiplication, having them illustrate these on the flannel board and identify the multiplication and its product.

Activity 2—Write this problem on the chalkboard: Bill was arranging chairs. He made 3 rows of 5 chairs each. How many chairs did he arrange? Have students read this problem. What are we to find? (The number of chairs Bill arranged.) Does the information given imply addition, multiplication, or subtraction? (Multiplication.) What words mean multiplication? (3 rows of 5 each.) What numbers should we multiply? (3×5.) What is the product? (15.) How many chairs did Bill arrange? (15.)

Continue with examples like those above in which students are to solve word problems in a group setting. In each case, make sure that you identify the phrase in the verbal problem that means multiplication.

Acting out the situation portrayed in the problem or drawing a picture of the situation is helpful for many students.

WORKTEXT® PAGE 78—For teaching suggestions, see the annotated pupil's page.

Page 79

OBJECTIVES

- Identify which of two whole numbers is greater
- Find sums for two 2-digit numbers
- Find sums for two 3-digit numbers
- Complete number patterns

MATERIALS

basic addition facts flash cards

PROCEDURE

Activity 1—Drill students on the basic addition facts using flash cards. Continuous review of these basic facts is essential to future recall and use of them. Identify those students who are having difficulty in responding to the facts. Remind these students how to complete addition facts using the number line.

Activity 2—Write $\begin{array}{r} 293 \\ +188 \\ \hline \end{array}$ on the chalkboard. Use this addition and others like it to review the procedure used for adding two 3-digit numbers.

WORKTEXT® PAGE 79—For teaching suggestions, see the annotated pupil's page.

As students are completing exercise C, check their work carefully. Watch for error patterns such as these:

Incorrect responses to addition facts.	$\begin{array}{r} 9 \\ +\ 7 \\ \hline 18 \end{array}$	$\begin{array}{r} 59 \\ +37 \\ \hline 98 \end{array}$
Adding in place.	$\begin{array}{r} 75 \\ +19 \\ \hline 814 \end{array}$	$\begin{array}{r} 23 \\ +58 \\ \hline 711 \end{array}$
Forgetting to rename ones as tens or tens as hundreds.	$\begin{array}{r} 78 \\ +45 \\ \hline 113 \end{array}$	$\begin{array}{r} 367 \\ +444 \\ \hline 701 \end{array}$

Pages 80-81

OBJECTIVE

- Find products for multiplications when 4 is one of the factors

BACKGROUND

As the size of the factors become larger, students are less familiar with the multiplication facts. As a result, more time is needed for the students to learn these facts. Only one factor per lesson will be presented from this point until all the basic facts are covered.

MATERIALS

11 index cards per student

PROCEDURE

Activity 1—Draw a number line on the chalkboard and have students help to label points from 0 to 36. Let's use the number line to find the product of 4 × 3. Where must we start? (0.) How many hops must we take to the right? (4.) How long should each of these hops be? (3 spaces.) Have a student draw arrows to show this multiplication. What is the product? (12.) Write 4 × 3 = 12 on the chalkboard. If we know 4 × 3 = 12, what other multiplication has a product of 12? (3 × 4.) Have another student show this on the number line.

Continue with examples in which students use the number line to find the products for multiplications which have one factor of 4. In each case, write the multiplication sentence on the chalkboard and then identify the related multiplication fact.

Activity 2—Distribute 11 index cards to each student. Have students write the multiplication fact $\begin{array}{r} 4 \\ \times 4 \end{array}$ on one side of a card and write the same fact with the product on the reverse side of that card. Complete the remainder of the cards in this same fashion so that the facts 4 × 4 through 4 × 9 and 5 × 4 through 9 × 4 are each on a single card.

After the multiplication flash cards have been completed, use a teacher set of cards with multiplications having one factor of 4 for drill. After students can respond rapidly to these facts, have pairs of students use their flash cards for more drill.

Activity 3—Draw a multiplication table like the one on Worktext® page 81 on the chalkboard. This is a convenient table in which we can record the multiplication facts we know. Let's fill in the first row of blanks. The first blank space should be completed by putting the product of 0 × 0. What is the product of 0 × 0? (0.) Write a 0 in the first blank space. The second blank should be completed with the product of 0 × 1. What is the product of 0 × 1? (0.) Write a 0 in this blank. Continue filling in the blanks in the table in this fashion. Make sure students recognize the multiplication that corresponds with each product. Complete the table through 4 × 9 and 9 × 4.

Let's find the product of 5 × 4 in our table. Find 5 in the column at the left and point to it with your left index finger. Find 4 in the row at the top and point to it with your right index finger. Now move your left index finger across and your right index finger down until they meet. What number is in the space where your fingers meet? (20.) This shows us that 5 × 4 = 20. Continue having students use the table until they can find products easily.

WORKTEXT® PAGES 80–81—For teaching suggestions, see the annotated pupil's pages.

ADDITIONAL ACTIVITIES

1. Materials: 1 set of pupil-made flash cards with factors of 0, 1, 2, 3, and 4 per pupil. Pair students and let them use the flash cards to drill each other on the multiplication facts.

2. Materials: spinners as constructed for Worktext® pages 74–75. Pair students who do not know their multiplication facts with students who do. The student who does not know the facts spins the pointer and must give the products for the multiplications involving the number pointed out and the factors 0, 1, 2, 3, and 4. The other student checks the products given.

Pages 82-83

OBJECTIVE

■ Find products for multiplication facts when 5 is one of the factors

BACKGROUND

Learning the multiplication facts when 5 is one of the factors can be easily accomplished by building on the knowledge that students already have of counting by fives. For example, to find the product of 4 × 5, which is 4 fives, we count 5, 10, 15, 20. This can also be shown conveniently on the number line by showing 4 hops of 5 spaces.

MATERIALS

9 index cards per student

PROCEDURE

Activity 1—Write the multiplication 7 × 5 on the chalkboard. How do we read this? (7 × 5 or 7 fives.)

If we want to find what 7 fives is equal to, we could count by fives. To count by fives, the first number we say is 5. What number would we say next? (10.) What would the next number be? (15.) Continue this process of counting by fives until the number 45 is reached. Write the sequence of numbers on the chalkboard. To find 7×5, we need to count 5 seven times. What number in this sequence is 5 counted seven times? (35.) Continue using this sequence of numbers to identify products for which 5 is the second factor. The other factor should not exceed 9.

We have already found that $7 \times 5 = 35$. What is 5×7 equal to? (35.) How do you know? (Changing the order of the factors does not change the product.) Continue with exercises emphasizing multiplication facts in which 5 is the first factor and the second factor does not exceed 9.

Activity 2—Distribute 9 index cards to each student. Have them make multiplication flash cards for the 9 new multiplication facts which have a factor of 5.

Take a teacher set of these flash cards, shuffle them, and drill the class on these multiplication facts for a short period of time. Make sure that each student has the opportunity to respond to one or more of the facts at least once.

Activity 3—Draw a number line on the chalkboard. Label each point which is a multiple of 5. Use this number line to show multiplications such as 5×7, 5×9, 5×3, and so on. In each case have students draw arrows to show the hops and find the product.

WORKTEXT® PAGES 82–83—For teaching suggestions, see the annotated pupil's pages.

ADDITIONAL ACTIVITIES

Materials: flash cards developed in the preceding lessons. Pair students and have them drill each other on multiplication facts using the flash cards. Have drills on multiplication facts for a few minutes each day until students can readily recall the product for each of the previously learned multiplication facts.

Page 84

OBJECTIVES

■ Write expanded names in which 1 ten must be renamed as 10 ones or 1 hundred must be renamed as 10 tens

■ Subtract 2- or 3-digit numbers when regrouping is required

■ Check subtractions by addition

MATERIALS
flash cards with the basic subtraction facts

PROCEDURE
Review the short form for subtracting a 3-digit number from a 3-digit number. (See the material for Worktext® pages 65–66.)

Continue until all students readily recall the procedure for subtracting two numbers and for checking subtraction by addition. In several of these exercises write the subtraction on the chalkboard in the form $293 - 175$. Have students write this subtraction in column form before they begin the subtraction.

WORKTEXT® PAGE 84—For teaching suggestions, see the annotated pupil's page.

As students are completing exercise C, check their success. Some common errors that students might make are:

Incorrect responses to facts.	79 −22 ‾‾ 56	96 −24 ‾‾ 62
Always subtracting the smaller digit from the larger digit.	75 −29 ‾‾ 54	281 −165 ‾‾ 124
Renaming incorrectly.	2⅟5 −163 ‾‾ 152	17² − 85 ‾‾ 97
Renaming when not necessary.	4²⁸ −104 ‾‾ 3114	4²⁸ −104 ‾‾ 314

Depending upon which skill is causing the difficulty, repeat activity 1 or activity 2. You may also wish to use some of the activities associated with Worktext® pages 62–66.

Page 85

OBJECTIVE

■ Estimate answers by first rounding each number to the nearest 10 and then subtracting

MATERIALS

flannel board
2 flannel dots and 1 flannel car
several pieces of yarn of different lengths

PROCEDURE

Activity 1—Draw a number line on the chalkboard and label points with the numbers from 110 to 120, inclusive. Which numbers on this number line are closer to 110? (111, 112, 113, and 114.) These numbers are rounded to 110. Which numbers are closer to 120? (116, 117, 118, 119.) These numbers are rounded to 120. What is 115 rounded to? (120.) When we round a number to the nearest 10, we are writing an approximate value for the actual number. Rounding to the nearest 10 means replacing the number by the multiple of 10 which is closest to the number. What is 78 rounded to? (80.) What is 176 rounded to? (180.) What is 95 rounded to? (100.) Remember that when a number is halfway between two multiples of 10, you round it to the higher multiple of 10. Continue asking questions requiring students to round numbers to the nearest 10.

Activity 2—Put two dots on the flannel board and connect them with a piece of yarn. This is to represent a road map. On road maps distances between cities are sometimes given in kilometers. A kilometer is about 1,000 big steps long. Suppose the distance between these two cities is 432 kilometers. Put the car on the yarn. This car has traveled part way between the two cities. It has gone 128 kilometers. We want to find how many kilometers it has yet to travel. What would we have to do to find the number of kilometers that the car must still travel? (Subtract 432 − 128.) Let's do that. Have students help you perform the subtraction on the chalkboard. Suppose we only wanted to find about how far the car has to travel. We could do that by rounding 432 to the nearest 10 and rounding 128 to the nearest 10 and then subtracting. What is 432 rounded to the nearest 10? (430.) What is 128 rounded to the nearest 10? (130.) What is the difference when 130 is subtracted from 430? (300.) Solving the problem this way, we say that we have found an approximate distance that the car has left to travel. Which of the two subtractions is easier? (The second.)

Continue making up problems of this type, using the different pieces of yarn and the two dots to represent cities. It may be helpful to let students supply the names for the cities and the distance that the car has traveled.

WORKTEXT® PAGE 85—For teaching suggestions, see the annotated pupil's page.

Page 86

OBJECTIVE

■ Use the distributive property of multiplication over addition to find products

BACKGROUND

The distributive property of multiplication over addition is an important property in mathematics. A specific example of the distributive property is $5 \times (3 + 4) = (5 \times 3) + (5 \times 4)$. One way of interpreting this property is that it gives us two ways to find products. We could find the answer to the above exercise by computing on either the left side of the sentence or on the right side of the sentence. If we computed on the left side of the sentence, we would first have to add $3 + 4$ and then multiply this sum times 5. If we computed on the right side of the sentence, we would first multiply 5×3 and 5×4. These two products, 15 and 20, would then be added to obtain the sum, 35. In either case, the answer is the same.

The use of the distributive property is basic to the procedure that we use to multiply. For example, to multiply 5×12 we could write $5 \times 12 = 5 \times (10 + 2)$ and then use the distributive property to obtain $(5 \times 10) + (5 \times 2)$.

PROCEDURE

Activity 1—Have several students come to the chalkboard and draw dot pictures in array form. One example might be to have a student draw 3 rows of 8 dots. What multiplication is illustrated by this dot picture? ($3 \times 8 = 24$.) Now watch as I draw a line between the third and fourth columns from the left. Do this. What multiplication is illustrated by the dot picture to the left of the line? ($3 \times 3 = 9$.) What multiplication is illustrated by the dot picture to the right of the line? ($3 \times 5 = 15$.) Does $9 + 15 = 24$? (Yes.) Does $3 \times 8 = (3 \times 3) + (3 \times 5)$? (Yes.) Write this last sentence on the chalkboard. Continue illustrating various examples of the distributive property using the dot pictures that the students have drawn on the chalkboard. It is not necessary to use the term distributive property with students at this time.

Activity 2—Write the sentence $4 \times (6 + 2) = (4 \times 6) + (4 \times 2)$ on the chalkboard. Have students compute to verify that $4 \times (6 + 2) = (4 \times 6) + (4 \times 2)$. Using different numbers, have students verify several more sentences of this type.

Now write $4 \times (2 + 3)$ on the chalkboard. How could we rewrite this multiplication? Help the students to see that the quantity $4 \times (2 + 3)$ can be rewritten as $(4 \times 2) + (4 \times 3)$. Have students compute to verify that this is a true sentence. Continue with exercises in which students use the distributive property to rewrite multiplication sentences.

We can use these two ways of writing multiplications to find forgotten facts. Suppose I wanted to find 4×8 but forgot the product. One way to find the product would be to rename 8 as $5 + 3$. Write $4 \times 8 = 4 \times (5 + 3)$. We can rewrite $4 \times (5 + 3)$ as $(4 \times 5) + (4 \times 3)$. Write this on the chalkboard and have students help find the product for 4×8.

WORKTEXT® PAGE 86—For teaching suggestions, see the annotated pupil's page.

Pages 87-88

OBJECTIVE

■ Find products for multiplication facts when 6 is one of the factors

MATERIALS

7 index cards per student
multiplication flash cards made in previous lessons which have 6 as one of the factors

PROCEDURE

Activity 1—Draw a number line on the chalkboard. Label the points named by multiples of 6. Use the number line to develop the multiplication facts having 6 as one of the factors.

Activity 2—Distribute 7 index cards to each student. Have the students make flash cards for each of the new multiplication facts having 6 as one of the factors.

Take a set of multiplication flash cards which have all multiplications with 6 as one of the factors. Show these to the class and have students respond to each multiplication fact. Go through the deck several times so that each student has an opportunity to respond at least once. As the activity progresses, remove the easier facts and continue drilling on the more difficult facts.

WORKTEXT® PAGES 87–88—For detailed teaching suggestions, see the annotated pupil's pages.

ADDITIONAL ACTIVITIES

Materials: 1 set of the flash cards made up to this point for each pair of students. Have the children drill each other on the multiplication facts in this deck. Continue these drills periodically until students are able to respond to all of these facts automatically.

Page 89

OBJECTIVE

■ Solve verbal problems involving the use of multiplication facts

BACKGROUND

Students will need to use multiplication facts to solve the problems on this page. Some of the problems require more than one step. When this is the case, students are asked to perform each step in a separate question. The results of these steps are then put together to solve the original problem. In this way, students are introduced to multiple-step problems while having to complete only a single step of each problem at a time.

PROCEDURE

Have this problem written on the chalkboard: Elaine bought 6 erasers. Each eraser cost 8¢. How much did she pay for all of the erasers? To solve a verbal problem, we must first read the problem carefully. Let's all read this problem together. Have the class read the problem with you in unison. What are we to find in this probelm? (How much money Elaine spent.) What information are we given? (The number of erasers she bought and the cost of each eraser.) Should we add, subtract, or multiply to find the answer? (Multiply.) What numbers should we multiply? (6×8.) What is the product of 6×8? (48.) How much money did Elaine spend altogether? (48¢.) After this problem has been solved, review the procedure for solving problems given in the background information for Worktext® page 42. These include reading the problem, determining what is to be found, what information is given, and how to solve the problem, solving the problem, and stating the answer.

WORKTEXT® PAGE 89—For teaching suggestions, see the annotated pupil's page.

Page 90

OBJECTIVE

■ Identify which months have 31 days and which months have less than 31 days

BACKGROUND

This lesson provides a handy method of determining the number of days in a month. Matching the months in order to the knuckles and the spaces between them provides a way. Months matched to knuckles have 31 days; the others have less. After July, which corresponds to the knuckle of the index finger on the left hand, begin with the knuckle of the index finger on the right hand.

MATERIALS

calendar showing all the months of the year on one page

PROCEDURE

WORKTEXT® PAGE 90—For teaching suggestions, see the annotated pupil's page.

Page 91

OBJECTIVE

■ Review the concepts and skills developed in chapter 4

PROCEDURE

WORKTEXT® PAGE 91—Direct students to complete the exercises in the chapter review. Worktext® page references for the exercises in this chapter review are: exercise A, pages 70–71, 74, 80, and 82; exercise B, pages 73, 76, 77, 80, and 83; exercise C, page 86; and exercise D, pages 72, 77, 80, 82, 83, and 87.

Page 92

The last page of each chapter is a check-up designed to indicate the pupils' understanding of the concepts and skills that were presented in the chapter. Have the students complete Worktext® page 92.

Multiplication and Division

5

OBJECTIVES

- Solve division sentences given physical descriptions or dot pictures
- Identify divisor, dividend, and quotient

BACKGROUND

Multiplication and division are inverse operations. In multiplication, we take the number of equal sets and the number of objects in each set and multiply to find the product. In division, we do the opposite. We take the total number of objects and either the number of equal sets or the number of objects in each set and divide to find the other number.

In this lesson, students are introduced to the words which name the parts of a division sentence.

MATERIALS

flannel board
30 flannel dots

PROCEDURE

Activity 1—Have a student come to the flannel board and put 12 dots on it. How many dots has (name of student) put on the flannel board? (12.) Suppose we want to separate these 12 dots into 3 equal sets. Let's do that by forming 3 rows of dots, with each row having the same number of dots in it. Have a student arrange the 12 dots in 3 rows of 4 dots each. How many rows of dots did (name of student) form? (3.) Are there the same number of dots in each row? (Yes.) How many dots are in each row? (4.) This activity illustrates a division. 12 dots were divided into 3 rows each containing 4 dots. We write 12 ÷ 3 = 4. Write this division on the chalkboard. Read the division sentence to the class, pointing to each symbol as it is read. Then have the class read this division sentence. Point to the

division sign. A line with a dot over it and a dot under it tells us to divide. Continue doing exercises of this type. Have students divide a set of dots into two or more rows, each having the same number of dots. In each case, write the division sentence on the chalkboard for students to read.

Activity 2—Write 15 ÷ 3 on the chalkboard. How many dots should we put on the flannel board? (15.) How many rows of dots should there be? (3.) Have a student demonstrate this. How many dots are in each row? (5.) Have a student complete the division sentence on the chalkboard and read it for the class. 15 tells us how many dots to put on the flannel board. The number 15 is called the dividend in the division sentence. Below 15 on the chalkboard write the word *dividend*. The 3 in the division sentence tells us the number of equal rows we should form. 3 is called the divisor. Write the word *divisor* beneath the 3. The answer to the division sentence tells us how many dots are in each row. It is called the quotient of the division. Write the word *quotient* beneath 5.

Continue illustrating divisions in this way. For each division, write the division sentence on the chalkboard and identify each part of the division sentence.

WORKTEXT® PAGE 93—For teaching suggestions, see the annotated pupil's page.

OBJECTIVES

- Show division as repeated subtraction
- Divide using the number line

BACKGROUND

Previous chapters showed that multiplication may be regarded as repeated addition. In like manner, division can be regarded as repeated subtraction. One way to find the quotient in a division is to determine the number of times that the divisor can be subtracted from the dividend. For example, if we wish to divide 18 by 6, we could write $18 - (6 + 6 + 6) = 0$. This shows that we have subtracted 3 sixes from 18 to arrive at a difference of 0. The quotient for the division $18 ÷ 6$ is 3, the number of sixes that can be subtracted from 18 to obtain a difference of 0.

We can use the fact that division is repeated subtraction to obtain the answers to divisions on the number line. For example, if we wish to divide 12 by 2 on the number line, we start at 12 and take hops of 2 spaces each to the left. The number of hops that it takes us to get to 0—six—is the quotient. This is illustrated on Worktext® page 94.

MATERIALS

30 counters per student

PROCEDURE

Activity 1—Give each student 30 counters. Put a set of 16 counters on your desk. Take sets of 4 counters from this set and see how many sets of 4 counters you can take away from the 16. How many sets of 4 can you take away from the 16? (4.) We can show this by writing 16 − (4 + 4 + 4 + 4) = 0. Write that on the chalkboard. How many fours were subtracted from 16? (4.) Since 4 fours can be subtracted from 16, we write 16 ÷ 4 = 4. Continue illustrating divisions by having students form a set of counters on their desks and then determining how many equal sets can be taken away from this original set. Write the sentence which shows the repeated subtraction on the chalkboard. Write the division sentence on the chalkboard. Have students relate the divisor to the number being subtracted and the quotient to the number of times the divisor was subtracted to obtain 0.

Activity 2—Write the division 14 ÷ 2 on the chalkboard. To find the quotient for this division, we must determine how many twos can be subtracted from 14. How many twos equal 14? (7.) How can we write 7 twos as an addition? (2 + 2 + 2 + 2 + 2 + 2 + 2.) Does 14 − (7 twos) equal zero? (Yes.) We can write the subtraction sentence 14 − (2 + 2 + 2 + 2 + 2 + 2 + 2) = 0, and this tells us that 14 ÷ 2 = 7. 7 is the number of twos that can be subtracted from 14. Continue writing divisions on the chalkboard and finding the quotient by determining the number of times the divisor can be subtracted from the dividend.

Activity 3—Draw a number line on the chalkboard. Have students help to name points from 0 to 25 on this number line. We can use the number line to show division. Suppose we wanted to perform the division 8 ÷ 4 on the number line. We would start at 8 and take hops of 4 spaces each to the left. Each hop is subtracting a 4 from 8. Use arrows to show consecutive hops of 4 spaces to the left. How many hops did we have to take to get to 0? (2.) This tells us that 8 ÷ 4 = 2. Write 8 ÷ 4 = 2 on the chalkboard. How would we solve the division 12 ÷ 2? At what number should we start? (12.) In what direction should we hop? (To the left.) How long should each hop be? (2 spaces.) Show these hops using arrows.

How many hops did we take to get to 0? (6.) What is the answer for the division 12 ÷ 2? (6.) Write 12 ÷ 2 = 6 on the chalkboard. When we take hops of 2 spaces to the left, we are actually subtracting 2. How many twos did we subtract from 12 in this example? (6.) Continue with exercises of this type having students demonstrate the procedure for dividing on the number line.

Activity 4—Show the division 18 ÷ 6 on the number line. Are all of the hops shown by the arrows the same number of spaces? (Yes.) At what number did we start? (18.) What is the number of spaces in each hop? (6.) How many hops did we take to get to 0? (3.) What division sentence should we write for this picture? (18 ÷ 6 = 3.) Continue with exercises of this type until students can identify the division sentence from a given number line picture.

WORKTEXT® PAGES 94–95—For teaching suggestions, see the annotated pupil's pages.

Page 96

OBJECTIVES

■ Recognize multiplication and division as opposite operations
■ Write three related facts, given a multiplication or division fact

BACKGROUND

If the two factors in a multiplication sentence are not equal, the sentence has one related multiplication sentence and two related division sentences. For the multiplication sentence 6 × 3 = 18, the related sentences are 3 × 6 = 18, 18 ÷ 6 = 3, and 18 ÷ 3 = 6. Since multiplication and division are related in this way, we say that division is the opposite of multiplication, or division is the inverse operation of multiplication. Students should be able to use this relationship to obtain division facts as well as to check computations.

MATERIALS

cards with rectangular dot arrays

PROCEDURE

Activity 1—Show a dot picture with 4 rows of 6 dots. What multiplication sentences are illustrated by this dot picture? (4 × 6 = 24 and 6 × 4 = 24.) If students cannot see both of these immediately, rotate the card so that instead of showing 4 rows of 6 dots, it shows 6 rows of 4 dots. The dot picture also shows 24 dots divided into 4 equal rows. What division sentence does this dot picture show? (24 ÷ 4 = 6.) Is there another division sentence illustrated by this dot picture? (Yes.) What is it? (24 ÷ 6 = 4.) Continue showing different dot pictures and having students identify the multiplication sentences and the division sentences which are illustrated. In each case, write these four sentences on the chalkboard. Make sure that students recognize that each multiplication sentence has a related division sentence and vice versa.

Activity 2—We know that each multiplication sentence has a related division sentence, and each division sentence has a related multiplication sentence. Write the multiplication sentence 6 × 2 = 12 on the chalkboard. What is the related multiplication sentence? (2 × 6 = 12.) What are the related division sentences? (12 ÷ 2 = 6 and 12 ÷ 6 = 2.) Draw a chart on the chalkboard similar to the one shown in exercise B, Worktext® page 96. Continue completing the entries in this chart by identifying one of the four sentences and having students complete the other three sentences.

WORKTEXT® PAGE 96—For teaching suggestions, see the annotated pupil's page.

Page 97

OBJECTIVES

- Find quotients for division facts in which 1 is the divisor
- Find quotients for division facts in which 2 is the divisor

MATERIALS

18 index cards per student

PROCEDURE

Activity 1—Draw a picture of a number line on the chalkboard and label points from 0 to 20. Write 7 ÷ 1 on the chalkboard. To find the answer for this division, we must find how many ones are in 7. How many ones are in 7? (7.) If students have difficulty in answering this question, draw 7 dots on the chalkboard and have a student circle sets of 1 dot. How many sets of 1 dot are in 7 dots? (7.) How can we show 7 ÷ 1 on the number line? (Start at 7 and take hops of 1 space to the left until we get to 0. The quotient is the number of hops.) Have a student show this. How many hops did it take to get to 0? (7.) Complete the division sentence 7 ÷ 1 = 7 on the chalkboard. Discuss each of the remaining eight division facts in which 1 is a divisor in the same way. Write each sentence on the chalkboard as it is discussed.

Remember that we can show divisions in another way. For the sentence 7 ÷ 1 = 7, we can write $1\overline{\smash{)}7}$ with quotient 7. Remind students that the 1 is the divisor and is written outside of the sign, the 7 underneath the sign is the dividend, and the 7 written above the sign is the quotient. When we read this, we say 1 into 7 is 7. Have students write each of the division facts using this notation.

Activity 2—Distribute 9 index cards to each student. Using 1 as the divisor and dividends from 1 through 9, have students write division facts without the answers on one side of the cards and the same division facts with the answers on the opposite sides of the cards. Check to make sure that each student is doing this correctly. After students have completed their cards, check to make sure that they have the correct answer on the opposite side of each card.

Give students a few minutes to study their fact cards. Tell them to look at the division fact, think of the quotient, and turn the card over to check to see if their quotient was correct. After they have had several minutes to do this, take a set of division fact cards with 1 as the divisor and have students respond to these fact cards.

Activities 3 and 4—Adapt the procedures used in activities 1 and 2 to teach the division facts in which the divisor is 2.

WORKTEXT® PAGE 97—For teaching suggestions, see the annotated pupil's page.

ADDITIONAL ACTIVITIES

Materials: 1 set of division flash cards with the facts having a divisor of 1 or 2. Shuffle the cards and show them one at a time. Go through the deck several times so that each student has a chance to respond one or more times. Remove the easy facts and continue drilling on the more difficult facts. Continue this process daily until students can respond readily and correctly to these facts.

Page 98

OBJECTIVES

- Find quotients for division facts in which 3 is the divisor
- Find quotients for division facts in which 4 is the divisor

MATERIALS

18 index cards per student

PROCEDURE

Activity 1—Use the number line to develop the division facts which have 3 as one of the factors. As you are developing these facts, write the division sentences and the divisions using the division symbol on the chalkboard. If students have difficulty in obtaining any quotient using the number line, have them draw a dot picture and separate the dots into sets of 3. Then ask pupils to find the number of sets of 3.

Activity 2—Distribute 9 index cards to each student. Have them write a division fact on the front of the card and the division fact with its answer on the opposite side of the card. Have them complete a card for each of the division facts having a divisor of 3.

After they have completed their cards, have them study the cards for a few minutes. Then drill the class using a demonstration set of flash cards. Go through the deck several times so that each student has a chance to respond to one or more of the division facts in which 3 is the divisor.

Activities 3 and 4—Modify activities 1 and 2 to teach the division facts in which 4 is the divisor.

WORKTEXT® PAGE 98—For teaching suggestions, see the annotated pupil's page.

ADDITIONAL ACTIVITIES

1. Materials: 1 set of division flash cards with divisors 1, 2, 3, and 4. Shuffle the cards and show these to the students. Have the students respond. Give each person a chance to respond several times to division facts. After going through the deck several times, remove the easier division facts and continue drilling on the more difficult facts.

2. Materials: sets of division flash cards with divisors 1, 2, 3, and 4. Group students in pairs and have them use the flash cards to drill each other on the division facts.

3. Materials: sets of index cards cut in half with division facts with divisors 1, 2, 3, and 4 written on them and sets of index cards cut in half with the answers for these divisions written on them. Form pairs of students. Today we are going to play a game. Shuffle the cards that I have given you and place them face down in four equal rows. The first player is to pick two cards and turn them over. If you pick a division fact and its answer, you may keep the cards and play again. If you do not pick a division fact and its answer, you must turn the cards face down. Then it is the other person's turn. The person who ends the game with the most cards is the winner. Have the students play several games. Then have students exchange sets of cards to drill on different division facts.

Page 99

OBJECTIVES

- Find quotients for division facts in which 5 is the divisor
- Find quotients for division facts in which 6 is the divisor

MATERIALS

18 index cards per student

PROCEDURE

Adapt the activities for Worktext® page 98 to develop the division facts in which 5 or 6 is the divisor.

WORKTEXT® PAGE 99—For teaching suggestions, see the annotated pupil's page.

ADDITIONAL ACTIVITIES

1. Materials: 1 set of division fact flash cards with divisors 1, 2, 3, 4, 5, and 6. Shuffle the cards and display them one at a time. Call on individual students to state the quotients.

2. Materials: 1 set of division flash cards with divisors 1, 2, 3, 4, 5, and 6 for each pair of students. Give each pair of students a set of student-made flash cards. Have students drill each other on the division facts.

3. Materials: sets of index cards cut in half with division facts in which the divisors are 1, 2, 3, 4, 5, and 6 written on them and sets of index cards cut in half with answers for the divisions written on them. Pair the students and have them use the cards to play the game described in additional activity 3 for Worktext® page 98.

Page 100

OBJECTIVES

- Translate verbal phrases that mean to divide
- Solve verbal problems describing division situations

BACKGROUND

Students should learn the words that mean to divide and how to translate these words. It is essential that these words be translated in the proper order, since $8 \div 2$ is not equal to $2 \div 8$.

When solving division problems, students should recognize that there are basically two kinds. In one type of problem, the total number of objects and the size of each group of objects to be formed is given. The number of groups is to be found. This is sometimes called comparison or measurement division. An example of this type of problem is: 12 desks are separated into rows with 6 desks in each row. How many rows are there? The second type of division situation is that in which the total number of objects and the number of groups to be formed is given. Here the number of objects in each group is to be found. This is sometimes called partitioning division. Rephrasing the above example: 12 desks are divided into 2 equal rows. How many desks are in each row?

Students should recognize both of these types of situations as problems requiring division and should be able to identify the division to be performed to solve the problem. It is not necessary that they distinguish between measurement and partitioning situations.

PROCEDURE

WORKTEXT® PAGE 100—For detailed teaching suggestions, see the annotated pupil's page.

Page 101

OBJECTIVES

- Add 2- and 3-digit numbers
- Subtract 2- and 3-digit numbers
- Solve verbal problems involving addition or subtraction

PROCEDURE

Activity 1—Review the procedure for adding two 3-digit numbers. Write $\begin{array}{r} 447 \\ +183 \end{array}$ on the chalkboard. Make sure that students remember to work in the ones' column first, the tens' column second, and the hundreds' column third. Emphasize the procedure used when 10 ones must be renamed as 1 ten and when 10 tens must be renamed as 1 hundred. Perform several additions for the class.

Activity 2—Review the procedure for subtracting a 3-digit number from a 3-digit number. Emphasize that students should first determine if there are enough ones to subtract from. If there are not, 1 ten must be renamed as 10 ones. Then subtract in the tens' column, renaming hundreds as tens if necessary. Finally, subtract in the hundreds' column. Have students help in the completion of subtractions in which renaming is necessary and not necessary.

WORKTEXT® PAGE 101—For teaching suggestions, see the annotated pupil's page.

ADDITIONAL ACTIVITIES

Materials: 1 set of addition flash cards and 1 set of subtraction flash cards. Drill the students on the addition facts and the subtraction facts separately for several minutes. Then mix the two sets of cards and tell them to look very carefully to determine which operation to perform. After they have found the sign which tells them to add or to subtract, they should state the answer.

Pages 102-3

OBJECTIVES

- Find products for multiplication facts in which 7 is one of the factors

■ Find quotients for division facts in which 7 is the divisor

BACKGROUND

Students should already know almost all of the multiplication facts which has 7 as one of the factors. The only new multiplication facts introduced in this lesson are 7×7, 7×8, 7×9, 8×7, and 9×7. All of the other facts having 7 as one of the factors should be reviewed. These multiplication facts will then be used to help develop the division facts in which the divisor is 7.

MATERIALS

14 index cards per student

PROCEDURE

Activity 1—Draw a number line on the chalkboard. Use the number line to develop the multiplication facts having a factor of 7. Write the multiplication sentences on the chalkboard. Have students write each multiplication fact in column form. Erase the multiplication sentences and the products for the multiplications written in column form and have students supply these products again. Place special emphasis on the new multiplication facts.

Activity 2—Distribute 5 index cards to each student. Have students make flash cards for the new multiplication facts. Have students study these facts at their desks for a few minutes. Then drill the class on the multiplication facts which have a factor of 7 by displaying flash cards and having students respond to these multiplication facts. If students still have difficulty in responding to these facts, group the students in pairs and have them drill each other on the multiplication facts which have 7 as one of the factors.

Activity 3—Use a number line drawn on the chalkboard to develop the division facts in which 7 is the divisor. After the 9 division facts with 7 as a divisor have been developed and the division sentences have been written on the chalkboard, erase the quotients and have students give the quotient of each division fact. If they have difficulty with any division facts, let them use the number line. Continue this process until all of the students can find the quotients for these division facts.

Activity 4—Give each student 9 index cards. Have students make flash cards for division facts having 7 as the divisor. After they have completed their flash cards, have them study these division facts by themselves. Then provide a brief class drill on these division facts using flash cards.

WORKTEXT® PAGES 102–3—For teaching suggestions, see the annotated pupil's pages.

ADDITIONAL ACTIVITIES

Materials: 1 set of multiplication flash cards and 1 set of division flash cards with all of the facts previously developed. (These are multiplication facts in which one of the factors is 7 or less and division facts in which the divisor is 7 or less.) Drill students on the multiplication flash cards and then on the division flash cards. Now I am going to try to trick you. Mix up the two sets of cards. You will have to look very carefully to see if you must multiply or divide, and then you will have to find either the product or the quotient. Continue drilling students with this deck of cards. After going through the deck several times, remove the easier facts and continue working on the more difficult facts.

If students are still having difficulty, group them in pairs. Then have them use the sets of flash cards that they have developed to drill each other on multiplication and division facts.

Pages 104-5

OBJECTIVES

■ Find products for multiplication facts in which 8 is one of the factors
■ Find quotients for division facts in which 8 is the divisor

BACKGROUND

The new multiplication facts to be developed in this lesson are 8×8, 8×9, and 9×8. The previously learned multiplication facts with 8 as a factor should be reviewed. There are also 9 new division facts for students to learn. Each of these division facts has a divisor of 8.

MATERIALS

12 index cards per student

PROCEDURE

Modify the activities for Worktext® pages 102–3

to teach students multiplication facts in which 8 is a factor and division facts in which 8 is the divisor.

WORKTEXT® PAGES 104–5—For teaching suggestions, see the annotated pupil's pages.

ADDITIONAL ACTIVITIES

Materials: 1 set of multiplication flash cards and 1 set of division flash cards with all of the facts that have previously been developed. Display the multiplication flash cards and have them respond to these facts. Then display the division flash cards and have them respond to these facts. Put the two decks together. **Now you must determine first if you must multiply or if you must divide. Then find the product or quotient.** Display these cards in random order. Go through the deck several times. Then remove the easier facts and continue drilling with the more difficult facts.

Pages 106-7

OBJECTIVES

- Find products for multiplication facts in which 9 is one of the factors
- Find quotients for division facts in which 9 is the divisor

BACKGROUND

There is only one new multiplication fact with factors of 9, that is, $9 \times 9 = 81$. The other facts which have 9 as one of the factors should be reviewed. In addition to this one new multiplication fact, there are 9 new division facts to be learned in this lesson. These are the division facts which have 9 as the divisor.

MATERIALS

10 index cards per student

PROCEDURE

Modify the activities for Worktext® pages 102–3 to teach students multiplication facts in which 9 is a factor and division facts in which 9 is the divisor.

WORKTEXT® PAGES 106–7—For teaching suggestions, see the annotated pupil's pages.

ADDITIONAL ACTIVITIES

Materials: 1 set of multiplication flash cards and 1 set of division flash cards. Drill the class first on the multiplication flash cards, then on the division flash cards, finally on the mixed set of flash cards. If students continue to have difficulty with specific facts, redevelop these facts using the number line. It is essential that students continue to drill on these facts until they can respond to them correctly and rapidly. After students have learned these facts, there should be periodic drills on them so that the skills are maintained.

Page 108

OBJECTIVES

- Identify the operation to perform in a given situation as multiplication or division
- Write a multiplication or division sentence from a verbal statement

BACKGROUND

There are three quantities in either a multiplication or a division situation: the number of equal sets, the number in each equal set, and the total number of objects. When we are given the number of equal sets and the number of objects in each set, we have a multiplication situation. When we are given the total number of objects and either the number of equal sets or the number of objects in each set, we have a division situation. Students should recognize these types of situations and be able to write the resulting multiplication or division sentence.

PROCEDURE

Today I am going to try to trick you. I will ask a question, and you tell me if we must multiply or divide to find the answer to the question. Then we will write the multiplication or division sentence. Listen very carefully to find out which operation should be performed. Here is the first question. How many objects are in 3 equal sets of 7 objects each? Do we multiply or divide? (Multiply.) Why do we multiply? (Because we know the number of sets and the number of objects in each set.) What multiplication sentence do we write? ($3 \times 7 = 21$.) How many equal sets of 5 objects each are in 30 objects? Do we multiply or divide to find the answer? (Divide.) Why do we divide? (Because we know the total number of objects and the number of objects in each set.) What division sentence do we write? ($30 \div 5 = 6$.) What does the 6 tell us? (There are 6 equal sets of 5 objects in 30.) 12 equals 4 equal sets of how many objects? Do we multiply or divide to find the answer? (Divide.) Why do we divide? (Because we know the total number of objects and the number of equal sets.) What division sentence do we write? ($12 \div 4 = 3$.) Continue with exercises of this type. In each case, emphasize the number of equal sets, the number in each set, and the total number of objects.

WORKTEXT® PAGE 108—For teaching suggestions, see the annotated pupil's page.

Page 109

OBJECTIVE
■ Find the products for the 100 basic multiplication facts

BACKGROUND
This lesson is designed to review the 100 basic multiplication facts. One of the most convenient ways for representing all 100 of these facts is the multiplication chart shown on Worktext® page 109.

PROCEDURE

WORKTEXT® PAGE 109—For teaching suggestions, see the annotated pupil's page.

Page 110

OBJECTIVE
■ Find quotients for 81 basic division facts

BACKGROUND
The students have learned 81 basic division facts. Seventy-two of these facts are shown in the tables on Worktext® page 110. The other 9 facts that students have learned have a divisor of 1. All of these facts should be reviewed and practiced so that students can respond readily to them.

PROCEDURE

WORKTEXT® PAGE 110—For teaching suggestions, see the annotated pupil's page.

Page 111

OBJECTIVE
■ Solve word problems involving multiplication and division

MATERIALS
30 counting blocks

PROCEDURE
Let's solve some multiplication and division problems. We will use the blocks to help us. Here is the first problem: Bob had 27 blocks. He put them in 3 equal rows. How many blocks did he put in each row? What are we to find? (The number of blocks in each row.) What information do we know? (Bob had 27 blocks and was forming 3 rows.) Have a student show this using the blocks. How many blocks are in each row? (9.) How could we use the given information to find this same answer? (Divide 27 by 3.) Write this division on the board. When we know the total number of objects and the number of equal sets, we divide to find the number of blocks in each set. Now let's try another problem. Peggy formed 6 rows of 4 blocks each. How many blocks did she use? Develop this problem in the same way, guiding students to see that this problem must be solved by multiplication. Continue with additional problems in the same manner.

WORKTEXT® PAGE 111—For teaching suggestions, see the annotated pupil's page.

Pages 112-13

OBJECTIVES

- Measure temperature to the nearest degree
- Interpret the meaning of different temperatures

BACKGROUND

The two scales commonly used for measuring temperature are the Celsius and the Fahrenheit scales. The Celsius scale is used with the metric system of measurement and will be presented in this lesson. Water freezes at 0 degrees Celsius, 32 degrees Fahrenheit. Normal body temperature is 37 degrees Celsius, 98.6 degrees Fahrenheit. Water boils at 100 degrees Celsius, 212 degrees Fahrenheit. The formula which shows the relationship between the Celsius (C) scale and the Fahrenheit (F) scale is $F = 9/5 C + 32$. The presentation of this conversion formula and the comparisons between the two scales are for the teacher's benefit only.

MATERIALS

1 classroom demonstration thermometer
2 large Celsius thermometers

PROCEDURE

Activity 1—Display the classroom model of a thermometer. This is a model of a thermometer. There is a real thermometer inside the classroom and another outside the classroom for us to use after we have learned to read the thermometer. What does a thermometer tell us? (How cold or how hot it is.) Most thermometers have a glass tube filled with mercury. As the temperature gets warmer, what happens to the liquid in the tube? (It rises higher.) As the temperature gets colder, what happens to the liquid in the tube? (It goes down.) There is a scale at the side of the glass tube which has numbers marked on it. This is similar to a number line. There are numbers above zero and numbers below zero. These numbers tell us the temperature. Temperature is measured in degrees. A small circle written above and to the right of a number stands for degrees. Write 40° on the chalkboard. How is this symbol read? (40 degrees.) Write *40 degrees* on the chalkboard next to the other symbol. Continue writing temperatures on the chalkboard and having students read the temperatures. Then have a student give a temperature and have another student write the symbol for this temperature on the chalkboard.

Now let's use the thermometer to read temperatures. Suppose the thermometer looked like this. The demonstration thermometer should show 50 degrees. We say that the thermometer reads 50 degrees. Continue illustrating various temperatures which are multiples of 10. The little lines between the numbers mark every 2 degrees. If the mercury in the thermometer is 1 mark above 40, that means it is 2 degrees above 40. Show this on the thermometer. What would be the temperature? (42°.) Continue having the students read the temperatures on the thermometer.

Activity 2—Use the indoor and outdoor thermometers to measure temperatures at various times during the day. Have students record the temperatures on a chart on the chalkboard. After the indoor and outdoor temperatures have been recorded for a day, have students look at the chart and interpret the meanings of the temperatures. For example, they may find that the temperature inside the classroom remains fairly constant throughout the day. The outside temperature in the morning is generally lower than the outside temperature at noon and so on. The emphasis on this activity should be on developing the skills necessary to read and write temperatures correctly.

WORKTEXT® PAGES 112–13—For detailed teaching suggestions, see the annotated pupil's pages.

Page 114

OBJECTIVE

- Review the concepts and skills developed in chapter 5

PROCEDURE

WORKTEXT® PAGE 114—Direct students to complete the exercises. Worktext® page references for the exercises in this chapter review are: exercise A, page 96; exercise B, pages 94, 95, 97, 98, and 99; exercise C, pages 103, 105, 107, and 109; exercise D, pages 95, 97, 98, 99, 103, 105, 107, and 110; and exercise E, pages 100, 101, and 111.

Page 115

The last page of each chapter is a check-up de-

signed to indicate the pupils' understanding of the concepts and skills that were presented in the chapter. Have the students complete Worktext® page 115 independently.

6 Geometry and Measurement

PROCEDURE

WORKTEXT® PAGES 116–17—For teaching suggestions, see the annotated pupil's pages.

ADDITIONAL ACTIVITIES

Materials: 1 model each of a line, a ray, a line segment, and a point cut from tagboard; 3 tagboard cards having one of the words *line, line segment,* or *ray* written on each.

Display the model of the line for the class to see. What is this a model of? (A line.) How do you know it is a model of a line? (Because it is straight and has arrows on the ends.) Continue discussing each of the models.

Put the models of the geometric figures and the cards with the names in a convenient place. Have individuals match figures with names.

Page 116-17

OBJECTIVES

■ Identify pictures which suggest lines, rays, and line segments
■ Draw pictures of lines, rays, and line segments

BACKGROUND

Geometry is an important part of everyday life. We encounter shapes in everything we see. We need to measure the length of objects, the size of regions, or the capacity of containers. All of these activities are a part of geometry.

Shapes and marks on paper are the starting points for imagining geometric figures such as points, lines, circles, or rectangles. The pictures that we draw are the physical representations of geometric figures and are used to make us think of the abstract geometric ideas. Thus, the things we speak of in geometry are imagined from physical surroundings.

This lesson provides instruction on the sets of points called lines, rays, and line segments. The purpose of this lesson is to identify and draw pictures of these three sets of points. Students should also realize that the things we speak of in geometry are imagined from our physical surroundings or from pictures.

Page 118

OBJECTIVES

■ Compare the lengths of line segments visually
■ Compare the lengths of line segments by making a model

BACKGROUND

Measurement is an important part of geometry. To find the measure of geometric configurations, students must learn to assign a number to represent the size property of the figure. When we measure line segments, we assign a number to tell how long the object is. The steps to be taken in developing measurement of line segments are: (1) compare segments visually to determine which is longer or shorter; (2) compare segments by making a model of one segment and moving it alongside the other to determine which is longer; (3) choose a unit line segment and lay off copies of it to see how many copies are contained in the segment; (4) choose a standard unit line segment such as a centimeter or inch; and (5) construct an instrument (ruler) to quickly read the number of standard units in the line segment.

Although these steps are stated for line segments, they are also used in developing measurement of angles, weight, capacity, or the size of regions. In this lesson, the first two steps in the measurement process are developed.

MATERIALS

1 strip of tagboard or paper about 2″ × 12″ per student
variety of straight sticks of different lengths

PROCEDURE

Give a stick (crayon, pencil, etc.) to each student. I have given each of you a stick. What geometric figure does it remind you of? (A line segment.) Today I want to determine if you can tell which of two line segments is longer. Ask two students to hold up their sticks for the class to see. Which stick is longer? How can you tell? How could you be really sure? (Compare the sticks by bringing them together and matching one set of end points to see which stick extends farther.) Have the class do this.

Now draw two line segments on the chalkboard. Which of these line segments is longer? How can you tell? How can you really be sure? Help the students to see that they cannot pick up one line segment and compare it to the other but must make a model of one line segment on a piece of paper and compare this model with the other line segment. Continue having students compare line segments on the chalkboard using this method.

WORKTEXT® PAGE 118—For detailed teaching suggestions, see the annotated pupil's page.

Pages 119-20

OBJECTIVE

■ Find the lengths of line segments using non-standard units of measure

BACKGROUND

Measurement implies finding a number to represent a property of a set. To measure the lengths of line segments, we need a unit of measure. Copies of this unit segment are laid end-to-end until they form a segment as long as or longer than the segment to be measured. The length is the number of units needed to form a segment as long as the segment to be measured.

The length of a line segment is often not exactly a whole number of units. When this occurs, the whole number of units closest to the length of the segment may be chosen as the measure.

MATERIALS

10 paper clips $1\frac{1}{4}$″ long per student
15 paper clips $\frac{15}{16}$″ long per student
3 strips of paper of varying lengths per student

PROCEDURE

Activity 1—Give each student the paper clips and the strips of paper. Take the longest of the three strips of paper. Use the big paper clips to make a line segment which has the same length as the longest piece of paper (insofar as possible). Was the line segment that you formed exactly the same length as the length of the strip of paper? (No.) How many paper clips formed a line segment about as long as the length of the paper? We say that this is the length of the strip of paper in big paper clips. Will the number be the same if you use little paper clips? (No.) Use your little paper clips to form a segment as long as the strip of paper. How many paper clips did you use? Did you use more little paper clips or big paper clips? (More little paper clips.) Continue with this activity by having students measure the other strips of paper. Have students generalize that when measuring an object the smaller the unit of measure the larger the number which is used to specify the length.

Activity 2—Have students take the longest strip of paper and form a big-paper-clip ruler on one of the long edges and a little-paper-clip ruler on the other long edge. Have them do this by laying a paper clip on the strip of paper so that the left edge touches the left edge of the paper. Make a mark at the right edge of the paper clip. Then slide the paper clip over so that the left edge of the paper clip touches the mark that was made. Then make a second mark at the edge of the paper clip, and so on. After these marks have been made, they should be numbered as points on a number line. Have students use their rulers to measure the lengths of common objects which you have provided or which may be found in the classroom.

ADDITIONAL ACTIVITIES

Materials: 20 index cards per pair of students. Direct pairs of students to measure the length of a desk by laying the index cards end-to-end. Record the measurement obtained by each pair on the chalkboard. There will probably be differences in their results even when measuring desks of the same length. Differences could result from using different units of measure, that is, some students might use one edge of the index cards while other pairs of students might use the other edge; not using the same unit consistently, that is, some may use the width sometimes and the length other times; overlapping the index cards rather than laying them end-to-end; or not choosing the number of units closest to the length of the desk.

Have students remeasure the length of a desk, making sure that each pair of students is using the same unit of measure. Record these results and note the consistency. Continue by having students measure other objects using either the width or length of index cards. When they report their measures, make sure that they state the unit of measure that was used, for example, 5 index-card widths or 3 index-card lengths.

Summarize by stressing the following concepts: (1) to find the length of line segments we need a unit of measure which is a line segment; (2) the length of a line segment is the number of units in the given line segment and is stated as the number of units closest to the length of the object measured; and (3) different units of measure result in different numbers for the length of the same line segment, so we must always state the unit of measure that was used.

Pages 121-22

OBJECTIVES

- Measure line segments to the nearest millimeter
- Measure line segments to the nearest centimeter
- Draw line segments having a given length in millimeters
- Draw line segments having a given length in centimeters

BACKGROUND

In the last lesson we saw that any line segment may be used as a unit to measure other line segments. Usually we use a standard unit of measure to find lengths. Use of a standard unit of measure facilitates communication. When we say that a line segment is 5 centimeters long, it means the same thing to everyone; when we say that a line segment is 5 paper clips long, it may mean different things to different people. For this reason, it is preferable to find lengths using a standard unit of measure.

One standard unit of linear measure is the meter. Other standard units of measure, such as the centimeter, decimeter, or millimeter, are defined in terms of a meter. When the word *meter* has the prefix *deci-*, it means one-tenth of a meter. Thus, there are 10 decimeters in a meter. In like fashion, the prefix *centi-* means one-hundredth and the prefix *milli-* means one-thousandth.

To facilitate the measurement process, we use a ruler. A ruler is an instrument consisting of standard units laid end-to-end. Names of numbers are written on the ruler so that it is not necessary to count the number of units each time. If the ruler is used properly, we can read the length of a segment directly from the numbers on the ruler.

In this lesson, students will learn to read rulers that are marked in centimeters and in millimeters. Emphasis should first be placed on reading the lengths of line segments to the nearest centimeter and then to the nearest millimeter.

MATERIALS

rulers cut from the bottom of Worktext® pages 121–22
variety of sticks

PROCEDURE

Activity 1—Have students cut out the ruler at the bottom of Worktext® pages 121–22. Have students use the side of the ruler marked in centimeters. Emphasize that the distance between two marks on the ruler is called a centimeter and is a standard unit of length. Have students use the centimeter ruler to find the lengths of various sticks. Make sure that they state the measure to the nearest centimeter.

Activity 2—Have students use the millimeter ruler on the reverse side of the centimeter ruler. Tell students that this ruler is marked in millimeters, which is another standard unit of measure. Have the students measure sticks using this ruler.

Activity 3—I would like you to use your ruler to draw a line segment 3 centimeters long. Which side of the ruler would you use? (The side marked in centimeters.) How would you do this? (Draw a line segment which extends from the left end of the ruler to the point on the ruler marked 3.) Continue having students draw segments when the measures of these segments are given in either centimeters or millimeters. In each case, make sure that they use the correct side of the ruler to draw the line segment.

WORKTEXT® PAGES 121–22—For teaching suggestions, see the annotated pupil's pages.

Page 123

OBJECTIVES

■ Recognize the relationships between millimeters, centimeters, decimeters, and meters

BACKGROUND

One of the advantages of the metric system is that each standard unit contains ten of the next smaller size standard unit. This means that each meter contains 10 decimeters, each decimeter contains 10 centimeters, and each centimeter contains 10 millimeters. To change or convert from one unit of measure to another is very simple, since all that is needed is to multiply by a power of 10. Knowing the relationship between these prefixes is essential in converting one metric unit to another.

MATERIALS

1 meter stick for each group of students

PROCEDURE

Activity 1—Form groups of students and give a meter stick to each group. The stick that you have is called a meter stick. Its length is 1 meter long. The meter is a standard unit of length. Have each group measure the length and width of the room in meters. Have each group report the measure that they found. If there is any discrepancy among the measures obtained by the different groups, discuss how this may have happened.

Activity 2—Discuss the meanings of the numbers on the meter stick. Have students identify two marks which are end points for a line segment 1 millimeter long, two marks which are end points for a line segment 1 centimeter long, and two marks which are end points for a line segment 1 decimeter long. After students have identified these marks, have them

count the number of millimeters in a centimeter, the number of centimeters in a decimeter, and the number of decimeters in a meter. Then ask questions based on these relationships.

Review the symbols mm, cm, dm, and m. Have the students use the meter sticks to complete sentences such as 50 mm = _____cm, 7 dm = _____cm, 34 mm = _____cm + _____mm, and so on. Extend the process to include lengths greater than a meter.

WORKTEXT® PAGE 123—For teaching suggestions, see the annotated pupil's page.

Page 124

OBJECTIVES

■ Identify and draw pictures of angles
■ Identify and draw pictures of right angles

BACKGROUND

An angle consists of two rays with a common end point. The common end point of the two rays is called the vertex of the angle, and the rays are called the sides of the angle. A physical model of an angle would be the hour hand and the minute hand of a clock. This lesson emphasizes a special kind of angle called a right angle. Models of a right angle are the hands of a clock when the time is nine o'clock, two adjacent edges of a window pane, or two adjacent edges of a page in a book.

MATERIALS

2 strips of tagboard per pupil
1 paper fastener per pupil

PROCEDURE

Activity 1—Have pupils join the two strips of tagboard using the paper fastener to form a model of an angle. You have made a model of an angle. Write the word *angle* on the chalkboard. Have students show different-sized angles with their model. Demonstrate how to show a right angle. Write the words *right angle* on the chalkboard.

Activity 2—Draw an angle on the chalkboard and label the sides and the vertex. An *angle* is formed when two rays have a common end point. The rays are called the *sides* of the angle and the common end point is called the *vertex* of the angle. Have students draw pictures of angles.

To draw a picture of a right angle we use a square corner. Take a sheet of paper or other square object and lay it against the chalkboard. Trace the segments formed by two adjacent sides. Put arrows at the ends of these line segments to indicate rays. This is a right angle. It makes a square corner. Have students draw pictures of right angles using the corner of a square object.

Draw several angles on the chalkboard. How could we tell which of these angles are right angles? (By using a piece of paper to see if it forms a square corner.) Have students bring a piece of paper to the chalkboard and test to see which of the angles are right angles.

WORKTEXT® PAGE 124—For teaching suggestions, see the annotated pupil's page.

Page 125

OBJECTIVES
- Identify parallel line segments
- Draw parallel line segments

BACKGROUND

Two lines are said to be parallel if they are lines in the same plane and they do not intersect. Parallel line segments are line segments lying on parallel lines. Models of parallel line segments are straight sections of two railroad tracks or two slats in a venetian blind. Other examples of parallel line segments are opposite sides of rectangles, squares, or parallelograms.

MATERIALS

2 tongue depressors per student

PROCEDURE

Activity 1—Give each student 2 tongue depressors. Lay one of your sticks on a sheet of paper. Use the straight edges of the stick to draw a line segment on each side of the stick. Look at these two line segments. What do you notice about them? Help the students to see that they would never intersect if they were extended indefinitely. Another way of

stating this is that they are the same distance apart at all of their points. When two lines lie in a plane and never cross regardless of how far they are extended, they are called parallel lines. Draw a picture of parallel lines on the chalkboard and underneath it write *parallel lines*. Can you find any models of parallel lines or parallel line segments in the classroom? (Some examples are slats on venetian blinds, the top and bottom of the chalkboard, tops and bottoms of windows, or the mortar joints between bricks.)

Activity 2—Draw several pairs of line segments on the chalkboard. Some of the segments should be parallel; others should not. Choose students to draw a ring around those pairs of segments which are parallel. Ask students to tell why the other segments are not parallel. Now take your sticks and place them on your desk so that they represent parallel segments. Now show two segments that are not parallel.

WORKTEXT® PAGE 125—For detailed teaching suggestions, see the annotated pupil's page.

ADDITIONAL ACTIVITIES

Draw pictures of geometric shapes made up of line segments on the chalkboard. Have students identify the parallel line segments in each figure.

Pages 126-27

OBJECTIVES
- Identify triangles, squares, rectangles, and parallelograms
- Draw triangles, squares, rectangles, and parallelograms

BACKGROUND

In previous levels of *Succeeding in Mathematics*, students were taught to recognize and to draw triangles, squares, and rectangles. Parallelograms are introduced for the first time in this lesson. All of these figures are plane figures in that they lie in a flat surface. They are also called closed figures because they separate the plane into an inside and an outside. These figures are shown on Worktext® page 126.

MATERIALS

meter stick
1 ruler marked in millimeters for each student

PROCEDURE

Activity 1—Draw pictures of triangles, rectangles, parallelograms, and squares on the chalkboard. Ask students to identify each figure. After each figure has been identified, write its name underneath the figure. How many sides does a triangle have? (3.) How many angles does a triangle have? (3.) How many sides does a rectangle have? (4.) How many angles does it have? (4.) What type of angles are in a rectangle? (Right angles.) What is the difference between a rectangle and a parallelogram? (Rectangles have right angles and parallelograms may have angles which are not right angles.) How are rectangles and parallelograms alike? (They have 4 sides, 4 angles, and opposite sides are parallel.) Ask students to come to the chalkboard and shade the insides and outsides of the figures.

Activity 2—Have students come to the chalkboard and draw pictures of triangles, rectangles, parallelograms, and squares. Have other students measure the length of each of the sides with a meter stick to the nearest centimeter and record the figures in columns. Have students at their desks add the measures of the sides. Students should recognize that the lengths of opposite sides of a parallelogram or rectangle are the same and that the lengths of all sides of a square are the same.

Have students draw figures with specified dimensions. Make sure that the angles for rectangles and squares are approximately right angles and that opposite sides of rectangles and parallelograms have approximately the same measure.

WORKTEXT® PAGES 126-27—For teaching suggestions, see the annotated pupil's pages.

Page 128

OBJECTIVE

■ Construct triangles, rectangles, squares, and parallelograms

BACKGROUND

Students can gain a better understanding of geometric shapes by constructing them. Many plane figures can be constructed using strips of poster board and paper fasteners. In addition to the concrete representation of geometric figures, it is possible for students to learn that triangles are rigid figures and that four-sided figures are not rigid.

MATERIALS

strips of poster board
1 centimeter ruler per student
paper fasteners

PROCEDURE

Divide the class into groups. Give each group a variety of poster board strips and paper fasteners. Direct students to use the paper fasteners to put three strips of poster board together. Have each group show its construction to the rest of the class. What type of figure have you constructed? (A triangle.)

Ask students to put four pieces of poster board together. Have each group show its construction to the class. Some of these will probably be four-sided figures that are not rectangles, squares, or parallelograms. Others may show the class a parallelogram, a rectangle, or a square. See if students can identify the figures. If they cannot, help them identify parallelograms, squares, and rectangles. If one group has a parallelogram, ask if they can make a rectangle from it. (They can since it is not a rigid figure.) If a group shows a rectangle or square, ask if they can make a parallelogram from it.

WORKTEXT® PAGE 128—For teaching suggestions, see the annotated pupil's page.

Page 129

OBJECTIVES

■ Identify circles
■ Draw circles
■ Identify the center, the radius, and the diameter of a circle

MATERIALS

1 strip of poster board per student
2 pencils per student
1 millimeter ruler per student
1 chalkboard compass

PROCEDURE

Activity 1—Draw a model of a circle on the chalkboard. Ask students how they can identify a circle. Students might give some of the following answers: It is round. It has no sides. It is curved. It is a closed figure. It has an inside and an outside. Every point on a circle is the same distance from a point called its center. Mark the center of the circle on the chalkboard. This point is the center. Have students measure the distance from the center to points on the circle. Make sure that all students understand that these lengths should be the same for each point on the circle.

There are many objects in the room that make us think of circles. Have students identify objects that make them think of circles. Some objects that might be in the room are: the clockface, the hole in the pencil sharpener, the top of a can, the letter *O* in a poster, or counting discs. Let each student who can find a model of a circle tell the class what the model is.

Activity 2—Give each student a strip of poster board. Make sure that each student has two pencils. Have students use their pencils to punch a hole near each end of the strip of paper. We are going to use two pencils and the strip of paper with holes punched in it to draw pictures of a circle. Put a pencil through each hole and place one pencil near the center of a piece of paper. This pencil will mark the center of the circle. Use the other pencil to draw a picture of a circle as the strip of paper goes around the first pencil. Let students experiment drawing pictures of circles.

How could we make a picture of a smaller circle using the strip of poster board? (Punch holes closer together.) After they have several circles on their paper, have them use a straightedge to draw a radius of a circle. Draw a line segment with one end point the center of the circle and the other end point on the circle. Demonstrate this on the chalkboard. This line segment is called a radius of the circle. Write the word *radius* under the line segment on the chalkboard. Have students copy this word on their paper. Have a student come to the chalkboard and draw a different radius of the circle. Continue having students draw different radii of the same circle. What do you know about each radius of the circle? (It has the same length as every other radius.) Repeat this same procedure to teach students about the diameter of a circle.

WORKTEXT® PAGE 129—For detailed teaching suggestions, see the annotated pupil's page.

Pages 130-31

OBJECTIVES

- Measure objects using the inch as the unit of measure
- Draw line segments having a specified length in inches
- Identify relationships between inches, feet, and yards

BACKGROUND

The units of length in the English or customary system of measurement (inches, feet, and yards) are reviewed in this lesson. Students should learn the approximate size of each of these units and the relationships in size among the units. The best way for students to learn these things is to have a wide variety of experience in measuring objects and estimating the length of objects.

MATERIALS

1-foot ruler marked in inches for each student
1 yardstick for each group of students
objects to be measured

PROCEDURE

Activity 1—Form groups of children and give each group a yardstick. This is a yardstick. The length of the stick is called 1 yard. The yard is divided into smaller units of measure. Find the numbers 9 and 10 on the yardstick. The length of the segment between 9 and 10 is 1 inch. Have students select other consecutive inch marks and tell the length of the segment between these marks. Have students find the marks 12 and 24 on the yardstick. How many inches are in the segment between the marks 12 and 24 on the yardstick? (12.) We say that 12 inches is 1 foot. Have students use their yardsticks to identify other segments that are 12 inches or 1 foot long. Write the words *inch, foot,* and *yard* on the chalkboard. Have students draw segments with these lengths. Have students measure the classroom and various classroom features.

Activity 2—Draw a line segment $4\frac{3}{8}$ inches long on the chalkboard. Have a student measure this segment in inches. Is the line segment closer to 4 inches long or closer to 5 inches long? (4 inches.) We say that the length of this line segment is 4 inches to the nearest inch. Continue having students measure line segments to the nearest inch for segments that have been drawn on the chalkboard. Then give each student a ruler. Have each student measure the length of a pencil to the nearest inch, the length of a book to the nearest inch, and the width of a book to the nearest inch. Have students compare answers to check their work. Have them measure a variety of objects in the classroom to the nearest inch.

Activity 3—Write 12 inches = 1 foot, 3 feet = 1 yard, 36 inches = 1 yard on the chalkboard. How many inches are in 2 feet? (24.) How did you find 24? (Added 12 + 12.) How many feet are in 3 yards? (9.) How did you find 9? (Multiplied 3 × 3.) How many yards are in 27 feet? (9.) How did you find 9? (Divided 27 by 3.) Continue asking questions like this.

Write 2 yards ○ 2 feet on the chalkboard. Have a student come to the chalkboard and draw a line segment 2 yards long and a line segment 2 feet long. Which is longer? (The segment 2 yards long.) Fill the circle with the sign >. Continue writing relations such as this and have students complete the sentence with one of the symbols <, > or =. Have students draw segments when needed.

WORKTEXT® PAGES 130–31—For teaching suggestions, see the annotated pupil's pages.

Page 132

OBJECTIVES
- Recognize that perimeter is the distance around a plane figure
- Find the perimeters of plane figures by measuring the sides and adding

MATERIALS
- 1 centimeter ruler showing millimeters for each student
- 1 meter stick for each group of students

PROCEDURE

Activity 1—Draw a picture of a triangle on the chalkboard. Have a student use a meter stick to measure the length of one side in centimeters. Write this length on the chalkboard. Have a second student measure a second side of the triangle and write this length on the chalkboard, and a third student do the same for the third side. How could we find the distance around the triangle? (By adding the three lengths.) Do this. The distance around the tri-

angle is _____ centimeters. This is called the *perimeter* of the triangle. Write perimeter = _____ cm on the chalkboard. Continue finding the perimeter of triangles, parallelograms, rectangles, and squares on the chalkboard.

Activity 2—Divide the class into groups and give each group a meter stick. Have each group find the perimeters of shapes in the classroom such as the chalkboard, the door, or a table top. After the groups have computed the perimeters, have a reporting session and compare the results obtained by the different groups. If there is a wide disparity in responses, have groups recompute the perimeters.

WORKTEXT® PAGE 132—For teaching suggestions, see the annotated pupil's page.

Page 133

OBJECTIVES
- Recognize that a kilometer is a unit of measure used in measuring long distances
- Recognize that a mile is a unit of measure used in measuring long distances

BACKGROUND

In the metric system, kilometers are used to measure long distances. A kilometer is 1,000 meters. In the customary system, a mile is used to measure long distances. A mile is 5,280 feet or 1,760 yards. The approximate relationship between miles and kilometers is 1 kilometer = .62 mile. This information is for teacher use only and should not be a part of the student lesson.

PROCEDURE

It is not convenient to measure long distances in meters. Why not? (We would have to lay the meter stick end-to-end too many times.) For this reason, we define another standard unit of measure. A kilometer is 1,000 meters long. Write 1 kilometer = 1,000 meters on the chalkboard. How could we find about how long a kilometer is? Help students to see that they could take 1,000 large steps in a straight line.

When traveling, we can use kilometers to measure distances. Draw a map on the chalkboard and state the distances between cities in kilometers. Have students read and interpret the map. Use local cities and distances if possible.

WORKTEXT® PAGE 133—For detailed teaching suggestions, see the annotated pupil's page.

Page 134

OBJECTIVES

- Distinguish between plane regions and their boundaries
- Compare plane regions to determine which is larger

BACKGROUND

A plane figure together with its inside is called a plane region. For example, a triangle consists of three line segments in a plane. The triangular region consists of these three line segments along with all of the points of the plane that are inside the triangle. To make a model of a plane region, we use a sheet of paper or some such physical entity that suggests that the inside is included along with the boundary. In this book, shading is used to indicate that the inside of a figure is included with the boundary. The measure of a plane region is the number of square regions needed to cover it. This number is called the area of the plane region.

MATERIALS

models of triangles, rectangles, squares, and parallelograms
several sheets of construction paper

PROCEDURE

Activity 1—Show students the models and have them identify each shape. These figures are made up of line segments.

Give sheets of construction paper to various students in the class and have them draw a picture of a triangle, a rectangle, a square, a parallelogram, or a circle on their paper. Show one of these pictures to the class. What do the pencil marks on this paper form? Watch as I cut along the pencil marks. Show the cutouts to the class. This piece of paper is called a region. It contains the points of the plane figure and all of the points inside that plane figure. Compare the model of the triangle made with strips and the model of the triangular region. What is the difference in the two shapes? (The triangle is the boundary and

the triangular region is the boundary along with its inside.) Continue until you have several models of each shape of region.

Hold up two triangular regions of different sizes. Which is larger? How can you tell? (Just by looking or by placing one on top of the other.) Continue comparing the size of regions. Sometimes it may be necessary to cut one region into two or more pieces in order to be able to show that it fits completely inside another region.

Activity 2—Draw a region of 8 squares and a region of 9 squares of the same size to its right on the chalkboard. Which region is larger? (The one on the right.) How can you tell? (It is made up of 9 squares, and the other is made up of only 8 squares.) Continue drawing pictures of this type on the chalkboard and comparing regions by counting squares.

WORKTEXT® PAGE 134—For detailed teaching suggestions, see the annotated pupil's page.

Pages 135-36

OBJECTIVES

- Find the area of plane regions by counting the number of square regions needed to form them
- Find the area of rectangular regions by multiplying the number of rows of squares times the number of squares in each row

BACKGROUND

When measuring the size of plane regions, we choose a square region as the unit of measure. The area is then the number of square regions that are needed to cover the given plane region. Standard units for measuring area are square regions which have as the length of their edges a standard unit of linear measure.

In this lesson, students will learn to find area using two techniques. The first is by counting the number of square regions needed to form the region. If the original region is bounded by a rectangle, it is possible to find the area by multiplying rather than by counting. This is the forerunner of the formula for finding the area of a rectangular region: area = length × width.

PROCEDURE

WORKTEXT® PAGES 135–36—For teaching suggestions, see the annotated pupil's page.

Page 137

OBJECTIVE

■ Review the concepts and skills developed in chapter 6

PROCEDURE

WORKTEXT® PAGE 137—Have students com-
plete the chapter review. Worktext® page references for the exercises in this chapter review are: exercise A, pages 116, 117, 124, 125, 126, and 129; exercise B, page 122; and exercise C, pages 127 and 132.

Page 138

The last page of each chapter is a check-up designed to indicate the pupils' understanding of the concepts and skills that were presented in the chapter. Have students complete Worktext® page 138 independently.

7 Fractions

Pages 139-40

OBJECTIVES

■ Recognize that fractions tell us about parts of a whole

■ Recognize that the parts in a whole must all be the same size

■ Identify fractions from pictures representing parts of a whole

BACKGROUND

Whole numbers tells us *how many* when we are talking about the number of objects in a set. This chapter introduces fractional numbers. Fractional numbers are named with fractions.

The need for fractions grew out of physical situations. If we wish to share an apple with a friend, or to cut a pizza into pieces, or to subdivide a set of objects into smaller sets, we use fractions to name the part of the whole or the part of the set. Fractions tell us *how much of the whole* or *how much of the set* by comparing a part to the whole. For example, when a pizza is cut into six pieces of the same size, we say that each piece is one-sixth of the pizza. The *one* tells us that we are concerned with one piece, and the *six* tells us there are six pieces of the same size. The fraction designating this part of the pizza is $\frac{1}{6}$.

Throughout this chapter, pictures of fractions are used to give meaning to symbols and new ideas. Pictures also enlarge and strengthen the student's concept of fractions.

The first lesson in this chapter focuses on fractions that name parts of a whole. This lesson emphasizes three key ideas: (1) fractions name a different kind of number than whole numbers; (2) a fraction names a part of a whole; and (3) a fraction such as $\frac{3}{4}$ means that the whole has been divided into four parts of the same size, and the fraction is concerned with three of these parts.

MATERIALS

construction paper
envelopes

PROCEDURE

Activity 1—Today we are going to begin to study numbers named with fractions. Ask students for examples of fractions. Some examples that they might suggest are one-half centimeter, half-dollar, one-third cup, and so on. Ask students what these numbers mean. Help the students to understand that fractions tell us about parts of a whole. Continue discussing fractions and their uses with the class.

Take a piece of construction paper and show it to the class. How could I show one-fourth of this piece of paper? In the discussion, bring out that the paper must be divided into four parts of the same size. How can I divide the paper into four equal parts? (By folding it.) After the paper has been divided into four equal parts, unfold it. Has the paper been divided into four equal parts? (Yes.) Cut the paper along the folds and show the students one part. This part is called one-fourth of the original piece of paper. Write $\frac{1}{4}$ on the piece of construction paper. Hold it up so the class can see. Pick up another of the pieces. What fraction names this part? ($\frac{1}{4}$.) Have a student write $\frac{1}{4}$ on this piece of paper. Continue this procedure with the other pieces. Write $\frac{1}{4}$ on the chalkboard. This fraction tells us that we have one of four equal parts. Write $\frac{3}{4}$ on the chalkboard. This fraction tells us that we have three of four equal parts. Ask a student to show the class $\frac{3}{4}$ of the paper. Write $\frac{2}{4}$ on the chalkboard. Have a student show $\frac{2}{4}$ of the piece of paper.

Take a second sheet of paper and cut it into four unequal parts. Does each part show $\frac{1}{4}$ of the paper? (No.) Why not? (Because the pieces are not the same size.)

Develop halves, thirds, and eighths in the same manner.

Activity 2—Give each student four strips of construction paper of equal size and a pair of scissors. Fold a strip of paper into halves. Cut along the fold. After you have cut this strip, check to make sure that your two pieces are the same size. What is each part called? (One-half.) Place the part called one-half on a whole strip of paper. Is the part called one-half smaller than or larger than the whole strip? (Smaller than.) That is why one-half is called part of a whole.

Continue by having students cut another strip of paper into fourths and another strip into eights. Have them show fractions such as $\frac{2}{4}$, $\frac{3}{4}$, $\frac{5}{8}$, and so on against

the one whole remaining strip of construction paper.

Students will be using these representations for fractions in succeeding lessons. After this activity has been completed, give each student an envelope in which to store the fractional pieces.

WORKTEXT® PAGES 139–40—For teaching suggestions, see the annotated pupil's pages.

ADDITIONAL ACTIVITIES

Materials: several objects that can be cut into parts. Show one of the objects. Suppose that two people want to share this object. How could we arrange this? (Cut the object into two equal parts.) What would each part be called? (One-half.) As you are doing this, emphasize that numbers named with fractions show parts of a whole, and that the parts in the object must all be the same size.

Pages 141-42

OBJECTIVES

■ Name the numerator, the denominator, and the fraction from pictures representing part of a whole

■ Write a fraction given its word name

BACKGROUND

The symbol $\frac{3}{4}$ compresses a great deal of meaning into a compact form. This fraction is composed of three parts: the 3, which is called the numerator, the dividing line, and the 4, which is called the denominator. The numerator tells us the number of parts in which we are interested, while the denominator tells us the total number of equal parts. The fraction itself tells us how the part is related to the whole.

In this lesson, students will continue to write fractions that are suggested from pictures. They will be expected to identify the numerator and the denominator for each of these fractions and to identify the fraction when given the word name. It is essential that the meaning of each fraction, as part of a whole, is emphasized each time the students write a fraction.

MATERIALS

fraction flash cards for halves, thirds, fourths, fifths, sixths, and eighths

fraction parts made by students
construction paper

PROCEDURE

Make the fraction flash cards by showing a bar divided into parts with the appropriate number of parts shaded. Show the name of the fraction on the reverse of each card. Prepare three strips of construction paper for each student. Each strip must be equal in length to those cut into parts by the students in the activity for Worktext® pages 139–40. Use a marking pen to divide the strips into thirds, fifths, and sixths.

Activity 1—Show the flash card illustrating $\frac{1}{4}$. The bar is divided into how many parts? (4.) How many of these parts are shaded? (1.) What fraction is shown on this card? ($\frac{1}{4}$.) Write $\frac{1}{4}$ on the chalkboard. What does the top number in the fraction tell us? (The number of pieces in which we are interested.) What does the bottom number in the fraction tell us? (The number of equal parts in the whole.) Continue drilling with the flash cards in this fashion until students are able to answer quickly.

Write $\frac{3}{8}$ on the chalkboard. In the fraction $\frac{3}{8}$ we call 3 the numerator. Write *numerator* next to the 3. What does the numerator tell us? (The number of parts in which we are interested.) The 8 is called the denominator. Write *denominator* next to the 8. What does the denominator tell us? (The number of equal parts in the whole.) Continue drilling with the flash cards. Ask students to identify the numerator, the denominator, and the fraction for each flash card.

Activity 2—Give students their envelopes of fraction parts and strips of paper marked into thirds, fifths, and sixths. Find the strip of paper that has been marked with lines dividing it into three equal parts. Cut the paper on the lines. What is each piece called? (One-third.) Have students write $\frac{1}{3}$ on each piece. Put two of these three pieces together on the whole strip of paper from your envelope. What fraction is represented? ($\frac{2}{3}$.) Develop fractions with denominator 5 and denominator 6 in the same way. Students should now have fraction parts for halves, thirds, fourths, fifths, sixths, and eighths in their envelope. Have them illustrate fractions using these parts and the whole number strip.

Activity 3—Write *seven-eighths* on the chalkboard. Ask a student to write the fraction for this word name. What is the numerator for this fraction? (7.) What is the denominator for this fraction? (8.) What does the fraction $\frac{7}{8}$ mean? (The part contains seven of eight equal pieces.) Continue having students write fractions for word names and identify the numerator, the denominator, and the meaning for each fraction.

WORKTEXT® PAGES 141–42—For teaching suggestions, see the annotated pupil's pages.

Pages 143-44

OBJECTIVES

■ Identify the fraction that names a part of a set

■ Identify the numerator as the number of objects in the part and the denominator as the total number of objects in the set

BACKGROUND

Fractions may designate a part of a set. For example, if we have a set of four objects and two of them are red, we say that two-fourths of the set is red. When fractions are used to name part of a set, the numerator is the number of objects in the part and the denominator is the total number of objects in the set. The objects in the set do not have to be the same size or shape.

MATERIALS

8 red counters per student
8 blue counters per student
8 half-inch circles
8 one-inch circles
8 half-inch squares
8 one-inch squares
overhead projector

PROCEDURE

Activity 1—Distribute 8 red and 8 blue counters to each student. Form a set of 4 red and 2 blue counters. How many objects are in this set? (6.) How many of these objects are red? (4.) The part of this set that is red is named by the fraction $\frac{4}{6}$. Write $\frac{4}{6}$ on the chalkboard. The numerator 4 tells us that there are 4 red counters in this part of the set. The denominator 6 tells us the number of objects in the set. What fraction tells us the part of the set that is blue? ($\frac{2}{6}$.) What does the 6 tell us? (There are 6 objects in the set.) Continue with examples of this type using sets made up of red and blue counters. Use sets which have 2, 3, 4, 5, 6, or 8 counters in them. In each case, emphasize the numerator, the denominator, and the meaning of the fraction.

Activity 2—Put a set of 3 half-inch circles and 5

one-inch circles on the overhead projector. How many small circles are in the set? (3.) How many circles are in the set altogether? (8.) What fraction names the part of the set that is small circles? ($\frac{3}{8}$.) Have a student come to the chalkboard and write $\frac{3}{8}$. What is the numerator of this fraction? (3.) What does it tell us? (The number of small circles in the set.) What is the denominator of this fraction? (8.) What does it tell us? (The number of circles in the set.) Continue using the small and large circles and squares to illustrate fractions.

Suppose we want to show a set in which two-thirds of the set is small squares. How many members should the set have? (3.) How many of these members should be small squares? (2.) Does it matter what the other member is? (Not as long as it is not a small square.) Have a student come to the overhead projector and illustrate a set in which two-thirds of the set is small squares. Continue giving students fractions and having them illustrate the sets on the overhead projector.

Form a set consisting of 2 half-inch circles, 3 one-inch circles, 4 half-inch squares, and 3 one-inch squares. What part of the set is large squares? ($\frac{3}{12}$.) What part of the set is small squares? ($\frac{4}{12}$.) Continue asking questions about various subsets of this set. Then form different sets with a variety of subsets and ask students to identify the fraction which designates each part of the set.

WORKTEXT® PAGES 143–44—For teaching suggestions, see the annotated pupil's pages.

ADDITIONAL ACTIVITIES

Materials: fraction flash cards for halves, thirds, fourths, fifths, sixths, eighths, and tenths. These flash cards should be similar to those made earlier, but these cards should show parts of sets. Show the flash cards and have students state the fractions that name different parts of the set. Students should also state the numerator and the denominator of each fraction and the meaning of the fraction.

Page 145

OBJECTIVES

- Recognize that fractions such as $\frac{2}{2}$, $\frac{3}{3}$, and $\frac{4}{4}$ are all names for a whole
- Recognize that a whole is named by the whole number 1

MATERIALS

fraction parts for halves, thirds, fourths, fifths, sixths, and eighths
flash cards showing the fractions $\frac{2}{2}$, $\frac{3}{3}$, $\frac{4}{4}$, $\frac{5}{5}$, $\frac{6}{6}$, $\frac{8}{8}$, and $\frac{10}{10}$

PROCEDURE

Activity 1—Give students their envelopes of fraction parts. Find the whole strip of paper in your envelope. Now find four fraction parts named $\frac{1}{4}$. Put these on the whole strip of paper side by side. Do they cover the whole strip exactly? (Yes.) How many fourths did you put on the whole? (4.) Write $\frac{4}{4}$ on the chalkboard. The fraction $\frac{4}{4}$ is a name for a whole. What is another name for a whole? Help the students to see that they could write a whole as 1, $\frac{2}{2}$, and so on. Illustrate other names for a whole by using other fraction cards. Write the fractions that name a whole on the chalkboard. Emphasize that a whole may be named by the number 1, or it may be named by many different fractions.

Erase the fractions on the chalkboard. Then have students come to the chalkboard and write different names for a whole. What do you notice about the numerator and the denominator in the fractions that name a whole? (They are equal.) Whenever the numerator and the denominator are equal, the fraction is a name for a whole, or the number 1.

Activity 2—Display the flash cards showing fractions that name a whole. Have students identify the fraction illustrated by each flash card. Then mix these cards with the other flash cards that illustrate fractions and have students identify the fraction illustrated by each flash card.

WORKTEXT® PAGE 145—For teaching suggestions, see the annotated pupil's page.

Page 146

OBJECTIVES

- Write standard names or expanded names for whole numbers
- Complete number patterns
- Complete number sentences by using the symbols <, >, and =

BACKGROUND

It is essential that students continually review previously learned skills. In this lesson, skills that were developed in chapter 1 are reviewed. The symbols $<$, $>$, and $=$ should be emphasized, because these symbols will be used with fractions hereafter.

PROCEDURE

Draw a number line on the chalkboard with eleven marks on it. Name the first two successive points with the numbers 495 and 496. Have students complete the number line. After the points on this number line have been named, write 495 on the chalkboard. Have students come to the chalkboard and write different expanded names for 495, that is, 4 hundreds, 9 tens, 5 ones or $400 + 90 + 5$. Continue to review writing expanded names.

Which is larger, 495 or 501? (501.) How do you know? (Because 501 is to the right of 495.) Write 495 is less than 501. Then write 495 ◯ 501. What symbol goes in the circle? ($<$.) Continue illustrating sentences of this type on the chalkboard.

After several exercises of this type have been completed, use the same number line and name two successive points 190 and 200. Not all of the numbers have been named on this number line. This time we are counting by tens on the number line. Have students complete this number pattern on the number line.

WORKTEXT® PAGE 146—For teaching suggestions, see the annotated pupil's page.

Page 147

OBJECTIVE

■ Compare fractions with the same denominator to determine which names the larger part

BACKGROUND

Just as we can tell which of two whole numbers is larger, we can also tell which of two fractional numbers is larger. When the denominators are alike, it is easy to tell which fraction names the larger part. In this case, all we need to do is look at the numerators and determine which numerator is larger. For example, $\frac{7}{10}$ and $\frac{5}{10}$ have a common denominator. Since this is the case, we look at the numerators. Since 7 is larger than 5, we know that $\frac{7}{10}$ is larger than $\frac{5}{10}$.

In this lesson, students should learn to determine which fraction names the larger part using pictures. The teacher should encourage students to discover the rule stated above.

MATERIALS

fraction flash cards showing wholes divided into parts

PROCEDURE

Show the flash cards for $\frac{1}{6}$ of a whole and $\frac{3}{6}$ of a whole. Ask students to identify the fractions that name the shaded parts. Then ask students to compare the shaded regions. Which of the two shaded regions is larger? (The one named by $\frac{3}{6}$.) Which of the shaded regions is smaller? (The one named by $\frac{1}{6}$.) Since the region named by the $\frac{1}{6}$ is smaller than the region named by $\frac{3}{6}$, we say that the fraction $\frac{1}{6}$ is less than the fraction $\frac{3}{6}$. Write $\frac{1}{6}$ is less than $\frac{3}{6}$ on the chalkboard. Beneath it write $\frac{1}{6} < \frac{3}{6}$. Continue comparing the parts named by other sixths, such as $\frac{3}{6}$ compared to $\frac{5}{6}$, $\frac{4}{6}$ compared to $\frac{3}{6}$, and so on. In each case have students name the fractions, identify which names the larger part, and write the sentence using the proper symbol. Does anyone see how we can tell which fraction names the larger part when the denominators are both 6? (By looking at the numerators.)

Continue with this activity using flash cards with denominators of 8 and those with denominators of 10.

If any students ask about comparing fractions with unequal denominators, let them experiment with the flash cards while you continue to teach other students how to compare fractions with like denominators.

WORKTEXT® PAGE 147—For teaching suggestions, see the annotated pupil's page.

ADDITIONAL ACTIVITIES

Materials: 1 centimeter ruler per student. Ask students to draw two rectangles 2 centimeters wide by 5 centimeters long. How could we divide this rectangular region into five parts of the same size? (Measure 1 centimeter segments along the length and draw 4 line segments to show 5 pieces.) Have students complete these pictures. In one of your pictures, show the fraction $\frac{3}{5}$ by shading. In the other picture, show the fraction $\frac{2}{5}$ by shading. Which is the larger fraction? ($\frac{3}{5}$.) Write the sentence which compares the fractions $\frac{3}{5}$ and $\frac{2}{5}$ using the symbol for is less than or is greater than. Continue having students draw pairs of rectangles and divide these rectangles into parts of the same size to show given fractions. After they have completed several of these pairs of rectangles, choose correct pictures and pin them on the bulletin board. This activity reinforces some of the concepts developed in the geometry chapter and applies them to fraction concepts.

Page 148

OBJECTIVE

■ Compare fractions with like denominators to determine which names the larger part of a set

BACKGROUND

In the preceding lessons, students compared fractions to determine which named the larger part of a whole. In this lesson, similar procedures will be used to compare fractions to determine which names the larger part of a set. As before, students should be encouraged to discover the rule that if two fractions have the same denominator, the fraction which has the larger numerator names the larger fraction.

PROCEDURE

Draw 2 sets of 5 squares each on the chalkboard. Have a student shade 3 in one set and 4 in the other set. Have a second student identify the fractions that name the shaded parts of the sets and a third student write these fractions on the chalkboard. Which fraction names the larger part of a set? ($\frac{4}{5}$.) Write $\frac{3}{5} < \frac{4}{5}$ and $\frac{4}{5} > \frac{3}{5}$. Leave these sets on the chalkboard and draw 3 more sets of 5 objects. Shade $\frac{1}{5}$ of one set, $\frac{2}{5}$ of one set, and $\frac{5}{5}$ of one set. Continue comparing pairs of fractions by determining which fraction names the larger or smaller part of the set.

Have 10 students come to the chalkboard and draw sets of 10 objects. Then have one of the students show $\frac{1}{10}$ of the set by shading, a second student show $\frac{2}{10}$ of the set by shading, and so on until the last student shows $\frac{10}{10}$ of the set by shading. After the students have shaded the correct number of objects in the sets, have them write the fraction that names the part of the set that is shaded. Use these pictures to help students compare pairs of fractions with the denominator 10 to determine which fraction names the larger or smaller part of the set. For each comparison write a sentence such as $\frac{3}{10} < \frac{5}{10}$.

WORKTEXT® PAGE 148—For teaching suggestions, see the annotated pupil's page.

ADDITIONAL ACTIVITIES

Materials: 8 red counters and 8 blue counters per student. Form one set of 5 red and 3 blue counters and a second set of 5 blue and 3 red counters. What part of the first set is blue? ($\frac{3}{8}$.) What part of the second set is blue? ($\frac{5}{8}$.) Which set has the most blue counters? (The second set.) Which fraction names the larger part of a set? ($\frac{5}{8}$.) Write the sentence $\frac{5}{8} > \frac{3}{8}$ on the chalkboard. Continue with this activity, having students construct sets using the red and blue counters, identify the fraction for parts of each set, and write a sentence comparing the fractions.

Page 149

OBJECTIVES

■ Name points on the number line using fractions
■ Use the number line to determine which of two fractions names the larger number

BACKGROUND

Each fraction has a corresponding point on the number line. To find the points which correspond to fourths, we begin with a unit interval, the end points of which are named 0 and 1. This unit interval is separated into four equal parts. The points of separation are named by the fractions $\frac{1}{4}$, $\frac{2}{4}$, and $\frac{3}{4}$. Although it is not essential at this time, it may be convenient to name the end points of the unit segment in two ways. Name the left end point 0 above the line and $\frac{0}{4}$ below the line. The right end point of the unit segment is named 1 and $\frac{4}{4}$. This introduces students to alternative ways to name the number 0 and the number 1.

PROCEDURE

Draw the picture shown below on the chalkboard.

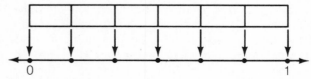

The bar has been divided into how many equal parts? (6.) How much of the bar is to the left of the first arrow? (0 or none.) Note that the left end of the bar

is directly above the point labeled 0 on the number line. What part of the bar is to the left of the second arrow? ($\frac{1}{6}$.) We name the point on the number line under this arrow $\frac{1}{6}$. What part of the bar is to the left of the next arrow? ($\frac{2}{6}$.) What fraction should name the point directly under this arrow? ($\frac{2}{6}$.) Continue until all points under the arrows have been named. What fraction would be another name for 1? ($\frac{6}{6}$.)

Remember that larger numbers appear to the right of smaller numbers on the number line. Look at the number line and find the fractions $\frac{2}{6}$ and $\frac{4}{6}$. Which fraction is farther to the right? ($\frac{4}{6}$.) Which fraction names the larger number? ($\frac{4}{6}$.) Write the sentences $\frac{2}{6} < \frac{4}{6}$ and $\frac{4}{6} > \frac{2}{6}$ on the chalkboard. Read these sentences with the class. Continue discussing the size of fractions on this number line.

Put another bar on the chalkboard and divide it into eight equal parts. Use the same procedures as described above to name fractions with denominators of 8 on the number line.

WORKTEXT® PAGE 149—For teaching suggestions, see the annotated pupil's page.

Page 150

OBJECTIVES

- Interpret the meanings of fractions
- Identify fractions from verbal descriptions

BACKGROUND

In previous work with fractions, the students have always had a visual representation to work with. The exercises on this page are more abstract. There are no pictures, but each fraction refers to a concrete object or set. Students are asked to use their knowledge of fractions in answering questions about situations described verbally. Students should be encouraged to answer the questions without drawing pictures; however, if they cannot answer them from the verbal description alone, they should answer them after drawing pictures.

PROCEDURE

WORKTEXT® PAGE 150—For teaching suggestions, see the annotated pupil's page.

Page 151

OBJECTIVES

- Complete multiplication facts and the related division facts
- Complete division facts using the number line

MATERIALS

set of multiplication fact flash cards
set of division fact flash cards

PROCEDURE

Activity 1—Draw a number line with points labeled from 0 to 60 on the chalkboard. Ask students to come to the chalkboard and identify the marks on the line which correspond to numbers such as 30, 42, 57, and so on.

Illustrate multiplications such as 5×6 and divisions such as $32 \div 8$ on the number line. Continue with these exercises until students recall how to multiply and divide on the number line.

Activity 2—Divide the class into four teams. Mix the multiplication and division flash cards. Show one of the flash cards. The first team is to give the product (or quotient), the second team is to write a related multiplication (or division), the third team is to write a related division (or multiplication), and the fourth team is to write another related division (or multiplication) on the chalkboard. Proceed through the deck of flash cards. Teams get one point for each correct response. Make sure that all members of the class participate in finding the product or quotient and writing the related facts.

WORKTEXT® PAGE 151—For detailed teaching suggestions, see the annotated pupil's page.

Pages 152-53

OBJECTIVES

- Identify the number of objects in one-half of a set
- Identify the number of objects in one-third of a set

BACKGROUND

To divide a set of objects into halves, we divide the set into two subsets, each of which has the same number of objects. For example, when dividing a set of eight objects into halves, we form two subsets, each with four objects in it. We say that one-half of 8 is 4. In like manner, to divide a set into thirds, we divide the set of objects into three subsets, each of which has the same number of elements. If the set originally had nine elements, we form three subsets, each with three elements in it. We say one-third of 9 is 3.

MATERIALS

9 white counters per student
9 red counters per student
9 green counters per student

PROCEDURE

Activity 1—Distribute 9 white and 9 red counters to each student. Form a set that contains 1 red counter and 1 white counter. What part of the set is red? (One-half.) What part of the set is white? (One-half.) Now form a set of 2 red counters and 2 white counters. Are there the same number of white counters as red counters in your set? (Yes.) When a set is divided into two parts, each of which has the same number of objects, we say that each part is one-half of the set. The red part of your set is named by one-half, and the white part is named by one-half. How many objects are in the red part of your set? (2.) How many objects are in your set altogether? (4.) How many objects are in one-half of your set? (2.) We say one-half of 4 is 2. Continue developing the idea of one-half of a set by forming sets with 3 red and 3 white counters, 4 red and 4 white counters, and so on up to 9 red and 9 white counters. In each case, emphasize that the red part of the set is one-half of the set. Write sentences such as $\frac{1}{2}$ of 8 is 4 for each set.

Now have students form a set of 8 white objects. How could we find one-half of this set? (Divide it into two smaller sets, each with the same number of elements.) Do that. What is one-half of 8? (4.) Continue having students form sets of objects and divide them into halves.

Activity 2—Distribute 9 white, 9 red, and 9 green counters to each student. Develop the notion of one-third of a set in the same way that one-half of a set was developed in activity 1.

Activity 3—Have a student come to the chalkboard and draw a set of 12 dots. What must we do to find one-half of this set? (Separate the set into two parts, each with the same number of dots.) Have a student come to the chalkboard and draw lines around two sets of dots to show one-half of the set. How many dots are in one-half of this set? (6.) What is one-half of 12? (6.) Write $\frac{1}{2}$ of 12 is 6. Continue with this activity showing halves and thirds.

Draw a set of 15 objects on the chalkboard and divide it into sets of 6 and 9. Has this set been divided into halves? (No.) Why not? (Because the two sets do not have the same number of objects.) Continue with examples which show sets that are *not* divided into halves or *not* divided into thirds. Be sure that some of these examples show a set divided into parts which have unequal numbers of objects in each part.

Write $\frac{1}{3}$ of 18 is _____ on the chalkboard. If we wanted to show this with a picture, how many dots would we have to draw? (18.) Into how many sets should we divide the 18 dots? (3.) Should each of these sets have the same number of elements? (Yes.) Have a student show this. How many dots are in each of these smaller sets? (6.) Have a student come to the chalkboard and complete the sentence by writing 6 in the blank. Continue with examples of this type.

WORKTEXT® PAGES 152–53—For teaching suggestions, see the annotated pupil's pages.

Pages 154-55

OBJECTIVES

■ Identify the number of objects in one-fourth of a set

■ Identify the number of objects in one-fifth of a set

MATERIALS

30 counters per student

PROCEDURE

Activity 1—Distribute the counters. Form a set of 20 counters. Separate the set of 20 counters into 4 smaller sets, each of which has the same number of counters. If students have difficulty, suggest that they form the 4 sets by first putting 1 counter in each of the 4 sets, then a second counter in each of the 4 sets, and so on. How many counters are in each of the 4 sets? (5.) What is one-fourth of 20? (5.) Continue this activity, having students divide the counters into 4 or 5 smaller sets. In each case, write the sentence, such as $\frac{1}{4}$ of 20 is 5, or $\frac{1}{5}$ of 20 is 4, on the chalkboard.

Activity 2—Draw a set of 30 dots on the chalkboard. Have a student draw rings around dots to show 5 sets, each with the same number of dots. How many dots are in each set? (6.) What is one-fifth of 30? (6.) Continue with exercises showing either one-fourth or one-fifth of the original set.

WORKTEXT® PAGES 154–55—For teaching suggestions, see the annotated pupil's pages.

Page 156

OBJECTIVES

- Write fractions for various parts of a meter
- Identify the number of centimeters in a fractional part of a meter

BACKGROUND

Use of the metric system provides an excellent means for developing the concepts of tenths and hundredths. Since there are 10 decimeters in 1 meter, each decimeter is one-tenth of a meter. Since there are 100 centimeters in a meter, each centimeter is one-hundredth of a meter. The fractional part of a meter represented by 42 centimeters is $\frac{42}{100}$. Given any number of centimeters between 0 and 100, we can write the fraction which denotes this part of a meter by writing the number of centimeters over 100. Using this technique, it is quite simple to change from the number of centimeters to a fractional part of a meter or vice versa.

MATERIALS

meter sticks
1 strip of paper, 10 cm wide by 1 m long, per student

PROCEDURE

Activity 1—Give each student a strip of paper. I want each of you to mark your strip of paper into decimeters. Remember that a decimeter is 10 centimeters long. After students have done this, have them fold the strip of paper along each decimeter mark. The folds of the paper separate the meter strip into how many pieces? (10.) Are each of these pieces the same length? (Yes.) What fraction names the part

of a meter for each of these pieces? ($\frac{1}{10}$.) How do you know that? (There are ten equal pieces and so each piece is one-tenth of a meter.) Tell the students that the word *decimeter* means one-tenth of a meter.

Have students use their strips of paper to measure objects in decimeters. Have them state the results in terms of fractional parts of a meter. If a student finds that the edge of a desk is 7 decimeters long, ask what part of a meter that is. (Seven-tenths of a meter.)

Activity 2—Arrange students in groups and give each group a meter stick. Look at the meter stick. How many centimeters are there in 1 meter? (100.) Are each of these centimeters the same length? (Yes.) What fraction names the part of the meter for 1 centimeter? ($\frac{1}{100}$.) We say that 1 centimeter is one-hundredth of a meter because there are 100 centimeters in a meter. What fraction would name the length of an object that is 5 centimeters long? ($\frac{5}{100}$.) Have students measure various objects in the room and give the length in centimeters and then in fractional parts of a meter. Remind them that they can change centimeters to a fractional part of a meter by writing the number of centimeters over 100.

How many centimeters are in seven-hundredths of a meter? (7.) How many centimeters are in one hundred-hundredths of a meter? (100.) Continue asking questions which require students to identify the number of centimeters in a fractional part of a meter.

WORKTEXT® PAGE 156—For teaching suggestions, see the annotated pupil's page.

Page 157

OBJECTIVES

- Write fractions for various parts of a dollar
- Identify the number of cents in a fractional part of a dollar

BACKGROUND

Use of our monetary system provides another excellent means of reinforcing the concept of fractions. Halves and fourths can be illustrated using half-dollars and quarters; tenths and hundredths can be illustrated using dimes and pennies. It is also possible to illustrate equivalent fractions using money. We know that a quarter is one-fourth of a dollar. We also know that a quarter is twenty-five cents or twenty-five hundredths of a dollar. This shows us that we can write $\frac{1}{4} = \frac{25}{100}$. In a similar manner, we can show $\frac{1}{2} = \frac{50}{100}$ by using half-dollars and pennies.

PROCEDURE

How many half-dollars are in a dollar? (2.) What fraction names the part of a dollar represented by a half-dollar? ($\frac{1}{2}$.) How many quarters are in a dollar? (4.) What fraction names the part of a dollar represented by a quarter? ($\frac{1}{4}$.) What fraction names the part of a dollar represented by 3 quarters? ($\frac{3}{4}$.) How many dimes are in a dollar? (10.) Each dime is one-tenth of a dollar. What fraction names the part of a dollar represented by 5 dimes? ($\frac{5}{10}$.) What fraction names the part of a dollar represented by 7 dimes? ($\frac{7}{10}$.) Each penny is one-hundredth of a dollar. What fraction names the part of a dollar represented by 23 pennies? ($\frac{23}{100}$.) Continue asking questions about the fraction that names parts of a dollar when you have several quarters, several dimes, or several pennies. Suppose Bob has fifty-hundredths of a dollar. How many cents does Bob have? (50.) What coins might Bob have? (1 half-dollar, 2 quarters, 5 dimes, 50 pennies, or other combinations of coins.) Continue asking questions in which you tell the fractional part of a dollar and ask students to identify the number of cents that this fractional part of a dollar represents.

WORKTEXT® PAGE 157—For teaching suggestions, see the annotated pupil's page.

Page 158

OBJECTIVE

■ Read and write symbols for money using the dollar sign and the decimal point

BACKGROUND

In this lesson, names for money will be written using the dollar sign and the decimal point. This notation has not been used in this text but has been introduced in previous levels of *Succeeding in Mathematics*. When we write $3.65, we mean three dollars and sixty-five cents. This is the conventional way of writing amounts of money when there is more than one dollar. It is often used when the amount of money is less than one dollar. In the latter case, we would write $.75. Sometimes a 0 is written before the decimal point in amounts less than one dollar.

PROCEDURE

Write $3.75 on the chalkboard. How do we read this symbol? (Three dollars and seventy-five cents.) Point to the dollar sign. This symbol is called a dollar sign. It tells us that we are reading an amount of money. Point to the decimal point. This symbol is called a decimal point. It separates the dollars and cents in an amount of money. Continue having students read various amounts of money.

Suppose we want to write five dollars and thirty cents using the dollar sign and the decimal point. Have a student come to the chalkboard and write $5.30. Give as much help as is needed. Continue stating amounts of money and having students write the amount of money on the chalkboard using the dollar sign and the decimal point. Write $.20 on the chalkboard. How many dollars are in this amount of money? (0.) How many cents are in the amount of money? (20.) Write $.02 on the chalkboard. How many dollars are in this amount of money? (0.) How many cents are in this amount of money? (2.) Which of these two amounts of money is larger? ($.20.) Continue writing different amounts of money on the chalkboard and having students identify the number of dollars, the number of cents, and which of the two amounts is larger.

WORKTEXT® PAGE 158—For teaching suggestions, see the annotated pupil's page.

Pages 159-60

OBJECTIVE

■ Read and interpret picture graphs

BACKGROUND

A picture graph is a pleasing and convenient way to represent certain types of data. A picture graph itself is composed of three main parts: the title, which tells the subject of the picture graph, the pictures, which represent the actual data, and the key, which describes what each picture represents. In order to interpret a picture graph, the key and the pictures must be used to find the actual number of objects that are represented.

This lesson is intended to be completed individually by students. It may be completed by the more capable students as the teacher is continuing to develop some fraction ideas with less capable students. It may also be used as a class exercise.

PROCEDURE

WORKTEXT® PAGES 159–60—For teaching suggestions, see the annotated pupil's pages.

ADDITIONAL ACTIVITIES

After students have completed the exercises on Worktext® pages 159–60, you may wish to have a group of students construct a picture graph for some set of data that is available in your classroom. You might have students make a graph showing the number of different types of fish in the aquarium.

Page 161

OBJECTIVE

■ Review the skills and concepts developed in chapter 7

PROCEDURE

WORKTEXT® PAGE 161—Have students complete the chapter review. Worktext® page references for the exercises in this chapter review are: exercise A, pages 139-42, 145, and 147; exercise B, pages 143, 144, 148, 152, 153, 154, and 155; exercise C, pages 147, 148, and 149; and exercise D, pages 152, 153, 154, and 155.

Page 162

The last page of each chapter is a check-up designed to indicate the pupils' understanding of the concepts and skills that were presented in the chapter. Have the students complete Worktext® page 162 independently.

Addition and Subtraction

Page 163

OBJECTIVES

■ Add 2-digit numbers when renaming is required

■ Add 3-digit numbers when renaming ones as tens and tens as hundreds is required

BACKGROUND

Students have had a great deal of experience with the processes used in adding and subtracting numbers. In this chapter, these processes will be extended to adding and subtracting 4-digit numbers, adding and subtracting money using the dollar sign and decimal point, and renaming when zeros are involved in subtraction. Emphasis in all of this work should be placed on addition and subtraction as abstract operations to be completed without the use of manipulative aids and pictures. To be sure, there still may be some students who need these types of activities; however, students should be encouraged to compute at the abstract level.

The present lesson reviews addition of 2- and 3-digit numbers. The learning activities for this lesson will be paper and pencil type activities. If students need work using concrete learning aids, the teacher should use activities similar to those described in chapter 2. The same basic instructions and materials may be used to extend instruction to 4-digit numbers.

PROCEDURE

Activity 1—In the following paragraphs, two games for drilling addition facts and easy addition exercises are described. These may be used as quick drills throughout the chapter.

Let students form teams. On the chalkboard, write a 1-digit number for each team. These numbers may be different for different teams. Give students the following directions: The first student in each team comes to the chalkboard and adds 4 to the number named in front of your team. The second student checks and corrects, if necessary, the first student's sum and then adds 4 to the correct sum on the chalkboard. This new sum is written in the column beneath the first student's sum. Each pupil in the row checks the previous sum and adds 4 to it, all in the same column. The row with the largest correct sum when I say stop is the winner. Pupils may have more than one turn before I say stop. Have a practice game until students understand the rules. Then play several games using constant addends other than 4.

The second game also encourages students to find sums for addition facts or simple addition exercises mentally. As before, students are divided into teams. Each team should have a piece of paper with the same addition fact on it. The first member on the team is given the paper and writes the sum on the piece of paper. The paper is then handed to the second player. The teacher states a number such as 5 and the second student is to add 5 to the sum written by the first student. The second student is to write his sum beneath the first player's sum. This continues until each member of the team has had a turn. The team(s) with the correct sum at the end of the game win(s). While students are completing this game, the teacher should walk about the room and identify those students who are having difficulty writing the correct sums. These students should be given more drill with basic addition facts and simple addition exercises.

Activity 2—Explain the addition algorithm for adding 2- and 3-digit numbers. Write an addition such as

$$\begin{array}{r} 394 \\ +178 \\ \hline \end{array}$$

on the chalkboard. Have students help to complete this and emphasize that the ones are added first, the tens second, and the hundreds last. Also emphasize the renaming process that is needed when there are 10 or more ones as the sum in the ones' column and 10 or more tens as the sum in the tens' column. Review several exercises of this type and have students complete more and more of the work.

WORKTEXT® PAGE 163—For teaching suggestions, see the annotated pupil's page.

Pages 164-65

OBJECTIVE

■ Add amounts of money when each amount is written using the dollar sign and the decimal point

BACKGROUND

Students have already had a great deal of experience with numbers written to show amounts of money. Sometimes these are written with the cent symbol and other times they are written with the dollar sign and the decimal point. In this Worktext®, students have not previously been required to add amounts of money when they were stated with the dollar sign and the decimal point. The important concept for students to learn is that the decimal points must be aligned in a column. Then the addition is performed similar to adding two 3-digit numbers. The decimal point and the dollar sign must be placed in the answer to indicate the amount of money.

This lesson is divided into three distinct parts. The first part is a review of the meaning of the dollar sign and the decimal point. Then students are asked to add two amounts of money without renaming. Finally, students are asked to add two amounts of money when renaming pennies as dimes and dimes as dollars is required. As in the previous lesson, students should be encouraged to perform these activities as paper and pencil activities without resorting to physical materials.

MATERIALS

objects with "price tags" on which the amount is shown using the dollar sign and the decimal point

PROCEDURE

Activity 1—Show one of the objects with its price tag to the class. Ask a student to tell how much the object costs. Write this amount of money on the chalkboard using the dollar sign and the decimal point. Ask the students what each of these symbols mean. How many dollars are needed to buy this object? How many dimes are needed to buy this object? How many pennies are needed to buy this object? Continue with this activity using the other objects.

Activity 2—The drill games described in the teaching activities for Worktext® page 163 may be modified and used to provide students with the opportunity to add small amounts of money.

$2.35

Activity 3—Write the addition +1.43 on the chalkboard. When adding two amounts of money, we must add the pennies to the pennies, the dimes to the dimes, and the dollars to the dollars. This means that when we write the additions, we should write the decimal points in a column. Then the digits representing pennies will be in the same column, the digits representing dimes will be in the same column, and the digits representing dollars will be in the same column. To complete the addition, we add the pennies first, the dimes second, and then the dollars. Do this. We must now write the dollar sign and the decimal point in the answer to show the correct amount of money. Have students complete several more examples.

WORKTEXT® PAGES 164–65—For teaching suggestions, see the annotated pupil's pages.

Page 166

OBJECTIVES

- Subtract a 2-digit number from a 2-digit number when it is necessary to rename 1 ten as 10 ones
- Subtract a 3-digit number from a 3-digit number when it is necessary to rename 1 hundred as 10 tens

BACKGROUND

This lesson is a review of previously learned skills in subtraction. Students should have the opportunity to review subtraction facts and the subtraction algorithm used for subtracting 2- and 3-digit numbers. Emphasize that students should subtract the ones first, the tens second, and the hundreds third. The process of renaming in subtraction should also be emphasized. As in addition, students should be encouraged to perform these subtractions in an abstract setting.

PROCEDURE

Activity 1—The two drill games described for Worktext® page 163 should be modified for subtraction. The first of these games is not only excellent practice for subtraction but also lays the groundwork for division as repeated subtraction.

83

Activity 2—Write a subtraction such as −65 on

the chalkboard. Explain the subtraction and renaming process by asking students questions and having them complete this exercise on the chalkboard. Continue with examples in which 2-digit numbers are subtracted from 3-digit numbers and 3-digit numbers are subtracted from 3-digit numbers.

WORKTEXT® PAGE 166—For teaching suggestions, see the annotated pupil's page.

Pages 167-68

OBJECTIVES

- Subtract amounts of money when the amounts are written using the dollar sign and the decimal point
- Check subtraction using addition

BACKGROUND

After the student has learned how to add amounts of money using the dollar sign and the decimal point and has reviewed subtraction, it should be a simple matter to teach subtraction of amounts of money using the dollar sign and the decimal point. When subtracting amounts of money, students should write the decimal points in a column. Then the subtraction is similar to the subtraction of whole numbers. Students must write the decimal point and the dollar sign in the difference to show that the difference is an amount of money.

PROCEDURE

Activity 1—Write $.35 on the chalkboard. How can we read this amount of money? (35 cents.) Continue writing various amounts of money on the chalkboard and having students read these amounts of money. Suppose we want to write the symbol for $3.75 on the chalkboard. Have a student write this amount. Continue having students come to the chalkboard and write amounts of money using the dollar sign and the decimal point.

Activity 2—Modify the drill games for Worktext® page 163 so that students have an opportunity to subtract small amounts of money.

$9.87

Activity 3—Write the subtraction −2.35 on the chalkboard. Explain the process for subtracting amounts of money. Have students help complete several examples.

Remind students that they can check a subtraction by adding. Write the addition check for the first subtraction on the chalkboard and have students help to add these two amounts of money. Then have them help to complete each of the addition checks for the subtractions that are written on the chalkboard.

WORKTEXT® PAGES 167–68—For teaching suggestions, see the annotated pupil's pages.

Page 169

OBJECTIVE
■ Solve verbal problems involving amounts of money by adding or subtracting

BACKGROUND
Some of the very real applications of mathematics for young children are money problems. Students are required to handle money almost daily as they go to the store, pay for their lunch, or buy things with their own money. Students should be encouraged to find the amount of money they are spending for two or more items or to determine the amount of change they should receive when they are shopping. This may develop into a play-store activity in the classroom or into an assignment requiring students to report on a trip to the store.

As students are solving the word problems on this page, they should be reminded of the steps that should be followed to complete the solution to word problems. These steps are listed in the background information for Worktext® page 42.

PROCEDURE

WORKTEXT® PAGE 169—For teaching suggestions, see the annotated pupil's page.

Pages 170-71

OBJECTIVES
■ Rename 1 hundred as 9 tens and 10 ones

■ Subtract a 3-digit number from a 3-digit number when it is necessary to rename 1 hundred as 9 tens and 10 ones

BACKGROUND
In previous subtraction exercises students have had to rename tens as ones or hundreds as tens. They have not had any subtraction exercises in which they needed more ones and there were no tens to rename. When this occurs, students must learn to rename 1 hundred as 10 tens and then rename one of these tens as 10 ones. This process may be shortened somewhat by renaming 1 hundred as 9 tens and 10 ones.

MATERIALS
5 green counters per pupil
10 red counters per pupil
18 white counters per pupil

PROCEDURE
Activity 1—Distribute the counters. Remind students that each green counter represents 100, each red counter represents 10, and each white counter represents 1. Have students show the number 432 with their counters. Make sure that each student shows 4 green, 3 red, and 2 white counters. Now have students show the number 200. Make sure that each student shows 2 green counters. Suppose that I would like to use some white counters to represent this same number. How could I do it? Help the students to see that one way to do this would be to exchange 1 green counter for 10 red counters and then to exchange 1 red counter for 10 white counters. Have students do this. How is the number 200 represented now? (By 1 green, 9 red, and 10 white counters.) The number sentence that we have just demonstrated is 200 = 100 + 90 + 10. Write this number sentence on the chalkboard. Continue with examples in which 1 hundred must first be renamed as 10 tens and then 1 ten renamed as 10 ones. Make sure that you write a number sentence on the chalkboard for each example done.

Activity 2—Put a chart similar to the one shown below on the chalkboard.

Standard Name	Rename 1 Hundred as 10 Tens	Rename 1 Ten as 10 Ones
400	300 + 100	300 + 90 + 10
400	3 hundreds, 10 tens	3 hundreds, 9 tens, 10 ones

Write the standard names and have students fill in the second and third columns.

602

Activity 3—Write −175 on the chalkboard. Are there enough ones to subtract from? (No.) Are there any tens to rename? (No.) How could we rewrite 602 so that there are some tens? (Rename 1 hundred

5 10
6Ø2

as 10 tens.) Show −175 on the chalkboard. Now can we rename 1 ten as 10 ones? (Yes.) Show

9
5 1Ø 12
6Ø2 on the chalkboard. We have rewritten 602
−175

as 5 hundreds, 9 tens, 12 ones. Now are there enough ones to subtract from? (Yes.) What is the difference in the ones' column? (7.) Are there enough tens to subtract from? (Yes.) What is the difference in the tens' column? (2.) Are there enough hundreds to subtract from? (Yes.) What is the difference in the hundreds' column? (4.) When there are not enough ones to subtract from and there are no tens to rename, we rename 1 hundred as 10 tens first and then rename 1 ten as 10 ones. Continue with exercises in which there are not enough ones to subtract from and there are no tens to rename.

Activity 4—Repeat activity 3 using amounts of money.

WORKTEXT® PAGES 170–71—For teaching suggestions, see the annotated pupil's pages.

Page 172

OBJECTIVES

- Write expanded names for 4-digit numbers
- Determine which of two 4-digit numbers is larger

BACKGROUND

This lesson reviews 4-digit numbers so that students will readily recall both the meaning of each digit and the expanded names for 4-digit numbers. These concepts will be needed as students learn how to add and subtract 4-digit numbers in subsequent lessons.

Students should have an intuitive understanding of how many things there are in 1,000. Some models that have previously been used are the number of pennies in ten dollars, or the number of spaces on a meter stick marked off in millimeters.

PROCEDURE

Activity 1— What number comes after 999? (1,000.) Can anyone tell me what 1,000 is? Be sure students understand that 1,000 is 10 hundreds or 100 tens or 1,000 ones. Other responses that might be given by students are the number of grams in a kilogram or the number of pennies in ten dollars. Let's see if we can count starting with large numbers. Have a student start counting with 1,285. Have the next student count 1,286, and so on.

After students have counted using word names, have them write the numerals for numbers between 1,000 and 10,000 on the chalkboard. Make sure that some of the examples you call out are numbers with zero as one of the digits, such as 1,045, 2,304, or 1,630.

Activity 2—Which number is larger, 1,432 or 1,324? (1,432.) Write the sentence 1,432 is greater than 1,324 on the chalkboard. Then write 1,432 > 1,324. Continue comparing the sizes of two numbers and writing the sentence using the symbol for is less than or is greater than.

WORKTEXT® PAGE 172—For detailed teaching suggestions, see the annotated pupil's page.

ADDITIONAL ACTIVITIES

Materials: three jars; one filled with lima beans, one filled with paper clips, and one filled with marbles. Have students guess the number of objects in each of the jars. Then have teams of students count the number of objects in each of the jars. Let students form their own procedures. If their procedures are too inefficient, give constructive help, such as suggesting that students count piles of 100 and then group the thousands, hundreds, tens, and ones together as in expanded names. This activity provides good experience in estimation and may also lead to other mathematical ideas, such as adding columns of 3-digit numbers or estimating the number of beans in the jar by counting how many beans are in a cup and seeing how many cups of beans fill the jar.

Page 173

OBJECTIVE

- Add two 4-digit numbers when renaming is not required

PROCEDURE

WORKTEXT® PAGE 173—For teaching suggestions, see the annotated pupil's page.

Pages 174-75

OBJECTIVES

- Rename 10 ones as 1 ten, 10 tens as 1 hundred, and 10 hundreds as 1 thousand
- Add two 4-digit numbers when renaming is required

PROCEDURE

WORKTEXT® PAGES 174–75—For teaching suggestions, see the annotated pupil's pages.

ADDITIONAL ACTIVITIES

Materials: counters of four different colors. If students have excessive difficulty in adding two 4-digit numbers, the process of addition should be developed through the use of concrete objects. Counters can be used to develop the notions of addition. In all cases, the teacher should remember that the ultimate goal of this instruction is to make students capable of adding two or more 4-digit numbers in an abstract setting.

Page 176

OBJECTIVES

- Identify fractions which name parts of a set
- Write fractions which name parts of a set
- Compare fractions having like denominators when physical representations of these fractions are available
- Find fractional parts of sets

MATERIALS

1 set of fraction flash cards
30 counters per student

PROCEDURE

Activity 1—Show the fraction flash cards to the class and have students respond by stating the word name for the fraction and by writing the fraction on the chalkboard. Go through the deck several times until students readily recall how to read and write fractions.

Activity 2—Use the flash cards which show parts of a whole divided into eighths. Show the class the flash card representing one-eighth of a whole and the flash card representing five-eighths of a whole. Which of these pictures shows the greater part of a whole? (The one showing five-eighths of the whole.) Write the sentence $\frac{5}{8} > \frac{1}{8}$. Continue comparing parts of a whole as represented by two of these cards and writing the sentence comparing the two fractions on the chalkboard.

Activity 3—Give each student 30 counters. Form a set of 18 counters. Now divide the set into three equal parts. How many counters are in each part? (6.) The sentence that tells us this is $\frac{1}{3}$ of 18 is 6. Continue with this activity, having students form sets of objects, separate them into an equal number of parts, and write the sentence.

WORKTEXT® PAGE 176—For teaching suggestions, see the annotated pupil's page.

Page 177

OBJECTIVE

- Subtract a 4-digit number from a 4-digit number when no renaming is required

PROCEDURE

WORKTEXT® PAGE 177—For teaching suggestions, see the annotated pupil's page.

Pages 178-79

OBJECTIVES

- Rename 1 thousand as 10 hundreds or 1 hundred as 10 tens or 1 ten as 10 ones

■ Subtract a 4-digit number from a 4-digit number when renaming is required

PROCEDURE

> WORKTEXT® PAGES 178–79—For detailed teaching suggestions, see the annotated pupil's pages.

ADDITIONAL ACTIVITIES

1. If students have excessive difficulty in subtracting two 4-digit numbers, the process of subtraction should be developed through the use of concrete objects and pictures. Concrete objects should be used initially before proceeding to the use of pictures.

2. If students have difficulty with the subtraction facts, they should complete short drill periods using subtraction flash cards.

Page 180

OBJECTIVES

■ Interpret data reported in a table
■ Differentiate between addition and subtraction situations
■ Solve addition and subtraction problems stated verbally

BACKGROUND

Counting birds as they migrate is one of the ways in which bird populations are estimated. The problems on this page indicate how students in schools might use mathematics. If an actual experiment of this type were conducted, it would provide students with excellent applications of counting, estimation, addition, and ways to report data. It would help to relate mathematical skills to the world in which we live.

PROCEDURE

> WORKTEXT® PAGE 180—For detailed teaching suggestions, see the annotated pupil's page.

Pages 181-82

OBJECTIVE

■ Read and interpret bar graphs

BACKGROUND

This lesson is intended to be completed by the students individually. It may be completed by the more capable students as the teacher is continuing to develop addition and subtraction of 4-digit numbers with less capable students. It may also be used as a class exercise for all students.

PROCEDURE

> WORKTEXT® PAGES 181–82—For detailed teaching suggestions, see the annotated pupil's pages.

ADDITIONAL ACTIVITIES

After students have completed the exercises on Worktext® pages 181–82, you may wish to have them construct bar graphs for sets of data that are available in the classroom.

Page 183

OBJECTIVE

■ Review the concepts and skills developed in Chapter 8

PROCEDURE

> WORKTEXT® PAGE 183—Have students complete the chapter review. Worktext® page references for the exercises in this chapter review are: exercise A, pages 163, 164, 165, 173, and 175; exercise B, pages 166, 167, 168, 171, 177, 178, and 179; and exercise C, pages 163, 166, 169, and 180.
>
> Error patterns for addition are given in the material for Worktext® page 79; those for subtraction are given in the material for Worktext®

page 84. If students need more practice after completing the chapter review, they may be assigned exercises in chapter 13, pages 275, 276, 278, and 279. These exercises provide additional practice applications on the skills involved.

Page 184

The last page of each chapter is a check-up designed to indicate the pupils' understanding of the concepts and skills that were presented in the chapter. Have the students complete Worktext® page 184 independently.

Multiplication

Page 185

OBJECTIVE
■ Find the products for multiplication facts

MATERIALS
1 classroom set of multiplication flash cards
1 set of multiplication flash cards for each pair of students

PROCEDURE
Activity 1—Draw a number line on the chalkboard and label every fifth point with a multiple of 5. There should be points on the number line to 80. Remind students how to find points which correspond to such numbers as 20, 37, 45, and so on. Then write multiplications such as 3×9 on the chalkboard. Have students find the products on the number line.

Activity 2—Show flash cards and call on students to give the products. Go through the deck several times. Then remove the easier facts and continue drilling.

If this drill indicates that students need more drill to remember the multiplication facts, group students in pairs and have them continue drilling on multiplication facts.

Activity 3—Draw a multiplication table on the chalkboard. Have students complete the table. After the table has been completed, write multiplications in column form on the chalkboard and have students give the products. For any multiplication that presents difficulty, have students use the multiplication table to find the product.

WORKTEXT® PAGE 185—For teaching suggestions, see the annotated pupil's page.

Page 186

OBJECTIVE
■ Multiply a 1- or 2-digit number by 10 or 100

BACKGROUND
Students should learn to recognize that the product of 10 times any number is the number with a zero after it; for example, $17 \times 10 = 170$. They should also learn that the product of 100 times any number is the number with two zeros after it.

MATERIALS
20 green counters per student
20 red counters per student
10 white counters per student

PROCEDURE

Activity 1—Distribute the counters. Remind students that each white counter represents 1, each red counter represents 10, and each green counter represents 100. Have students use their counters to show 374. How many green counters did you use? (3.) How many red counters did you use? (7.) How many white counters did you use? (4.) Continue representing numbers using the counters.

Activity 2—Show 70 with your counters. What counters did you use? (7 red counters.) This says that you have 7 tens. Suppose you want to write 7 tens as a multiplication. Who can write this on the chalkboard? Have a student come to the chalkboard and write 7×10. 7 tens and 7×10 are two names for the same number. What is the standard name for this number? (70.) Complete the sentence $7 \times 10 = 70$ on the chalkboard. Continue illustrating multiplications which have 10 as one of the factors and a 1-digit number as the other factor. How are the number of zeros in the product related to the number of zeros in 10? (They are the same.) How many places will there be in the answer if you multiply a 1-digit number by 10? (2.) Do you think this would be true if you multiplied a 2-digit number times 10? Let's see if you can show this using your counters. Put 12 red counters on your desk. This shows the multiplication 12×10. What is the standard name for 12×10? (120.) Does the product have one more digit than 12? (Yes.) What is this digit? (0.) After students understand this process, go back and work with the multiplication 10×10. Make sure that students understand that when they have 10 tens it should be written as 100.

Use the same procedure with the green counters to teach multiplication by 100. Can anyone tell an easy way for writing the product when multiplying by 10? Help students to see that the product can be written by writing the number and putting a zero to the right of it. Emphasize this rule with several examples. Can anyone tell an easy way for writing the product when multiplying by 100? Help the students to see that to write the product when multiplying by 100, you write the number and put two zeros to the right of it. Have students use this rule with several examples.

WORKTEXT® PAGE 186—For teaching suggestions, see the annotated pupil's page.

ADDITIONAL ACTIVITIES

Materials: 2 pieces of paper, one with $\times$ *10* and the other with $\times$ *100* written on it in large characters.

I'm going to try to trick you in this game. I'm going to tell you a number and hold up one of these cards. Show the cards to the class. You will have to write on your paper the product of the number times the number on the card. Say "five" and hold up the card $\times$ *10*. Have students write the product on their paper and then choose a student to come to the board and write the product. Continue this drill until students can multiply correctly and rapidly by 10 and by 100.

Page 187

OBJECTIVES

- Multiply a 1-digit number times a multiple of 10
- Multiply a 1-digit number times a multiple of 100

BACKGROUND

Multiplying a 1-digit number times multiples of 10 or 100 is an essential skill used in multiplying a 1-digit number times either a 2- or a 3-digit number. This skill can be learned by using the basic multiplication facts and extending the pattern that was developed in the last lesson.

PROCEDURE

Activity 1—Write the pattern 10, 20, 30, ____, ____, ____ on the chalkboard. Have different students fill in the blanks. The pattern here is counting by tens. If we continued this pattern, would 90 be written? (Yes.) Would 75 be written? (No.) Have students extend this pattern until they get to 100. The numbers that we have written in this pattern are called multiples of 10. Is 40 a multiple of 10? (Yes.) Is 4 a multiple of 10? (No.)

Develop multiples of 100 in the same way.

Activity 2—Write 3×3 on the chalkboard. Have a student write this as a repeated addition. What is the product? (9.) Then write 3×30. This means 3 thirties. Have a student write this as a repeated addition. What is the product of 3×30? (90.) Write 3×300 on the chalkboard. Have a student write this as a repeated addition and find the sum. What is the product of 3×300? (900.) Write these three multiplications in column form next to each other. Does anyone see a pattern? If no one responds, complete several more examples. Then have students study the pattern and try to describe it in their own words. Stress that the pattern is the same for each set of multiplications.

WORKTEXT® PAGE 187—For detailed teaching suggestions, see the annotated pupil's page.

Page 188

OBJECTIVE

■ Find products such as 3×25 using the distributive property

BACKGROUND

The distributive property is used to find the product of 3×25 by following the steps below.

1. Replace 25 by its expanded name.
   $3 \times 25 = 3 \times (20 + 5)$
2. Use the distributive property.
   $3 \times 25 = (3 \times 20) + (3 \times 5)$
3. Multiply 3×20 and 3×5.
   $3 \times 25 = 60 + 15$
4. Add $60 + 15$.
   $3 \times 25 = 75$

This procedure is used in the ordinary method for multiplication of a 1-digit number times a 2-digit number but is written in a different form. The purpose of this lesson is to prepare students to understand the short form of multiplying a 1-digit number times a 2-digit number.

MATERIALS

15 red counters per student
15 white counters per student

PROCEDURE

Distribute the counters. Use your counters to show the number 21. Check to make sure that each student shows 2 red counters and 1 white counter. Write the sentence $21 = 20 + 1$ on the chalkboard. Let's use our counters to multiply 3×21. 3×21 means that we have 3 groups of 21. Show 21 three times using the counters. How many ones are in the three groups? (3.) How many tens are in the three groups? (6.) Six tens equals what number? (60.) The product for 3×21 is found by adding $60 + 3$. What is this sum? (63.) Let's show what we did by writing number sentences on the chalkboard. Write the following number sentences on the chalkboard and explain them using the verbal descriptions.

$3 \times 21 = 3 \times (20 + 1)$	Replace 21 by its expanded name.
$= (3 \times 20) + (3 \times 1)$	Rename the multiplication since $3 \times (20 + 1) = (3 \times 20) + (3 \times 1)$.
$= 60 + 3$	Multiply 3×20 and 3×1.
$= 63$	Add $60 + 3$.

Continue with examples of this type.

WORKTEXT® PAGE 188—For teaching suggestions, see the annotated pupil's page.

Page 189

OBJECTIVE

■ Use partial products to multiply a 1-digit number times a 2-digit number

BACKGROUND

Students could continue to find products by using repeated addition or by using the distributive property as they did in the last lesson. However, these methods are quite long. In this lesson students will begin to learn a faster and more efficient way to find products for multiplications in which one factor is a 1-digit number and the other factor is a 2-digit number.

In this lesson, students will use a long form to find products for multiplications such as 4×34. This procedure will require students to carry through three steps: (1) multiply 4 times 4 ones and write the product 16; (2) multiply 4 times 3 tens and then write the product 120; and (3) add $16 + 120$ and write the sum 136. This is the product of 4×34.

In this procedure, each of the partial products is written. In the next lesson, students will learn to multiply without writing each of the partial products.

PROCEDURE

WORKTEXT® PAGE 189—For teaching suggestions, see the annotated pupil's page.

ADDITIONAL ACTIVITIES

Materials: duplicated sheets of multiplication exercises. Prepare multiplication exercises with 1-

digit numbers times multiples of 10 and 1-digit numbers times 2-digit numbers. Have students complete the multiplications as homework.

Page 190

OBJECTIVE

■ Multiply a 1-digit number times a 2-digit number using the short form when no renaming is required

BACKGROUND

Multiplying using the short form uses all of the steps learned in the previous lesson but does not require the student to write the results of intermediate steps. This savings in writing requires the student to remember more while completing the multiplication. The procedure introduced in this lesson is the beginning of the pattern that we ordinarily use in multiplication. This step-by-step procedure is called the multiplication algorithm. Using the basic multiplication facts and this rule permits us to find the product for any two whole numbers.

PROCEDURE

Write $\begin{array}{r} 72 \\ \times\ 3 \\ \hline \end{array}$ on the chalkboard. Have students find the product for this multiplication using the long form previously developed. After students have found the product, erase the two partial products. Show students that they could find the product for 3 × 72 without writing the partial products. Continue this procedure using a variety of examples. Make sure that the product of the ones' digits is always less than 10.

WORKTEXT® PAGE 190—For teaching suggestions, see the annotated pupil's page.

Pages 191-92

OBJECTIVE

■ Multiply a 1-digit number times a 2-digit number when renaming ones as tens is required

BACKGROUND

The process of renaming in the short form of multiplication is introduced in this lesson. Students should learn to recognize that when the product of the ones is greater than 10, each set of 10 ones must be renamed as 1 ten. The number of tens must be remembered and must be added to the product that is obtained when multiplying the tens. We sometimes write a small digit in the tens' column to indicate the number of tens to remember to add.

PROCEDURE

Activity 1—What is the product of 6 × 7? (42.) Write 42 = ____ tens, ____ones on the chalkboard. Have a student come to the chalkboard and complete this sentence. If we have 42 ones, we can rename 40 of the ones as 4 tens, giving us 4 tens and 2 ones. Continue drilling students on multiplication facts, writing the expanded name for each product. In each case, emphasize that you are renaming 10 ones as 1 ten.

You may also at this time wish to review multiplying a 1-digit number times a multiple of 10, for example, 7 × 30. This product is 21 tens, and 20 of these tens are renamed as 2 hundreds.

Activity 2—Write $\begin{array}{r} 83 \\ \times\ 7 \\ \hline \end{array}$ on the chalkboard. Have students complete this multiplication by writing partial products and then adding to find the answer. Let's see if we can find the product without writing the partial products. First we multiply the ones. When we multiply 7 times 3 ones, what do we get? (21.) 21 is how many tens and how many ones? (2 tens and 1 one.) We write 1 in the product and write the 2 above the 8 to remind us that we have 2 tens to be added in the tens' column. Now we multiply the tens. 7 times 8 tens is how many tens? (56.) How many tens do we have to add to this? (2.) What is 56 tens plus 2 tens? (58 tens.) We write 58 tens as 5 hundreds and 8 tens. Continue practicing multiplication of a 1-digit number times a 2-digit number using the short form. Let students complete more and more of the work in each multiplication. Make sure that in each multiplication you emphasize the renaming of ones as tens.

WORKTEXT® PAGES 191-92—For teaching suggestions, see the annotated pupil's pages.

ADDITIONAL ACTIVITIES

Materials: 9 green counters, 19 red counters, and 19 white counters per student. Write $\begin{array}{r} 47 \\ \times\ 4 \\ \hline \end{array}$ on the chalkboard. First we multiply the ones. If we multiply 4 times 7 ones, how many ones do we get? (28.) Represent 28 using red and white counters. How many red counters did you use? (2.) How many white counters did you use? (8.) If we use the short form to multiply, where do we write the 8 ones? (In the ones' column.) Where do we write the 2 tens? (In the tens' column above the 4.) Now we multiply 4 times 4 tens. How many tens do we get? (16.) Show this with red counters. We must add to these 16 tens the 2 tens that we already have. How many tens do we have then? (18.) Write 18 tens in the product. Show how this multiplication is finished using the short form. Continue using counters to help find the products for a 1-digit number times a 2-digit number. In each case, emphasize the way that the product is found using the short form.

Page 193

OBJECTIVES

- Add columns of three numbers
- Subtract 3-digit numbers from 3-digit numbers
- Check subtraction by addition

MATERIALS

basic addition facts flash cards
basic subtraction facts flash cards
basic multiplication facts flash cards

PROCEDURE

Activity 1—Today we are going to review addition, subtraction, and multiplication facts. I am going to try to trick you by showing you cards. You will have to look very carefully to determine if you should add, subtract, or multiply. After you have found which operation to perform, find the answer. Show the first card. What operation should you perform? What is the answer? Continue going through the cards, first asking what operation to perform and then asking what the answer is. After several examples of this type, just ask students to find the answers.

Activity 2—Review the procedure for addition and have students help to complete several additions involving adding two 2- or 3-digit numbers with renaming. Also review the procedure for adding columns of three numbers.

Activity 3—Review the procedure for subtracting a 3-digit number from a 3-digit number. Emphasize that renaming is sometimes necessary in subtraction. Have students help to complete several sub-

tractions in which renaming is necessary. After the differences have been found, remind them that they can check a subtraction by adding the difference to the subtrahend. Check each of the subtractions that were worked on the chalkboard.

WORKTEXT® PAGE 193—For teaching suggestions, see the annotated pupil's page.

Page 194

OBJECTIVE

- Solve problems requiring two operations

PROCEDURE

When you are asked to find the sum, what operation should you perform? (Addition.) When you are asked to find the difference, what operation should you perform? (Subtraction.) When you are asked to find the product, what operation should you perform? (Multiplication.) I am going to give you some problems. I will call on one of you to work each problem on the board while the rest of you work the problem at your seats. You can then check your work with the problem that is on the board. Let's begin. Find the sum of 16 and 43. (name of student), please come to the board and do this problem. After the student has completed the problem, have the students at their seats check their work. Now multiply this sum times 5. Have a student come to the board and do this while the rest of the students are doing it at their seats. What is the product? (295.) Remind students that they first added 16 and 43 and then multiplied 5 times this sum. Continue with problems of this type.

WORKTEXT® PAGE 194—For teaching suggestions, see the annotated pupil's page.

Pages 195-96

Objectives

- Multiply a 1-digit number times a 3-digit number using expanded names

■ Multiply a 1-digit number times a 3-digit number by writing partial products and adding

PROCEDURE

WORKTEXT® PAGES 195–96—For teaching suggestions, see the annotated pupil's pages.

Page 197

OBJECTIVE

■ Multiply a 1-digit number times a 3-digit number using the short form when no renaming is required

BACKGROUND

When using the short form, the individual partial products are not written. This requires students to remember more as they are completing the multiplication and to be careful about the placement of digits in the product. This lesson is the first in a series which develops the short form. Students must learn to multiply the ones and write the product in the ones' column, multiply the tens and write the product in the tens' column, and multiply the hundreds and write the product in the hundreds' column.

PROCEDURE

Write $\begin{array}{r} 423 \\ \times\ 3 \end{array}$ on the chalkboard. Let's find the product using partial products. Have students complete this multiplication by writing all three partial products and then adding. Let students do as much of the work as possible and give help only where needed. After this multiplication is written on the board, erase the zeros as shown below.

$$\begin{array}{r} 423 \\ \times\ 3 \\ \hline 9 \\ 60 \quad \text{Erase} \\ 1200 \\ \hline 1269 \end{array}$$

Does anyone see how we might have written the answer without writing all of the partial products? Help students to see that they could write the product of the ones in the ones' place, the product of the

tens in the tens' place, and the product of the hundreds in the hundreds' place.

WORKTEXT® PAGE 197—For teaching suggestions, see the annotated pupil's page.

Page 198

OBJECTIVE

■ Multiply a 1-digit number times a 3-digit number when renaming tens as hundreds is necessary

PROCEDURE

Activity 1—Write 4 × 60 on the chalkboard. Have a student complete this multiplication. Nearby, write 4 × 6 tens. Six tens is another way to write 60. When we multiply 4 × 6 tens, how many tens do we get? (24.) Write 24 tens. Is 240 equal to 24 tens? (Yes.) That means that we can write 24 tens as blank hundreds, blank tens. What numbers go in the blanks? (2 in the hundreds' blank and 4 in the tens' blank.) Continue illustrating multiplications of this type. In each case, multiply a 1-digit number times a multiple of 10 and write the expanded name for the product.

Activity 2—Write the multiplication $\begin{array}{r} 372 \\ \times\ 4 \end{array}$ on the chalkboard. Have students complete this multiplication using partial products. Nearby, write the same multiplication. Let's see if we can use the short form to find this product. First, we multiply 4 × 2. What is the product? (8.) We put 8 in the ones' column. Next, we multiply 4 × 7 tens. How many tens do we get? (28 tens.) Twenty of these tens can be renamed as how many hundreds? (2.) How many tens are left? (8.) We write the 8 in the tens' column and a small 2 above the 3 in the hundreds' column to remind us that we have renamed these 20 tens as 2 hundreds. Next, we multiply 4 × 3 hundreds. What is the product? (12 hundreds.) How many hundreds must we add to this? (2 hundreds.) What is the sum? (14 hundreds.) We write 4 in the hundreds' column and 1 in the thousands' column. What is the product of 4 × 372? (1,488.) Continue with examples of this type. For each example, have students complete the multiplication using partial products. Then have them help complete the multiplication using the short form. Emphasize the renaming of 10 tens as 1 hundred.

Pages 199-200

OBJECTIVE

- Multiply a 1-digit number times a 3-digit number when renaming ones as tens and tens as hundreds is required

PROCEDURE

Adapt the procedure used for Worktext® page 198 to develop renaming ones as tens and tens as hundreds.

ADDITIONAL ACTIVITIES

For additional practice, prepare duplicated sheets similar to those in exercises B and C.

Page 201

OBJECTIVE

- Solve verbal problems requiring multiplication

BACKGROUND

The problems on this page are all measurement conversions that can be solved by multiplication. These not only provide practice in solving verbal problems but also provide a way to compute useful information. All of the problems are written in the same general style to help students recognize that they are to multiply to solve the problem and to emphasize this particular type of measurement conversion.

PROCEDURE

Page 202

OBJECTIVE

- Find quotients for division facts

PROCEDURE

Page 203

OBJECTIVE

- Find the product of a 1-digit number times a 1-, 2-, or 3-digit number

BACKGROUND

The multiplications on this page are of a variety of types. Those in exercise A are multiplication facts. Exercise B contains multiplication of a 1-digit number times a multiple of 10, multiplication of a 1-digit number times a 2-digit number when renaming is not required, and multiplication of a 1-digit number times a 2-digit number when renaming is required. In exercise C, students are asked to multiply a 1-digit number times a 3-digit number. The multiplications included in this exercise are multiplication of a 1-digit number times a multiple of 100, multiplication of a 1-digit number times a 3-digit number when renaming is not required, and multiplication of a 1-digit number times a 3-digit number when single or double renaming is required.

Responding incorrectly to a multiplication fact.	$\begin{array}{r} 5 \\ 27 \\ \times 8 \\ \hline 4 \end{array}$	$\begin{array}{r} 5 \\ 371 \\ \times 8 \\ \hline 48 \end{array}$
Multiplying in place.	$\begin{array}{r} 27 \\ \times 8 \\ \hline 1,656 \end{array}$	$\begin{array}{r} 371 \\ \times 8 \\ \hline 24,568 \end{array}$
Forgetting to rename ones as tens or tens as hundreds.	$\begin{array}{r} 27 \\ \times 8 \\ \hline 166 \end{array}$	$\begin{array}{r} 371 \\ \times 8 \\ \hline 2,468 \end{array}$
Adding incorrectly.	$\begin{array}{r} 5 \\ 27 \\ \times 8 \\ \hline 116 \end{array}$	$\begin{array}{r} 5 \\ 371 \\ \times 8 \\ \hline 2,868 \end{array}$

If any of these error patterns are observed, it is essential that the skill be retaught.

Additional practice in multiplying a 1-digit number times a 2- or 3-digit number is found in chapter 13, page 281.

Page 204

OBJECTIVE

■ Complete number patterns involving an addition rule, a multiplication rule, a subtraction rule, or a division rule

BACKGROUND

It is not essential that all students complete this page. It is intended to be a fun page that students may complete when they have time. You may wish to assign this page to more capable students while you reteach skills to less capable students.

PROCEDURE

WORKTEXT® PAGE 204—For detailed teaching suggestions, see the annotated pupil's page.

Page 205

OBJECTIVE

■ Review the concepts and skills developed in chapter 9

PROCEDURE

WORKTEXT® PAGE 205—Have students complete the chapter review. Worktext® page references for the exercises in this chapter review are: exercise A, pages 186 and 187; exercise B, page 188; exercise C, pages 190, 192, 196, 197, 200, and 203; and exercise D, pages 190 and 201.

Page 206

The last page of each chapter is a check-up designed to indicate the pupils' understanding of the concepts and skills that were presented in the chapter. Have the students complete Worktext® page 206 independently.

 Division

multiplication and division facts on the chalkboard and having students supply the related multiplication and division facts.

WORKTEXT® PAGE 207—For teaching suggestions, see the annotated pupil's page.

Page 207

OBJECTIVES
- Find quotients using dot pictures
- Find quotients using repeated subtraction
- Find quotients using the number line

BACKGROUND
The purpose of this lesson is to review the meaning of division and the processes which may be used to find quotients. The divisions used will serve as a review of division facts. Division facts will be reviewed in more detail in the next lesson. These facts will then be used as students are learning to divide in the subsequent lessons of this chapter.

MATERIALS
overhead projector
50 small opaque disks

PROCEDURE
Activity 1—Put 24 disks on the overhead projector. If an overhead projector is not available, this activity can be completed by drawing dots on the chalkboard. How many sets of 6 can be formed? (4.) Write the division sentence $24 \div 6 = 4$ on the chalkboard. Discuss this as a comparative situation in which we know the total number of objects (24), the number of objects in each set (6), and want to find the number of sets (4). Remind students that 24 is called the dividend, 6 the divisor, and 4 the quotient.

Continue with divisions illustrating either the comparative or partitioning type (see the background material for Worktext® page 100).

Activity 2—Write 8×6 on the chalkboard. What is the product? (48.) What other multiplication could you write? ($6 \times 8 = 48$.) Write this. What divisions are suggested by these multiplication sentences? ($48 \div 8 = 6$ and $48 \div 6 = 8$.) Write these. Continue writing

Page 208

OBJECTIVE
- Find quotients for division facts

BACKGROUND
Some students will readily recall the division facts, while other students will have difficulty. For this latter group of students, drill and review is necessary. The review may require that they go through a relearning process beginning with the manipulation of concrete objects and progressing to pictures and then to abstract division facts. Students who cannot remember the division facts should be encouraged to use either repeated subtraction or division on the number line.

It is important for students to be able to complete division facts rapidly before they progress to more complex divisions.

MATERIALS
1 classroom set of division fact flash cards
1 student set of division fact flash cards for each pair of students

PROCEDURE
Before playing a game using the flash cards, let's review the division facts. Go through the classroom deck several times. Call on students to respond to division facts.

Divide the class into five teams and divide the classroom set of division flash cards into five equal stacks. Lay each stack with the divisions facing up. Have a student from each team look at the top card of their team's stack and go to the chalkboard and write the quotient for that division fact. After they have written the quotient, they must check their work with the answer on the back of the card. If their answer is correct, they place the card to one side and return to their seats. If their answer is incorrect, they must return to the chalkboard, erase their first written quotient, and write the correct quotient. Students take turns completing the division facts, and the first team to work through its stack of division facts wins.

Play this game several times, changing the division facts that each team must complete after each game.

If some students need additional practice on division facts, distribute student sets of division flash cards and have the students work in pairs completing division facts.

WORKTEXT® PAGE 208—For detailed teaching suggestions, see the annotated pupil's page.

Page 209

OBJECTIVE

■ Find quotients using repeated subtraction

BACKGROUND

When using repeated subtraction to find quotients, students should be encouraged to subtract larger multiples of the divisor, because this makes the division process shorter. The three examples below illustrate this.

a.
```
        6
    7 )42
       −7     1 seven
       35
       −7     1 seven
       28
       −7     1 seven
       21
       −7     1 seven
       14
       −7     1 seven
        7
       −7    +1 seven
        0     6 sevens
```

b.
```
        6
    7 )42
      −14     2 sevens
       28
      −14     2 sevens
       14
      −14    +2 sevens
        0      6 sevens
```

c.
```
        6
    7 )42
      −28     4 sevens
       14
      −14    +2 sevens
               6 sevens
```

PROCEDURE

WORKTEXT® PAGE 209—For detailed teaching suggestions, see the annotated pupil's page.

Pages 210-11

OBJECTIVE

■ Find quotients and remainders for simple divisions

BACKGROUND

In this lesson, students are taught the concept of division with remainders. Students find quotients and remainders by referring to concrete situations, by performing divisions on the number line, and by subtracting multiples of the divisor.

It is important for students to learn that the remainder is always less than the divisor. They should also be introduced to the principle that the dividend equals the quotient times the divisor plus the remainder.

MATERIALS

30 counters per student

PROCEDURE

Activity 1—Give each student 30 counters. Form a set of 27 counters. How many sets of 5 counters can you make from these 27? (5.) How many counters are left over? (2.) When we divide 27 by 5, we say that the quotient is 5 and the remainder is 2. Write the complete division on the chalkboard. Continue with examples of this type. Emphasize that the remainder must always be less than the number of objects in each of the equal subsets.

Activity 2—Draw a number line with every fifth point labeled, up to 40. Let's use the number line to find the quotients and the remainders for some divisions. Write the division 4)31 on the chalkboard. To find the quotient, where should we start? (At 31.) The hops that we take to the left should be how many spaces long? (4.) Have a student show this. After the hops take the student to 3, ask: Can (name of student) take another hop of 4 spaces to the left? (No.) How many hops of 4 spaces has (name of student) taken? (7.) How many spaces are left? (3.) The quotient for this division is 7, and the remainder is 3. Is 3 less than the divisor, 4? (Yes.)

After several of these divisions have been completed and are written on the chalkboard, have students multiply the quotient times the divisor and add the remainder to this product. In each case, point out that the result of this computation is the dividend. Emphasize that this is the method used to check division.

$$
\begin{array}{ccccc}
8 & 7 & 5 & 6 & 5 \\
3\overline{)22} & 7\overline{)60} & 8\overline{)50} & 5\overline{)33} & 9\overline{)40} \\
-24 & -49 & -40 & -30 & -45
\end{array}
$$

Have students tell if the trial quotient shown for each division is too large, correct, or too small.

2. To test the students' comprehension of the concepts of quotient and remainder, you might use exercises such as $6\overline{)\Box}^{\,5r\bigcirc}$ In this division, what is the quotient? (5.) What is the divisor? (6.) What symbol stands for the dividend? (Box.) What symbol stands for the remainder? (Circle.) What do we know about the size of the number that must be put in the circle? (It must be less than 6.) If we put 34 in the box, what number would go in the circle? (4.) If we put 3 in the circle, what number would go in the box? (33.) If we put zero in the circle, what number would go in the box? (30.) Continue with examples of this type.

Page 212

OBJECTIVE

■ Identify the correct trial quotients in simple divisions

BACKGROUND

One of the major difficulties in division is the identification of the correct trial quotient. As students are learning to find quotients, they should be taught to guess the number of times the divisor can be subtracted from the dividend. This guess may be either too small, correct, or too large. Students must be taught to recognize these three situations and to correct the situation when the trial quotient is too large or too small.

PROCEDURE

Write the division $6\overline{)47}$ on the chalkboard. Suppose that we guess that the quotient of this division is 8. What is the product of 6×8? (48.) Complete the division on the chalkboard thusly: $6\overline{)47}^{\,8}$
-48 (8×6)
Can we subtract 48 from 47? (No.) What is wrong with the guess? (It is too large.) What would be a better guess? (7.) What is 7×6? (42.) Write
$$
6\overline{)47}^{\,7}
$$
-42 (7×6) on the chalkboard. Can we subtract 42 from 47? (Yes.) What is the difference? (5.) Is 5 smaller than 6? (Yes.) What is the quotient and the remainder for this division? (The quotient is 7, the remainder is 5.) Complete the division on the chalkboard. Continue with this type of division. Make sure that some trial quotients are too small.

ADDITIONAL ACTIVITIES

1. Materials: duplicated sheets with divisions like those shown below:

Page 213

OBJECTIVES

■ Find the quotients and the remainders for simple divisions
■ Check divisions

BACKGROUND

Students should continue to find quotients on a trial and error basis. It is not unusual for students not to find the correct quotient on the first try. Emphasis should still be placed on how to determine if a trial quotient is correct.

After a division has been completed and the correct quotient and remainder have been found, the students should learn to check their work by multiplying the quotient times the divisor and adding to this product the remainder. The result of this computation should equal the dividend.

PROCEDURE

Write $7\overline{)44}$ on the chalkboard. Select the trial quotient 5 and show that this is too small. Select trial quotient 7 and show that this is too large. Then select the correct quotient, 6. Have students help with this work and tell how we know that the trial quotient is either too large or too small. Emphasize that finding the correct quotient is a trial and error procedure in which people often make mistakes. To check this division, we first multiply 7×6. What is the product of 7 × 6? (42.) To this product we add the remainder, 2. What is the sum of 42 + 2? (44.) The result of this computation is the dividend, 44, so we say we have checked the division. Continue with divisions of this type.

WORKTEXT® PAGE 213—For teaching suggestions, see the annotated pupil's page.

Page 214

OBJECTIVE

■ Find quotients when the divisors are 1-digit numbers and the dividends and the quotients are multiples of 10

BACKGROUND

Divisions in which the quotients are multiples of 10 constitute the first step in finding 2-digit quotients. In this lesson, students will be asked first to relate this type of division to multiplication and then to recognize the relationship between divisions such as $3\overline{)24}$ and $3\overline{)240}$.

As students complete divisions in which the quotients are multiples of 10, it is important that they write the quotients in the proper position. The most convenient way to do this is to write the tens' digit in the quotient over the tens' digit in the dividend and the ones' digit in the quotient over the ones' digit in the dividend.

PROCEDURE

Write 6 × 10, 6 × 20, 6 × 30, 6 × 40, 6 × 50, 6 × 60, 6 × 70, 6 × 80, and 6 × 90 on the chalkboard. Have students write the products. We are going to use these multiplications to help us find quotients. Let's find the quotient for the division $6\overline{)240}$. Which of these multiplications has a product of 240? (6 × 40.) What is the quotient for this division? (40.) Watch as I write this quotient in the division. Write 40 so that the 4 is above the 4 in the dividend and the 0 is above the 0 in the dividend. Continue with examples in which the divisor is 6 and the quotient is a multiple of 10. Leave all of these divisions on the chalkboard.

Study the examples on the chalkboard and see if you can find an easier way to find the quotients. Help students to see that they could find the quotients by dividing the divisor into the first two digits of

the dividend. Do this by showing the relationship between the divisions $6\overline{)24}$ and $6\overline{)240}$. After students have made this generalization, write $8\overline{)160}$ on the chalkboard. To find this quotient, what division should we think of? ($8\overline{)16}$.) What is the quotient for this division? (2.) What is the quotient for $8\overline{)160}$? (20.) Write the quotient for this division. Make sure that the 2 is written above the 6 in the dividend and the 0 is written above the 0 in the dividend. Continue with examples of this type.

WORKTEXT® PAGE 214—For teaching suggestions, see the annotated pupil's page.

Pages 215-16

OBJECTIVES

■ Determine if there are one or two digits in quotients

■ Complete divisions when the quotients are either a 1-digit number or a multiple of 10

BACKGROUND

One way to determine if the quotient is a 1- or 2-digit number is to use the trial quotients 1, 10, and 100. If the use of these trial quotients indicates that the quotient is larger than 1 but smaller than 10, the correct quotient is a 1-digit number. If the use of these trial quotients indicates that the quotient is larger than 10 but smaller than 100, the correct quotient is a 2-digit number.

To effectively use this lesson, students must recall the procedures for multiplying a 1-digit number times 1, times 10, and times 100; the meaning of trial quotients; and how to order numbers. Short oral reviews of these concepts are provided.

PROCEDURE

Activity 1—Write 7 × 1, 7 × 10, and 7 × 100 on the chalkboard. Have students give the products for each of these orally. What pattern do you see for these three multiplications? (The product is the 1-digit factor 7 followed by the number of zeros in the other factor.) Continue having students find products such as 9 × 1, 8 × 10, and 6 × 100.

Activity 2—I am thinking of a number. The number is larger than 1 but smaller than 10. What could the number be? (2, 3, 4, . . ., 9.) How many digits do each of these numbers have? (1.) Now I'm thinking of a number that is larger than 10 but smaller than 100. What number might this be? (11, 12,. . .,99.) How many digits do each of these numbers have? (2.) If a number is between 1 and 10, how many digits does it have? (1.) If a number is between 10 and 100, how many digits does it have? (2.) Continue asking questions about the size of numbers and the number of digits needed to write the name for these numbers.

Activity 3—Write 5$\overline{)43}$ on the chalkboard. Try the trial quotient 1 and the trial quotient 10. Is the trial quotient 1 too large or too small? (Too small.) Is the trial quotient 10 too large or too small? (Too large.) The quotient is between what two numbers? (1 and 10.) How many digits does the quotient have? (1.) Continue reviewing the idea of trial quotients using 1, 10, and 100.

WORKTEXT® PAGES 215–16—For detailed teaching suggestions, see the annotated pupil's pages.

Pages 217-19

OBJECTIVE

■ Solve divisions in which there are 2-digit quotients and no remainders

BACKGROUND

In this lesson, students are introduced to divisions in which the quotient has two digits. Since students have already learned to determine if the quotient has one or two digits, to find quotients which are multiples of ten, and to find 1-digit quotients, the skills in this lesson are a combination of previously learned skills and techniques.

The exercises on these pages are developmental. Students should not be permitted to go on to exercise C before they have learned how to complete the exercises in B. The same is true for each succeeding exercise on the pages.

PROCEDURE

WORKTEXT® PAGES 217–19—For detailed teaching suggestions, see the annotated pupil's pages.

ADDITIONAL ACTIVITIES

Materials: duplicated sheets. Students may need additional practice in finding 2-digit quotients. Here are some more divisions that the teacher might reproduce for the students.

8$\overline{)224}$ 4$\overline{)140}$ 3$\overline{)141}$ 7$\overline{)392}$ 5$\overline{)370}$ 6$\overline{)228}$
2$\overline{)58}$ 6$\overline{)252}$ 3$\overline{)285}$ 9$\overline{)162}$ 7$\overline{)266}$ 8$\overline{)328}$

Pages 220-21

OBJECTIVES

■ Solve divisions in which there are 2-digit quotients and remainders
■ Check divisions with remainders

BACKGROUND

Much of the difficulty in division is the amount of computation and reasoning that must be completed. For this reason, it is essential that students have a sufficient amount of practice in division. The exercises on these pages provide additional practice as well as introducing the idea of remainders other than zero in divisions with 2-digit quotients.

PROCEDURE

WORKTEXT® PAGES 220–21—For teaching suggestions, see the annotated pupil's pages.

ADDITIONAL ACTIVITIES

Assign students to teams of three and call each team a calculator. The functions of the three students are:
1. Keyboard and digits estimator—this pupil writes the dictated division and finds if the quotient has one or two digits.
2. Tens divider—this pupil finds the number of tens in a quotient, multiplies, and finds the remainder after dividing the tens. If the quotient has one digit, this person is idle.
3. Ones divider—this pupil finds the ones' digit, multiplies, and finds the remainder after dividing the ones. If the quotient is a multiple of 10, this person is idle.

Have one or two teams come to the chalkboard and tell each of the students their title and job in the calculator. Dictate division (some with 1-digit quotients, some with multiples of 10 as quotients, and some with 2-digit quotients). Let the students carry out their jobs to find the answers. Let students change titles and jobs for different divisions. While some teams are at the chalkboard, the remaining students should be performing the divisions on paper.

Page 222

OBJECTIVE

■ Solve verbal problems involving division

PROCEDURE

WORKTEXT® PAGE 222—For teaching suggestions, see the annotated pupil's page.

Pages 223-24

OBJECTIVE

■ Complete divisions in which the divisor is a multiple of 10 and the quotient is a 1-digit number

BACKGROUND

This lesson introduces a method for finding trial quotients when dividing by a special type of 2-digit divisor, namely, a multiple of 10. Each division in this lesson has a 1-digit quotient and a remainder of zero. Students are expected to find these quotients using a pattern. In an example like $30\overline{)180}$, students are led to see that it has the same quotient as $3\overline{)18}$. They are beginning the practice of extracting the first digit in a divisor and the first one or two digits of the dividend to find trial quotients.

PROCEDURE

WORKTEXT® PAGES 223–24—For teaching suggestions, see the annotated pupil's pages.

Page 225

OBJECTIVES

■ Solve divisions with 1-digit quotients and 1-digit divisors

■ Solve divisions with 2-digit quotients and 1-digit divisors

■ Solve divisions with 1-digit quotients and multiples of 10 as divisors

PROCEDURE

WORKTEXT® PAGE 225—For detailed teaching suggestions, see the annotated pupil's page.

If students have difficulty with any type of exercise included on this page, they should refer to pages in the chapter dealing with that type of division. For rows 1 and 2, students should refer to Worktext® pages 212 and 213. For rows 3, 4, and 5, they should refer to Worktext® pages 218–21. For row 6, they should refer to Worktext® pages 223 and 224.

Below are some of the error patterns to watch for in division.

Incorrect responses to division or multiplication facts.

$$\begin{array}{r} 6 \\ 8\overline{)56} \\ -56 \\ \hline 4 \end{array}$$

Failure to complete the division process or failure to understand that the remainder must be less than the divisor.

$$\begin{array}{r} 10 \quad 14\text{ r }8 \\ 5\overline{)78} \\ -50 \\ \hline 28 \\ -20 \\ \hline 8 \end{array}$$

Quotient written in the wrong place (tens' digit in the ones' column, etc.).

$$\begin{array}{r} 2 \\ 7\overline{)140} \\ -14 \\ \hline 0 \end{array}$$

Page 226

OBJECTIVES

■ Identify the operation needed to solve verbal problems

■ Find solutions to verbal problems mentally

PROCEDURE

I am going to say some phrases. You are to decide if you should add, subtract, multiply, or divide to find the answer. Listen carefully. Here's the first phrase: 7 increased by 8. What operation do you perform? (Addition.) What is the sum? (15.) Continue calling out phrases. Require students to calculate the answers mentally.

> WORKTEXT® PAGE 226—For teaching suggestions, see the annotated pupil's page.

Page 227

OBJECTIVES

■ Measure temperatures in degrees Fahrenheit

BACKGROUND

There are two scales commonly used for measuring temperature—Fahrenheit and Celsius. The students have already worked with temperature using the Celsius scale.

The formula which shows the relationship between temperatures expressed in degrees Celsius (C) and degrees Fahrenheit (F) is $F = (9/5 \times C) + 32$. It is important for students to have an intuitive idea of the difference between degrees Fahrenheit and degrees Celsius, but they need not know the conversion formula. For example, students should recognize that for most temperatures, the number of degrees Fahrenheit is larger than the number of degrees Celsius. They should also know the approximate meanings of temperatures.

MATERIALS

1 Fahrenheit thermometer
1 Celsius thermometer

PROCEDURE

Activity 1—Display the thermometers. These thermometers both measure temperature in degrees. The scales of the thermometers are different. One of the thermometers measures temperature in degrees Celsius. You have already learned to use this type of thermometer. The other thermometer measures temperature in degrees Fahrenheit. We read this thermometer in the same way that we read the Celsius thermometer, but the numbers that we obtain mean different things. Have students read the thermometers. Write on the chalkboard the room temperature in degrees Fahrenheit and degrees Celsius. On a warm day, the thermometers might read 86° Fahrenheit, 30° Celsius. Water boils at 212° Fahrenheit, 100° Celsius. Water freezes at 32° Fahrenheit, 0° Celsius.

Activity 2—Draw a chart on the chalkboard with spaces to record the outside temperature three times a day for a week. Place both of the thermometers outdoors. At the times designated on the chart, have students read the temperatures in degrees Celsius and degrees Fahrenheit. Record the readings on the chart. After the chart has been completed, ask: When is it usually warmer, in the middle of the day or in the morning? Which day was the warmest day? Which day was the coolest?

> WORKTEXT® PAGE 227—For teaching suggestions, see the annotated pupil's page.

Page 228

OBJECTIVE

■ Review the concepts and skills developed in chapter 10

PROCEDURE

> WORKTEXT® PAGE 228—Have students complete the chapter review. Worktext® page references for the exercises in this chapter review are: exercise A, pages 207 and 208; exercise B, page 212; exercise C, pages 215 and 216; exercise D, pages 211, 217, 218, 219, 220, 221, and 225; and exercise E, pages 213, 216, 219, 221, and 225.

Page 229

The last page of each chapter is a check-up designed to indicate the pupils' understanding of the concepts and skills that were presented in the chapter. Have the students complete Worktext® page 229 independently.

Geometry and Measurement

Page 230

OBJECTIVES
- Identify pictures of planes
- Identify pictures of plane figures

BACKGROUND

The objects in our world are three-dimensional shapes. In geometry, not all geometric shapes have three dimensions. The geometric figures presented in chapter 6 were one-dimensional or two-dimensional. Some one-dimensional shapes are lines, rays, and line segments. Two-dimensional shapes include figures such as angles, triangles, circular regions, and parallelograms.

In this lesson, students will learn that a plane is represented by any flat surface. Geometric figures that can be drawn on a plane, such as a line, an angle, a circle, or a square region, are called plane figures. Geometric figures such as a box or a ball are not plane figures, because all of their points do not lie in the same plane.

MATERIALS
poster board
ruler
felt-tip marker
small three-dimensional objects

PROCEDURE

We have studied about geometric sets of points called lines, triangles, and circles. Another geometric set of points is a plane. Write *plane* on the chalkboard. Flat surfaces such as the top of a table or the surface of the chalkboard make us think of planes. What other objects in the room make us think of planes? (The floor, the walls, the ceiling, desk tops.) Explain that these are only parts of planes because the flat surface extends on beyond the edges of the table top or the edges of the chalkboard, just as a line extends beyond the mark that we draw to represent it.

Hold up a piece of poster board. Does this piece of poster board make you think of a plane? (Yes.) Have a student use the ruler and the felt-tip marker to draw a line on the poster board. Make sure that the student draws a straight mark and puts arrows on the ends to show that the line goes on indefinitely in both directions. Are all of the points of this line in the plane? (Yes.) Have another student draw a picture of a triangular region. Are all of the points of the triangular region in the plane? (Yes.) Continue having students draw pictures of plane figures on the poster board. In each case, ask if all of the points of the picture are in the plane. All of the geometric figures that you have drawn are plane figures, because all of their points are in the plane. Title the poster board *plane figures* for display later.

Turn the poster board over and lay a small box on it. Are all of the points of the box in the plane? (No.) Do this with other three-dimensional objects. These objects are not plane figures, because all of their points do not lie in the plane.

WORKTEXT® PAGE 230—For teaching suggestions, see the annotated pupil's page.

Page 231

OBJECTIVE
- Identify space figures

BACKGROUND

Figures which do not have all of their points in a plane are called space figures. Some physical objects which represent space figures are a ball, a box, an ice cream cone, and a tin can.

MATERIALS
poster board
small three-dimensional objects

PROCEDURE

Show the poster board with pictures of plane figures on it. Ask students to identify each of the plane figures. In the last lesson, we saw that there were some geometric figures which were not plane figures.

Hold up a box or a ball for them to see. These objects make us think of space figures. Hold up an object such as a ball, cone, or tin can. Does this make you think of a plane figure or a space figure? (A space figure.) Glue or tape several of these objects on a piece of poster board and label this piece of poster board *space figures*.

WORKTEXT® PAGE 231—For detailed teaching suggestions, see the annotated pupil's page.

ADDITIONAL ACTIVITIES

Divide the class into two teams. Have one team identify an object in the room and state its name for the other team. The other team must determine if this object represents a plane figure or a space figure. Interchange the roles of the teams.

Pages 232-33

OBJECTIVES

■ Identify objects which represent rectangular boxes or cubes
■ Identify the parts of a rectangular box
■ Draw pictures of boxes or cubes

MATERIALS

models of boxes and cubes
construction paper

PROCEDURE

Show a model of a rectangular box. Is this a plane figure or a space figure? (A space figure.) We call the sides of a space figure its *faces*. Write *faces* on the chalkboard. Point to the faces of the rectangular box. What shape is each face of this box? (A rectangular region.) If students say a rectangle, remind them that the face contains the points inside the rectangle also. How many faces does this rectangular box have? (6.) Write *a rectangular box is made up of 6 rectangular regions as faces*. Describe the edges and vertices of a rectangular box in the same way.

Describe a cube as a special type of rectangular box in which all of the faces are square regions. Give students an opportunity to examine a model of a rectangular box and a cube individually.

WORKTEXT® PAGES 232–33—For teaching suggestions, see the annotated pupil's pages.

Page 234

OBJECTIVE

■ Identify space figures as cylinders, cones, or spheres

BACKGROUND

Three additional space figures that students should know by name are cylinders, cones, and spheres. There are a wide variety of objects in the physical world which can serve as models for these space figures. For example, tin cans are excellent models of cylinders, some paper drinking cups are models of cones, and balls are models of spheres.

MATERIALS

models of cylinders, cones, and spheres

PROCEDURE

Show models of cylinders, cones, and spheres to the class. Identify each object, give its mathematical name, and write the name on the chalkboard. Give students the opportunity to identify the objects by their mathematical names. Discuss the distinguishing attributes of each figure. For example, a cylinder has two flat parts which are circular regions, a cone has one flat circular region and slopes up to a point, and a sphere has no flat surfaces.

Have students identify objects that serve as models of cylinders, cones, or spheres. Have them name the object and tell what it represents.

WORKTEXT® PAGE 234—For teaching suggestions, see the annotated pupil's page.

Page 235

OBJECTIVES

■ Distinguish between space figures and solid regions

■ Compare solid regions visually to determine which is larger

BACKGROUND

Rectangular boxes, cubes, cylinders, spheres, and cones are boundaries of solid regions. A solid region is a space figure together with its inside.

Measurement of solid regions follows the same basic steps used to measure line segments or areas. As applied to solid regions, the steps are: (1) visual comparison; (2) a physical comparison (filling one space figure with a substance and pouring this into the other space figure); (3) finding the number of nonstandard cubic units contained in the region; (4) using standard cubic units to find volume; and (5) using formulas to find volume. The first four of these steps are considered in Level 4 of *Succeeding in Mathematics*.

MATERIALS

space figures that can be filled with sand or water
sand or water

PROCEDURE

Activity 1—Show a model of a cone. Is this a space figure or a plane figure? (A space figure.) What is its name? (A cone.) Is it empty or full? (Empty.) Watch as I fill it with sand. The sand fills the inside of the cone. We say that the cone, along with the inside of the cone, is a solid region. The cone is called the boundary of the solid region.

Activity 2—Hold up two space figures of obviously different sizes. Fill them with sand. Which space figure holds the most sand? Which solid region is larger? If students cannot tell which is larger by looking, pour the sand out of one container and transfer the sand from the second container into the first container.

WORKTEXT® PAGE 235—For teaching suggestions, see the annotated pupil's page.

Pages 236-37

OBJECTIVE

■ Find the volume of a solid region by counting the number of cubes needed to build or fill it.

BACKGROUND

To measure solid regions, select a unit solid region such as one bounded by a cube. The number of units contained in the solid region is called its volume. Volume is a measure of the space occupied by or contained in a solid region.

MATERIALS

several small boxes
15 cubes (counting blocks) per pupil

PROCEDURE

Activity 1—Show one of the small boxes. Is this the boundary of a solid region, or is it a solid region? (The boundary.) Why? (Because it is empty.) How many blocks do you think we would need to fill this box? Let students guess. Then fill the box with blocks. Does the box filled with blocks represent a solid region? (Yes.) Why? (Because it is full.) We say that it takes (number of blocks) blocks to fill the box. Continue this process with the other small boxes. The number of blocks needed to fill a box is called its volume. Have students give the volume for each of the boxes in terms of blocks. Using these volumes, order the boxes by size.

Activity 2—Give each student 15 blocks. On the chalkboard, draw stacks of blocks like those shown below.

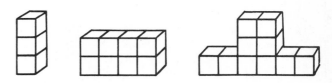

Have students use the blocks to make stacks like those shown in the drawings. Then have them identify the number of blocks needed to make each stack of blocks.

WORKTEXT® PAGES 236–37—For teaching suggestions, see the annotated pupil's pages.

ADDITIONAL ACTIVITIES

Materials: boxes and counting blocks. Have students find the volume of each box by filling it with blocks. As a discovery exercise, you might have several boxes which will hold more blocks than are available. Students should be able to find the volume of these boxes by putting in one layer of blocks at the bottom of the box and then finding how many layers of blocks would be needed to fill the box.

Page 238

OBJECTIVES

- Review addition facts and skills
- Review subtraction facts and skills
- Solve verbal problems involving addition or subtraction

PROCEDURE

WORKTEXT® PAGE 238—For teaching suggestions, see the annotated pupil's page.

Pages 239-40

OBJECTIVES

- Recognize that liter and milliliter are standard units of liquid capacity
- Identify the approximate capacity of familiar objects

BACKGROUND

Measuring liquid capacity is developed in a pattern similar to that used for developing the measurement of other types of quantities. The first step is to compare two containers visually to determine which will hold the most. Next, a physical comparison is developed, such as filling one container with liquid and pouring it into the other. To find a number which tells the measure of a liquid quantity, we need to choose a container as a unit of measure. The number of units in the amount of liquid is its measure. For communication purposes, we need to choose standard units of measure, and those developed in this lesson are the liter and the milliliter.

MATERIALS

watertight containers of various sizes
coffee cup
poster board
meter sticks
1 cubic centimeter block

PROCEDURE

Activity 1—Show two containers. Which of these will hold the most water? In the beginning, make sure that the comparisons can be made visually. Then show two containers which have approximately the same capacity. Which will hold the most liquid? Sometimes it is difficult to tell which container will hold the most liquid. We can find out which one holds the most liquid by filling one with water and then pouring this water into the second container. Do this. Which of the two containers is larger? Continue comparing the liquid capacity of various containers using water.

Place a variety of containers filled with water on a table and ask students to arrange them in order from the one containing the least water to the one containing the most. If students disagree about the ordering, have them use an additional clear container. Suggest that they pour the water from one container into this and mark the height with a piece of tape. They should do this for each of the amounts of liquid. The comparisons can then be made by comparing the heights of liquid in the glass reference container.

Activity 2—Show the class a fairly large container partially filled with water. How can we tell someone how much water we have in this container? Help students to see that they need some unit container to measure the amount of liquid. Can we use this coffee cup to measure the amount of liquid in the container? (Yes.) How can we do that? (See how many times the coffee cup can be filled with the water in the container.) Continue measuring amounts of liquid using nonstandard units of measure.

Have students use a nonstandard unit of measure to find the liquid capacity of several larger containers. Have them compare the amounts of liquid in these containers.

Activity 3—Divide the class into groups. One standard unit of liquid capacity is the liter. A liter is defined as the capacity of a cube that is 1 decimeter on each side. We are going to make such a cube from poster board. Find page 233 in your Worktext®. On that page is a pattern for making a cube. We will use this pattern but enlarge it to make a cube that is 1 decimeter on each side. Have students enlarge this pattern. Give help as needed. Make sure that each group has their pattern checked before they cut it out. After students have constructed their cubes, reemphasize that the capacity of this cube is 1 liter. Write the word *liter* on the chalkboard and have students copy this on their container as a label.

To measure smaller amounts of liquid, we use a standard unit of measure called a milliliter. A milliliter is the capacity of a cube that is 1 centimeter on each side. Hold up the 1 cubic centimeter block. The capacity of the inside of this cube is 1 milliliter. Write the word *milliliter* on the chalkboard. Then write 1,000 milliliters = 1 liter.

Page 241

OBJECTIVES

- Identify the relationships between the gallon, the quart, the pint, and the cup
- Identify the approximate capacity of common containers

BACKGROUND

Some common standard units of liquid capacity in the English system are the gallon, the quart, the pint, and the cup. Students should know and be able to interpret the relationships between these units of measure. They should also be able to estimate the capacity of familiar containers using these units of measure.

MATERIALS

watertight containers of various sizes
several containers of gallon, quart, pint, and cup capacity

PROCEDURE

Activity 1—Use the standard unit containers to measure amounts of liquid in the other containers. Have students compare the amounts of liquid in these other containers by pouring their contents into the standard unit containers. Have them state the measure of the liquid in each container.

Activity 2—Have groups of students experiment with the capacity of standard unit containers. The results of these experiments should be used to develop the following relationships: 1 gallon = 4 quarts, 1 quart = 2 pints, 1 pint = 2 cups, 1 gallon = 8 pints, 1 gallon = 16 cups, 1 quart = 4 cups. As the students discover these relationships by measuring, write them on the chalkboard. How many cups are in 2 pints? (4.) How many gallons are in 8 quarts? (2.) Continue asking questions of this type.

WORKTEXT® PAGE 241—For teaching suggestions, see the annotated pupil's page.

ADDITIONAL ACTIVITIES

Materials: containers with capacity marked in gallons, quarts, pints, or cups. Have students find these containers at home to bring to school. Display the containers around the room and have students use water or sand to compare the capacity of various containers.

Page 242

OBJECTIVE

- Find the product of three 1-digit factors

BACKGROUND

Finding the product of three 1-digit factors provides excellent review of multiplication facts and skills. Students must learn to first multiply any pair of the 1-digit factors. This requires that they can recall and use the multiplication facts. This product must then be multiplied times the third factor. This requires that students know how to multiply a 1-digit number times a 2-digit number.

In each of the exercises on this page, parentheses are used. Students should learn to multiply the two factors inside the parentheses first, and then to multiply this product times the factor outside the parentheses. There are also exercises which illustrate the associative property for multiplication, that is, $a \times (b \times c) = (a \times b) \times c$. Students should recognize this property from the examples provided on this page but need not know the name of the property.

PROCEDURE

WORKTEXT® PAGE 242—For teaching suggestions, see the annotated pupil's page.

Page 243

OBJECTIVES

- Compare the weights of two objects using a balance
- Find the weights of objects using a balance and nonstandard units of measure

BACKGROUND

One method for comparing weights is to lift each of the objects and judge which is heavier. This is an efficient way to compare weights that are quite different. When the weights are nearly the same, it may be impossible to determine which is heavier by lifting. Under these circumstances, it may be necessary to compare the weights of the two objects using a pan balance.

Students will also learn to find the weights of objects using nonstandard units. This can be done by placing the object to be weighed in one pan of the balance and one or more of the units of measure in the other pan of the balance. The number of units of measure necessary to balance the object to be weighed is its weight.

Comparing weights and finding the weight using nonstandard units are the first steps in developing the concept of weight. In the next lesson, standard units of weight will be developed.

MATERIALS

variety of objects to be weighed
20 paper clips of the same size
20 small blocks of the same size
1 pan balance

PROCEDURE

Activity 1—Show two objects. Have students guess which is heavier. Have a student lift the objects and predict which is heavier. Initially, make sure that the objects have markedly different weights. In later examples, encourage some conflict by having the objects similar in weight.

What is another way to tell which object is heavier? (By weighing them or by comparing them on a balance.) Look at this balance. We can put one object on one side of the balance and the other object on the other side. The side of the balance that goes down indicates the object that is heavier. Have students use the balance to determine which of two objects is heavier.

Activity 2—We can also use the balance to measure the weights of objects. To do this we need a unit of measure. Any weight can serve as a unit of measure. Let's use paper clips to find the weight of a pencil. Put the pencil in one pan of the balance and start placing paper clips in the other pan. When the two pans balance, have a student count the number of paper clips in the one pan. The unit of measure is paper clips and the weight of the pencil in paper clips is (number of paper clips). Continue weighing other objects using paper clips and blocks. In each case, emphasize the unit of measure and the weight.

WORKTEXT® PAGE 243—For detailed teaching suggestions, see the annotated pupil's page.

Pages 244-45

OBJECTIVES

- Recognize that the gram and the kilogram are standard units of weight
- Identify the approximate weight of common objects

BACKGROUND

In this lesson, students should recognize that a standard unit of weight agreed upon and used by everyone is necessary. In the metric system, two standard units of weight are the gram and the kilogram. Grams are used to measure light objects, and kilograms are used to measure heavier objects. Students should be encouraged to think of the gram as about the weight of a paper clip and the kilogram as about the weight of a liter of water. This will give them concrete referents for these abstract units of weight.

MATERIALS

50 paper clips
4 liter containers filled with water
1 balance
1 bath scale marked in kilograms
variety of objects to be weighed

PROCEDURE

Activity 1—To tell other people the weight of objects, we need a standard unit of weight which is understood by everyone. Two such standard units are the gram and the kilogram. A gram weighs about the same as one paper clip. Is a gram a heavy or a light weight? (Light.) To find the weight of an object such as a nickel, put the nickel in one pan of the balance and see how many paper clips are needed to balance it. Demonstrate this. The number of paper clips is approximately the weight of the nickel in grams. What is the approximate weight of the nickel in grams? (5.) Continue illustrating the weights of objects by using paper clips to balance them.

To weigh heavier objects, we use a standard unit of weight called a kilogram. A kilogram is 1,000 grams. Write 1 kilogram = 1,000 grams on the chalkboard. A liter of water weighs about 1 kilogram. Show the class a liter container filled with water. The water in this weighs about 1 kilogram. If an object is balanced by two kilogram weights, what is the weight of this object in kilograms? (2.) What is the weight of the object in grams? (2,000.) Continue with this activity. Make sure that all students have a chance to participate in balancing objects using kilogram weights and gram weights.

Activity 2—Have available the bath scale marked in kilograms. This scale is marked in kilograms. When we place an object on it, it measures the weight in kilograms. Use the scale to weigh objects in the room. Have students guess the approximate weight of each object before they put it on the scale. Then have them check their guess by weighing the object. Have students guess the approximate weight of each object before they put it on the scale. Then have them check their guess by weighing the object. Have students weigh themselves.

WORKTEXT® PAGES 244–45—For detailed teaching suggestions, see the annotated pupil's pages.

ADDITIONAL ACTIVITIES

Have students collect containers which have the weight marked in grams. Have them bring these containers to class. Make a chart that shows the name of the object and the weight of the object in grams or kilograms.

Page 246

OBJECTIVES

- Recognize pounds and ounces as standard units of weight
- Identify the approximate weights of familiar objects
- Recognize the relationship between pounds and ounces

MATERIALS

scale marked in pounds and ounces
objects to be weighed

PROCEDURE

Activity 1—Ounces and pounds are also standard units used to measure weights. Have available an object which weighs approximately 1 ounce. (A silver dollar is ideal for this purpose.) The weight of this object is about 1 ounce. Pass the object around the room for the children to lift so that they get an approximate idea of the weight. Hold up an object which weighs approximately 1 pound. This object weighs about 1 pound. Pass this around the room for the students to lift. Is a pound heavier than an ounce? (Yes.) If we wanted to weigh something that was light, would we use ounces or pounds? (Ounces.) If we wanted to weigh something that was heavy, would we use ounces or pounds? (Pounds.) Show the class several other objects and ask if they should use ounces or pounds to weigh them.

Activity 2—Show the scale marked in pounds and ounces. Illustrate how they should use and read this scale. Have members of the class weigh objects which may be found in the classroom.

One pound is the same weight as 16 ounces. Write 1 pound = 16 ounces on the chalkboard. Have students weigh objects in pounds. For objects that weigh less than 10 pounds, have them find the weight of each object in ounces by multiplying 16 times the weight in pounds.

WORKTEXT® PAGE 246—For detailed teaching suggestions, see the annotated pupil's page.

Page 247

OBJECTIVE

- Review division facts and skills

MATERIALS

division fact flash cards

PROCEDURE

Activity 1—Use the division fact flash cards to review division facts. Go through the deck several times and make sure that each student has a chance to respond to several division facts. As you are doing this, identify the numbers which are called the divisor, the dividend, and the quotient.

Activity 2—Review the procedure for determining

if a quotient has one or two digits. Then review several divisions in which you must first determine the number of digits in the quotient and then find the quotient and remainder. As you are doing this, ask students questions and have them do more and more of the work.

WORKTEXT® PAGE 247—For detailed teaching suggestions, see the annotated pupil's page.

Page 248

OBJECTIVES

- Identify the unit of measure that should be used to measure length, weight, liquid capacity, or temperature
- Solve problems involving addition, subtraction, multiplication, or division

WORKTEXT® PAGE 248—For teaching suggestions, see the annotated pupil's page.

Page 249

OBJECTIVE

- Review the concepts and skills developed in chapter 11

PROCEDURE

WORKTEXT® PAGE 249—Have students complete the chapter review. Worktext® page references for the exercises in this chapter review are: exercise A, pages 230–36; exercise B, page 237; exercise C, pages 239–41; and exercise D, pages 243–46.

Page 250

The last page of each chapter is a check-up designed to indicate the pupils' understanding of the concepts and skills presented in the chapter. Have the students complete Worktext® page 250.

Fractions

Pages 251-52

OBJECTIVES

- Identify fractions from pictures of parts of a whole or parts of a set
- Identify the numerator and denominator of a fraction
- Write the names for fractions

BACKGROUND

The concepts and skills already developed pertaining to fractions will be extended in this chapter. In order to do this successfully, students must readily recall the meaning of fractions, the ways fractions are written, and the interpretation of fractions. The first lesson in this chapter provides a review of fractions. Subsequent lessons develop the concepts of equivalent fractions, comparing the size of fractions, improper fractions, mixed numerals, fractions on the number line, adding fractions with like denominators, and subtracting fractions with like denominators.

Students who need a more extensive review of fractions may be referred to chapter 7.

MATERIALS

fraction flash cards (see material for chapter 7)

PROCEDURE

Shuffle the decks of fraction flash cards. Show the cards one at a time. Have students tell the fraction that names the part of the whole or the part of the set that is shown. After a student has responded correctly to a given flash card, ask what the fraction means. For example, the flash card $\frac{3}{4}$ *of a whole* means three of the four equal parts. The flash card $\frac{3}{4}$ *of a set* means three of the four members in the set. Remind students that when a fraction describes a part of a set, the objects in the set may have different sizes. When the fraction names a part of a whole, the pieces must be equal in size.

Write $\frac{5}{8}$ on the chalkboard. This fraction is composed of three parts. The 5 is called the numerator; the 8 is called the denominator; and the bar divides the numerator from the denominator. The fraction itself tells us about a part of a whole or a part of a set. Write several fractions on the chalkboard and have students identify the numerator and the denominator. Then state word names for fractions and have students write the fractions on the chalkboard.

> WORKTEXT® PAGES 251–52—For detailed teaching suggestions, see the annotated pupil's pages.

Page 253

OBJECTIVE

■ Identify fractions which show equal parts of a whole

BACKGROUND

Equivalent fractions can be shown using parts of a whole. Exercise A on Worktext® page 253 shows $\frac{1}{2}$, $\frac{2}{4}$, $\frac{3}{6}$, and $\frac{4}{8}$, which all name the same amount of the circular region. When two fractions such as $\frac{1}{2}$ and $\frac{4}{8}$ show the same amount of a region, we say that these fractions are equivalent and write $\frac{1}{2} = \frac{4}{8}$.

MATERIALS

several pieces of rectangular white paper
felt-tip marker

PROCEDURE

I am going to fold a piece of paper into halves. Do this. Open it and use the marker to trace the fold. Look at the piece of paper. The fold that I have colored separates the paper into how many parts? (2.) What fraction names each part? ($\frac{1}{2}$.) Watch as I shade $\frac{1}{2}$. Now I am going to fold the paper in half as I did before and fold this in half again. Do this. Open the paper and trace the second fold with the marker. The folds divide the paper into how many parts? (4.) Is each of these four parts the same size? (Yes.) How many fourths are shaded? (2.) Remember that we shaded $\frac{1}{2}$ of the paper. Now we see that we have also shaded $\frac{2}{4}$ of the paper. Are these two regions the same? (Yes.) What can we say about $\frac{1}{2}$ and $\frac{2}{4}$? (They are equal.) Write the sentence $\frac{1}{2} = \frac{2}{4}$ on the chalkboard. Refold the paper and fold it in half one more time to show $\frac{4}{8} = \frac{2}{4}$ or $\frac{4}{8} = \frac{1}{2}$. Continue with a second sheet of paper, first folding it in thirds and then folding it in sixths. Use this to show that $\frac{2}{3}$ of the paper is the same amount as $\frac{4}{6}$ of the paper. Continue using different sheets of paper to show different pairs of equal fractions.

> WORKTEXT® PAGE 253—For teaching suggestions, see the annotated pupil's page.

Page 254

OBJECTIVE

■ Identify fractions which show the same part of a set

MATERIALS

15 lima beans per student

PROCEDURE

Give each student 15 lima beans. Put 8 beans on your desk. How many beans are in $\frac{3}{8}$ of the set? (3.) How many beans are in $\frac{2}{8}$ of the set? (2.) Now separate the 8 beans into 4 sets, each containing the same number of beans. How many beans are in each set? (2.) We have already said that $\frac{2}{8}$ of the 8 beans is 2. How many beans are in $\frac{1}{4}$ of the original set? (2.) Since there are the same number of beans in $\frac{1}{4}$ of the set and in $\frac{2}{8}$ of the set, we write $\frac{1}{4} = \frac{2}{8}$. Write this on the chalkboard. Continue with examples of this type. In each case, identify the number of beans in the fractional part of the set. When two fractions denote the same number from a specified set, we can write a sentence stating that these two fractions name the same number.

WORKTEXT® PAGE 254—For teaching suggestions, see the annotated pupil's page.

ADDITIONAL ACTIVITIES

Materials: flannel board and 12 white flannel dots. Let students form arrangements of several rows of several dots each. Using these arrangements, identify fractions which show the same number of dots. For example, if an arrangement of 3 rows of 4 dots each are shown on the flannel board, ask: How many dots are in $\frac{1}{3}$ of the set? (4.) How many dots are in $\frac{4}{12}$ of the set? (4.) What two fractions can we write in a sentence? ($\frac{1}{3} = \frac{4}{12}$.) Have a student write this sentence on the chalkboard. Continue with examples of this type.

Pages 255-56

OBJECTIVES

■ Compare the size of numbers named by fractions with common denominators

■ Compare the size of numbers named by fractions which do not have common denominators

MATERIALS

fraction flash cards showing wholes divided into eighths

6 sheets of construction paper of the same size but different colors

PROCEDURE

Activity 1—Show students the flash cards on which $\frac{1}{8}$ and $\frac{3}{8}$ of a whole have been shaded. Ask them to identify the fractions which name the shaded parts. Then place one of these flash cards underneath the other so that students can compare the shaded regions. Which of the two shaded regions is larger? (The one named by $\frac{3}{8}$.) Which of the shaded regions is smaller? (The one named by $\frac{1}{8}$.) Since the region named by $\frac{1}{8}$ is smaller than the region named by $\frac{3}{8}$, we say that $\frac{1}{8}$ is less than $\frac{3}{8}$. Write $\frac{1}{8}$ is less than $\frac{3}{8}$ on the chalkboard and underneath it write

$\frac{1}{8} < \frac{3}{8}$. Emphasize that these sentences are read the same way. After several examples like this have been considered, write $\frac{7}{8}$ and $\frac{6}{8}$ on the chalkboard. Which of these two fractions names the larger number? ($\frac{7}{8}$.) Help students to arrive at the generalization that the fractions have like denominators and 7 is larger than 6. Continue with examples and help students to learn that when both denominators are the same, the larger fraction can be identified by finding the larger numerator.

Activity 2—Draw a number line on the chalkboard and divide the segment between 0 and 1 into five equal pieces. Have students help to name the points on this number line. Remind students that larger numbers are named to the right of smaller numbers on the number line. Have students complete sentences such as $\frac{1}{5} \bigcirc \frac{4}{5}$.

When two fractions have like denominators, we can determine the fraction which names the larger number by looking at the numerators. The one with the larger numerator names the larger number.

Activity 3—Take a sheet of construction paper and cut it into halves. Hold up one of the pieces. What part of the paper is this? ($\frac{1}{2}$.) Write the fraction $\frac{1}{2}$ on one of the pieces of paper. Hold up the other part. What part of the piece of paper is left? ($\frac{1}{2}$.) Continue cutting paper showing thirds, fourths, fifths, sixths, and eighths, using a different color for each. Suppose we were to compare the piece of paper named $\frac{1}{2}$ with the piece of paper named $\frac{1}{4}$. Have students compare these regions by placing one on top of the other. Which region is larger? (The one with $\frac{1}{2}$ on it.) Which region is smaller? (The one with $\frac{1}{4}$ on it.) We say that $\frac{1}{2}$ is greater than $\frac{1}{4}$. Write the sentence $\frac{1}{2} > \frac{1}{4}$ on the chalkboard and read it for the class. Continue comparing the size of fractions by comparing the regions which represent them.

WORKTEXT® PAGES 255–56—For teaching suggestions, see the annotated pupil's pages.

Page 257

OBJECTIVES

■ Write standard names and expanded names given word names

■ Complete number patterns

BACKGROUND

The purpose of this lesson is to review number

and numeration skills. You may wish to use this page without any prior activities as a review sheet for students to complete. If you feel the need for initial teaching activities, follow those given below. In any case, students should be able to complete these exercises without using manipulatives or pictures.

PROCEDURE

Activity 1—I am going to give you some word names for numbers. I will call on one person to write the standard name on the chalkboard while the rest of you write the standard name for this number on your paper. You can then check your work with the work on the chalkboard. Give numbers such as 279, 5,065, and 402. After students have demonstrated the capability for writing standard names, have them write the expanded name for each of the numbers that you give orally.

Activity 2—Draw a number line on the chalkboard and mark 7 points. Have students complete number patterns on the number line. Begin with ones' patterns using 3- and 4-digit numbers. After students have demonstrated the capability of completing ones' patterns, have them complete twos' patterns, fives' patterns, tens' patterns, and hundreds' patterns.

WORKTEXT® PAGE 257—For teaching suggestions, see the annotated pupil's page.

Pages 258-59

OBJECTIVES

■ Identify mixed numerals and their parts
■ Name numbers larger than 1 using mixed numerals

BACKGROUND

Students have considered mixed numerals intuitively when measuring objects. In this lesson, students will learn to name numbers greater than 1 with mixed numerals. When students are asked to identify and write a mixed numeral in this lesson, they will always have a pictorial representation available.

MATERIALS

construction paper

PROCEDURE

Use whole and fractional part pieces of construction paper to illustrate mixed numerals. After students can identify a mixed numeral when given the pieces of construction paper, have individual students select the correct pieces of construction paper to show a given mixed numeral. Each student should have an opportunity to participate in these activities.

WORKTEXT® PAGES 258–59—For teaching suggestions, see the annotated pupil's pages.

ADDITIONAL ACTIVITIES

Materials: ruler divided into quarter inches. Have pupils find the lengths of a variety of objects and state the measures using mixed numerals.

Pages 260-61

OBJECTIVES

■ Name numbers larger than 1 with mixed numerals and fractions
■ Where appropriate, change a fraction to a mixed numeral by shading pictures

BACKGROUND

Students have previously learned that one whole can be named by a fraction. *One* has been the largest number named by a fraction. Numbers greater than one have been named with standard names or with mixed numerals. This lesson develops the concept that numbers greater than one can be named with fractions.

Fractions that name numbers greater than one are easy to recognize. The numerator names a larger number than the denominator. The interpretation of these symbols may be more difficult than the interpretation of mixed numerals. Sometimes students do not have an intuitive feeling for the meaning of a fraction such as $\frac{9}{5}$, whereas they do have an intuitive feeling for the meaning of the equivalent mixed numeral $1\frac{4}{5}$. For this reason, it is essential that students have a rich experience with pictures that can be used to interpret fractions in which the numerator is larger than the denominator. These pictures will be similar to those used to teach mixed numerals, but each whole will be divided into the number of pieces specified by the denominator. In this way, students can write the fraction by writing the number of pieces shaded over the number of pieces in one whole.

MATERIALS

construction paper

PROCEDURE

Suppose that I wished to give each of you $\frac{1}{8}$ of a piece of construction paper. How many eighths are there in one whole? ($\frac{8}{8}$.) Write this fraction on the chalkboard. Are $\frac{8}{8}$ enough to give each member of the class $\frac{1}{8}$ of a piece of construction paper? (No.) How many eighths would I need? (The number of students in the class.) Cut pieces of construction paper into eighths until you have enough pieces to give each student $\frac{1}{8}$ of a sheet of construction paper. What fraction could I write to name this amount? (Answer depends on number of students in the class.) What mixed numeral could I write to show this number? (Answer depends on number of students in the class.) Write on the chalkboard the number sentence that shows these two numbers are equal.

Continue working with construction paper, illustrating mixed numerals and fractions in which the numerator is greater than the denominator. In each case, write the number sentence that is illustrated.

WORKTEXT® PAGES 260–61—For teaching suggestions, see the annotated pupil's pages.

ADDITIONAL ACTIVITIES

Materials: rulers divided into quarter inches. Have pupils measure objects in the room and give the measure as a mixed number or as a fraction in which the numerator is larger than the denominator.

Page 262

OBJECTIVE

■ Name points on a number line with fractions

BACKGROUND

Each time that we use a ruler, we are using a number line on which fractions are implied but not written. Whenever we measure we choose some unit and denote it as a whole. Each of these units is subdivided into smaller parts which are fractional parts of the unit. On a ruler, the marks between the whole numbers represent these fractional parts.

In a previous chapter, students wrote fractions between 0 and 1 on the number line. In this lesson, students will learn to write fractions that name numbers greater than 1 on the number line.

PROCEDURE

Activity 1—Draw the picture shown below on the chalkboard.

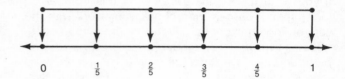

The bar has been divided into how many equal parts? (5.) How much of the bar is to the left of the first arrow? (0 or none.) Note that the left end of the bar is directly above the point labeled 0 on the number line. We also name this point $\frac{0}{5}$. How much of the bar is to the left of the second arrow? ($\frac{1}{5}$.) We name the point on the number line under this arrow $\frac{1}{5}$. Continue naming the points on the number line. Emphasize that 0 and $\frac{0}{5}$ are two names for the same point and that 1 and $\frac{5}{5}$ are two names for the same point.

Repeat this activity for a bar divided into 8 equal pieces and have students name the points on the number line with fractions having the denominator 8.

Activity 2—Draw the picture shown below on the chalkboard.

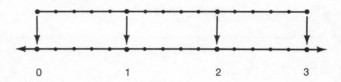

Name points on the number line between 0 and 1 with the fractions $\frac{1}{5}$, $\frac{2}{5}$, $\frac{3}{5}$, and $\frac{4}{5}$. What fraction could we use to name the point labeled 1? ($\frac{5}{5}$.) Label the points on the number line between 1 and 2. How many fifths are to the left of the first arrow to the right of 1? (6.) We can name this point $\frac{6}{5}$. Continue naming the rest of the points on the number line. After you have named the points on the number line with fractions, go back and name selected points using mixed numerals.

WORKTEXT® PAGE 262—For teaching suggestions, see the annotated pupil's page.

Page 263

OBJECTIVE
- Measure line segments to the nearest eighth inch

MATERIALS
rulers marked in eighths of an inch

PROCEDURE
Give a ruler to each student. Ask students to find the longest mark between the left edge of the ruler and the mark labeled 1. Into how many parts does this mark divide the inch? (2.) Each of the two parts is called a half inch. Draw line segments on the chalkboard that are $3\frac{1}{2}$ inches long, $5\frac{1}{2}$ inches long, etc. Have students find the measure of these. Have students state the lengths as mixed numerals.

Follow the same procedure to develop the idea of fourth inches and eighth inches.

WORKTEXT® PAGE 263—For teaching suggestions, see the annotated pupil's page.

Page 264

OBJECTIVES
- Complete addition facts on the number line
- Complete subtraction facts on the number line
- Find sums or differences
- Find the sums or differences for verbal problems involving addition and subtraction

BACKGROUND
The purpose of this lesson is to review the procedure for adding and subtracting on the number line. This procedure will be used in subsequent lessons in this chapter when students learn to add and subtract on the number line with fractions having like denominators.

PROCEDURE
Activity 1—Draw a number line on the chalkboard and review the procedure for adding and subtracting on the number line.

Activity 2—Review the procedure for adding and subtracting 2-, 3-, and 4-digit numbers. Write exercises on the chalkboard and have students complete parts of each of the exercises. Emphasize the renaming process. Make sure that some of the subtractions require the students to rename 100 as 10 tens and rename one of these tens as 10 ones.

WORKTEXT® PAGE 264—For teaching suggestions, see the annotated pupil's page.

Page 265

OBJECTIVE
- Add fractions with common denominators using pictures

BACKGROUND
In this lesson, pictures are used to teach students to add fractions with common denominators. For example, to add $\frac{1}{5} + \frac{3}{5}$, a whole object is divided into five equal pieces. One of these equal pieces is shaded to show $\frac{1}{5}$, and 3 different pieces are shaded to show $\frac{3}{5}$. Altogether the student has shaded four of the five equal pieces, so the sum is $\frac{4}{5}$. Using pictures, students are expected to add fractions with common denominators and sums less than or equal to 1. With sufficient experience, students may recognize the rule that to add fractions with a common denominator, add the numerators and place this sum over the common denominator. In this lesson, students will not be held responsible for adding fractions using this rule.

PROCEDURE
Draw a picture of a rectangle on the chalkboard and divide it into four equal parts. Have a student shade one of the four equal parts. What fraction names the part that (name of student) shaded? ($\frac{1}{4}$.) Have a second student shade another $\frac{2}{4}$ of the rectangle using chalk of another color. What fraction names the part of the rectangle that (name of student) shaded? ($\frac{2}{4}$.) Altogether, how much did both of the students shade? ($\frac{3}{4}$.) We can write this whole procedure as the addition sentence $\frac{1}{4} + \frac{2}{4} = \frac{3}{4}$. Write this. Continue illustrating various addition sentences of fractions with common denominators in this fashion.

Page 266

OBJECTIVE

■ Add two fractions with common denominators on the number line

BACKGROUND

In this lesson, students will learn a different model for adding fractions. As in the previous lesson, the addition of fractions is limited to fractions with common denominators and a sum less than or equal to 1.

In this lesson, students are expected to learn and use the rule that to add fractions with a common denominator, add the numerators and place this sum over the common denominator. Application of this rule permits students to add fractions with like denominators without having a pictorial or number line model.

PROCEDURE

Draw a number line on the chalkboard and make the unit segment about two feet long. Mark off this unit segment in six equal spaces. Above the number line, label the end points 0 and 1. Below the number line, label the points $\frac{0}{6}$, $\frac{1}{6}$, $\frac{2}{6}$, . . ., $\frac{6}{6}$. Write $\frac{1}{6} + \frac{4}{6}$ on the chalkboard. **Today we are going to learn how to add fractions on the number line. To add two fractions such as $\frac{1}{6} + \frac{4}{6}$, start at 0 and take a hop of $\frac{1}{6}$ of a unit to the right.** Have a student draw an arrow to show this hop. **Next take a hop of $\frac{4}{6}$ of a unit to the right.** Have another student draw an arrow to show this hop. **The stopping point is the sum. What is the sum for the addition $\frac{1}{6} + \frac{4}{6}$?** ($\frac{5}{6}$.) Continue illustrating addition of fractions having the common denominator 6. **How can we find the sum for the two fractions $\frac{2}{6} + \frac{3}{6}$ without using the number line?** (Add the numerators and write this sum over the common denominator 6.)

Repeat the above procedure for a number line that has been divided into eighths.

Page 267

OBJECTIVE

■ Subtract fractions with common denominators using pictures

BACKGROUND

In this lesson, pictures will be used to teach students to subtract fractions with common denominators. For example, to subtract $\frac{5}{8} - \frac{3}{8}$, a whole object is divided into eight equal pieces, and five of these are shaded. To show that $\frac{3}{8}$ is subtracted, we put an *X* on three of the five shaded pieces. The fraction that tells the part of the whole that is left, $\frac{2}{8}$, is the difference. Using pictures, students are expected to subtract fractions with common denominators when the minuend is less than 1. The difference in some cases may be 0, or 0 over the common denominator. With sufficient experience, students may recognize the rule that to subtract two fractions with a common denominator, subtract the numerators and place this difference over the common denominator. In this lesson, students will not be required to use this rule when subtracting fractions.

PROCEDURE

Draw a picture of a rectangle on the chalkboard and divide it into eight equal parts. Beneath this rectangle write $\frac{5}{8} - \frac{4}{8}$. **To show this subtraction using the picture, we must first show $\frac{5}{8}$ of the rectangle.** Have a student shade $\frac{5}{8}$ of the rectangle. **Now we want to take away $\frac{4}{8}$ from what we have. We can show this by putting *X*s on part of the shaded region.** Have a student put *X*s on $\frac{4}{8}$ of the whole that was shaded. **What part of the whole is left?** ($\frac{1}{8}$.) **What is the difference of $\frac{5}{8} - \frac{4}{8}$?** ($\frac{1}{8}$.) Have a student complete the subtraction sentence by writing this difference.

Page 268

OBJECTIVE

■ Subtract two fractions with a common denominator using the number line

BACKGROUND

Subtracting fractions on the number line is similar to subtracting whole numbers on the number line. In this lesson, students subtract two fractions with a common denominator on the number line. The minuend for each subtraction is less than or equal to 1. After some experience with subtracting fractions on the number line, students are expected to learn the rule that to subtract fractions with a common denominator, subtract the numerators and place the difference over the common denominator. This rule is analagous to the rule for adding fractions with a common denominator.

PROCEDURE

Draw a number line on the chalkboard with a unit segment about two feet long. Subdivide the unit segment into six equal parts. Above the number line label the end points 0 and 1. Below the number line label the points $\frac{0}{6}$, $\frac{1}{6}$, $\frac{2}{6}$, . . . , $\frac{6}{6}$. Write $\frac{5}{6} - \frac{2}{6}$ on the chalkboard. Today we are going to subtract two fractions with a common denominator using the number line. Find the difference for the subtraction that I have written on the board. Start at $\frac{5}{6}$ and take a hop of $\frac{2}{6}$ to the left. Draw an arrow starting at $\frac{5}{6}$ and going $\frac{2}{6}$ of a unit to the left. The stopping point is the difference. What is the difference? ($\frac{3}{6}$.) Have a student complete the subtraction sentence by writing the difference. Continue explaining examples of subtraction of fractions having the denominator 6. In each case, have students draw arrows on the number line and identify the difference. What is an easy way to subtract two fractions with a common denominator? (Subtract the numerators and write the difference over the common denominator.)

Repeat the activity using a number line divided into eighths. Emphasize the rule for subtracting fractions with a common denominator. After students understand this rule, erase the number lines and provide several practice exercises in which students must use the rule to find the difference.

WORKTEXT® PAGE 268—For teaching suggestions, see the annotated pupil's page.

Page 269

OBJECTIVES

■ Complete multiplication and division facts

■ Find products when multiplying a 1-digit number times a 2- or 3-digit number

■ Find quotients when dividing by a 1-digit number or a multiple of 10

MATERIALS

multiplication flash cards
division flash cards

PROCEDURE

Activity 1—Review the basic multiplication and division facts using the flash cards.

Activity 2—Review the multiplication and division algorithms developed in this book. This should be done at the chalkboard with students completing sample exercises at their desks.

WORKTEXT® PAGE 269—For teaching suggestions, see the annotated pupil's page.

Page 270

OBJECTIVE

■ Solve verbal problems involving fractions

BACKGROUND

In previous work with fractions, students have usually had a visual representation of the part of the whole or the part of the set that was under consideration. The exercises on this page are more abstract in that there are no pictures. Students are asked to read and interpret verbal situations and then solve each problem. They may draw pictures of each situation if necessary.

PROCEDURE

Have this problem written on the chalkboard. Jill ate $\frac{2}{6}$ of a pizza and Chuck ate $\frac{3}{6}$ of the pizza. How much of the pizza did they eat? Have a student read the problem. What are we given? (Jill ate $\frac{2}{6}$ of a pizza and Chuck ate $\frac{3}{6}$ of the pizza.) Who can draw a picture of this situation on the chalkboard? Have a student draw a circular region on the chalkboard, divide it into six equal pieces, shade two of the pieces to show the pizza that Jill ate, and shade three of the pieces to show the pizza that Chuck ate. How can we find the amount of pizza that the two ate? (Add the fractions.) What fractions should we add? ($\frac{2}{6} + \frac{3}{6}$.)

What is the sum? ($\frac{5}{6}$.) Have a student state this answer as a complete sentence.

WORKTEXT® PAGE 270—For teaching suggestions, see the annotated pupil's page.

Page 271

OBJECTIVES

- Check to determine if a square of numbers is a magic square
- Complete a square of numbers so that it will form a magic square

BACKGROUND

A magic square is a square of numbers in which the sums of the numbers in each row, each column, and each diagonal are equal. Checking to determine if a square of numbers is a magic square provides practice in finding sums for columns of numbers.

If a square of numbers is a magic square and each number in the magic square is multiplied by a constant, the new square of numbers is also a magic square. Using this principle, a variety of different magic squares can be created given a single magic square.

Placing numbers in a square so that it forms a magic square is a difficult task, one that develops problem-solving strategies. In this lesson, students will be asked to complete a magic square when some of the numbers are given and they know the magic sum. This provides practice in searching for a missing addend or in subtraction. Students are also required to add columns of numbers, multiply a 1-digit number times a 1- or 2-digit number, and find missing addends. In this way, a good review of previously learned skills is provided in a novel setting.

The exercises on this page were designed for students to complete independently. This may be done by more advanced students as the teacher continues to develop fraction concepts with less capable students, or it may be used by the entire class.

PROCEDURE

WORKTEXT® PAGE 271—For teaching suggestions, see the annotated pupil's page.

Page 272

OBJECTIVE

- Review the concepts and skills developed in chapter 12

PROCEDURE

WORKTEXT® PAGE 272—Have students complete the chapter review. Worktext® page references for the exercises in this chapter review are: exercise A, pages 253, 254; exercise B, pages 255, 256; exercise C, pages 258–61; exercise D, pages 266, 268.

Page 273

The last page of each chapter is a check-up designed to indicate the pupils' understanding of the concepts and skills that were presented in the chapter. Have the students complete Worktext® page 273 independently.

13 Additional Exercises

Pages 274-284

The exercises in this chapter should be used to provide students with additional practice on the basic concepts and skills developed in this Worktext.® The exercises deal predominantly with the four fundamental operations stressed in *Succeeding in Mathematics*—addition, subtraction, multiplication, and division.

Teachers should assign these additional exercises carefully. If a student does not need to practice a particular skill, the exercises related to that skill should not be assigned. It is suggested that those students who need a lot of practice write the answers to the exercises on a separate piece of paper. This will enable them to work each exercise several times.

Suggestions for using these exercises are annotated on the pupil's pages bound into this Teacher's Edition.

Index for Student Pages

Succeeding in Mathematics
Revised

WORKTEXT

Otto C. Bassler
Professor of Mathematics Education
George Peabody College for Teachers of Vanderbilt University
Nashville, Tennessee

John R. Kolb
Professor of Mathematics and Mathematics Education
North Carolina State University
Raleigh, North Carolina

Mary S. Craighead
Primary Teacher, St. Vincent School
Nashville, Tennessee

William L. Gray
Associate Professor of Education
University of Maryland Baltimore County
Baltimore, Maryland

Illustrated by Ellen Goins

Steck-Vaughn Company   Austin, Texas

ISBN 0-8114-0974-0

9 0 HG 91

Contents

1 • NUMBERS AND NUMERATION

COUNTING

A Use the picture to answer these questions.

1. How many cows does the farmer have? _____8_____

2. How many baby chicks does the farmer have? _____8_____

3. How many pigs are in the mud? _____4_____

4. How many spotted horses does the farmer have? _____2_____

B Use marks like | to show the numbers.

1. pigs ||||||| **2.** cows |||||||| **3.** farmer |

4. chickens ||||||| **5.** horses |||| **6.** trees ||||||

C Use the picture to answer these questions.

1. Are there enough trees for each horse to get under a different tree?

_____yes_____

2. Are there enough trees for each cow to get under a different tree?

_____no_____

3. Are there more horses or cows? _____cows_____

4. Are there more chickens or pigs? _____chickens_____

Direct students' attention to the picture. Have them identify the various sets shown. Then
have students respond to the questions. After students have completed the page, read the
correct answers aloud and have students check their work.

1

NAMING NUMBERS

 Tell how many puppies are in each box.

1. ____2____ puppies   **2.** ____3____ puppies   **3.** ____5____ puppies

---

The symbols 0, 1, 2, 3, 4, 5, 6, 7, 8, and 9 are called **digits**. Each digit names a number less than ten.

 Look at the ★s. How many groups of ten? ____1____ How many groups of one? ____2____ The name for the number of ★s in this set is **12**. The name 12 means 1 ten and 2 ones.

C Complete each sentence.

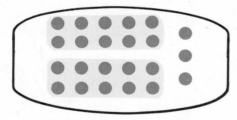   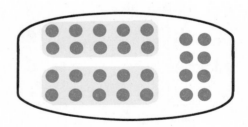

1. ___2___ tens, ___3___ ones = ___23___   **2.** ___2___ tens, ___8___ ones = ___28___

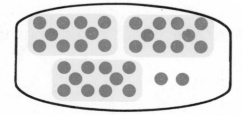   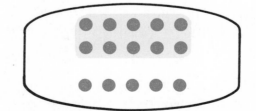

3. ___3___ tens, ___2___ ones = ___32___   **4.** ___1___ ten, ___5___ ones = ___15___

---

2   Explain that when there are more than 9 objects in a set, we use two digits to name the number of objects. The digit on the left tells us the number of groups of 10 objects, and the digit on the right tells us the number of groups of 1 object.

D Complete each sentence.

1. 42 = __4__ tens, __2__ ones   **2.** 35 = __3__ tens, __5__ ones

3. 63 = __6__ tens, __3__ ones   **4.** 72 = __7__ tens, __2__ ones

5. 20 = __2__ tens, __0__ ones   **6.** 49 = __4__ tens, __9__ ones

When two digits are written side by side, the digit on the **left** tells the number of **tens**. The digit on the **right** tells the number of **ones**.

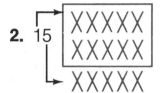

number of tens

36

number of ones

E Make Xs to show the groups of tens and ones. Box each group of ten.

1. 32
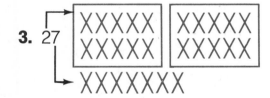

2. 15
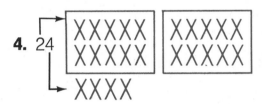

3. 27

4. 24

F Complete each sentence.

1. The 4 in 46 tells the number of __tens__.

2. The 6 in 46 tells the number of __ones__.

3. In 58 there are __5__ groups of ten.

4. In 29 there are __2__ groups of ten and __9__ ones.

5. The number name for 3 groups of ten and 6 ones is __36__.

6. The number name for 9 groups of ten and 9 ones is __99__.

7. 70 means __7__ groups of ten and __0__ ones.

Students who have difficulty with any of these exercises should have additional experiences with the activities for this page.

3

NUMBERS LESS THAN 100

| Standard Name 35 | Expanded Names 3 tens, 5 ones **or** 30 + 5 | Word Name thirty-five |

A Write standard names to complete each sentence.

1. 4 tens = __40__   **2.** 9 ones = __9__   **3.** 6 tens = __60__

4. thirty = __30__   **5.** sixty-one = __61__   **6.** twelve = __12__

7. 40 + 2 = __42__   **8.** 80 + 8 = __88__   **9.** 30 + 7 = __37__

10. 4 tens, 9 ones = __49__   **11.** 5 tens, 3 ones = __53__

12. 1 ten, 3 ones = __13__   **13.** 9 tens, 1 one = __91__

B Fill the blanks to complete each expanded name.

1. 55 = __50__ + __5__   **2.** 84 = __80__ + __4__   **3.** 79 = __70__ + __9__

4. 15 = __1__ ten, __5__ ones   **5.** 96 = __9__ tens, __6__ ones

C Complete the chart.

	Standard Name	Expanded Names		Word Name
1.	43	4 tens, 3 ones	40 + 3	forty-three
2.	15	1 ten, 5 ones	10 + 5	fifteen
3.	37	3 tens, 7 ones	30 + 7	thirty-seven
4.	34	3 tens, 4 ones	30 + 4	thirty-four
5.	86	8 tens, 6 ones	80 + 6	eighty-six
6.	79	7 tens, 9 ones	70 + 9	seventy-nine
7.	72	7 tens, 2 ones	70 + 2	seventy-two

COMPARING NUMBERS

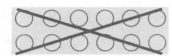

How many circles? ____12____   How many squares? ____15____

Put an *X* on the set which has the smaller number of objects.

We know 12 **is less than** 15. We write 12 < 15. We know 15
is greater than 12.   We write 15 > 12. The symbol < or >
always points to the smaller number.

Read the material inside the border. Stress that the symbols < and > always point to the
smaller number.

A Draw a ring around the larger number in each pair.

1. 6 (9)   **2.** 17 (27)   **3.** (36) 35

4. (12) 8   **5.** 42 (53)   **6.** 84 (90)

7. (84) 64   **8.** (20) 9   **9.** (47) 43

B Put the symbol < (is less than) or > (is greater than) in each ●.

1. 7 > 2   **2.** 96 < 98   **3.** 63 > 36

4. 9 < 10   **5.** 27 > 19   **6.** 47 < 50

7. 52 > 42   **8.** 40 < 51   **9.** 16 < 21

←———————————————————————————→
  0 1 2 3 4 5 6 7 8 9 10 11 12 13 14 15 16 17 18 19 20 21 22 23 24 25

Students who have difficulty with exercise A or B should have additional experiences with
activities 1 and 2.

C Name the counting number that is two **less** than each of these numbers.

1. __5__ 7   **2.** __12__ 14   **3.** __23__ 25   **4.** __9__ 11

5. __19__ 21   **6.** __71__ 73   **7.** __47__ 49   **8.** __28__ 30

D Complete each number line by filling each ▪.

1. ←—•—•—•—•—•—→   **2.** ←—•—•—•—•—•—•—→
      17 18   21   58 59   62
         19 20   60 61   63

Discuss the number line. Then have students complete the page.
Students having difficulty with the last sets of exercises should have additional experiences with activity 3.

USING NUMBERS

A We count to find **how many** objects are in a set.

1. How many steps are in the picture? _____8_____

2. How many children are in the picture? _____2_____

B The boy is on the fourth step from the bottom. **Fourth** tells the **position** of the boy on the steps.

What step is the girl on? _____sixth_____

C Read each sentence. Write *how many* or *position* in the blank to show how the number is used.

1. There are *twelve* months in a year. _____how many_____

2. Jan is reading the *fifth* page in her book. _____position_____

D Write names that show position.

first	second	third	fourth	fifth	sixth	seventh	eighth	ninth
1st	2nd	3rd	4th	5th	6th	7th	8th	9th

E Write names that tell how many.

one	two	three	four	five	six	seven	eight	nine	ten
1	2	3	4	5	6	7	8	9	10

F Answer these questions.

1. Carl was the 12th person in line. Jack stood next in line.

   What position did Jack have? _____13th_____

2. Angelina is reading page 89. What will she read next? _____90_____

GROUPING BY TENS

10 ones   form   1 ten

 Draw a ring around each group of 10 ones. Then complete the sentence.

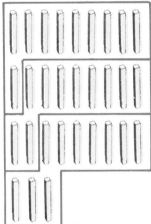 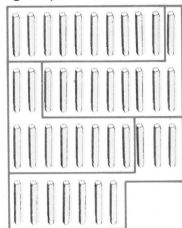 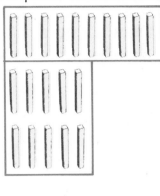

1. _3_ tens = _30_   **2.** _4_ tens = _40_   **3.** _2_ tens = _20_

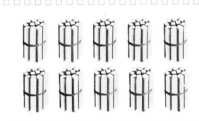

10 tens = 1 hundred = 100

Discuss the example. Have students complete the exercises on pages 7 and 8. Read the statement at the bottom of page 8.

 Draw a box around each group of 10 tens (1 hundred). Then complete the sentence.

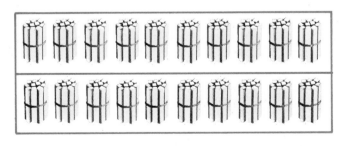 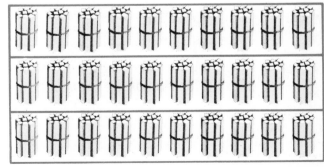

1. _2_ hundreds = _200_   **2.** _3_ hundreds = _300_

C Study the picture.

How many hundreds? ____1____ How many tens? ____6____ How many ones? ____3____

1 hundred, 6 tens, 3 ones = 163

D Draw a ring around each group of 10∗s. Draw a box around each group of 1 hundred (10 tens)∗s. Then complete the sentence.

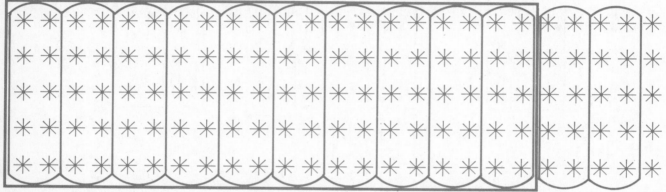

1. ____1____ hundred, ____2____ tens, ____5____ ones = ____125____

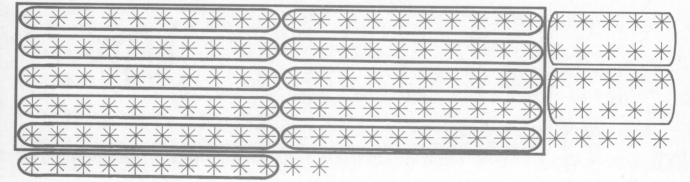

2. ____1____ hundred, ____3____ tens, ____7____ ones = ____137____

When three digits are written side by side, each digit has a different place value.

245

→ number of hundreds
→ number of tens
→ number of ones

Write 3-digit numbers on the chalkboard. Ask what each digit stands for—hundreds, tens, or ones.

NUMBERS LESS THAN 1,000

 Complete the chart.

	Standard Name	Expanded Name	Hundreds	Tens	Ones
1.	483	400 + 80 + 3	4	8	3
2.	562	500 + 60 + 2	5	6	2
3.	898	800 + 90 + 8	8	9	8
4.	236	200 + 30 + 6	2	3	6
5.	640	600 + 40 + 0	6	4	0
6.	769	700 + 60 + 9	7	6	9
7.	837	800 + 30 + 7	8	3	7
8.	914	900 + 10 + 4	9	1	4

B Write the standard name for each word name.

1. five hundred thirty-seven ___537___ **2.** two hundred seventy-one ___271___

3. nine hundred sixty ___960___ **4.** four hundred twelve ___412___

5. six hundred four ___604___ **6.** eight hundred fifty-five ___855___

7. one hundred eleven ___111___ **8.** seven hundred ninety ___790___

C Name the counting number that comes just **after** each number.

1. 481 ___482___ **2.** 695 ___696___ **3.** 439 ___440___

4. 599 ___600___ **5.** 263 ___264___ **6.** 119 ___120___

D Name the counting number that comes just **before** each number.

1. ___572___ 573 **2.** ___368___ 369 **3.** ___180___ 181

4. ___144___ 145 **5.** ___189___ 190 **6.** ___235___ 236

If students have difficulty with any of these exercises, they should have additional experiences with activities 1 and 2.

9

E Fill the blank to complete each pattern.

1. 137   138   139   _140_

2. 470   480   490   _500_

3. 273   274   275   _276_

4. 897   898   899   _900_

5. 390   391   392   _393_

6. 700   710   720   _730_

7. 180   190   200   _210_

8. 698   699   700   _701_

 F Draw a ring around the larger number.

1. 37   (38)

2. (87)   67

3. (52)   51

4. (128)   126

5. 538   (838)

6. (264)   244

7. (425)   415

8. 600   (900)

9. 108   (109)

> Remember: < means **is less than**. > means **is greater than**.
> 70 < 90 is read "seventy is less than ninety."

G Write <, >, or = in each ● to make the sentence true.

1. 84   >   64

2. 30 + 4   =   34

3. 185   <   188

4. 915   >   899

5. 40 + 5   <   54

6. 68   <   101

7. 351   <   357

8. 287   >   278

9. 202   =   200 + 2

10. 200 + 90 + 5   >   259

11. 483   =   400 + 80 + 3

H Answer these questions.

1. What is the largest 3-digit counting number? _999_

2. What is the smallest 3-digit counting number? _100_

3. If 948 < 94▢ is true, what digit must be written in the box? _9_

4. If 213 > 2▢3 is true, what digit must be written in the box? _0_

DOLLARS, DIMES, AND PENNIES

 100¢   10¢   1¢

A Name the amount of money in cents.

1. 234¢

2. 115¢

3. 352¢

4. 103¢

B Complete each sentence.

1. The number of dollars is the __hundreds'__ digit in the amount of money.

2. The number of dimes is the __tens'__ digit in the amount of money.

3. The number of pennies is the __ones'__ digit in the amount of money.

C Complete the chart.

	Number of Dollars	Number of Dimes	Number of Pennies	Number of Cents
1.	4	3	1	431¢
2.	5	6	2	562¢
3.	1	0	5	105¢
4.	7	2	9	729¢
5.	6	8	0	680¢

Discuss how in our system of naming numbers, each time we have 10 things of one kind we put them together to form a new thing. Relate this discussion to the picture showing 10 hundreds = 1 thousand.

NAMING LARGER NUMBERS

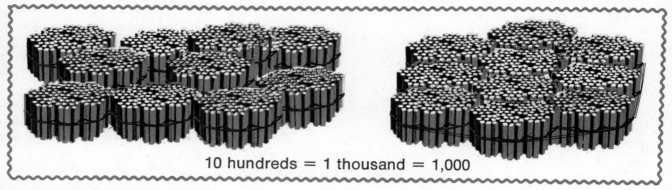

10 hundreds = 1 thousand = 1,000

Treat exercise A orally.

 A Complete each sentence.

1. __10__ hundreds = 1 thousand   **2.** __10__ tens = 1 hundred

3. 100 tens = __1__ thousand   **4.** __1,000__ ones = 1 thousand

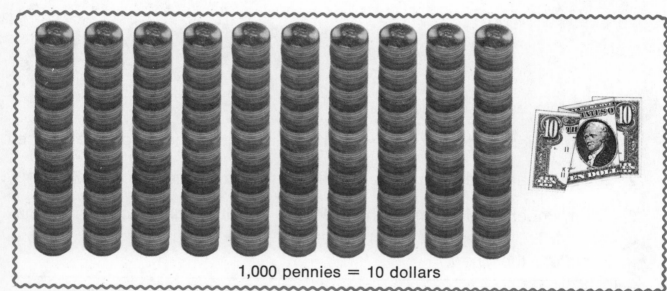

1,000 pennies = 10 dollars

Discuss this picture. Each stack of 100 pennies is 1 dollar. Ten hundred pennies = 1,000 pennies, or 10 dollars.

B Another way to picture 1,000 objects is with money.

1. A ten-dollar bill = __1,000__ pennies.

2. The number of ten-dollar bills is the __thousands'__ digit.

3. The number of dollars is the __hundreds'__ digit.

4. The number of dimes is the __tens'__ digit.

5. The number of pennies is the __ones'__ digit.

12   Have students complete these exercises individually.

C Fill the blanks. Write the standard name for the number.

thousands hundreds tens ones

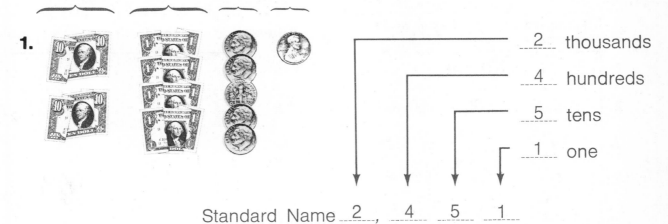

1.

_2_ thousands
_4_ hundreds
_5_ tens
_1_ one

Standard Name _2_, _4_ _5_ _1_

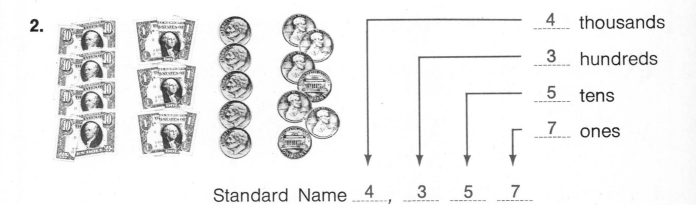

2.

_4_ thousands
_3_ hundreds
_5_ tens
_7_ ones

Standard Name _4_, _3_ _5_ _7_

D Complete each sentence.

1. In 4,737 there are ____7____ hundreds.

2. In 5,269 there are ____5____ thousands.

3. In 2,641 there are ____4____ tens.

4. In 1,289 there are ____9____ ones.

5. The 4 in 2,649 tells the number of ____tens____.

6. The 7 in 7,511 tells the number of ____thousands____.

7. The 5 in 2,135 tells the number of ____ones____.

8. The 9 in 1,957 tells the number of ____hundreds____.

Use 3,568 as an example to discuss writing the expanded names of 4-digit numbers. Then have students complete the exercises on pages 14 and 15.

NUMBERS LESS THAN 10,000

 A Complete the chart.

	Standard Name	Expanded Name	Thousands	Hundreds	Tens	Ones
1.	6,527	6,000 + 500 + 20 + 7	6	5	2	7
2.	8,139	8,000 + 100 + 30 + 9	8	1	3	9
3.	5,672	5,000 + 600 + 70 + 2	5	6	7	2
4.	4,493	4,000 + 400 + 90 + 3	4	4	9	3
5.	6,508	6,000 + 500 + 0 + 8	6	5	0	8
6.	2,570	2,000 + 500 + 70 + 0	2	5	7	0

B Name the counting number that comes just **after** each of these numbers.

1. 999 _1,000_   **2.** 1,999 _2,000_   **3.** 4,899 _4,900_

4. 1,023 _1,024_   **5.** 2,769 _2,770_   **6.** 5,672 _5,673_

7. 1,069 _1,070_   **8.** 2,909 _2,910_   **9.** 6,499 _6,500_

C Name the counting number that comes just **before** each of these numbers.

1. _1,199_ 1,200   **2.** _2,999_ 3,000   **3.** _5,719_ 5,720

4. _1,389_ 1,390   **5.** _3,608_ 3,609   **6.** _5,999_ 6,000

7. _1,588_ 1,589   **8.** _4,000_ 4,001   **9.** _7,587_ 7,588

D Write the standard name.

1. Four thousand, six hundred fifty-five _____ 4,655

2. Two thousand, five hundred seventy _____ 2,570

3. Nine thousand, ninety-five _____ 9,095

E Complete each pattern.

Ones' Patterns

1. 1,785   1,786   1,787   _1,788_   **2.** 1,007   1,008   1,009   _1,010_

3. 2,447   2,448   2,449   _2,450_   **4.** 6,997   6,998   6,999   _7,000_

5. 4,600   4,601   4,602   _4,603_   **6.** 4,097   4,098   4,099   _4,100_

Tens' Patterns

7. 2,480   2,490   2,500   _2,510_   **8.** 3,590   3,600   3,610   _3,620_

9. 4,710   4,720   4,730   _4,740_   **10.** 5,970   5,980   5,990   _6,000_

11. 1,670   1,680   1,690   _1,700_   **12.** 8,070   8,080   8,090   _8,100_

Hundreds' Patterns

13. 3,400   3,500   3,600   _3,700_   **14.** 1,000   1,100   1,200   _1,300_

15. 2,700   2,800   2,900   _3,000_   **16.** 6,700   6,800   6,900   _7,000_

17. 4,000   4,100   4,200   _4,300_   **18.** 9,600   9,700   9,800   _9,900_

F Draw a ring around the larger number.

1.   879   (1,223)   **2.** (1,879)   1,779   **3.** (4,631)   4,579

4. 4,081   (4,082)   **5.** 7,754   (7,764)   **6.** 6,221   (6,321)

7. (2,022)   2,020   **8.** 4,263   (5,183)   **9.** (4,527)   3,527

G Answer these questions.

1. What is the smallest 4-digit counting number?   _1,000_

2. What is the largest 4-digit counting number?   _9,999_

3. If 2,47■ < 2,471 is true, what digit must be written in the box?   _0_

4. What counting numbers are larger than 4,798 and smaller than 4,802?

   _4,799   4,800   4,801_

PROBLEM SOLVING

 In the blank after each word name, write the standard name for the number. Then answer the questions.

The Empire State Building has one hundred two __102__ stories, six thousand, five hundred __6,500__ windows, and one thousand, eight hundred sixty __1,860__ steps. The building is one thousand, four hundred seventy-two __1,472__ feet tall.

1. The smallest number in the story is __102__.

2. The largest number in the story is __6,500__.

3. Are there more steps or windows? __windows__

The S. S. *United States* was a large, fast ocean liner. It was nine hundred ninety __990__ feet long. It carried one thousand, ninety __1,090__ crew members and one thousand, nine hundred thirty __1,930__ passengers. Nine thousand __9,000__ meals a day could be prepared in its galleys.

4. The largest number in this story is __9,000__.

5. The smallest number in this story is __990__.

One of the great players in major league baseball was Ty Cobb. In his career he played in three thousand, thirty-three __3,033__ games, had four thousand, one hundred ninety-one __4,191__ hits, scored two thousand, two hundred forty-four __2,244__ runs, and stole eight hundred ninety-two __892__ bases.

6. The largest number in this story is __4,191__.

7. The smallest number in this story is __892__.

ROUNDING TO THE NEAREST TEN

 Use the picture to answer.

1. Without counting, guess how many objects are pictured. What is your guess? _____

2. Count the objects. How many are there? ___32___

3. Carlos guessed there were 20 objects. Sam guessed 30, and Phil guessed 40. Whose guess was best? _____Sam's_____

✳·✳

Sometimes we do not need to know the exact number. We might say there are about so many objects. When we tell the nearest ten to a number we have **rounded the number to the nearest ten.**

✳·✳

Discuss the material above and the example in exercise B. Then have students complete exercises B, C, and D.

 Study each number line. Choose the nearest ten to the number named in color. Complete the sentence.

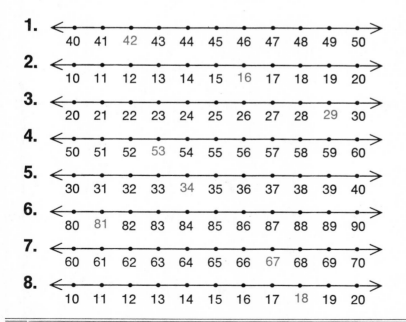

1. 40 41 42 43 44 45 46 47 48 49 50   42 is rounded to __40__.

2. 10 11 12 13 14 15 16 17 18 19 20   16 is rounded to __20__.

3. 20 21 22 23 24 25 26 27 28 29 30   29 is rounded to __30__.

4. 50 51 52 53 54 55 56 57 58 59 60   53 is rounded to __50__.

5. 30 31 32 33 34 35 36 37 38 39 40   34 is rounded to __30__.

6. 80 81 82 83 84 85 86 87 88 89 90   81 is rounded to __80__.

7. 60 61 62 63 64 65 66 67 68 69 70   67 is rounded to __70__.

8. 10 11 12 13 14 15 16 17 18 19 20   18 is rounded to __20__.

Answer these questions about this number line.

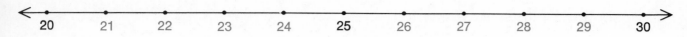

20 21 22 23 24 **25** 26 27 28 29 30

1. Which numbers named in color are rounded to 20? _21, 22, 23, 24_

2. Which numbers named in color are rounded to 30? _26, 27, 28, 29_

3. Which number is halfway between 20 and 30? _25_

> When a number is halfway between two tens, it is rounded to the larger ten. **25 is rounded to 30.**

D Round each number named in color to the nearest ten.

1.

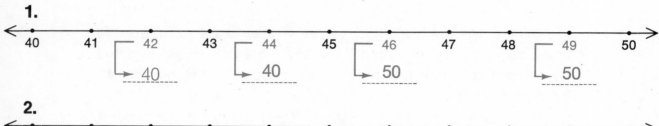

40 41 42 43 44 45 46 47 48 49 50
        40   40   50   50

2.

80 81 82 83 84 85 86 87 88 89 90
     80   90   90

3.

110 111 112 113 114 115 116 117 118 119 120
          110 110   120 120   120

Before students begin exercise E, explain how numbers are rounded to the nearest ten.

E Round to the nearest ten.

1. 157 _160_   45 _50_   184 _180_   38 _40_   76 _80_

2. 101 _100_   409 _410_   52 _50_   555 _560_   33 _30_

3. 243 _240_   686 _690_   287 _290_   194 _190_   22 _20_

4. 994 _990_   14 _10_   88 _90_   63 _60_   118 _120_

5. 111 _110_   777 _780_   302 _300_   275 _280_   92 _90_

Students having difficulty with any of these exercises should have additional experiences with activities 2 and 3.

ANOTHER WAY TO NAME NUMBERS

Long ago, Egyptians used pictures to name numbers.

Egyptian Numeral	Standard Name
/	1
∩	10
9	100
⚮	1,000

1. What picture did the Egyptians use to name 10? __∩__ 100? __9__

2. What is the value for each of these pictures? / __1__ ⚮ __1,000__

To find the value of an Egyptian numeral, add the values of its pictures.

$$9∩∩∩// = 9 + ∩ + ∩ + ∩ + / + /$$
$$= 100 + 10 + 10 + 10 + 1 + 1 = 132$$

A Find the value for each Egyptian numeral.

1. ∩∩/// means 10 + __10__ + 1 + __1__ + __1__ = __23__

2. 99∩// means 100 + __100__ + __10__ + __1__ + __1__ = __212__

3. ⚮9∩∩// means __1,000__ + __100__ + __10__ + __10__ + __1__ + __1__ = __1,122__

To find the Egyptian numeral for 235, think: 235 = 2 hundreds, 3 tens, 5 ones. Then draw 2 pictures for 100, 3 pictures for 10, and 5 pictures for 1. The Egyptian numeral for 235 is 99∩∩∩/////.

B Complete the chart.

	Standard Name	Thousands	Hundreds	Tens	Ones	Egyptian Numeral
1.	47	—	—	4	7	∩∩∩∩///////
2.	35	—	—	3	5	∩∩∩/////
3.	182	—	1	8	2	9∩∩∩∩∩∩∩∩//
4.	1,233	1	2	3	3	⚮99∩∩∩///

Lead students to see that this system is more cumbersome than the system we use.

19

Treat exercises A and B orally before having students complete the rest of the exercises.

TELLING TIME

 A Use clock A to answer these questions.

A

1. The hour hand is between _____9_____ and _____10_____.

2. How many minutes is it past 9? __20__
(Remember that it takes 5 minutes for the minute
hand to move from one number to the next.)

> The time shown is written 9:20 and read
> nine-twenty. It means 20 minutes past 9.

 B Use clock B to answer these questions.

B

1. The hour hand is between _____6_____ and _____7_____.

2. How many minutes is it past 6? __50__

3. How many minutes is it before 7? __10__

> The time shown is written 6:50 and read
> six-fifty. It means 10 minutes to 7.

 **C** Tell how many minutes past the hour.

1. _____5_____ past 3   **2.** __25__ past _____8_____   **3.** __30__ past __12__

 D Tell how many minutes before the hour.

1. __10__ before __3__   **2.** __25__ before __10__   **3.** __20__ before __5__

Students who have difficulty with these exercises should have additional experiences with
the demonstration clock-face.

CHAPTER REVIEW

(A) We use ten digits to write number names. Write these digits.

0, 1, 2, 3, 4, 5, 6, 7, 8, 9

(B) Complete each sentence.

1. 1 ten = ___10___ ones

2. 1 hundred = ___100___ ones

3. 1 hundred = ___10___ tens

4. 1 thousand = ___10___ hundreds

(C) Numbers have many different names. Complete the chart.

	Standard Name	Expanded Name	Word Name
1.	4,860	4,000 + 800 + 60	four thousand, eight hundred sixty
2.	95	90 + 5	ninety-five
3.	784	700 + 80 + 4	seven hundred eighty-four
4.	2,614	2,000 + 600 + 10 + 4	two thousand, six hundred fourteen

(D) < means **is less than**. > means **is greater than**. Write <, >, or = in each ⬤ to make the sentence true.

1. 168 < 178   40 + 7 = 47   32 > 30

2. 184 = 100 + 80 + 4   1,647 > 1,247   700 + 3 < 706

(E) Complete these number patterns.

1. 47 48 49 ___50___

2. 970 980 990 ___1,000___

3. 82 81 80 ___79___

4. 1,897 1,898 1,899 ___1,900___

5. 197 198 199 ___200___

6. 4,000 5,000 6,000 ___7,000___

(F) Round each of these numbers to the nearest ten.

1. 146 ___150___   432 ___430___   71 ___70___   327 ___330___

2. 869 ___870___   85 ___90___   1,892 ___1,890___   14 ___10___

CHECK-UP

 A Name the counting number that comes just **after** each of these numbers.

899 ___900___   4,728 ___4,729___   5,999 ___6,000___   8,620 ___8,621___

 B Write the standard name to complete each sentence.

1. 3 thousands, 5 hundreds, 6 tens, 7 ones = ___3,567___

2. $4,000 + 800 + 70 + 3 =$ ___4,873___

C Write an expanded name to complete each sentence.

1. $475 =$ ___$400 + 70 + 5$___

2. $1,836 =$ ___$1,000 + 800 + 30 + 6$___

3. $2,047 =$ ___$2,000 + 40 + 7$___

D Write >, <, or = in each ●

1. 47 < 49

2. 10 hundreds = 1 thousand

3. $2,000 + 3$ = 2,003

4. 7 tens < 700

5. 4,837 > 4,637

6. $900 + 40 + 3$ > 934

E Round each number to the nearest ten.

1. 79 ___80___   **2.** 582 ___580___   **3.** 45 ___50___   **4.** 198 ___200___

 F Write the standard names for the numbers. Then answer the questions.

Judy, Charlie, and Manuel were saving bottle caps. Judy had one hundred seventy-nine ___179___, Charlie had two hundred twelve ___212___, and Manuel had one hundred seventy ___170___.

1. Who saved the most bottle caps? ___Charlie___

2. Who saved the fewest bottle caps? ___Manuel___

2 · ADDITION

UNDERSTANDING ADDITION

A Sally and Joan saw some large raccoons and some small raccoons in a cage. Joan **counted** to find the total number of raccoons. Sally **added** to find the total number of raccoons.

1. What numbers did Joan say when she counted? ___1___, ___2___,

___3___, ___4___, ___5___, ___6___, ___7___

2. What numbers did Sally add? ___2___ and ___5___

3. How many raccoons were there in all? ___7___

> Sally thought: 2 raccoons plus 5 raccoons equals 7 raccoons.
> Sally wrote this addition sentence: $2 + 5 = 7$.

B Write an addition sentence for each picture.

1. △ △ △ △   △ △   **2.** ▢ ▢ ▢   ▢ ▢ ▢ ▢ ▢

___4___ + ___2___ = ___6___   ___3___ + ___5___ = ___8___

C For each addition, use the sticks to help complete the sentence.

| | | | | | | | | | | | | | | | | | | | | | | | | | |

1. $6 + 4 =$ ___10___   **2.** $5 + 2 =$ ___7___   **3.** $8 + 1 =$ ___9___

| | | | | | | | | | | | | | | | | | | | | |

4. $2 + 3 =$ ___5___   **5.** $7 + 3 =$ ___10___   **6.** $2 + 6 =$ ___8___

D For each addition, complete the sentence.

1. $4 + 7 =$ ___11___   **2.** $1 + 6 =$ ___7___   **3.** $5 + 5 =$ ___10___

Students having difficulty with any of these exercises should have additional experiences with activities 1 and 2.

23

Discuss the example showing addition on the number line. Then treat exercise A orally.

ADDITION ON THE NUMBER LINE

Add 3 + 6 on the number line.
First: Start at 3.
Second: Count 6 spaces to the right.
Third: The sum is 9.

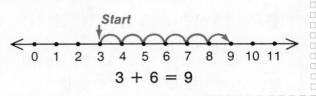

$3 + 6 = 9$

 A Fill the blanks to add 5 + 2 on the number line.

First: Start at ___5___. (Draw an arrow pointing to the starting number.)

Second: Hop ___2___ spaces to the right. (Use an arrow to show this.)

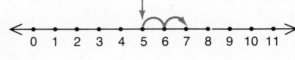

Third: The sum is ___7___.

Use number 1 in exercise B to stress the procedure for adding on the number line. Ask questions of students as to what to do in each step.

 B Complete the sentence for each addition shown by the number line.

1. $4 + 4 = 8$

2. $2 + 6 = 8$

3. $5 + 1 = 6$

4. $5 + 6 = 11$

5. $3 + 7 = 10$

6. $6 + 3 = 9$

24

C Use the number line to help you add.

0 1 2 3 4 5 6 7 8 9 10 11 12 13 14 15 16 17 18

1. 3 + 1 = __4__   4 + 5 = __9__   7 + 2 = __9__   2 + 6 = __8__

2. 4 + 2 = __6__   3 + 3 = __6__   3 + 5 = __8__   7 + 5 = __12__

3. 7 + 4 = __11__   6 + 2 = __8__   5 + 5 = __10__   8 + 8 = __16__

4. 8 + 5 = __13__   6 + 6 = __12__   4 + 8 = __12__   9 + 7 = __16__

The addition sentence 4 + 5 = 9 is also written $\begin{array}{r} 4 \\ +5 \\ \hline 9 \end{array}$. In these addition sentences, 4 and 5 are called **addends** and 9 is called the **sum**.

 **D** Complete the charts.

1.

	Sentence	Addends		Sum
a.	1 + 4 = 5	1	4	5
b.	2 + 6 = 8	2	6	8
c.	7 + 3 = 10	7	3	10
d.	4 + 3 = 7	4	3	7
e.	3 + 1 = 4	3	1	4

2.

	Sentence	Addends		Sum
a.	4 + 5 = 9	4	5	9
b.	1 + 6 = 7	1	6	7
c.	6 + 1 = 7	6	1	7
d.	5 + 2 = 7	5	2	7
e.	3 + 8 = 11	3	8	11

E Find the sum for each addition. Use the number line in exercise C if you need it.

1.
$\begin{array}{r} 6 \\ +1 \\ \hline 7 \end{array}$
$\begin{array}{r} 3 \\ +4 \\ \hline 7 \end{array}$
$\begin{array}{r} 1 \\ +8 \\ \hline 9 \end{array}$
$\begin{array}{r} 4 \\ +2 \\ \hline 6 \end{array}$
$\begin{array}{r} 5 \\ +7 \\ \hline 12 \end{array}$
$\begin{array}{r} 7 \\ +3 \\ \hline 10 \end{array}$
$\begin{array}{r} 2 \\ +6 \\ \hline 8 \end{array}$

2.
$\begin{array}{r} 7 \\ +2 \\ \hline 9 \end{array}$
$\begin{array}{r} 8 \\ +3 \\ \hline 11 \end{array}$
$\begin{array}{r} 6 \\ +7 \\ \hline 13 \end{array}$
$\begin{array}{r} 2 \\ +8 \\ \hline 10 \end{array}$
$\begin{array}{r} 1 \\ +9 \\ \hline 10 \end{array}$
$\begin{array}{r} 5 \\ +3 \\ \hline 8 \end{array}$
$\begin{array}{r} 3 \\ +9 \\ \hline 12 \end{array}$

Students having difficulty with any of these exercises should have additional experiences with activities 1 and 2.

25

ADDITION FACTS

 Use the picture of the number line to help you find the sums.

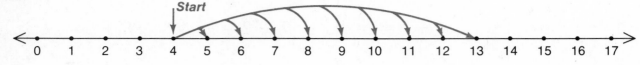

4	4	4	4	4	4	4	4	4
+ 1	+ 2	+ 3	+ 4	+ 5	+ 6	+ 7	+ 8	+ 9
5	6	7	8	9	10	11	12	13

B Find the sums. Look for a pattern in each row.

1.

2	2	2	2	2	2	2	2	2
+ 1	+ 2	+ 3	+ 4	+ 5	+ 6	+ 7	+ 8	+ 9
3	4	5	6	7	8	9	10	11

2.

7	7	7	7	7	7	7	7	7
+ 1	+ 2	+ 3	+ 4	+ 5	+ 6	+ 7	+ 8	+ 9
8	9	10	11	12	13	14	15	16

3.

9	9	9	9	9	9	9	9	9
+ 1	+ 2	+ 3	+ 4	+ 5	+ 6	+ 7	+ 8	+ 9
10	11	12	13	14	15	16	17	18

C Addition facts may be shown in tables. Complete each table.

1.

+	0	1	2	3	4	5	6	7	8	9
3	3	4	5	6	7	8	9	10	11	12

2.

+	0	1	2	3	4	5	6	7	8	9
5	5	6	7	8	9	10	11	12	13	14

3.

+	0	1	2	3	4	5	6	7	8	9
8	8	9	10	11	12	13	14	15	16	17

D Complete this addition facts table.

+	0	1	2	3	4	5	6	7	8	9
0	0	1	2	3	4	5	6	7	8	9
1	1	2	3	4	5	6	7	8	9	10
2	2	3	4	5	6	7	8	9	10	11
3	3	4	5	6	7	8	9	10	11	12
4	4	5	6	7	8	9	10	11	12	13
5	5	6	7	8	9	10	11	12	13	14
6	6	7	8	9	10	11	12	13	14	15
7	7	8	9	10	11	12	13	14	15	16
8	8	9	10	11	12	13	14	15	16	17
9	9	10	11	12	13	14	15	16	17	18

Check your addition facts table with the addition facts table printed on the inside back cover of this book.

E Use your addition facts table to find the sums.

1.

8	2	6	7	7	6	5	5
+ 3	+ 3	+ 7	+ 9	+ 5	+ 8	+ 6	+ 8
11	5	13	16	12	14	11	13

2.

4	5	7	3	6	7	0	7
+ 6	+ 7	+ 4	+ 5	+ 0	+ 6	+ 9	+ 8
10	12	11	8	6	13	9	15

3.

1	8	4	0	1	9	9	1
+ 8	+ 7	+ 3	+ 4	+ 9	+ 9	+ 6	+ 6
9	15	7	4	10	18	15	7

Additional practice on the addition facts can be found in chapter 13, page 274.

27

PROPERTIES OF ADDITION

A Answer the questions.

1. How many squares? ___6___

2. How many triangles? ___8___

3. How many shapes in all? ___14___

> We write the addition sentences $6 + 8 = 14$ or $8 + 6 = 14$.

B Complete the addition sentences for each picture.

1. ☆ ☆ ☆ ☆ ☆ $7 + 5 =$ ___12___   2. ☆ ☆ ☆ ☆ ☆ ☆ $3 + 8 =$ ___11___
   ☆ ☆ ☆ ☆ ☆ $5 + 7 =$ ___12___   ☆ ☆ ☆ ☆ ☆ $8 +$ ___3___ $= 11$

3. ★ ★ ★ ★ ★ $6 + 9 =$ ___15___   4. ★ ★ ★   ___6___ $+$ ___4___ $= 10$
   ★ ★ ★ ★ ★   ★ ★ ★
   ★ ★ ★ ★ ★ ___9___ $+$ ___6___ $= 15$ ★ ★ ★ ★ ___4___ $+$ ___6___ $= 10$

C Complete each sentence.

1. If $7 + 5 = 12$, then $5 + 7 =$ ___12___.   2. If $9 + 6 = 15$, then $6 + 9 =$ ___15___.

3. If $4 + 9 = 13$, then $9 + 4 =$ ___13___.   4. If $8 + 4 = 12$, then $4 + 8 =$ ___12___.

> Changing the order of the addends does not change the sum.

D Find each sum. Then write the related addition by changing the order of the addends.

1.
$$\begin{array}{cc} 8 & 5 \\ +5 & +8 \\ \hline 13 & 13 \end{array}$$

2.
$$\begin{array}{cc} 9 & 3 \\ +3 & +9 \\ \hline 12 & 12 \end{array}$$

3.
$$\begin{array}{cc} 7 & 8 \\ +8 & +7 \\ \hline 15 & 15 \end{array}$$

4.
$$\begin{array}{cc} 2 & 9 \\ +9 & +2 \\ \hline 11 & 11 \end{array}$$

5.
$$\begin{array}{cc} 4 & 7 \\ +7 & +4 \\ \hline 11 & 11 \end{array}$$

6.
$$\begin{array}{cc} 3 & 6 \\ +6 & +3 \\ \hline 9 & 9 \end{array}$$

E Answer the questions.

1. How many squares? ___5___ □ □ □ □ □

2. How many triangles? ___3___ ▲ ▲ ▲

3. How many circles? ___7___ ○ ○ ○ ○ ○ ○ ○

4. How many shapes in all? ___15___

> We write the addition sentences (5 + 3) + 7 = 15 or
> 5 + (3 + 7) = 15. The parentheses ( ) tell us which
> numbers to add first.

F Find the sums. Look for a pattern.

1. a. 6 + (3 + 5) = 6 + __8__ = __14__   **b.** (6 + 3) + 5 = __9__ + 5 = __14__

2. a. 4 + (5 + 2) = __11__   **b.** (4 + 5) + 2 = __11__

3. a. 7 + (1 + 5) = __13__   **b.** (7 + 1) + 5 = __13__

4. Were the answers to parts a and b of each exercise the same? __yes__

G Complete each sentence.

1. If 9 + (5 + 4) = 18, then (9 + 5) + 4 = __18__.

2. If 6 + (4 + 7) = 17, then (6 + 4) + 7 = __17__.

3. If 9 + (1 + 6) = 16, then (9 + 1) + 6 = __16__.

H Find the sums by adding down the column. Check by adding up the column.

4	7	6	5	9	3	8	2
3	2	4	3	1	4	1	6
+ 2	+ 4	+ 6	+ 7	+ 8	+ 6	+ 7	+ 3
9	13	16	15	18	13	16	11

Students having difficulty with these exercises should complete the additional activity.

PROBLEM SOLVING

 Several words mean "to add." Write the addition and the sum for each phrase.

	Phrase	Addition	Sum
1.	6 and 7	6 + 7	13
2.	5 added to 9	5 + 9	14
3.	3 more than 5	5 + 3	8
4.	7 plus 8	7 + 8	15
5.	4 increased by 6	4 + 6	10

Discuss the directions for exercise B. Work number 1 with the students.

B Solve each word problem. As you read each problem, underline the words that tell you to add.

1. Sam had 3 quarters <u>more than</u> Bill. Bill had 7 quarters. How many quarters did Sam have? __10__ quarters

2. Laura had 9 pencils. Isabel had 6 pencils. How many pencils did they have <u>together</u>? __15__ pencils

3. Enrique had 8 rocks in his collection. He <u>increased</u> his collection by 5 rocks. How many rocks are in his collection? __13__ rocks

4. Lisa Cree put 7 stamps in her album. She <u>added</u> 4 more stamps to those already in the album. How many stamps are in the album? __11__ stamps

5. There are 9 guppies <u>plus</u> 5 goldfish in a fish tank. How many fish are in the tank? __14__ fish

REVIEWING NUMBERS LESS THAN 1,000

A Complete the chart.

	Standard Name	Expanded Name	Hundreds	Tens	Ones
1.	507	500 + 7	5	0	7
2.	843	800 + 40 + 3	8	4	
3.	269	200 + 60 + 9	2	6	
4.	482	400 + 80 + 2	4	8	2

B Fill the blank to complete each pattern.

1. 572   571   570   __569__

2. 15   17   19   __21__

3. 140   150   160   __170__

4. 400   500   600   __700__

C Write <, >, or = in each ● to make the sentence true.

1. 729 **>** 725   30 + 4 **=** 34   238 **>** 218

2. 6 + 8 **<** 6 + 9   690 **<** 890   800 + 9 **<** 908

D Complete each number line by filling each

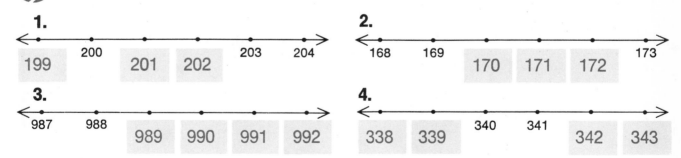

1.
199 200 201 202 203 204

2.
168 169 170 171 172 173

3.
987 988 989 990 991 992

4.
338 339 340 341 342 343

E Answer these questions.

1. If 289 < 2☐3 is true, what digit must be written in the box? __9__

2. If 471 > 47☐ is true, what digit must be written in the box? __0__

3. If 298 > ☐98 is true, what digit must be written in the box? __1__

If students have difficulty with exercise E, remind them to compare the digits beginning on the left. In number 1, we know that 289 is less than 2☐3, so the digit in the blank must be greater than 8. The only choice is 9.

31

REVIEWING MONEY

 How much money?

1.   _____35_____ cents

2.  _____27_____ cents

 Complete the charts.

1.

	Dimes	Pennies	Cents
a.	5	9	59¢
b.	3	7	37¢
c.	9	0	90¢
d.	8	3	83¢
e.	6	5	65¢

2.

	Tens	Ones	Expanded Name	Standard Name
a.	5	9	50 + 9	59
b.	4	6	40 + 6	46
c.	7	3	70 + 3	73
d.	8	8	80 + 8	88
e.	6	0	60 + 0	60

 Study the example. Find the sums.

	Had This Much	Got This Much More	How Much Now
1.			32¢ + 25¢ 57¢
2.			53¢ + 34¢ 87¢
3.			16¢ + 42¢ 58¢
4.			50¢ + 17¢ 67¢

Students who have difficulty with exercise C may need each of these situations illustrated using models of money.

2-DIGIT ADDITION—NO RENAMING

 A Complete each sentence.

1. 48 = 4 tens, ___8___ ones = 40 + ___8___

2. 53 = ___5___ tens, ___3___ ones = ___50___ + 3

B Find the sums. Look for a pattern.

1.
```
  7    70
+ 2  + 20
───  ────
  9    90
```

2.
```
  4    40
+ 3  + 30
───  ────
  7    70
```

3.
```
 5 ones    5 tens
+ 3 ones  + 3 tens
────────  ────────
 8 ones    8 tens
```

Three Ways To Add 62 and 25

Expanded Name I
```
  62 = 6 tens, 2 ones
+ 25 = 2 tens, 5 ones
       8 tens, 7 ones = 87
```
First: Add the ones.
Second: Add the tens.
  Write the standard name for the sum.

Expanded Name II
```
  62 = 60 + 2
+ 25 = 20 + 5
       80 + 7 = 87
```
First: Add the ones.
Second: Add the tens.
  Write the standard name for the sum.

Short Form
```
  62
+ 25
────
  87
```
First: Add the ones.
Second: Add the tens.

C Find the sums.

1.
```
  37 =  3  tens,  7  ones
+ 42 =  4  tens,  2  ones
         7  tens,  9  ones = 79
```

2.
```
  33 =  30  +  3
+ 60 =  60  +  0
         90  +  3  = 93
```

D Use the short form to find the sums. Remember: Add the ones first, and then add the tens.

1.
```
  83     77     63     42     36     15
+ 16   + 21   + 14   +  4   + 32   + 32
────   ────   ────   ────   ────   ────
  99     98     77     46     68     47
```

2.
```
  21     50     33     18     45     72
+ 43   + 39   + 46   + 50   + 44   + 15
────   ────   ────   ────   ────   ────
  64     89     79     68     89     87
```

2-DIGIT ADDITION WITH RENAMING

 A Complete the tables.

1. Rename 10 ones as 1 ten.

	Tens	Ones	Tens	Ones
a.	0	13 →	1	3
b.	3	15 →	4	5
c.	4	10 →	5	0
d.	0	18 →	1	8
e.	2	12 →	3	2

2. Rename 10 tens as 1 hundred.

	Hundreds	Tens	Hundreds	Tens
a.	0	12 →	1	2
b.	3	17 →	4	7
c.	0	14 →	1	4
d.	1	11 →	2	1
e.	5	16 →	6	6

B Find the sums.

1.
$$6 \text{ tens} = 60$$
$$+ 5 \text{ tens} = 50$$
$$\underline{11} \text{ tens} = \underline{110}$$

$$9 \text{ tens} = 90$$
$$+ 5 \text{ tens} = 50$$
$$\underline{14} \text{ tens} = \underline{140}$$

2.
$$35 = 30 + 5$$
$$+ 27 = 20 + 7$$
$$\underline{50} + \underline{12} = \underline{62}$$

$$78 = 70 + 8$$
$$+ 19 = 10 + 9$$
$$\underline{80} + \underline{17} = \underline{97}$$

3.
$$72 = 70 + 2$$
$$+ 94 = 90 + 4$$
$$\underline{160} + \underline{6} = \underline{166}$$

$$31 = 30 + 1$$
$$+ 85 = 80 + 5$$
$$\underline{110} + \underline{6} = \underline{116}$$

4.
$$58 = 50 + 8$$
$$+ 83 = 80 + 3$$
$$\underline{130} + \underline{11} = \underline{141}$$

$$67 = 60 + 7$$
$$+ 73 = 70 + 3$$
$$\underline{130} + \underline{10} = \underline{140}$$

Two Ways To Add 67 and 45

Expanded Name

$$67 = 60 + 7$$
$$+ 45 = 40 + 5$$
$$100 + 12 = 112$$

First: Add the ones.
Second: Add the tens.
  Write the standard
  name for the sum.

Short Form

$$\overset{1}{6}7$$
$$+ 45$$
$$112$$

First: Add the ones. $7 + 5 = 12$. Rename
12 ones as 1 ten and 2 ones.
Write 2 in the ones' column in the sum.
Write 1 in the tens' column above the 6.
  Second: Add the tens. $1 + 6 + 4 = 11$.
  Write 11 tens in the sum.

C Draw a ring around each addition in which 10 ones must be renamed as 1 ten.

⟨16 + 26⟩   ⟨35 + 48⟩   93 + 74   59 + 60   ⟨47 + 4⟩   ⟨39 + 21⟩   53 + 56   ⟨75 + 96⟩   62 + 6

D Complete the additions using the short form.

1.
$\overset{1}{7}5$	63	$\overset{1}{4}6$	$\overset{1}{3}2$	91	$\overset{1}{8}9$	$\overset{1}{\;}6$
+ 15	+ 75	+ 26	+ 8	+ 76	+ 34	+ 98
90	138	72	40	167	123	104

2.
58	28	54	30	86	47	65
+ 61	+ 46	+ 58	+ 99	+ 7	+ 53	+ 97
119	74	112	129	93	100	162

Treat the problems in exercise E orally. Have students discuss why each answer is correct.

E Answer each of these questions.

1. Bill said the sum of $40 + 13$ is 413. Jack said it is 4,013. What is it?   53

2. Sally said you rename 13 ones as 1 ten and 3 ones in the addition $65 + 8$. Sue said you don't. Who is right?   Sally

3. Emilio said the sum of $37 + 43$ is 70. Candida said it is 80. Who is right?   Candida

COLUMN ADDITION

 A Complete the sentences to find the sum.

Adding Down

Adding Up

Start ⟶ **a.** $8 + 3 =$ | 11 | 8

b. $11 + 5 =$ | 16 | 3

c. $16 + 7 =$ | 23 | 5

| + 7 |

23

c. $15 + 8 =$ | 23 | 8

b. $12 + 3 =$ | 15 | 3

Start ⟶ **a.** $7 + 5 =$ | 12 | 5

| + 7 |

Write the sum in the box. ⟶ 23

Have students complete exercise B.

B Find the sums by adding **up** the columns. Check your work by adding **down**.

3	5	6	4	2	5	6	7	5
8	7	3	7	6	5	2	8	2
9	4	8	9	5	8	4	1	3
+ 2	+ 4	+ 1	+ 3	+ 4	+ 5	+ 9	+ 6	+ 8
22	20	18	23	17	23	21	22	18

Discuss the example showing how to add a column of 2-digit numbers. Emphasize adding the ones first, then the tens.

Adding a Column of 2-Digit Numbers

```
  2
 64
 35
 27
+58
───
184
```

First: Add the ones. $4 + 5 + 7 + 8 = 24$. Rename 24 as 2 tens and 4 ones. Write 2 in the tens' column above the 6. Write 4 in the ones' column in the sum.

Second: Add the tens. $2 + 6 + 3 + 2 + 5 = 18$. Write 18 tens.

Have students complete exercise C.

C Find the sums.

35	25	63	68	44	36	34	62
22	41	84	47	21	45	34	84
36	57	27	13	69	84	34	84
+ 14	+ 32	+ 35	+ 27	+ 78	+ 27	+ 34	+ 62
107	155	209	155	212	192	136	292

Students having difficulty with any of these exercises should have additional work as indicated: exercise B, activity 1; exercise C, activity 2 or with counters. More practice adding columns of numbers can be found in chapter 13, pages 275 and 276.

ESTIMATING ANSWERS

 Brenda sees 3 items she needs to buy that cost 39¢, 27¢, and 21¢. She estimates how much she will need to pay. First she rounds the cost of each item to the nearest ten. Then she adds.

Cost	Estimate
39¢	40¢
27¢	30¢
+ 21¢	+ 20¢

Actual Cost	87¢	Estimated Cost	90¢

Tell students that the rest of the exercises on the page refer to these pictures of canned goods and their prices.

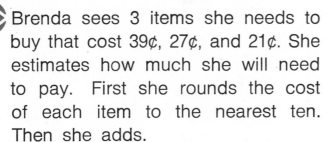

43¢	42¢	49¢	62¢	36¢	43¢

Have students complete exercise B, check their work, and correct any mistakes.

 Round the cost of each item to the nearest ten.

    40¢   40¢   50¢

    60¢   40¢   40¢

Discuss number 1. Teach students to use the rounded cost of each item from exercise B to arrive at the answer.

 Estimate the cost of each set of canned goods.   Do not write the addition.

1.   90¢   2.   80¢

3.   100¢   4.   100¢

5.   130¢   6.   140¢

7.   140¢   8.   130¢

Tell students to use the rounded costs from exercise B to arrive at the answer.

 Draw a ring around the sets of canned goods that cost less than a dollar.

1.   2.

3.   4.

DOLLARS, DIMES, AND PENNIES

 A How much money?

1.

212¢

2.

345¢

B Complete the charts.

1.

	Dollars	Dimes	Pennies	Cents
a.	5	7	3	573¢
b.	2	6	5	265¢
c.	1	0	6	106¢
d.	3	4	2	342¢
e.	1	7	0	170¢

2.

	Hundreds	Tens	Ones	Expanded Name	Standard Name
a.	5	7	3	500 + 70 + 3	573
b.	2	4	3	200 + 40 + 3	243
c.	5	4	9	500 + 40 + 9	549
d.	3	8	7	300 + 80 + 7	387
e.	2	0	4	200 + 4	204

C Study the example. Find the sums.

Had This Much	Got This Much More	How Much Now
1.		113¢ + 230¢ 343¢
2.		430¢ + 145¢ 575¢
3.		540¢ + 207¢ 747¢
4.		134¢ + 342¢ 476¢

Group students having difficulty with exercise C and illustrate each of the addition situations with models of money.

3-DIGIT ADDITION—NO RENAMING

 Find the sums. Look for a pattern.

1.
```
    6        6 tens        6 hundreds
  + 3      + 3 tens      + 3 hundreds
  ─────    ─────────     ────────────
    9        9 tens        9 hundreds
```

2.
```
    6        60           600
  + 3      + 30         + 300
  ───      ────         ─────
    9        90           900
```

3.
```
    4        4 tens        4 hundreds
  + 2      + 2 tens      + 2 hundreds
  ─────    ─────────     ────────────
    6        6 tens        6 hundreds
```

4.
```
    4        40           400
  + 2      + 20         + 200
  ───      ────         ─────
    6        60           600
```

Two Ways To Add 621 + 347

Expanded Name

$$621 = 600 + 20 + 1$$
$$+\ 347 = 300 + 40 + 7$$
$$900 + 60 + 8 = 968$$

First: Add the ones.
Second: Add the tens.
Third: Add the hundreds.
  Write the standard name
  for the sum.

Short Form

```
  621    First: Add the ones.
+ 347    Second: Add the tens.
─────
  968    Third: Add the hundreds.
```

 Find the sums using expanded names.

1.
```
  324 = 300 + 20 + 4
+ 163 = 100 + 60 + 3
─────────────────────
        400 + 80 + 7 = 487
```

2.
```
  284 = 200 + 80 + 4
+ 414 = 400 + 10 + 4
─────────────────────
        600 + 90 + 8 = 698
```

3.
```
  165 = 100 + 60 + 5
+ 713 = 700 + 10 + 3
─────────────────────
        800 + 70 + 8 = 878
```

4.
```
  240 = 200 + 40 + 0
+ 109 = 100 +  0 + 9
─────────────────────
        300 + 40 + 9 = 349
```

 Use the short form to find the sums. Remember: Add the ones first, add the tens second, and add the hundreds third.

```
   165      380      427      661      253      546      409
 + 224    + 416    + 152    + 307    + 313    + 341    + 180
 ─────    ─────    ─────    ─────    ─────    ─────    ─────
   389      796      579      968      566      887      589
```

Students having difficulty with these exercises should have more experience adding with counters or with felt models of money. **39**

3-DIGIT ADDITION WITH RENAMING

 A Complete the tables.

1. Rename 10 ones as 1 ten.

	Tens	Ones	Tens	Ones
a.	2	17 →	3	7
b.	0	10 →	1	0
c.	2	15 →	3	5
d.	1	12 →	2	2

2. Rename 10 tens as 1 hundred.

	Hundreds	Tens	Hundreds	Tens
a.	4	11 →	5	1
b.	3	14 →	4	4
c.	0	16 →	1	6
d.	1	13 →	2	3

3. Rename 10 ones as 1 ten. Then rename 10 tens as 1 hundred.

	Hundreds	Tens	Ones	Hundreds	Tens	Ones	Hundreds	Tens	Ones
a.	3	12	13 →	3	13	3 →	4	3	3
b.	2	15	11 →	2	16	1 →	3	6	1
c.	0	14	17 →	0	15	7 →	1	5	7
d.	1	13	10 →	1	14	0 →	2	4	0

B Find the sums.

1.
$$135 = 100 + 30 + 5$$
$$+ 247 = 200 + 40 + 7$$
$$300 + 70 + 12 = 382$$

2.
$$329 = 300 + 20 + 9$$
$$+ 426 = 400 + 20 + 6$$
$$700 + 40 + 15 = 755$$

3.
$$218 = 200 + 10 + 8$$
$$+ 755 = 700 + 50 + 5$$
$$900 + 60 + 13 = 973$$

4.
$$243 = 200 + 40 + 3$$
$$+ 475 = 400 + 70 + 5$$
$$600 + 110 + 8 = 718$$

5.
$$697 = 600 + 90 + 7$$
$$+ 152 = 100 + 50 + 2$$
$$700 + 140 + 9 = 849$$

6.
$$371 = 300 + 70 + 1$$
$$+ 286 = 200 + 80 + 6$$
$$500 + 150 + 7 = 657$$

Discuss the example showing two ways to add 476 + 295. By questioning, bring out that renaming is necessary when the sum of the ones or the tens is 10 or more. Then have students complete the page.

Two Ways To Add 476 + 295

Expanded Form

$$476 = 400 + 70 + 6$$
$$+ 295 = 200 + 90 + 5$$
$$600 + 160 + 11 = 771$$

First: Add the ones.
Second: Add the tens.
Third: Add the hundreds.
  Write the standard name for the sum.

Short Form

```
  1 1
  476
+ 295
  771
```

First: Add the ones.
  6 + 5 = 11. Rename 11 ones as 1 ten, 1 one. Write 1 in the sum. Write 1 in the tens' column above the 7.
Second: Add the tens.
  1 + 7 + 9 = 17. Rename 17 tens as 1 hundred, 7 tens. Write 7 in the sum. Write 1 in the hundreds' column above the 4.
Third: Add the hundreds.
  1 + 4 + 2 = 7. Write 7 in the sum.

C Ring each addition in which 10 ones must be renamed as 1 ten.

421	(438)	492	(379)	(406)	586	287
+ 263	+ 328	+ 163	+ 118	+ 176	+ 412	+ 562

D Ring each addition in which 10 tens must be renamed as 1 hundred.

(563)	257	(482)	(790)	246	(126)	328
+ 281	+ 418	+ 272	+ 150	+ 321	+ 480	+ 309

 Ring each addition in which 10 ones must be renamed as 1 ten and 10 tens must be renamed as 1 hundred.

395	(532)	536	(675)	(468)	(208)	239
+ 471	+ 278	+ 159	+ 139	+ 254	+ 197	+ 217

F Find the sums using the short form.

219	144	395	286	350	638	479
+ 247	+ 473	+ 405	+ 539	+ 490	+ 259	+ 96
466	617	800	825	840	897	575

Additional practice in adding 3-digit numbers can be found in chapter 13, page 275.

PROBLEM SOLVING

Gary and Tomás collect baseball trading cards. Gary has 75 cards. Tomás has 48 cards. How many cards do they have together?

1. What must be found? <u>The number of cards the boys have together.</u>

2. What facts are given? <u>Gary has 75 cards. Tomás has 48 cards.</u>

3. What operation can be used to solve the problem? <u>Addition</u>

4. Solve the problem.   75   or 75 + 48 = 123
$$\begin{array}{r} 75 \\ + 48 \\ \hline 123 \end{array}$$

5. What is the solution? <u>123 cards</u>

6. State the solution in a complete sentence. <u>Gary and Tomás have</u>

   <u>123 cards.</u>

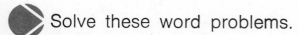 Solve these word problems.

1. A ship increased its cargo at a port by loading a lion and a tiger. The lion weighed 430 pounds and the tiger weighed 350 pounds. How much was the ship's weight increased? <u>780</u> pounds

2. Valentina identified 17 types of leaves, and George identified 16 different types of leaves. How many types of leaves did they identify together? <u>33</u> types

3. Rita is 9 years old. Her teacher is 18 years older than Rita. How old is Rita's teacher? <u>27</u> years old

4. Sandra swims laps each day. On Thursday she swam 27 laps, and on Friday she swam 35 laps. How many laps did she swim altogether?

   <u>62</u> laps

ROMAN NUMERALS

The ancient Romans used letters to name numbers. Study the chart which shows the symbols the Romans used to name numbers.

Roman Numeral	Standard Name
I	1
V	5
X	10
L	50
C	100

1. What symbol did the Romans use to name 5? __V__ 100? __C__

2. What is the value for the symbol I? __1__ X? __10__ L? __50__

> To find the value of a roman numeral, add the values of its letters.
> CCLXXVI = C + C + L + X + X + V + I
> = 100 + 100 + 50 + 10 + 10 + 5 + 1 = 276

A Write the value of each roman numeral. Use the chart to help you.

1. XXV means 10 + __10__ + 5 = __25__

2. LXI means 50 + __10__ + __1__ = __61__

3. CCCLX means 100 + __100__ + __100__ + 50 + __10__ = __360__

> To find the roman numeral for 21, think: 21 = 2 tens, 1 one, or 21 = 10 + 10 + 1. The roman numeral for 10 + 10 + 1 is XXI.

B Complete the chart.

	Standard Name	100s	50s	10s	5s	1s	Roman Numeral
1.	21	—	—	2	—	1	XXI
2.	215	2	—	1	1	—	CCXV
3.	18	—	—	1	1	3	XVIII
4.	57	—	1	—	1	2	LVII

CHAPTER REVIEW

 A Use the number line to help you find the addition facts.

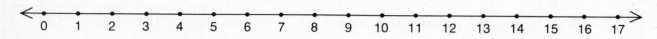

$7 + 5 =$ ___12___ $6 + 9 =$ ___15___ $4 + 6 =$ ___10___ $8 + 8 =$ ___16___

B Complete these sentences.

1. If $7 + 9 = 16$, then $9 + 7 =$ ___16___ .

2. $7 + (5 + 6) =$ ___18___ .

3. If $(6 + 9) + 8 = 23$, then $6 + (9 + 8) =$ ___23___ .

C Find the sums.

1.
$$\begin{array}{r} 45 \\ + 24 \\ \hline 69 \end{array} \qquad \begin{array}{r} 31 \\ + 56 \\ \hline 87 \end{array} \qquad \begin{array}{r} 47 \\ + 28 \\ \hline 75 \end{array} \qquad \begin{array}{r} 56 \\ + 72 \\ \hline 128 \end{array} \qquad \begin{array}{r} 85 \\ + 49 \\ \hline 134 \end{array}$$

2.
$$\begin{array}{r} 45 \\ 21 \\ + 30 \\ \hline 96 \end{array} \qquad \begin{array}{r} 52 \\ 64 \\ + 31 \\ \hline 147 \end{array} \qquad \begin{array}{r} 14 \\ 48 \\ + 15 \\ \hline 77 \end{array} \qquad \begin{array}{r} 153 \\ + 298 \\ \hline 451 \end{array} \qquad \begin{array}{r} 467 \\ + 43 \\ \hline 510 \end{array}$$

D Solve these problems.

1. John has 90¢. Does he have enough money to buy a 39¢ pen and a 46¢ pad of paper? ___yes___

2. Sally has 75¢. Jane has 39¢ more than Sally. How much money does Jane have? ___114¢___

3. The Cohen theater sold 137 tickets on Monday night and 158 tickets on Tuesday night. How many tickets were sold altogether?

___295___ tickets

CHECK-UP

 A Find the sums for these addition facts.

1. $2 + 5 =$ ___7___ $4 + 9 =$ ___13___ $8 + 1 =$ ___9___

2. $7 + 8 =$ ___15___ $3 + 8 =$ ___11___ $6 + 2 =$ ___8___

3. $7 + 7 =$ ___14___ $9 + 5 =$ ___14___ $6 + 8 =$ ___14___

 B Complete these sentences.

1. If $8 + 9 = 17$, then $9 + 8 =$ ___17___.

2. $6 + (5 + 9) =$ ___20___.

3. If $8 + (7 + 6) = 21$, then $(8 + 7) + 6 =$ ___21___.

 C Find the sums.

1.
```
  27        48        72        85        14
+ 51      + 43      + 63      + 49        37
----      ----      ----      ----      + 48
  78        91       135       134      ----
                                          99
```

2.
```
  126       142       365       186        64
+ 702     + 284     + 115     + 297        35
-----     -----     -----     -----      + 24
  828       426       480       483      ----
                                          123
```

D Solve these problems.

1. Dalia's mother is 23 years older than Dalia. Dalia is 9 years old. How old is her mother? ___32___ years old

2. The Sinquah family drove 325 miles on the first day of their vacation and 265 miles on the second day. How far did they drive altogether?

   ___590___ miles

3. Rodolfo has 4 dimes and 17 pennies. How much money does he have? ___57___ ¢

45

Discuss the example. Have students complete the exercises.

3 • SUBTRACTION

UNDERSTANDING SUBTRACTION

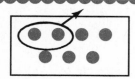 We think: 7 take away 2 equals 5.
We write the subtraction sentence,
7 − 2 = 5.

A Write the subtraction sentence for each picture.

1.   **2.**   **3.**   **4.**

10 − 3 = __7__   __6__ − __2__ = 4   __7__ − __4__ = 3   __9__ − __8__ = __1__

B Draw dots. Circle the dots and use arrows to show the subtractions.

1. 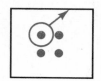 **2.**   **3.**   **4.**

4 − 1 = __3__   10 − 2 = __8__   6 − 3 = __3__   5 − 4 = __1__

C Circle and use arrows to show how many were taken away. Then write the subtraction sentence.

1. Sheila had 5 marbles. She lost 2 of them. How many marbles does she have left?

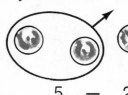

5 − 2 = 3

2. Margarita had 6 dimes. She spent 4 of them. How many dimes does she have left?

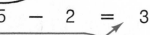

6 − 4 = 2

3. Ming had 8 raisins. He ate 3 raisins. How many raisins does he have left?

8 − 3 = 5

Students having difficulty with any of these exercises should repeat activities 1 and 2.

SUBTRACTION ON THE NUMBER LINE

Find 7 — 4 on the number line.
First: Start at 7.
Second: Count 4 spaces to the left.
The difference is 3.

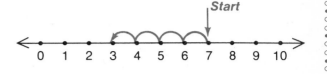

A Fill the blanks to subtract 9 — 3 on the number line.

1. **First:** Start at ___9___. (Draw an arrow pointing to the starting number.)

2. **Second:** Hop ___3___ spaces to the left. (Use an arrow to show this.)

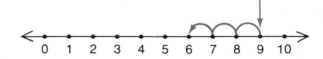

As students complete this exercise, check to make sure that they draw one arrow to 9 and another arrow which shows counting 3 spaces to the left.

3. **Third:** The difference is ___6___.

B Complete the sentence for each subtraction shown on the number line.

1. 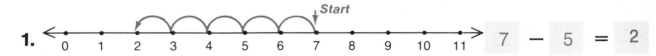 7 — 5 = 2

2.  6 — 2 = 4

3.  10 — 6 = 4

4. 11 — 4 = 7

5. 9 — 5 = 4

6.  8 — 5 = 3

7.  11 — 9 = 2

Have students complete exercise B. Stress that the starting point is the minuend, the number of spaces moved to the left is the subtrahend, and the stopping point is the difference.

47

C Subtract the following. Use the number line to help.

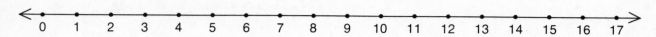

```
  0   1   2   3   4   5   6   7   8   9   10  11  12  13  14  15  16  17
```

1. $5 - 3 = \underline{2}$ $7 - 2 = \underline{5}$ $4 - 1 = \underline{3}$ $8 - 4 = \underline{4}$

2. $10 - 5 = \underline{5}$ $6 - 5 = \underline{1}$ $11 - 5 = \underline{6}$ $13 - 4 = \underline{9}$

Two Ways To Write Subtractions

$11 - 8 = 3$

Difference

Subtrahend

Minuend

$11 \longleftarrow$ Minuend

$- 8 \longleftarrow$ Subtrahend

$3 \longleftarrow$ Difference

D Complete the chart.

	Sentence	Minuend	Subtrahend	Difference
1.	$9 - 7 = 2$	9	7	2
2.	$12 - 8 = 4$	12	8	4
3.	$13 - 5 = 8$	13	5	8
4.	$10 - 9 = 1$	10	9	1

E 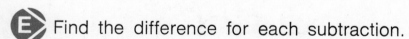 Find the difference for each subtraction.

1.
```
  7      9      5      8      6     10      4
 -4     -3     -1     -2     -6     -7     -2
 ---    ---    ---    ---    ---    ---    ---
  3      6      4      6      0      3      2
```

2.
```
 14     11     10     12     17     16     13
 -9     -7     -3     -5     -9     -7     -6
 ---    ---    ---    ---    ---    ---    ---
  5      4      7      7      8      9      7
```

After students have completed the exercises, review the ways in which subtractions are written and the names for the terms in a subtraction. Ask: Which is larger, the minuend or the subtrahend? The difference or the minuend? The difference or the subtrahend?

ADDITION AND SUBTRACTION

 Answer these questions.

1. How many blue squares? _____9_____

2. How many white squares? _____2_____

3. How many gray squares? _____7_____

The row of white squares and gray squares is as long as the row of blue squares.   The picture shows the addition sentences 2 + 7 = 9 and 7 + 2 = 9.   The picture also shows the subtraction sentences 9 − 2 = 7 and 9 − 7 = 2.

 Complete the sentences for each picture.

Addition Sentences		Subtraction Sentences

1. 4 + 3 = ___7___

3 + 4 = ___7___

7 − 3 = ___3___

7 − 4 = ___4___

2. 9 + 2 = ___11___

___2___ + ___9___ = ___11___

11 − 9 = ___2___

___11___ − ___2___ = ___9___

3. ___4___ + ___5___ = ___9___

___5___ + ___4___ = ___9___

___9___ − ___4___ = ___5___

___9___ − ___5___ = ___4___

4. ___1___ + ___5___ = ___6___

___5___ + ___1___ = ___6___

___6___ − ___1___ = ___5___

___6___ − ___5___ = ___1___

5. ___7___ + ___3___ = ___10___

___3___ + ___7___ = ___10___

10 − 7 = ___3___

10 − 3 = ___7___

6. ___3___ + ___5___ = ___8___

___5___ + ___3___ = ___8___

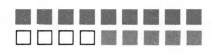

8 − 3 = ___5___

8 − 5 = ___3___

C Complete the table.

	Addition Facts		Subtraction Facts	
1.	$7 + 9 = 16$	$9 + 7 = 16$	$16 - 9 = 7$	$16 - 7 = 9$
2.	$4 + 5 = 9$	$5 + 4 = 9$	$9 - 5 = 4$	$9 - 4 = 5$
3.	$3 + 8 = 11$	$8 + 3 = 11$	$11 - 8 = 3$	$11 - 3 = 8$
4.	$9 + 5 = 14$	$5 + 9 = 14$	$14 - 5 = 9$	$14 - 9 = 5$
5.	$7 + 5 = 12$	$5 + 7 = 12$	$12 - 5 = 7$	$12 - 7 = 5$
6.	$6 + 7 = 13$	$7 + 6 = 13$	$13 - 7 = 6$	$13 - 6 = 7$

D Write all the addition and subtraction facts for each picture.

1.

$$\begin{array}{r} 8 \\ + 5 \\ \hline 13 \end{array} \quad \begin{array}{r} 5 \\ + 8 \\ \hline 13 \end{array} \quad \begin{array}{r} 13 \\ - 5 \\ \hline 8 \end{array} \quad \begin{array}{r} 13 \\ - 8 \\ \hline 5 \end{array}$$

2.

$$\begin{array}{r} 7 \\ + 7 \\ \hline 14 \end{array} \quad \begin{array}{r} 14 \\ - 7 \\ \hline 7 \end{array}$$

3.

$$\begin{array}{r} 6 \\ + 9 \\ \hline 15 \end{array} \quad \begin{array}{r} 9 \\ + 6 \\ \hline 15 \end{array} \quad \begin{array}{r} 15 \\ - 9 \\ \hline 6 \end{array} \quad \begin{array}{r} 15 \\ - 6 \\ \hline 9 \end{array}$$

4.

$$\begin{array}{r} 5 \\ + 5 \\ \hline 10 \end{array} \quad \begin{array}{r} 10 \\ - 5 \\ \hline 5 \end{array}$$

5.

$$\begin{array}{r} 7 \\ + 5 \\ \hline 12 \end{array} \quad \begin{array}{r} 5 \\ + 7 \\ \hline 12 \end{array} \quad \begin{array}{r} 12 \\ - 5 \\ \hline 7 \end{array} \quad \begin{array}{r} 12 \\ - 7 \\ \hline 5 \end{array}$$

6.

$$\begin{array}{r} 8 \\ + 8 \\ \hline 16 \end{array} \quad \begin{array}{r} 16 \\ - 8 \\ \hline 8 \end{array}$$

E Draw dots to show these facts.

1.

$$\begin{array}{r} 11 \\ - 8 \\ \hline 3 \end{array}$$

2.

$$\begin{array}{r} 9 \\ - 2 \\ \hline 7 \end{array}$$

3.

$$\begin{array}{r} 12 \\ - 6 \\ \hline 6 \end{array}$$

4.

$$\begin{array}{r} 13 \\ - 9 \\ \hline 4 \end{array}$$

5.

$$\begin{array}{r} 10 \\ - 7 \\ \hline 3 \end{array}$$

6.

$$\begin{array}{r} 14 \\ - 6 \\ \hline 8 \end{array}$$

If any students have continued difficulty in completing these exercises, group them and perform the additional activity.

SUBTRACTION FACTS

A Use the number line to help you find the differences.

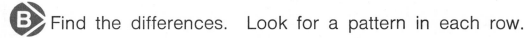

8	9	10	11	12	13	14	15	16	17
−8	−8	−8	−8	−8	−8	−8	−8	−8	−8
0	1	2	3	4	5	6	7	8	9

B Find the differences. Look for a pattern in each row.

1.
0	1	2	3	4	5	6	7	8	9
−0	−0	−0	−0	−0	−0	−0	−0	−0	−0
0	1	2	3	4	5	6	7	8	9

2.
4	5	6	7	8	9	10	11	12	13
−4	−4	−4	−4	−4	−4	−4	−4	−4	−4
0	1	2	3	4	5	6	7	8	9

3.
7	8	9	10	11	12	13	14	15	16
−7	−7	−7	−7	−7	−7	−7	−7	−7	−7
0	1	2	3	4	5	6	7	8	9

C Subtraction facts may be shown in tables. Complete each table.

1.
−	8	6	3	4	9	2	7	1	5
10	2	4	7	6	1	8	3	9	5

2.
−	6	8	9	7
15	9	7	6	8

3.
−	4	9	6	3	7	5	8
12	8	3	6	9	5	7	4

4.
−	9	6	7	5	8
14	5	8	7	9	6

5.
−	3	8	9	2	5	7	4	6
11	8	3	2	9	6	4	7	5

6.
−	6	4	8	9	7	5
13	7	9	5	4	6	8

1.

6	10	7	4	11	13	15	14	7	5
-3	-9	-2	-4	-6	-6	-9	-5	-4	-3
3	1	5	0	5	7	6	9	3	2

2.

10	13	16	13	9	8	14	9	12	9
-3	-9	-9	-8	-8	-3	-7	-7	-6	-6
7	4	7	5	1	5	7	2	6	3

3.

12	16	4	5	6	7	12	17	12	14
-7	-7	-2	-1	-2	-5	-3	-8	-8	-8
5	9	2	4	4	2	9	9	4	6

4.

10	7	9	8	10	13	15	11	18	8
-1	-6	-4	-2	-6	-7	-6	-4	-9	-8
9	1	5	6	4	6	9	7	9	0

E Complete each square by subtracting each row and each column.

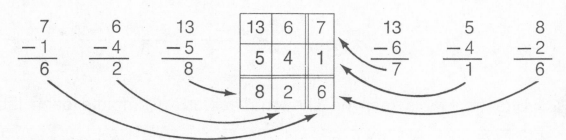

1.

17	9	8
8	7	1
9	2	7

2.

14	7	7
5	2	3
9	5	4

3.

11	5	6
6	2	4
5	3	2

4.

16	9	7
8	5	3
8	4	4

5.

12	3	9
7	1	6
5	2	3

6.

13	7	6
5	3	2
8	4	4

If students have difficulty in exercise E, explain the six subtractions for each square—across rows, down columns, and the differences of the rows and columns. Additional practice on the subtraction facts can be found in chapter 13, page 277.

PROBLEM SOLVING

 A Translate these phrases and subtract.

Words That Mean To Subtract

	Phrase	Subtraction	Difference
1.	9 less 5	9 − 5	4
2.	7 subtracted from 13	13 − 7	6
3.	12 take away 3	12 − 3	9
4.	8 decreased by 4	8 − 4	4
5.	The difference of 15 and 8	15 − 8	7
6.	16 subtract 9	16 − 9	7

Work the first problem in exercise B with the students. Use questioning to guide students through the problem-solving procedure.

B For each problem, underline the words that tell you to subtract. Then solve each word problem.

1. Courtney had twelve seashells. Kelly took away 7 of them. How many seashells did Courtney have left? __5__ seashells

2. Diego had 11 pages left to read in a book. He decreased this by 3 pages. How many pages did he have left to read? __8__ pages

3. Juanita has 15 butterflies in her collection. Timoteo has 9 butterflies. What is the difference in the number of butterflies in their collections?

__6__ butterflies

4. Trina and Heather had a contest doing pull-ups. Trina did 6 less pull-ups than Heather. Heather did 11 pull-ups. How many pull-ups did Trina do? __5__ pull-ups

5. Bob subtracted 5 from his present age of 10 years. How old was Bob 5 years ago? __5__ years

2-DIGIT SUBTRACTION—NO RENAMING

 Complete each sentence.

1. 57 = __5__ tens, __7__ ones = __50__ + __7__

2. 79 = __7__ tens, __9__ ones = __70__ + __9__

3. 32 = __3__ tens, __2__ ones = __30__ + __2__

B **Find the differences. Look for a pattern.**

1.	3 ones	3 tens	**2.**	6 ones	6 tens	**3.**	9	90
	− 2 ones	− 2 tens		− 3 ones	− 3 tens		− 4	− 40
							5	50
	__1__ one	__1__ ten		__3__ ones	__3__ tens			

Three Ways To Subtract 67 − 42

Expanded Name I

67 = 6 tens, 7 ones
−42 = 4 tens, 2 ones
    2 tens, 5 ones = 25
First: Subtract the ones.
Second: Subtract the tens.
  Write the standard name.

Expanded Name II

67 = 60 + 7
−42 = 40 + 2
    20 + 5 = 25
First: Subtract the ones.
Second: Subtract the tens.
  Write the standard name.

Short Form

  67
 −42
  25
First: Subtract
  the ones.
Second: Subtract
  the tens.

C **Find the differences.**

1.   39 = 3 tens, 9 ones
     − 12 = 1 ten, 2 ones

         __2__ tens, __7__ ones = __27__

2.   83 = 80 + 3
     − 70 = 70 + 0

         __10__ + __3__ = __13__

D **Use the short form to find the differences. Remember: Subtract the ones first. Then subtract the tens.**

78	45	65	89	46	53	39	68
−52	−24	−21	−54	−41	−30	−16	−33
26	21	44	35	5	23	23	35

Students who have difficulty with exercises C or D should complete the additional activity. More practice exercises can be found in chapter 13, page 278.

RENAMING TENS AS ONES

Tanya had

She exchanged for

Tanya then had

 Complete each sentence. Rename 1 ten as 10 ones.

1.   

   __2__ dimes, __2__ pennies = __1__ dime, __12__ pennies

2.   

   __3__ dimes, __0__ pennies = __2__ dimes, __10__ pennies

 Complete this chart. Exchange 1 dime for 10 pennies.

2 dimes, 1 penny		__1__ dime, __11__ pennies
3 dimes, 0 pennies	**Exchange 1 dime for 10 pennies**	__2__ dimes, __10__ pennies
5 dimes, 6 pennies		__4__ dimes, __16__ pennies

If students have difficulty with exercise A or B, they should have additional experience with activity 2.

C Complete each sentence by renaming 1 ten as 10 ones.

1. 3 tens, 5 ones = __2__ tens, __15__ ones. $30 + 5 = \underline{20} + \underline{15}$.

2. 5 tens, 0 ones = __4__ tens, __10__ ones. $50 + 0 = \underline{40} + \underline{10}$.

3. 9 tens, 3 ones = __8__ tens, __13__ ones. $90 + 3 = \underline{80} + \underline{13}$.

4. 1 ten, 4 ones = __0__ tens, __14__ ones. $10 + 4 = \underline{0} + \underline{14}$.

5. 2 tens, 1 one = __1__ ten, __11__ ones. $20 + 1 = \underline{10} + \underline{11}$.

6. 6 tens, 6 ones = __5__ tens, __16__ ones. $60 + 6 = \underline{50} + \underline{16}$.

SUBTRACTION—RENAMING TENS AS ONES

 Fill the blanks.

Not enough ones to subtract from.   Subtract ones first, then tens.

$$72 = 70 + \boxed{2}$$
$$-18 = 10 + \boxed{8}$$

Rename 1 ten as ten ones. ➡

$$72 = \boxed{60} + \boxed{12}$$
$$-18 = \underline{10} + \underline{8}$$

$$?$$

$$\underline{50} + \underline{4} = \underline{54}$$

 Subtract using expanded names. Fill the blanks and box.

$$34 = 30 + 4 = 20 + \boxed{14}$$
$$-16 = 10 + 6 = 10 + 6$$

$$\underline{10} + \underline{8} = \underline{18}$$

Discuss the example showing the short form to subtract. Explain that 43 must be renamed as 3 tens, 13 ones, and this is what is shown by crossing out 43 and writing above it.

Short Form To Subtract 43 — 19

Step 1	$\overset{3\ 13}{\cancel{43}}$ $-\ 19$	Look at the minuend. There are not enough ones to subtract from. Rename 1 ten as 10 ones. 43 = 3 tens, 13 ones.
Step 2	$\overset{3\ 13}{\cancel{43}}$ $-\ 19$ $\ \ \ \ 4$	Subtract ones. 13 ones — 9 ones = 4 ones. Write 4 in the difference.
Step 3	$\overset{3\ 13}{\cancel{43}}$ $-\ 19$ $\ \ 24$	Subtract tens. 3 tens — 1 ten = 2 tens. Write 2 in the difference.

 Find the differences. If there are not enough ones to subtract from, rename 1 ten as 10 ones.

51	76	34	42	85	53	72	77
− 24	− 48	− 15	− 23	− 47	− 25	− 43	− 38
27	28	19	19	38	28	29	39

CHECKING SUBTRACTION BY ADDITION

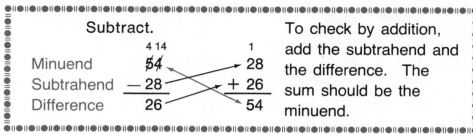

	Subtract.		To check by addition,
		4 14	1
Minuend		5̶4̶ → 28	add the subtrahend and the difference. The
Subtrahend	− 28 → + 26		sum should be the
Difference	26 → 54		minuend.

 Subtract. Check by addition.

1. 37 → 12
  − 12 → + 25
   25 → 37

2. 85   47
  − 47 + 38
   38   85

3. 71   25
  − 25 + 46
   46   71

4. 99   62
  − 62 + 37
   37   99

5. 64   56
  − 56 + 8
    8   64

6. 57   19
  − 19 + 38
   38   57

B Subtract and use the short check.

Short Check
  4 13
  5̶3̶
 − 38 ⎤
 + 15 ⎦ Add
  53

1. 98
  − 37 ⎤
  + 61 ⎦
   98

2. 63
  − 28 ⎤
  + 35 ⎦
   63

3. 47
  − 17 ⎤
  + 30 ⎦
   47

4. 34
  − 29 ⎤
  + 5 ⎦
   34

Students who have difficulty with exercise A or B should have more experience with the activity for this lesson.

C Solve these subtraction stories. Check each subtraction by addition.

1. Celia has 73 baseball trading cards. Glenn has 56 cards. How many more cards does Celia have than Glenn? __17__ cards

2. Gloria is 11 years old. Her father is 38 years old. What is the difference in their ages? __27__ years

3. Harry and John lifted weights. Harry lifted 47 pounds, and John lifted 38 pounds. How many more pounds did Harry lift? __9__ pounds

SUBTRACTING 1-DIGIT NUMBERS FROM 2-DIGIT NUMBERS

 A Study the first three subtractions in each row. Then complete the subtractions.

1.

9	19	29	39	49	59	69	79	89
−3	−3	−3	−3	−3	−3	−3	−3	−3
6	16	26	36	46	56	66	76	86

2.

15	1 15 25	2 15 35	45	55	65	75	85	95
−7	−7	−7	−7	−7	−7	−7	−7	−7
8	18	28	38	48	58	68	78	88

Discuss the example. Then have students complete exercises B and C.

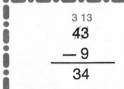

3 13 43	Step 1: Rename 1 ten as 10 ones.
−9	Step 2: Subtract the ones.
34	Step 3: Write the tens.

B Find the differences.

1.

27	34	69	56	48	19	75	38
−5	−1	−7	−6	−2	−4	−3	−7
22	33	62	50	46	15	72	31

2.

51	27	30	42	14	63	95	71
−8	−9	−4	−3	−8	−5	−7	−5
43	18	26	39	6	58	88	66

3.

47	35	27	84	69	52	70	19
−26	−8	−19	−4	−32	−7	−25	−15
21	27	8	80	37	45	45	4

C Subtract. Check by addition.

63	74	36	27	52	48	73	51
−47	−9	−18	−6	−4	−21	−69	−8
+16	+65	+18	+21	+48	+27	+4	+43
63	74	36	27	52	48	73	51

PROBLEM SOLVING

A Write *add* or *subtract* in the blank to tell what you must do to solve the problem.

1. What is left when 23 is taken from 39?   subtract

2. How much is 15 and 9?   add

3. How much is 17 plus 23?   add

4. How much larger is 35 than 8?   subtract

5. What is 35 increased by 17?   add

6. What is 35 decreased by 17?   subtract

7. 9 and how many more equal 32?   subtract

8. What is 53 minus 42?   subtract

B Solve these word problems.

1. Jim has 87 stamps in his collection. Linda has 59 stamps.

   a. How many stamps do they have together?   146   stamps

   b. Who has the most stamps?   Jim   How many more?

    28   stamps

2. Jim sold 8 of his 87 stamps. How many stamps does Jim have left?
   79   stamps

3. Linda bought 3 new stamps. The stamps cost 27¢, 45¢, and 21¢. How much did she pay for these 3 stamps?   93   ¢

4. Jim says 2 of his stamps together are worth 75¢. If one of them is worth 57¢, how much is the other stamp worth?   18   ¢

5. Linda went into a stamp shop and bought a stamp for 39¢. She gave the clerk 75¢. How much change should Linda get?   36   ¢

Students who have difficulty with these exercises should be grouped for teacher guidance in completing the problems.

59

3-DIGIT SUBTRACTION—NO RENAMING

Three Ways To Subtract 487 − 163

Expanded Name I

$$487 = 4 \text{ hundreds, } 8 \text{ tens, } 7 \text{ ones}$$
$$- 163 = 1 \text{ hundred, } 6 \text{ tens, } 3 \text{ ones}$$
$$\overline{3 \text{ hundreds, } 2 \text{ tens, } 4 \text{ ones}} = 324$$

First: Subtract the ones.
Second: Subtract the tens.
Third: Subtract the hundreds.
Write the standard name.

Expanded Name II

$$487 = 400 + 80 + 7$$
$$- 163 = 100 + 60 + 3$$
$$\overline{300 + 20 + 4} = 324$$

First: Subtract the ones.
Second: Subtract the tens.
Third: Subtract the hundreds.
Write the standard name.

Short Form

$$\begin{array}{r} 487 \\ - 163 \\ \hline 324 \end{array}$$

First: Subtract the ones.
Second: Subtract the tens.
Third: Subtract the hundreds.

A Find the differences.

1. $625 = 6$ hundreds, 2 tens, 5 ones
    $- 313 = 3$ hundreds, 1 ten, 3 ones

    <u>3</u> hundreds, <u>1</u> ten, <u>2</u> ones = <u>312</u>

2. $897 = 800 + 90 + 7$
    $- 251 = 200 + 50 + 1$

    <u>600</u> + <u>40</u> + <u>6</u> = <u>646</u>

B Use the short form to find the differences. Remember: Subtract the ones first. Subtract the tens second. Subtract the hundreds third.

1.

687	594	376	547	934	658
− 253	− 372	− 124	− 136	− 812	− 224
434	222	252	411	122	434

2.

846	417	463	842	142	963
− 313	− 114	− 322	− 312	− 120	− 132
533	303	141	530	22	831

RENAMING 1 HUNDRED AS 10 TENS

| 1 dollar   2 dimes | 0 dollars   12 dimes |

 A Complete the chart.   Exchange 1 dollar for 10 dimes.

3 dollars 4 dimes		__2__ dollars __14__ dimes
8 dollars 0 dimes	**Exchange 1 dollar for 10 dimes**	__7__ dollars __10__ dimes
1 dollar 3 dimes		__0__ dollars __13__ dimes
4 dollars 1 dime		__3__ dollars __11__ dimes

If students have difficulty with exercise A, they should have more experiences with activity 1.

 B Complete each sentence by renaming 1 hundred as 10 tens.

1. 5 hundreds, 3 tens = __4__ hundreds, __13__ tens. $500 + 30 = \underline{400} + \underline{130}$.

2. 7 hundreds, 6 tens = __6__ hundreds, __16__ tens. $700 + 60 = \underline{600} + \underline{160}$.

3. 2 hundreds, 0 tens = __1__ hundred, __10__ tens. $200 + 0 = \underline{100} + \underline{100}$.

4. 9 hundreds, 7 tens = __8__ hundreds, __17__ tens. $900 + 70 = \underline{800} + \underline{170}$.

C Complete each sentence by renaming 1 hundred as 10 tens or 1 ten as 10 ones.

1. $600 + 10 + 5 = 500 + \boxed{110} + 5$

2. $600 + 10 + 5 = 600 + 0 + \boxed{15}$

3. $400 + 80 + 0 = 400 + \boxed{70} + 10$

4. $100 + 60 + 7 = 0 + \boxed{160} + 7$

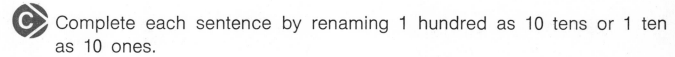

If students have difficulty with exercise B or C, more experience with activity 2 should be provided.

SUBTRACTION—RENAMING HUNDREDS AS TENS OR TENS AS ONES

> If there are not enough ones to subtract from, rename 1 ten as 10 ones. If there are not enough tens to subtract from, rename 1 hundred as 10 tens.

 Follow the directions to fill the blanks.

$$537 = 500 + 30 + 7$$
$$- 162 = 100 + 60 + 2$$

$$5$$

Are there enough ones to subtract from? ___yes___
Subtract the ones.
Are there enough tens to subtract from? ___no___
Rename 1 hundred as 10 tens.
Now are there enough tens to subtract from? ___yes___

$$537 = 400 + 130 + 7$$
$$- 162 = 100 + 60 + 2$$

$$300 + 70 + 5 = 375$$

Subtract the tens, then the hundreds.
Write the standard name.

B Follow the directions to fill the blanks.

$$861 = 800 + 60 + 1$$
$$- 454 = 400 + 50 + 4$$

Are there enough ones to subtract from? ___no___
Rename 1 ten as 10 ones.
Are there enough ones to subtract from? ___yes___

$$861 = 800 + 50 + 11$$
$$- 454 = 400 + 50 + 4$$

$$400 + 0 + 7 = 407$$

Are there enough tens to subtract from? ___yes___
Subtract the ones, then the tens, and then the hundreds.
Write the standard name.

Short Form To Subtract 915 — 562

Step 1	$\begin{array}{r} 915 \\ -562 \\ \hline 3 \end{array}$	Subtract ones. If there are not enough ones in the minuend, rename 1 ten as 10 ones. 5 ones — 2 ones = 3 ones. Write 3 ones.
Step 2	$\begin{array}{r} {}^{8\ 11}\!\!\not9\not15 \\ -562 \\ \hline 53 \end{array}$	Subtract tens. Since there are not enough tens to subtract from, rename 1 hundred as 10 tens. 11 tens — 6 tens = 5 tens. Write 5 tens.
Step 3	$\begin{array}{r} {}^{8\ 11}\!\!\not9\not15 \\ -562 \\ \hline 353 \end{array}$	Subtract hundreds. 8 hundreds — 5 hundreds = 3 hundreds. Write 3 hundreds.

C Find the differences. Rename 1 ten as 10 ones.

| $\begin{array}{r}491\\-163\\\hline 328\end{array}$ | $\begin{array}{r}873\\-524\\\hline 349\end{array}$ | $\begin{array}{r}566\\-238\\\hline 328\end{array}$ | $\begin{array}{r}648\\-319\\\hline 329\end{array}$ | $\begin{array}{r}475\\-247\\\hline 228\end{array}$ | $\begin{array}{r}794\\-478\\\hline 316\end{array}$ | $\begin{array}{r}432\\-218\\\hline 214\end{array}$ |

D Find the differences. Rename 1 hundred as 10 tens.

| $\begin{array}{r}738\\-284\\\hline 454\end{array}$ | $\begin{array}{r}627\\-372\\\hline 255\end{array}$ | $\begin{array}{r}448\\-168\\\hline 280\end{array}$ | $\begin{array}{r}835\\-641\\\hline 194\end{array}$ | $\begin{array}{r}756\\-572\\\hline 184\end{array}$ | $\begin{array}{r}687\\-394\\\hline 293\end{array}$ | $\begin{array}{r}529\\-244\\\hline 285\end{array}$ |

E Subtract. Use addition to check your work. You may have to rename 1 ten as 10 ones or 1 hundred as 10 tens.

| $\begin{array}{r}{}^{8\ 13}\!\!\not9\not36\\-574\\\hline +362\\\hline 936\end{array}$ | $\begin{array}{r}437\\-128\\\hline +309\\\hline 437\end{array}$ | $\begin{array}{r}646\\-371\\\hline +275\\\hline 646\end{array}$ | $\begin{array}{r}218\\-192\\\hline +\ 26\\\hline 218\end{array}$ | $\begin{array}{r}572\\-426\\\hline +146\\\hline 572\end{array}$ | $\begin{array}{r}769\\-284\\\hline +485\\\hline 769\end{array}$ |

Discuss the example. Emphasize the renaming process in each step. Point out that renaming is not necessary in step 1 or step 3. Have students complete some examples of this type before working page 63.

63

RENAMING 1 HUNDRED AS 10 TENS AND 1 TEN AS 10 ONES

 A Complete the chart. Exchange 1 dime for 10 pennies and 1 dollar for 10 dimes.

3	1	4		3	0	14		2	10	14
6	2	0	**Exchange 1 dime for 10 pennies**	6	1	10	**Exchange 1 dollar for 10 dimes**	5	11	10
9	8	2		9	7	12		8	17	12
4	4	7		4	3	17		3	13	17
6	2	5		6	1	15		5	11	15

Students having difficulty with exercise A should have more experiences with the activity involving models of money.

B Complete the chart.

	Expanded Name	Rename 1 Ten as 10 Ones	Rename 1 Hundred as 10 Tens
1.	500 + 60 + 4	500 + 50 + 14	400 + 150 + 14
2.	800 + 10 + 2	800 + 0 + 12	700 + 100 + 12
3.	400 + 80 + 0	400 + 70 + 10	300 + 170 + 10
4.	100 + 30 + 5	100 + 20 + 15	0 + 120 + 15
5.	700 + 70 + 7	700 + 60 + 17	600 + 160 + 17

C Complete each sentence by renaming 1 ten as 10 ones and 1 hundred as 10 tens.

1. 3 hundreds, 6 tens, 3 ones = ___2___ hundreds, ___15___ tens, ___13___ ones

2. 4 hundreds, 1 ten, 5 ones = ___3___ hundreds, ___10___ tens, ___15___ ones

3. 7 hundreds, 8 tens, 0 ones = ___6___ hundreds, ___17___ tens, ___10___ ones

4. 1 hundred, 1 ten, 1 one = ___0___ hundreds, ___10___ tens, ___11___ ones

Students having difficulty with exercise B or C should have more experiences with the activity involving counters.

SUBTRACTION—RENAMING HUNDREDS AS TENS AND TENS AS ONES

 A Fill the blanks.

$$314 = 300 + 10 + 4$$
$$- 168 = 100 + 60 + 8$$

$$314 = 300 + \ \ 0 + 14$$
$$- 168 = 100 + 60 + \ \ 8$$
$$\underline{\ \ \ \ \ \ 6\ \ \ \ }$$

$$314 = 200 + 100 + 14$$
$$- 168 = 100 + \ 60 + \ \ 8$$
$$\underline{100} + \underline{40} + \ 6 \ = \underline{146}$$

Are there enough ones to subtract from? __no__

Rename 1 ten as 10 ones. Now are there enough ones to subtract from? __yes__

Subtract the ones. Are there enough tens to subtract from? __no__

Rename 1 hundred as 10 tens. Now are there enough tens to subtract from? __yes__

Subtract tens and hundreds. Write the standard name.

B Fill the blanks to complete the subtractions.

Standard Name	Expanded Name	Rename 1 Ten as 10 Ones	Rename 1 Hundred as 10 Tens
1. $\begin{array}{r} 835 \\ -\ 367 \end{array}$	$\begin{array}{r} 800+30+5 \\ 300+60+7 \end{array}$	$\begin{array}{r} 800 + 20 + 15 \\ 300 + 60 + \ \ 7 \end{array}$	$\begin{array}{r} 700 + 120 + 15 \\ 300 + \ 60 + \ \ 7 \end{array}$ $\underline{400} + \underline{60} + \underline{8} = \underline{468}$
2. $\begin{array}{r} 321 \\ -\ 165 \end{array}$	$\begin{array}{r} 300+20+1 \\ 100+60+5 \end{array}$	$\begin{array}{r} 300 + 10 + 11 \\ 100 + 60 + \ \ 5 \end{array}$	$\begin{array}{r} 200 + 110 + 11 \\ 100 + \ 60 + \ \ 5 \end{array}$ $\underline{100} + \underline{50} + \underline{6} = \underline{156}$
3. $\begin{array}{r} 457 \\ -\ 198 \end{array}$	$\begin{array}{r} 400+50+7 \\ 100+90+8 \end{array}$	$\begin{array}{r} 400 + 40 + 17 \\ 100 + 90 + \ \ 8 \end{array}$	$\begin{array}{r} 300 + 140 + 17 \\ 100 + \ 90 + \ \ 8 \end{array}$ $\underline{200} + \underline{50} + \underline{9} = \underline{259}$

Students who have difficulty with exercise B should have more experiences with activities involving counters. Have them represent the minuend with counters and then perform the subtraction physically.

65

Short Form To Subtract 623 − 274

Step 1
$$\begin{array}{r} \overset{1\ 13}{6\cancel{2}\cancel{3}} \\ -\ 274 \\ \hline 9 \end{array}$$

Subtract ones. Since there are not enough ones to subtract from, rename 1 ten as 10 ones. $600 + 20 + 3 = 600 + 10 + 13$. Subtract the ones. 13 ones − 4 ones = 9 ones.
Write 9 ones.

Step 2
$$\begin{array}{r} \overset{11}{\overset{5\ 1\ 13}{6\cancel{2}\cancel{3}}} \\ -\ 274 \\ \hline 49 \end{array}$$

Subtract tens. Since there are not enough tens to subtract from, rename 1 hundred as 10 tens. $600 + 10 + 13 = 500 + 110 + 13$. Subtract the tens. 11 tens − 7 tens = 4 tens.
Write 4 tens.

Step 3
$$\begin{array}{r} \overset{11}{\overset{5\ 1\ 13}{6\cancel{2}\cancel{3}}} \\ -\ 274 \\ \hline 349 \end{array}$$

Subtract hundreds. 5 hundreds − 2 hundreds = 3 hundreds.
Write 3 hundreds.

C Ring subtractions in which 1 ten must be renamed as 10 ones.

839	(863	(584	748	968	(472	(973
− 682	− 535)	− 397)	− 275	− 146	− 287)	− 725)

D Ring subtractions in which 1 hundred must be renamed as 10 tens.

(517	386	(448	(683	(573	745	229
− 298)	− 137	− 162)	− 294)	− 375)	− 316	− 119

E Find the differences using the short form.

634	521	536	680	974	658	210
− 287	− 153	− 278	− 493	− 576	− 369	− 132
347	368	258	187	398	289	78

CROSS-NUMBER PUZZLE

ACROSS

1. Four hundred sixteen

4. Two thousand, three hundred forty-one

8. 871 — 241

9. 236 + 482

10. 897, 898, 899, _____

11. 600 + 50 + 7

13. One more than 999

15. 625 — 189

16. 456 + 257

18. 12 less than 70

20. 825, 830, 835, _____

21. One less than 1,280

23. 164 — 87

24. The number between 1,889 and 1,891

1.	2.	3.		4.	5.	6.	7.
4	1	6	✳	2	3	4	1
8. 6	3	0	✳	9. 7	1	8	✳
✳	10. 9	0	0	✳	11. 6	5	12. 7
✳	9	✳	✳	13. 1	0	0	0
14. 8	✳	15. 4	3	6	✳	✳	8
16. 7	17. 1	3	✳	✳	18. 5	19. 8	✳
20. 8	4	0	✳	21. 1	2	7	22. 9
✳	23. 7	7	✳	24. 1	8	9	0

DOWN

1. 6 more than 40

2. 1 less than 1,400

3. 200, 400, _____

4. 82 — 55

5. 3,000 + 100 + 60

6. 4,820, 4,830, 4,840, _____

12. 239 + 469

13. 7 + 9

14. 992 — 114

15. The number after 4,306

17. 3 less than 150

18. 259 + 269

19. 882, 881, 880, _____

21. 20 — 9

22. 9 tens

PUZZLER ???????????????????????????????

A bear is at the bottom of a hole 10 meters deep. Each day the bear climbs up 3 meters. Each night the bear slides back down 2 meters. How long will it take the bear to get out of the hole? ___8___ days

CHAPTER REVIEW

$12 - 4 = 8$ is shown on the number line.

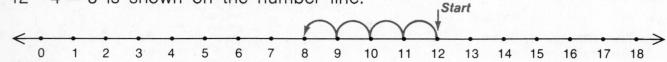

Start

| 0 | 1 | 2 | 3 | 4 | 5 | 6 | 7 | 8 | 9 | 10 | 11 | 12 | 13 | 14 | 15 | 16 | 17 | 18 |

A Use the number line to find the differences.

1. $10 - 6 = \underline{\ 4\ }$ $13 - 5 = \underline{\ 8\ }$ $9 - 4 = \underline{\ 5\ }$ $17 - 9 = \underline{\ 8\ }$

2. $14 - 7 = \underline{\ 7\ }$ $5 - 3 = \underline{\ 2\ }$ $15 - 6 = \underline{\ 9\ }$ $11 - 8 = \underline{\ 3\ }$

B Complete these tables showing subtraction facts.

1.

−	6	3	1	7	2	5	8
8	2	5	7	1	6	3	0

2.

−	6	5	8	3	7	9
12	6	7	4	9	5	3

3.

−	4	7	2	6	9	3	5
10	6	3	8	4	1	7	5

4.

−	6	8	9	7
15	9	7	6	8

C Rename 1 ten as 10 ones or 1 hundred as 10 tens.

1. $20 + 3 = \underline{\ 10\ } + 13$ **2.** $400 + 60 + 5 = 300 + \underline{\ 160\ } + 5$

3. $60 + 8 = 50 + \underline{\ 18\ }$ **4.** $700 + 10 + 1 = 700 + \underline{\ 0\ } + 11$

D Subtract the ones, then the tens, and then the hundreds.

264	93	471	267	713	957	95
−149	−45	−129	−83	−264	−482	−27
115	48	342	184	449	475	68

E Subtract. Check by addition.

$$
\begin{array}{c}
{}^{7\ 14} \\
\cancel{843} \\
-\ 161 \\
\hline
+\ 682 \\
\hline
843
\end{array}
$$

48	184	627	62	825
− 35	− 76	− 209	− 15	− 367
+ 13	+ 108	+ 418	+ 47	+ 458
48	184	627	62	825

CHECK-UP

 Find the difference for each subtraction fact.

1. $15 - 8 = \underline{7}$ $11 - 9 = \underline{2}$ $8 - 5 = \underline{3}$ $18 - 9 = \underline{9}$

2. $9 - 4 = \underline{5}$ $14 - 5 = \underline{9}$ $12 - 7 = \underline{5}$ $10 - 6 = \underline{4}$

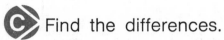 Complete each sentence.

1. $40 + 7 = \underline{30} + 17$ **2.** $400 + 30 + 5 = 300 + \underline{130} + 5$

3. $90 + 2 = 80 + \underline{12}$ **4.** $700 + 10 + 6 = \underline{600} + 100 + 16$

 Find the differences.

63	81	467	372	859	622
-42	-37	-121	-245	-274	-305
21	44	346	127	585	317

D Subtract. Check by addition.

93	74	190	263	634	314
$-\ 8$	-26	$-\ 85$	-182	-228	-176
85	48	105	81	406	138

Student answers to exercise D should include the short check.

E Solve each word problem.

1. Nina is 11 years old. Her father is 40 years old. What is the difference in their ages? $\underline{29}$ years

2. Eric and Marc were playing dominoes. Eric's score was 165. Marc's score was 198. Marc was winning by how many points? $\underline{33}$ points

3. Cruz was reading a book with 320 pages. He was on page 198. How many pages did he have left to read? $\underline{122}$ pages

4 • MULTIPLICATION

MULTIPLICATION AS REPEATED ADDITION

 Answer the questions about the picture.

1. How many boxes? _____3_____

2. How many crayons in each box? _____6_____

3. How many crayons in all? _____18_____

The addition sentence is 6 + 6 + 6 = 18.
The multiplication sentence is 3 × 6 = 18.

Go over the example in exercise B. Point out that since there are 2 sets of 5 objects, the total number of objects can be obtained by adding 5 + 5 *or* by multiplying 2 × 5.

B Complete the chart.

	Sets	Number of Sets	Number in Each Set	Total Number of Dots	Addition Sentence	Multiplication Sentence
1.	• • • • • • • • • •	2	5	10	5 + 5 = 10	2 × 5 = 10
2.	• • • • • • • • • • • • • • •	3	5	15	5 + 5 + 5 = 15	3 × 5 = 15
3.	• • • • • • • • • • • •	2	6	12	6 + 6 = 12	2 × 6 = 12
4.	• • • • • • • • • • • • • • • • • • • •	4	5	20	5 + 5 + 5 + 5 = 20	4 × 5 = 20
5.	• • • • • • • • • • • • • • • • • •	3	6	18	6 + 6 + 6 = 18	3 × 6 = 18
6.	• • • • • • • • • • • •	4	3	12	3 + 3 + 3 + 3 = 12	4 × 3 = 12

Read the statements before exercises C, D, and E with the class. Work additional examples if necessary. Then have students complete the page.

> The multiplication sentence for
> $2 + 2 + 2 + 2 = 8$ is $4 \times 2 = 8$.

 Complete each addition sentence. Then write the related multiplication sentence.

Addition Sentence	Multiplication Sentence
1. $3 + 3 + 3 + 3 = \underline{\ 12\ }$	$4 \times 3 = 12$
2. $5 + 5 + 5 + 5 + 5 = \underline{\ 25\ }$	$5 \times 5 = 25$

> The addition sentence for $3 \times 5 = 15$ is $5 + 5 + 5 = 15$.

 Complete each multiplication sentence. Then write the related addition sentence.

Multiplication Sentence	Addition Sentence
1. $4 \times 5 = \underline{\ 20\ }$	$5 + 5 + 5 + 5 = 20$
2. $2 \times 3 = \underline{\ 6\ }$	$3 + 3 = 6$

> In the multiplication sentence $5 \times 3 = 15$, 5 and 3 are **factors** and 15 is the **product**.

 Complete the chart.

	Repeated Addition	Multiplication Sentence	Factors		Product
1.	$6 + 6 + 6$	$3 \times 6 = 18$	3	6	18
2.	$4 + 4 + 4 + 4 + 4$	$5 \times 4 = 20$	5	4	20
3.	$2 + 2$	$2 \times 2 = 4$	2	2	4
4.	$2 + 2 + 2 + 2 + 2 + 2$	$6 \times 2 = 12$	6	2	12
5.	$3 + 3 + 3 + 3$	$4 \times 3 = 12$	4	3	12

Students having difficulty with any of these exercises should have repeated experiences with activities 2 or 3.

MULTIPLICATION ON THE NUMBER LINE

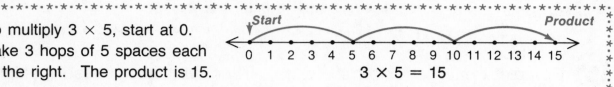

To multiply 3 × 5, start at 0.
Take 3 hops of 5 spaces each
to the right.   The product is 15.

Start   *Product*

0 1 2 3 4 5 6 7 8 9 10 11 12 13 14 15

3 × 5 = 15

Work through number 1 in exercise A with the class. Have students complete the rest of the page.

 Complete the multiplication sentence for each number line.

1. 0 1 2 3 4 5 6 7 8 9 10 11 12 13 14 15 16   ___4___ × ___3___ = ___12___

2. 0 1 2 3 4 5 6 7 8 9 10 11 12 13 14 15 16   ___2___ × ___5___ = ___10___

3. 0 1 2 3 4 5 6 7 8 9 10 11 12 13 14 15 16   ___6___ × ___1___ = ___6___

4. 0 1 2 3 4 5 6 7 8 9 10 11 12 13 14 15 16   ___5___ × ___2___ = ___10___

B Draw arrows on the number lines and solve the multiplications.

1. 0 1 2 3 4 5 6 7 8 9 10 11 12 13 14 15 16   4 × 4 = ___16___

2. 0 1 2 3 4 5 6 7 8 9 10 11 12 13 14 15 16   6 × 2 = ___12___

3. 0 1 2 3 4 5 6 7 8 9 10 11 12 13 14 15 16   5 × 3 = ___15___

4. 0 1 2 3 4 5 6 7 8 9 10 11 12 13 14 15 16   2 × 7 = ___14___

C Use the number line to help you find the products.

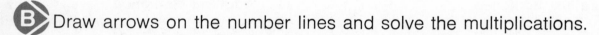

0 1 2 3 4 5 6 7 8 9 10 11 12 13 14 15 16 17 18 19 20 21 22 23 24 25

1. 4 × 3 = ___12___   3 × 4 = ___12___   5 × 5 = ___25___   3 × 8 = ___24___

2. 1 × 5 = ___5___   6 × 3 = ___18___   2 × 8 = ___16___   2 × 9 = ___18___

3. 4 × 6 = ___24___   3 × 6 = ___18___   5 × 4 = ___20___   4 × 4 = ___16___

4. 7 × 1 = ___7___   6 × 4 = ___24___   3 × 3 = ___9___   2 × 5 = ___10___

If students have difficulty completing the multiplications in exercise C, provide more experiences with the initial teaching activity. Students who need more practice in finding products with the number line or with sets of objects should complete the additional activity.

ORDER OF THE FACTORS

 Use the pictures to help you find the products.

1. 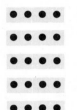   **2.**   **3.**   **4.**

$5 \times 4 =$ __20__ $4 \times 5 =$ __20__

$2 \times 6 =$ __12__ $6 \times 2 =$ __12__

5. Does $5 \times 4 = 4 \times 5$? __yes__   **6.** Does $2 \times 6 = 6 \times 2$? __yes__

 Draw dots in the boxes. Answer the questions.

1. In box W draw dots to show 4×2.

2. In box X draw dots to show 2×4.

3. Does $4 \times 2 = 2 \times 4$? __yes__

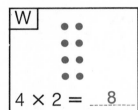 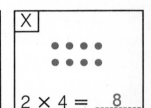

4. In box Y draw dots to show 3×5.

5. In box Z draw dots to show 5×3.

6. Does $3 \times 5 = 5 \times 3$? __yes__

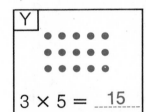 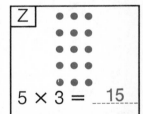

> The product for 6×3 is the same as the product for 3×6.
> Changing the order of the factors does not change the product.

Read the statement above to the class. Then have the students complete exercise C.

C Complete each sentence.

1. $4 \times 6 = 24$, so $6 \times 4 =$ __24__.   **2.** $1 \times 8 = 8$, so $8 \times 1 =$ __8__.

3. $5 \times 2 = 10$, so $2 \times 5 =$ __10__.   **4.** $3 \times 9 = 27$, so $9 \times 3 =$ __27__.

5. $6 \times 3 = 18$, so $3 \times 6 =$ __18__.   **6.** $7 \times 5 = 35$, so $5 \times 7 =$ __35__.

7. $9 \times 2 = 18$, so $2 \times 9 =$ __18__.   **8.** $8 \times 4 = 32$, so $4 \times 8 =$ __32__.

FACTORS OF 0 OR 1

 Use the picture to help you answer the questions.

1. How many rings? __4__

2. How many dots in each ring? __0__

3. How many dots in all? __0__

$4 \times 0 = 0$

 Complete each addition and multiplication sentence.

1. $0 + 0 + 0 + 0 + 0 + 0 =$ __0__ $6 \times 0 =$ __0__

2. $0 + 0 + 0 =$ __0__ $3 \times 0 =$ __0__

3. $0 + 0 + 0 + 0 + 0 + 0 + 0 + 0 =$ __0__ $8 \times 0 =$ __0__

> When 0 is a factor in a multiplication, the product is equal to 0.

 Multiply.

1. $1 \times 0 =$ __0__ $9 \times 0 =$ __0__ $0 \times 4 =$ __0__ $5 \times 0 =$ __0__

2. $0 \times 7 =$ __0__ $2 \times 0 =$ __0__ $0 \times 0 =$ __0__ $3 \times 0 =$ __0__

3. $0 \times 8 =$ __0__ $0 \times 2 =$ __0__ $7 \times 0 =$ __0__ $0 \times 1 =$ __0__

D Use the picture to help you answer the questions.

1. How many rows of ⭐s? __1__

2. How many ⭐s in each row? __7__ $1 \times 7 = 7$

3. How many ⭐s in all? __7__

E Complete each addition and multiplication sentence.

1. $1 + 1 + 1 =$ __3__ $3 \times 1 =$ __3__

2. $1 + 1 + 1 + 1 + 1 + 1 + 1 + 1 =$ __8__ $8 \times 1 =$ __8__

3. $1 + 1 + 1 + 1 =$ __4__ $4 \times 1 =$ __4__

When 1 is a factor in a multiplication, the product is equal to the other factor.

 Multiply.

1. $1 \times 8 = \underline{\ 8\ }$ $1 \times 0 = \underline{\ 0\ }$ $1 \times 1 = \underline{\ 1\ }$ $3 \times 1 = \underline{\ 3\ }$

2. $6 \times 1 = \underline{\ 6\ }$ $2 \times 1 = \underline{\ 2\ }$ $1 \times 2 = \underline{\ 2\ }$ $4 \times 1 = \underline{\ 4\ }$

3. $7 \times 1 = \underline{\ 7\ }$ $1 \times 9 = \underline{\ 9\ }$ $0 \times 1 = \underline{\ 0\ }$ $1 \times 5 = \underline{\ 5\ }$

The multiplication sentence $1 \times 7 = 7$ is often written like this:
$$\begin{array}{r} 1 \\ \times\ 7 \\ \hline 7 \end{array}$$

Point out the two ways to write a multiplication sentence. Then have students complete the page.

 Complete each sentence. Then write it in column form.

$9 \times 1 = \underline{\ 9\ }$ $0 \times 7 = \underline{\ 0\ }$ $4 \times 0 = \underline{\ 0\ }$ $1 \times 3 = \underline{\ 3\ }$ $6 \times 1 = \underline{\ 6\ }$

$$\begin{array}{r} 9 \\ \times\ 1 \\ \hline 9 \end{array} \qquad \begin{array}{r} 0 \\ \times\ 7 \\ \hline 0 \end{array} \qquad \begin{array}{r} 4 \\ \times\ 0 \\ \hline 0 \end{array} \qquad \begin{array}{r} 1 \\ \times\ 3 \\ \hline 3 \end{array} \qquad \begin{array}{r} 6 \\ \times\ 1 \\ \hline 6 \end{array}$$

H Write the products.

1.
$$\begin{array}{r} 0 \\ \times\ 5 \\ \hline 0 \end{array} \quad \begin{array}{r} 8 \\ \times\ 1 \\ \hline 8 \end{array} \quad \begin{array}{r} 1 \\ \times\ 5 \\ \hline 5 \end{array} \quad \begin{array}{r} 2 \\ \times\ 0 \\ \hline 0 \end{array} \quad \begin{array}{r} 9 \\ \times\ 0 \\ \hline 0 \end{array} \quad \begin{array}{r} 7 \\ \times\ 1 \\ \hline 7 \end{array} \quad \begin{array}{r} 0 \\ \times\ 8 \\ \hline 0 \end{array}$$

2.
$$\begin{array}{r} 1 \\ \times\ 1 \\ \hline 1 \end{array} \quad \begin{array}{r} 0 \\ \times\ 3 \\ \hline 0 \end{array} \quad \begin{array}{r} 4 \\ \times\ 1 \\ \hline 4 \end{array} \quad \begin{array}{r} 6 \\ \times\ 1 \\ \hline 6 \end{array} \quad \begin{array}{r} 1 \\ \times\ 6 \\ \hline 6 \end{array} \quad \begin{array}{r} 0 \\ \times\ 7 \\ \hline 0 \end{array} \quad \begin{array}{r} 7 \\ \times\ 0 \\ \hline 0 \end{array}$$

I Complete each table.

1.

×	0	1	3	4	7	9
0	0	0	0	0	0	0

2.

×	0	2	4	6	8	9
1	0	2	4	6	8	9

Do additional activity 1 with all of the students. Complete additional activity 2 with students having difficulty identifying the products for multiplications in which one of the factors is 0 or 1. A method for drilling on multiplication facts with one factor 0 or 1 is provided in additional activity 3.

FACTORS OF 2 OR 3

A Use the pictures to help you answer the questions.

1. How many rows of chess pieces? __2__

2. How many chess pieces in each row? __8__

3. How many chess pieces in all? __16__ $2 \times 8 = $ __16__

4. How many rows of marbles? __5__

5. How many marbles in each row? __2__

6. How many marbles in all? __10__ $5 \times 2 = $ __10__

Have students complete exercises B and C.

B Use the number line to help you find the products.

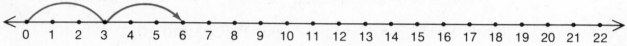

1. $2 \times 3 = $ __6__   2. $2 \times 8 = $ __16__   3. $2 \times 5 = $ __10__

4. $2 \times 9 = $ __18__   5. $2 \times 1 = $ __2__   6. $2 \times 4 = $ __8__

C Complete each sentence.

1. $2 \times 6 = 12$, so $6 \times 2 = $ __12__.   2. $2 \times 9 = 18$, so $9 \times 2 = $ __18__.

3. $2 \times 3 = 6$, so $3 \times 2 = $ __6__.   4. $2 \times 4 = 8$, so $4 \times 2 = $ __8__.

Complete exercise D orally.

D Use the pictures to help you answer the questions.

1. How many sets of flags? __3__

2. How many flags in each set? __4__

3. How many flags in all? __12__ $3 \times 4 = $ __12__

4. How many sets of dots? __4__

5. How many dots in each set? __3__

6. How many dots in all? __12__ $4 \times 3 = $ __12__

E Use the number line to help you find the products.

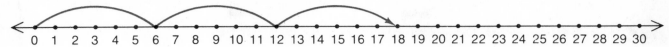

0 1 2 3 4 5 6 7 8 9 10 11 12 13 14 15 16 17 18 19 20 21 22 23 24 25 26 27 28 29 30

1. $3 \times 6 =$ __18__   **2.** $3 \times 2 =$ __6__   **3.** $3 \times 7 =$ __21__

4. $3 \times 1 =$ __3__   **5.** $3 \times 5 =$ __15__   **6.** $3 \times 4 =$ __12__

7. $3 \times 9 =$ __27__   **8.** $3 \times 8 =$ __24__   **9.** $3 \times 3 =$ __9__

F Complete each sentence.

1. $3 \times 5 = 15$, so $5 \times 3 =$ __15__.   **2.** $3 \times 6 = 18$, so $6 \times 3 =$ __18__.

3. $3 \times 8 = 24$, so $8 \times 3 =$ __24__.   **4.** $3 \times 2 = 6$, so $2 \times 3 =$ __6__.

5. $3 \times 4 = 12$, so $4 \times 3 =$ __12__.   **6.** $3 \times 7 = 21$, so $7 \times 3 =$ __21__.

7. $3 \times 9 = 27$, so $9 \times 3 =$ __27__.   **8.** $3 \times 0 = 0$, so $0 \times 3 =$ __0__.

G Write the products. Use the number line to help you.

1.
8	5	9	7	3	4	2
× 3	× 2	× 2	× 1	× 6	× 3	× 2
24	10	18	7	18	12	4

2.
6	3	1	5	0	8	2
× 3	× 2	× 9	× 3	× 3	× 2	× 8
18	6	9	15	0	16	16

3.
7	6	3	9	7	4	3
× 2	× 2	× 3	× 3	× 3	× 2	× 0
14	12	9	27	21	8	0

 Complete each table.

1.

×	0	3	4	6	8	9
2	0	6	8	12	16	18

2.

×	0	1	3	5	6	9
3	0	3	9	15	18	27

WORDS THAT MEAN TO MULTIPLY

 Translate these phrases and find the products.

	Phrase	Translation	Product
1.	3 times 7	3 × 7	21
2.	6 rows of 3	6 × 3	18
3.	The product of 1 and 9	1 × 9	9
4.	3 multiplied by 4	3 × 4	12
5.	2 groups of 8 each	2 × 8	16
6.	5 threes	5 × 3	15

Have students solve each problem in exercise B. Then discuss the words that mean to multiply in each problem.

B Solve each word problem. See if you can find the words that mean to multiply.

1. Judy's 3 rabbits had litters of 5 bunnies each. How many baby bunnies does she have? ___15___ bunnies

2. Paul had 2 six-packs of bottles. How many bottles did he have? ___12___ bottles

3. Dalia saw 2 cars with 4 passengers each. How many passengers did she see? ___8___ passengers

4. Juan had 3 boards, each of which was 5 decimeters long. How many decimeters of board did he have? ___15___ decimeters

5. There were 7 rows of 3 girl scouts marching in a parade. How many girl scouts were there? ___21___ girl scouts

6. Shirley found 6 four-leaf clovers. How many leaves were there? ___24___ leaves

---

Students who have difficulty solving these problems individually should solve them in a group.

Use number 1 in exercise A to review writing number names in expanded form.

ADDITION REVIEW

 A Complete each sentence.

1. 427 = 400 + 20 + 7   **2.** 35 = 30 + 5

3. 163 = 100 + 60 + 3   **4.** 89 = 80 + 9

5. 793 = 700 + 90 + 3   **6.** 50 = 40 + 10

Have students complete exercises B, C, and D after you work the first item in each exercise orally.

 B Put < (is less than), > (is greater than), or = (is equal to) in each ●.

1. 189 < 198   9 + 3 = 3 + 9   20 + 9 < 20 + 19

2. 2,465 > 2,365   7 + 8 > 5 + 9   70 + 3 = 60 + 13

3. 994 < 1,003   6 + 5 > 5 + 5   800 + 7 > 80 + 7

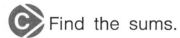 **C** Find the sums.

1.
5	0	8	6	5	8	3
3	9	4	8	7	8	7
+ 2	+ 7	+ 3	+ 7	+ 9	+ 5	+ 5
10	16	15	21	21	21	15

2.
56	72	94	59	68	79	24
+ 32	+ 35	+ 64	+ 37	+ 55	+ 97	+ 59
88	107	158	96	123	176	83

3.
245	308	450	546	415	157	396
+ 731	+ 570	+ 281	+ 207	+ 398	+ 657	+ 452
976	878	731	753	813	814	848

 **D** Complete each number pattern.

1. 42 44 46 __48__   **2.** 197 198 199 __200__

3. 4 8 12 __16__   **4.** 220 230 240 __250__

5. 15 18 21 __24__   **6.** 400 500 __600__ 700

Students having difficulty with exercise C should have more experiences with activities 1 and 2. Students having difficulty with exercises A, B, or D should have group instruction on the concepts presented in these exercises.

FACTORS OF 4

 A Complete each addition and multiplication sentence. Look for a pattern.

1. $4 + 4 =$ ___8___ $2 \times 4 =$ ___8___

2. $4 + 4 + 4 =$ ___12___ $3 \times 4 =$ ___12___

3. $4 + 4 + 4 + 4 =$ ___16___ $4 \times 4 =$ ___16___

4. $4 + 4 + 4 + 4 + 4 =$ ___20___ $5 \times 4 =$ ___20___

5. $4 + 4 + 4 + 4 + 4 + 4 =$ ___24___ $6 \times 4 =$ ___24___

6. $4 + 4 + 4 + 4 + 4 + 4 + 4 =$ ___28___ $7 \times 4 =$ ___28___

7. $4 + 4 + 4 + 4 + 4 + 4 + 4 + 4 =$ ___32___ $8 \times 4 =$ ___32___

8. $4 + 4 + 4 + 4 + 4 + 4 + 4 + 4 + 4 =$ ___36___ $9 \times 4 =$ ___36___

B Use the number line to help you find the products.

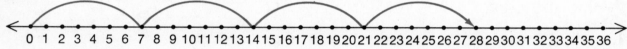

1. $4 \times 7 =$ ___28___ $4 \times 3 =$ ___12___ $4 \times 4 =$ ___16___

2. $4 \times 2 =$ ___8___ $4 \times 8 =$ ___32___ $4 \times 9 =$ ___36___

3. $4 \times 6 =$ ___24___ $4 \times 1 =$ ___4___ $4 \times 5 =$ ___20___

C Complete each sentence.

1. $4 \times 7 =$ ___28___, so $7 \times 4 = 28$.   **2.** $4 \times 0 = 0$, so $0 \times 4 =$ ___0___.

3. $4 \times 3 = 12$, so $3 \times 4 =$ ___12___.   **4.** $4 \times 9 =$ ___36___, so $9 \times 4 = 36$.

5. $4 \times 6 = 24$, so $6 \times 4 =$ ___24___.   **6.** $4 \times 2 =$ ___8___, so $2 \times 4 =$ ___8___.

D Write the products.   Use the number line to help you.

5	7	9	4	1	4	7
$\times 4$	$\times 2$	$\times 4$	$\times 6$	$\times 9$	$\times 3$	$\times 4$
20	14	36	24	9	12	28

E In the multiplication table below, the number name printed in color shows the product of 7 × 4; the number name printed in black shows the product of 3 × 6. Complete the open spaces in the table.

×	0	1	2	3	4	5	6	7	8	9
0	0	0	0	0	0	0	0	0	0	0
1	0	1	2	3	4	5	6	7	8	9
2	0	2	4	6	8	10	12	14	16	18
3	0	3	6	9	12	15	18	21	24	27
4	0	4	8	12	16	20	24	28	32	36
5	0	5	10	15	20	25	30	35	40	45
6	0	6	12	18	24	30				
7	0	7	14	21	28	35				
8	0	8	16	24	32	40				
9	0	9	18	27	36	45				

F Use the table in exercise E to help you find the products.

1.

$$\begin{array}{r} 3 \\ \times 4 \\ \hline 12 \end{array} \qquad \begin{array}{r} 7 \\ \times 3 \\ \hline 21 \end{array} \qquad \begin{array}{r} 4 \\ \times 9 \\ \hline 36 \end{array} \qquad \begin{array}{r} 8 \\ \times 2 \\ \hline 16 \end{array} \qquad \begin{array}{r} 6 \\ \times 3 \\ \hline 18 \end{array} \qquad \begin{array}{r} 0 \\ \times 9 \\ \hline 0 \end{array} \qquad \begin{array}{r} 4 \\ \times 8 \\ \hline 32 \end{array}$$

2.

$$\begin{array}{r} 7 \\ \times 4 \\ \hline 28 \end{array} \qquad \begin{array}{r} 2 \\ \times 9 \\ \hline 18 \end{array} \qquad \begin{array}{r} 6 \\ \times 4 \\ \hline 24 \end{array} \qquad \begin{array}{r} 3 \\ \times 5 \\ \hline 15 \end{array} \qquad \begin{array}{r} 4 \\ \times 4 \\ \hline 16 \end{array} \qquad \begin{array}{r} 2 \\ \times 5 \\ \hline 10 \end{array} \qquad \begin{array}{r} 4 \\ \times 5 \\ \hline 20 \end{array}$$

3.

$$\begin{array}{r} 5 \\ \times 0 \\ \hline 0 \end{array} \qquad \begin{array}{r} 2 \\ \times 7 \\ \hline 14 \end{array} \qquad \begin{array}{r} 9 \\ \times 3 \\ \hline 27 \end{array} \qquad \begin{array}{r} 3 \\ \times 8 \\ \hline 24 \end{array} \qquad \begin{array}{r} 6 \\ \times 2 \\ \hline 12 \end{array} \qquad \begin{array}{r} 1 \\ \times 7 \\ \hline 7 \end{array} \qquad \begin{array}{r} 3 \\ \times 3 \\ \hline 9 \end{array}$$

FACTORS OF 5

A Complete each addition and multiplication sentence. Look for a pattern.

1. 5 + 5 = __10__   2 × 5 = __10__

2. 5 + 5 + 5 = __15__   3 × 5 = __15__

3. 5 + 5 + 5 + 5 = __20__   4 × 5 = __20__

4. 5 + 5 + 5 + 5 + 5 = __25__   5 × 5 = __25__

5. 5 + 5 + 5 + 5 + 5 + 5 = __30__   6 × 5 = __30__

6. 5 + 5 + 5 + 5 + 5 + 5 + 5 = __35__   7 × 5 = __35__

7. 5 + 5 + 5 + 5 + 5 + 5 + 5 + 5 = __40__   8 × 5 = __40__

8. 5 + 5 + 5 + 5 + 5 + 5 + 5 + 5 + 5 = __45__ 9 × 5 = __45__

B Study the number line. Not all of the marks have been named. A ring has been drawn around the point for 48.

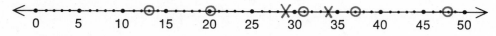

1. Put Xs on the points named 30 and 35.

2. The point on the number line for 32 is between 30 and 35. Put a ring around the point for 32.

3. The point on the number line for 14 is between 10 and 15. Put a ring around the point for 14.

4. Put rings around the points for 21 and 38.

C Use the number line to help you find the products.

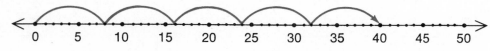

1. 5 × 8 = __40__   5 × 1 = __5__   5 × 4 = __20__

2. 5 × 3 = __15__   5 × 7 = __35__   5 × 2 = __10__

3. 5 × 6 = __30__   5 × 5 = __25__   5 × 9 = __45__

D Complete each sentence.

1. 5 × 3 = _15_, so 3 × 5 = 15.   **2.** 5 × 1 = _5_, so 1 × 5 = _5_.

3. 5 × 8 = 40, so 8 × 5 = _40_.   **4.** 5 × 4 = _20_, so 4 × 5 = 20.

5. 5 × 2 = _10_, so 2 × 5 = _10_.   **6.** 5 × 9 = 45, so 9 × 5 = _45_.

7. 5 × 7 = 35, so 7 × 5 = _35_.   **8.** 5 × 6 = _30_, so 6 × 5 = _30_.

 E Write the products. Use the number line to help you.

```
←•••••••••••••••••••••••••••••••••••••••••••••••••••→
  0    5    10   15   20   25   30   35   40   45   50
```

1.
$$\begin{array}{c} 7 \\ \times\ 5 \\ \hline 35 \end{array} \quad \begin{array}{c} 5 \\ \times\ 4 \\ \hline 20 \end{array} \quad \begin{array}{c} 6 \\ \times\ 3 \\ \hline 18 \end{array} \quad \begin{array}{c} 2 \\ \times\ 9 \\ \hline 18 \end{array} \quad \begin{array}{c} 5 \\ \times\ 3 \\ \hline 15 \end{array} \quad \begin{array}{c} 9 \\ \times\ 5 \\ \hline 45 \end{array} \quad \begin{array}{c} 4 \\ \times\ 6 \\ \hline 24 \end{array}$$

2.
$$\begin{array}{c} 5 \\ \times\ 2 \\ \hline 10 \end{array} \quad \begin{array}{c} 7 \\ \times\ 4 \\ \hline 28 \end{array} \quad \begin{array}{c} 5 \\ \times\ 5 \\ \hline 25 \end{array} \quad \begin{array}{c} 0 \\ \times\ 5 \\ \hline 0 \end{array} \quad \begin{array}{c} 6 \\ \times\ 2 \\ \hline 12 \end{array} \quad \begin{array}{c} 5 \\ \times\ 6 \\ \hline 30 \end{array} \quad \begin{array}{c} 8 \\ \times\ 5 \\ \hline 40 \end{array}$$

3.
$$\begin{array}{c} 1 \\ \times\ 8 \\ \hline 8 \end{array} \quad \begin{array}{c} 1 \\ \times\ 5 \\ \hline 5 \end{array} \quad \begin{array}{c} 4 \\ \times\ 9 \\ \hline 36 \end{array} \quad \begin{array}{c} 5 \\ \times\ 7 \\ \hline 35 \end{array} \quad \begin{array}{c} 7 \\ \times\ 3 \\ \hline 21 \end{array} \quad \begin{array}{c} 5 \\ \times\ 9 \\ \hline 45 \end{array} \quad \begin{array}{c} 6 \\ \times\ 5 \\ \hline 30 \end{array}$$

 F Write <, >, or = in each ● to make the sentence true.

1. 5 × 4 **>** 19   6 × 3 **=** 18   4 × 5 **<** 30

2. 9 × 5 **=** 45   8 × 2 **<** 18   7 × 3 **=** 21

3. 2 × 7 **>** 12   6 × 5 **=** 30   0 × 9 **<** 9

4. 8 × 5 **=** 40   5 × 2 **<** 12   5 × 1 **>** 0

G Complete the table.

×	0	1	2	3	4	5	6	7	8	9
5	0	5	10	15	20	25	30	35	40	45

SUBTRACTION REVIEW

 A Complete each sentence by renaming 1 ten as 10 ones.

1. 600 + 30 + 5 = 600 + 20 + 15   **2.** 300 + 10 + 2 = 300 + 0 + 12

3. 100 + 50 + 0 = 100 + 40 + 10   **4.** 400 + 70 + 6 = 400 + 60 + 16

B Complete each sentence by renaming 1 hundred as 10 tens.

1. 200 + 20 + 8 = 100 + 120 + 8   **2.** 500 + 40 + 3 = 400 + 140 + 3

3. 700 + 0 + 5 = 600 + 100 + 5   **4.** 300 + 30 + 9 = 200 + 130 + 9

C Subtract.   Check by addition.

1.
```
  7 12 11
   8̷3̷1̷
 − 168 ⌉
 + 663 ⌋
   831
```
```
  79
− 62
+ 17
  79
```
```
  84
− 37
+ 47
  84
```
```
  52
− 19
+ 33
  52
```
```
 785
−145
+640
 785
```
```
 396
−201
+195
 396
```

2.
```
 610
−240
+370
 610
```
```
 573
−169
+404
 573
```
```
 857
−163
+694
 857
```
```
 444
−288
+156
 444
```
```
 913
−478
+435
 913
```
```
 682
−153
+529
 682
```

D Copy in columns and subtract.

1. 82 − 64
2. 618 − 193
3. 843 − 246

1.
```
  82
− 64
  18
```
2.
```
 618
−193
 425
```
3.
```
 843
−246
 597
```

E Complete each number pattern.

1. 97 96 95 __94__   **2.** 350 348 346 __344__

3. 62 61 60 __59__   **4.** 170 160 150 __140__

5. 80 77 74 __71__   **6.** 900 800 700 __600__

84

ESTIMATING ANSWERS IN SUBTRACTION

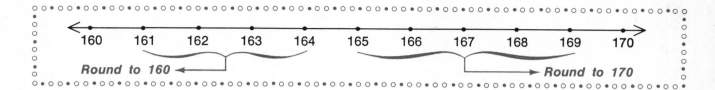

160   161   162   163   164   165   166   167   168   169   170

Round to 160 ←   → Round to 170

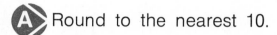 **A** Round to the nearest 10.

1. 264 ___260___   178 ___180___   442 ___440___   69 ___70___

2. 125 ___130___   433 ___430___   91 ___90___   186 ___190___

3. 593 ___590___   667 ___670___   705 ___710___   101 ___100___

If students have difficulty with exercise A, they should have more experiences with activity 1.

B Mr. Ross has driven 168 kilometers from Columbus. He estimates how much farther he has to travel by rounding to the nearest 10 and subtracting.

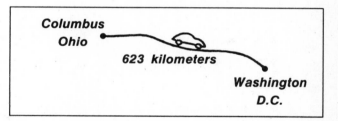

Columbus
Ohio

623 kilometers

Washington
D.C.

1. Fill the blanks in the sentences.

He rounds 623 kilometers to 620 kilometers.

He rounds 168 kilometers to ~~170~~ kilometers.

___455___   ~~450~~

2. Subtract the numbers in the shaded boxes. Write the differences on the blanks.

3. Draw a ring around the subtraction which is easier to do. Put an X on the subtraction Mr. Ross did.

4. The actual distance from Columbus to Washington is ___623___ kilometers.

5. The estimated (rounded) distance from Columbus to Washington is

___620___ kilometers.

FINDING PRODUCTS

A Use the dot pictures to help you find the products.

1. This shows $3 \times (3 + 4)$ This shows $(3 \times 3) + (3 \times 4)$

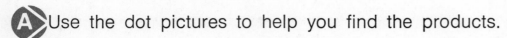

$3 \times (3 + 4)$

$3 \times \boxed{7} = \boxed{21}$

$(3 \times 3) = \boxed{9}$ $(3 \times 4) = \boxed{12}$

$\boxed{9} \quad + \quad \boxed{12} = \boxed{21}$

Does $3 \times (3 + 4) = (3 \times 3) + (3 \times 4)$? ___yes___

2. This shows $4 \times (6 + 2)$ This shows $(4 \times 6) + (4 \times 2)$

$4 \times (6 + 2)$

$4 \times \boxed{8} = \boxed{32}$

$(4 \times 6) = \boxed{24}$ $(4 \times 2) = \boxed{8}$

$\boxed{24} \quad + \quad \boxed{8} = \boxed{32}$

Does $4 \times (6 + 2) = (4 \times 6) + (4 \times 2)$? ___yes___

Explain the example in exercise B, stressing how each expression on the right sides of the equal signs was obtained. Have students complete exercise B.

B Complete each sentence.

1. $5 \times 7 = 5 \times (4 + 3)$

$\quad = (\boxed{5} \times 4) + (\boxed{5} \times 3)$

$\quad = \boxed{20} + 15$

$\quad = \boxed{35}$

2. $3 \times 8 = 3 \times (5 + 3)$

$\quad = (3 \times \boxed{5}) + (3 \times \boxed{3})$

$\quad = 15 + \boxed{9}$

$\quad = \boxed{24}$

Students having difficulty with any of these exercises should have more experiences with activities 1 and 2.

FACTORS OF 6

A Complete each addition and multiplication sentence. Look for a pattern.

1. 6 + 6 = ___12___   2 × 6 = ___12___

2. 6 + 6 + 6 = ___18___   3 × 6 = ___18___

3. 6 + 6 + 6 + 6 = ___24___   4 × 6 = ___24___

4. 6 + 6 + 6 + 6 + 6 = ___30___   5 × 6 = ___30___

5. 6 + 6 + 6 + 6 + 6 + 6 = ___36___   6 × 6 = ___36___

6. 6 + 6 + 6 + 6 + 6 + 6 + 6 = ___42___   7 × 6 = ___42___

7. 6 + 6 + 6 + 6 + 6 + 6 + 6 + 6 = ___48___   8 × 6 = ___48___

8. 6 + 6 + 6 + 6 + 6 + 6 + 6 + 6 + 6 = ___54___   9 × 6 = ___54___

B Study the number line. Not all of the marks have been named. A ring has been drawn around the point for 26.

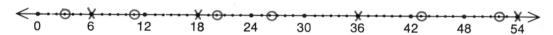

1. Put Xs on the points named below.

     6   18   36   54

2. Draw a ring around the points for the numbers named below.

     3   11   20   43   52

C Use the number line to help you find the products.

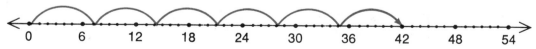

1. 6 × 7 = ___42___   6 × 3 = ___18___   6 × 8 = ___48___

2. 6 × 2 = ___12___   6 × 5 = ___30___   6 × 1 = ___6___

3. 6 × 9 = ___54___   6 × 6 = ___36___   6 × 4 = ___24___

D In the multiplication table below, the number name printed in color shows the product of 6 × 8. The number name printed in black shows the product of 7 × 6. Complete the open spaces in the table.

×	0	1	2	3	4	5	6	7	8	9
0	0	0	0	0	0	0	0	0	0	0
1	0	1	2	3	4	5	6	7	8	9
2	0	2	4	6	8	10	12	14	16	18
3	0	3	6	9	12	15	18	21	24	27
4	0	4	8	12	16	20	24	28	32	36
5	0	5	10	15	20	25	30	35	40	45
6	0	6	12	18	24	30	36	42	48	54
7	0	7	14	21	28	35	42			
8	0	8	16	24	32	40	48			
9	0	9	18	27	36	45	54			

E Use the table in exercise D to help you find the products.

1.

6	7	5	4	8	1	7
× 5	× 6	× 5	× 9	× 6	× 6	× 5
30	42	25	36	48	6	35

2.

9	0	6	3	5	6	0
× 6	× 9	× 6	× 6	× 3	× 9	× 6
54	0	36	18	15	54	0

3.

7	2	9	7	6	8	4
× 4	× 6	× 3	× 3	× 4	× 2	× 4
28	12	27	21	24	16	16

USING MULTIPLICATION

A Cindy and David collected empty bottles. Cindy found enough bottles to fill 4 cartons of 6 bottles. David found enough bottles to fill 3 cartons of 6 bottles.

1. How many bottles did Cindy find? ____24____ bottles

2. How many bottles did David find? ____18____ bottles

3. How many bottles were found altogether? ____42____ bottles

B Solve these word problems.

1. Judy has a penny collection. One page of her coin book has 5 rows of 6 pennies each. How many pennies are needed to fill this page?

____30____ pennies

2. Andy has a nickel collection. One page of his coin book has 3 rows of 4 nickels and 2 rows of 5 nickels.

  a. How many nickels are needed to fill the 3 rows of 4? ____12____ nickels

  b. How many nickels are needed to fill the 2 rows of 5? ____10____ nickels

  c. How many nickels are needed to fill the whole page? ____22____ nickels

3. Ruth's nickel book is not like Andy's. One page has 5 rows of 4 nickels each.

  a. How many nickels are needed to fill one page? ____20____ nickels

  b. Whose book has more nickels on a page, Ruth's or Andy's? ____Andy's____

  c. How many more nickels? ____2____ nickels

4. José has a dime collection. A page of his coin book has 5 rows of 5 dimes. How many dimes are needed to fill this page? ____25____ dimes

5. Elsie has a quarter collection. A page of her coin book has 4 rows of 3 quarters. How many quarters are needed to fill this page in her book? ____12____ quarters

If students experience difficulty with this page, it may be due to poor reading ability or inability to carry out the mathematical processes involved. Group such students and work several of the problems orally with them. You may then wish to have them attempt to solve some of the problems independently.

89

LENGTHS OF THE MONTHS

 A Get a calendar and look at the number of days in each month. Draw a ring around the months that have 31 days.

(January)   February   (March)   April

(May)   June   (July)   (August)

September   (October)   November   (December)

B Look at the picture of a right and a left hand drawn as fists. Starting with the left hand, count off the months for hills and valleys.

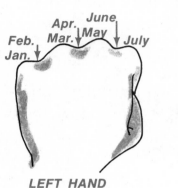 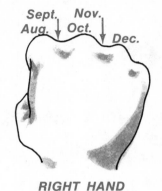

LEFT HAND   RIGHT HAND

1. How many days are in each month that corresponds to a hill? __31__

2. Except for February, how many days are in each month that corresponds to a valley? __30__

C Make a fist with your left hand and match the names of the months from January through July with hills and valleys as in the picture. Continue by making a fist with your right hand and matching the months August through December with hills and valleys.

> Months that match to hills have 31 days. Months that match to valleys have 30 days except for February, which has 28 or 29 days.

D Use the rule above to find the number of days in the months shown below.

August	__31__	May	__31__	December	__31__	October	__31__
March	__31__	September	__30__	April	__30__	July	__31__

CHAPTER REVIEW

A The addition sentence for $4 \times 6 = 24$ is $6 + 6 + 6 + 6 = 24$. Complete each multiplication sentence and write the related addition sentence.

1. $3 \times 7 = \underline{21}$ $\underline{7 + 7 + 7 = 21}$

2. $2 \times 9 = \underline{18}$ $\underline{9 + 9 = 18}$

3. $7 \times 4 = \underline{28}$ $\underline{4 + 4 + 4 + 4 + 4 + 4 + 4 = 28}$

B Complete each sentence.

1. $6 \times 8 = 48$, so $8 \times 6 = \underline{48}$.

2. $7 \times 4 = \underline{28}$, so $4 \times 7 = 28$.

3. $9 \times 5 = \underline{45}$, so $5 \times 9 = 45$.

4. $3 \times 5 = \underline{15}$, so $5 \times 3 = \underline{15}$.

C Fill the blanks.

1. $6 \times (4 + 3) = (6 \times 4) + (6 \times 3)$

$= 24 + 18$

$= 42$

2. $7 \times (3 + 4) = (7 \times 3) + (7 \times 4)$

$= 21 + \boxed{28}$

$= \boxed{49}$

3. $3 \times (5 + 2) = (3 \times \boxed{5}) + (3 \times 2)$

$= 15 + \boxed{6}$

$= \boxed{21}$

4. $5 \times (4 + 5) = (5 \times \boxed{4}) + (5 \times \boxed{5})$

$= \boxed{20} + \boxed{25}$

$= \boxed{45}$

D Use the number line to help you find the products.

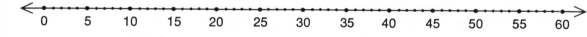

0 5 10 15 20 25 30 35 40 45 50 55 60

1.

4	6	0	7	9	4	5
$\times 4$	$\times 3$	$\times 5$	$\times 6$	$\times 1$	$\times 7$	$\times 6$
16	18	0	42	9	28	30

2.

3	7	1	4	5	6	2
$\times 2$	$\times 0$	$\times 6$	$\times 9$	$\times 3$	$\times 6$	$\times 5$
6	0	6	36	15	36	10

CHECK-UP

 A Complete these sentences.

1. $5 \times 9 = 45$, so $9 \times 5 = \underline{45}$.   **2.** $6 \times 7 = \underline{42}$, so $7 \times 6 = 42$.

3. $4 \times 3 = \underline{12}$, so $3 \times 4 = \underline{12}$.   **4.** $3 \times 5 = \underline{15}$, so $5 \times 3 = \underline{15}$.

B Draw arrows on the number line to show the multiplication fact. Then write the product.

1. $3 \times 7 = \underline{21}$

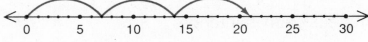

2. $4 \times 5 = \underline{20}$

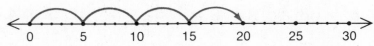

C Find the products for the multiplication facts.

1.

6	7	9	8	7	4	5
$\times 6$	$\times 2$	$\times 0$	$\times 3$	$\times 4$	$\times 8$	$\times 4$
36	14	0	24	28	32	20

2.

7	6	5	9	3	4	6
$\times 1$	$\times 3$	$\times 5$	$\times 2$	$\times 3$	$\times 6$	$\times 2$
7	18	25	18	9	24	12

D Solve these word problems.

1. Beth's stamp album has places for 6 rows of 5 stamps on each page.

How many stamps will fit on the page? __30__ stamps

2. Barry bought 3 pencils at the bookstore for 7¢ each. How much did

he have to pay for all of the pencils? __21__ ¢

3. Kate bought 9 cards of buttons. On each card there were 4 buttons.

How many buttons did she buy? __36__ buttons

4. Emilio and Betty stacked sacks of oranges in 8 rows. They put 5 sacks in each row. How many sacks of oranges did they stack?

__40__ sacks

5 • MULTIPLICATION AND DIVISION

UNDERSTANDING DIVISION

 Read each word problem and fill the blanks.

1. 10 children formed 2 teams to play kickball. How many children were on each team? __5__ The division sentence is 10 ÷ 2 = 5. It is read **ten divided by two equals five.**

2. 12 nickels were to be divided so each of 3 children received the same number of nickels. How many nickels did each child receive?

__4__ nickels   The division sentence is 12 ÷ 3 = __4__.

> A division sentence like 15 ÷ 5 = 3 has three parts.
> 15 is the **dividend.**
> 5 is the **divisor.**
> 3 is the **quotient.**

Explain number 1 in exercise B. In exercises B and C, the divisor always shows the number of equal rows of dots. The quotient is found by counting the number of dots in a row.

 Use the dot pictures to help you find the quotients.

1. 15 ÷ 3 = __5__   **2.** 10 ÷ 2 = __5__   **3.** 12 ÷ 4 = __3__   **4.** 20 ÷ 5 = __4__

 Complete the division sentence for each dot picture.

1.  24 ÷ 3 = 8   **2.**  30 ÷ 5 = 6

3.  25 ÷ 5 = 5   **4.** 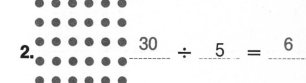 14 ÷ 2 = 7

Treat exercise A orally. Discuss the terms *dividend, divisor,* and *quotient.* Point out that the dividend tells the total number of objects while the divisor and the quotient tell the number of equal sets and the number of objects in each set.

93

DIVISION AS REPEATED SUBTRACTION

 A Mark each picture.   Then fill the blanks.

 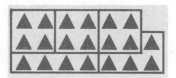

1. Look at the set of squares. Put the squares in groups of 6 by drawing rings around sets of 6 squares.

   a. $18 - (6 + 6 + 6) =$ ___0___

   b. How many 6s were subtracted? ___3___

   c. $18 \div 6 =$ ___3___

Have students complete exercise B.

2. Look at the set of triangles. Put the triangles in sets of 4 by drawing rings.

   a. $20 - (4 + 4 + 4 + 4 + 4)$
   $=$ ___0___

   b. How many 4s were subtracted? ___5___

   c. $20 \div 4 =$ ___5___

B Complete the chart.

	Repeated Subtraction	Division Sentence	Dividend	Divisor	Quotient
1.	$12 - (3 + 3 + 3 + 3) = 0$	$12 \div 3 = 4$	12	3	4
2.	$8 - (4 + 4) = 0$	$8 \div 4 = 2$	8	4	2
3.	$15 - (5 + 5 + 5) = 0$	$15 \div 5 = 3$	15	5	3
4.	$12 - (6 + 6) = 0$	$12 \div 6 = 2$	12	6	2
5.	$24 - (8 + 8 + 8) = 0$	$24 \div 8 = 3$	24	8	3

Remind students how to subtract on the number line. Explain the example showing how to divide $10 \div 5$ on the number line.

How To Do the Division $10 \div 5$ on the Number Line

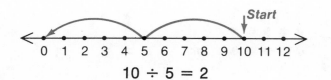

Start at 10.
Take hops of 5 spaces to the left.
Stop at 0.
The quotient is the number of hops.

$10 \div 5 = 2$

Have students complete exercises C and D.

 Complete the chart.

		Start	Length of Hops	Number of Hops	Division Sentence
1.	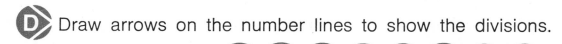	14	2	7	$14 \div 2 = 7$
2.		9	3	3	$9 \div 3 = 3$
3.		12	4	3	$12 \div 4 = 3$
4.		14	7	2	$14 \div 7 = 2$

 Draw arrows on the number lines to show the divisions.

1. $16 \div 2 = $ ___8___

2. $21 \div 7 = $ ___3___

3. $18 \div 3 = $ ___6___

The division sentence $21 \div 3 = 7$
is sometimes written like this:

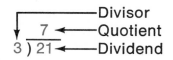

Discuss the two ways to write a division. Give several more examples. Then have students complete exercise E.

E Use the number line to help you find the quotients.

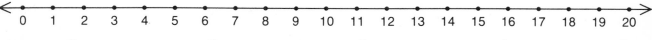

1. $3\overline{)6}$ = 2 $2\overline{)4}$ = 2 $2\overline{)10}$ = 5 $3\overline{)12}$ = 4 $2\overline{)6}$ = 3

2. $5\overline{)15}$ = 3 $2\overline{)18}$ = 9 $4\overline{)20}$ = 5 $4\overline{)8}$ = 2 $3\overline{)9}$ = 3

3. $2\overline{)16}$ = 8 $4\overline{)16}$ = 4 $5\overline{)5}$ = 1 $6\overline{)12}$ = 2 $4\overline{)12}$ = 3

MULTIPLICATION AND DIVISION

 A For each dot picture, write two multiplication and two division sentences.

		Multiplication Sentences		Division Sentences	
1.	•••••••• ••••••••	$2 \times 8 = 16$	$8 \times 2 = 16$	$16 \div 2 = 8$	$16 \div 8 = 2$
2.	••••• ••••• ••••• ••••• ••••• •••••	$6 \times 5 = 30$	$5 \times 6 = 30$	$30 \div 6 = 5$	$30 \div 5 = 6$
3.	••••••• ••••••• ••••••• •••••••	$4 \times 7 = 28$	$7 \times 4 = 28$	$28 \div 4 = 7$	$28 \div 7 = 4$

> Each time you know one multiplication fact, you also know another multiplication fact and two division facts.

 **B** Complete the table.

	Multiplication Facts		Division Facts	
1.	$4 \times 8 = 32$	$8 \times 4 = 32$	$32 \div 4 = 8$	$32 \div 8 = 4$
2.	$5 \times 9 = 45$	$9 \times 5 = 45$	$45 \div 5 = 9$	$45 \div 9 = 5$
3.	$5 \times 7 = 35$	$7 \times 5 = 35$	$35 \div 5 = 7$	$35 \div 7 = 5$
4.	$8 \times 3 = 24$	$3 \times 8 = 24$	$24 \div 8 = 3$	$24 \div 3 = 8$

C Complete each multiplication sentence. Use the multiplication sentence to find the missing numbers in the division sentence.

1. $4 \times 9 = 36$; $36 \div 4 = 9$ **2.** $7 \times 3 = 21$; $21 \div 7 = 3$

3. $2 \times 9 = 18$; $18 \div 9 = 2$ **4.** $6 \times 6 = 36$; $36 \div 6 = 6$

5. $5 \times 8 = 40$; $40 \div 5 = 8$ **6.** $3 \times 5 = 15$; $15 \div 3 = 5$

Students having difficulty should have more experiences with the introductory activities for this lesson.

DIVISION BY 1 OR 2

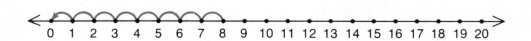

$$8 \div 1 = 8 \qquad 1\overline{)8}\,^{8}$$

 Division by 1. Use the number line to divide.

1. $6 \div 1 = \underline{6}$ $2 \div 1 = \underline{2}$ $5 \div 1 = \underline{5}$ $1 \div 1 = \underline{1}$

2. $3 \div 1 = \underline{3}$ $9 \div 1 = \underline{9}$ $7 \div 1 = \underline{7}$ $4 \div 1 = \underline{4}$

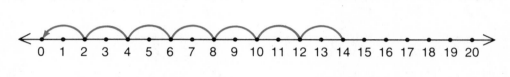

$$14 \div 2 = 7 \qquad 2\overline{)14}\,^{7}$$

 Division by 2. Use the number line to divide.

1. $4 \div 2 = \underline{2}$ $10 \div 2 = \underline{5}$ $6 \div 2 = \underline{3}$ $16 \div 2 = \underline{8}$

2. $8 \div 2 = \underline{4}$ $2 \div 2 = \underline{1}$ $18 \div 2 = \underline{9}$ $12 \div 2 = \underline{6}$

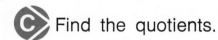 Find the quotients.

1. $1\overline{)6}\,^{6}$ $\qquad$ $2\overline{)10}\,^{5}$ $\qquad$ $2\overline{)4}\,^{2}$ $\qquad$ $1\overline{)8}\,^{8}$ $\qquad$ $2\overline{)16}\,^{8}$

2. $2\overline{)12}\,^{6}$ $\qquad$ $1\overline{)5}\,^{5}$ $\qquad$ $1\overline{)1}\,^{1}$ $\qquad$ $2\overline{)8}\,^{4}$ $\qquad$ $1\overline{)2}\,^{2}$

3. $1\overline{)4}\,^{4}$ $\qquad$ $2\overline{)2}\,^{1}$ $\qquad$ $1\overline{)3}\,^{3}$ $\qquad$ $1\overline{)9}\,^{9}$ $\qquad$ $2\overline{)6}\,^{3}$

DIVISION BY 3 OR 4

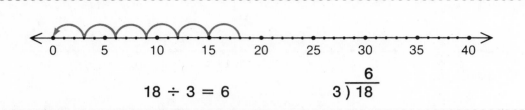

$18 \div 3 = 6$ $3 \overline{)\,18}$ with 6 on top

A Division by 3. Use the number line to divide.

1. $3 \div 3 = \underline{}\;1$ $12 \div 3 = \underline{}\;4$ $6 \div 3 = \underline{}\;2$ $21 \div 3 = \underline{}\;7$

2. $24 \div 3 = \underline{}\;8$ $15 \div 3 = \underline{}\;5$ $27 \div 3 = \underline{}\;9$ $9 \div 3 = \underline{}\;3$

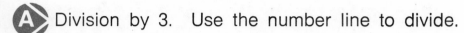

$36 \div 4 = 9$ $4 \overline{)\,36}$ with 9 on top

B Division by 4. Use the number line to divide.

1. $16 \div 4 = \underline{}\;4$ $24 \div 4 = \underline{}\;6$ $4 \div 4 = \underline{}\;1$ $28 \div 4 = \underline{}\;7$

2. $20 \div 4 = \underline{}\;5$ $8 \div 4 = \underline{}\;2$ $32 \div 4 = \underline{}\;8$ $12 \div 4 = \underline{}\;3$

C Find the quotients.

1. $4 \overline{)\,24} = 6$ $3 \overline{)\,24} = 8$ $3 \overline{)\,12} = 4$ $4 \overline{)\,36} = 9$ $2 \overline{)\,16} = 8$

2. $3 \overline{)\,9} = 3$ $4 \overline{)\,8} = 2$ $4 \overline{)\,32} = 8$ $3 \overline{)\,21} = 7$ $4 \overline{)\,4} = 1$

D Complete the multiplication first. Then do the related division.

1. $\begin{array}{r} 5 \\ \times\, 4 \\ \hline 20 \end{array}$ $4 \overline{)\,20} = 5$

2. $\begin{array}{r} 6 \\ \times\, 3 \\ \hline 18 \end{array}$ $3 \overline{)\,18} = 6$

3. $\begin{array}{r} 9 \\ \times\, 4 \\ \hline 36 \end{array}$ $4 \overline{)\,36} = 9$

DIVISION BY 5 OR 6

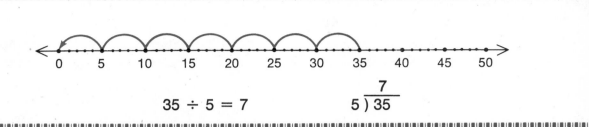

$$35 \div 5 = 7 \qquad 5)\overline{35} \;\; ^7$$

 A Division by 5. Use the number line to divide.

1. $10 \div 5 = \underline{\ 2\ }$ $25 \div 5 = \underline{\ 5\ }$ $40 \div 5 = \underline{\ 8\ }$ $5 \div 5 = \underline{\ 1\ }$

2. $45 \div 5 = \underline{\ 9\ }$ $15 \div 5 = \underline{\ 3\ }$ $30 \div 5 = \underline{\ 6\ }$ $20 \div 5 = \underline{\ 4\ }$

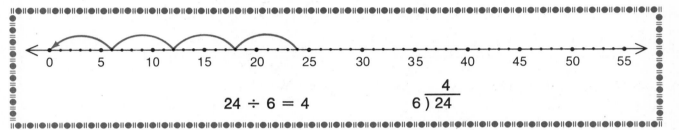

$$24 \div 6 = 4 \qquad 6)\overline{24} \;\; ^4$$

 B Division by 6. Use the number line to divide.

1. $36 \div 6 = \underline{\ 6\ }$ $12 \div 6 = \underline{\ 2\ }$ $30 \div 6 = \underline{\ 5\ }$ $48 \div 6 = \underline{\ 8\ }$

2. $6 \div 6 = \underline{\ 1\ }$ $54 \div 6 = \underline{\ 9\ }$ $18 \div 6 = \underline{\ 3\ }$ $42 \div 6 = \underline{\ 7\ }$

 C Find the quotients.

1. $5)\overline{30} \;\; ^6$ $6)\overline{48} \;\; ^8$ $4)\overline{24} \;\; ^6$ $5)\overline{35} \;\; ^7$ $5)\overline{45} \;\; ^9$

2. $6)\overline{24} \;\; ^4$ $5)\overline{10} \;\; ^2$ $6)\overline{18} \;\; ^3$ $3)\overline{21} \;\; ^7$ $6)\overline{42} \;\; ^7$

D Complete the multiplication first. Then do the related division.

1. $\begin{array}{r} 9 \\ \times\, 6 \\ \hline 54 \end{array}$ $6)\overline{54} \;\; ^9$
  2. $\begin{array}{r} 8 \\ \times\, 5 \\ \hline 40 \end{array}$ $5)\overline{40} \;\; ^8$
  3. $\begin{array}{r} 5 \\ \times\, 6 \\ \hline 30 \end{array}$ $6)\overline{30} \;\; ^5$

Check students' work. Have them use the number line to correct any mistakes. Then complete additional activity 1 with all students. Additional activity 2 or 3 may be used if necessary.

99

Work exercise A with the class. Emphasize the phrases which mean to divide. Have students write the translations and quotients on the chalkboard.

WORDS THAT MEAN TO DIVIDE

 Translate these phrases and find the quotients.

	Phrase	Translation	Quotient
1.	12 divided by 4	12 ÷ 4	3
2.	3 into 21	21 ÷ 3	7
3.	The number of fives in 30	30 ÷ 5	6
4.	18 divided by 2	18 ÷ 2	9
5.	24 objects separated into 4 equal sets	24 ÷ 4	6
6.	How many 2s equal 12	12 ÷ 2	6

Read the first problem with the class. Use questions to direct attention to the words which mean to divide and to point out how to set up the division sentence.

B Solve each word problem. See if you can find the words that mean to divide.

1. Jim has 32 rabbits divided equally between 4 hutches. How many rabbits are in each hutch? ___8___ rabbits

2. How many rows of 5 chairs each can be made using 20 chairs? ___4___ rows

3. Haruko cut a board of wood 35 inches long into 5 pieces of equal length. How long was each piece? ___7___ inches

4. There are 24 crayons in a box. The crayons are in 4 rows. How many crayons are there in each row? ___6___ crayons

5. Tina has 45 pennies. She wants to exchange them for nickels. How many nickels equal her 45 pennies? ___9___ nickels

 Students who have difficulty completing these exercises independently should solve them in a group setting. They may wish to draw a picture of the situation.

ADDITION—SUBTRACTION REVIEW

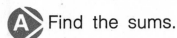 Find the sums.

1.

23	43	28	64	93	68	73
+ 45	+ 95	+ 49	+ 12	+ 44	+ 55	+ 97
68	138	77	76	137	123	170

2.

432	546	384	754	485	375
+ 264	+ 306	+ 390	+ 197	+ 287	+ 492
696	852	774	951	772	867

B Find the differences.

1.

85	42	92	31	64	61	92
− 23	− 9	− 63	− 4	− 34	− 49	− 76
62	33	29	27	30	12	16

2.

598	637	374	765	415	690
− 416	− 9	− 57	− 158	− 268	− 493
182	628	317	607	147	197

C Solve these word problems.

1. Phil had 93 newspapers to sell. He sold all but 15 of them. How many newspapers did he sell? __78__ newspapers

2. Esperanza read 173 pages in her book and still had 45 pages to read. How many pages are in the book? __218__ pages

3. Rex saves football trading cards. He has 39 Lions, 23 Bears, and 43 Packers. How many cards does he have? __105__ cards

4. Mike threw a football 27 meters. Janis threw a football 41 meters. How much farther did Janis throw the football? __14__ meters

MULTIPLICATION AND DIVISION BY 7

 Complete each sentence. Look for a pattern.

1. 7 + 7 = __14__   2 × 7 = __14__

2. 7 + 7 + 7 = __21__   3 × 7 = __21__

3. 7 + 7 + 7 + 7 = __28__   4 × 7 = __28__

4. 7 + 7 + 7 + 7 + 7 = __35__   5 × 7 = __35__

5. 7 + 7 + 7 + 7 + 7 + 7 = __42__   6 × 7 = __42__

6. 7 + 7 + 7 + 7 + 7 + 7 + 7 = __49__   7 × 7 = __49__

7. 7 + 7 + 7 + 7 + 7 + 7 + 7 + 7 = __56__   8 × 7 = __56__

8. 7 + 7 + 7 + 7 + 7 + 7 + 7 + 7 + 7 = __63__   9 × 7 = __63__

 Complete the table.

	Multiplication Facts		Division Facts	
1.	6 × 7 = 42	7 × 6 = 42	42 ÷ 7 = 6	42 ÷ 6 = 7
2.	1 × 7 = 7	7 × 1 = 7	7 ÷ 7 = 1	7 ÷ 1 = 7
3.	5 × 7 = 35	7 × 5 = 35	35 ÷ 7 = 5	35 ÷ 5 = 7
4.	2 × 7 = 14	7 × 2 = 14	14 ÷ 7 = 2	14 ÷ 2 = 7
5.	3 × 7 = 21	7 × 3 = 21	21 ÷ 7 = 3	21 ÷ 3 = 7
6.	8 × 7 = 56	7 × 8 = 56	56 ÷ 7 = 8	56 ÷ 8 = 7
7.	4 × 7 = 28	7 × 4 = 28	28 ÷ 7 = 4	28 ÷ 4 = 7
8.	9 × 7 = 63	7 × 9 = 63	63 ÷ 7 = 9	63 ÷ 9 = 7
9.	7 × 7 = 49		49 ÷ 7 = 7	

Have students cover the products and quotients in the table with a clean piece of paper and respond to each exercise again.

Complete the table.

X	0	1	2	3	4	5	6	7	8	9
7	0	7	14	21	28	35	42	49	56	63

D Write the products.

1.

$$\begin{array}{r} 7 \\ \times\,4 \\ \hline 28 \end{array} \qquad \begin{array}{r} 6 \\ \times\,7 \\ \hline 42 \end{array} \qquad \begin{array}{r} 5 \\ \times\,4 \\ \hline 20 \end{array} \qquad \begin{array}{r} 1 \\ \times\,7 \\ \hline 7 \end{array} \qquad \begin{array}{r} 9 \\ \times\,7 \\ \hline 63 \end{array} \qquad \begin{array}{r} 6 \\ \times\,6 \\ \hline 36 \end{array} \qquad \begin{array}{r} 7 \\ \times\,0 \\ \hline 0 \end{array}$$

2.

$$\begin{array}{r} 9 \\ \times\,5 \\ \hline 45 \end{array} \qquad \begin{array}{r} 7 \\ \times\,8 \\ \hline 56 \end{array} \qquad \begin{array}{r} 5 \\ \times\,7 \\ \hline 35 \end{array} \qquad \begin{array}{r} 4 \\ \times\,9 \\ \hline 36 \end{array} \qquad \begin{array}{r} 7 \\ \times\,3 \\ \hline 21 \end{array} \qquad \begin{array}{r} 8 \\ \times\,7 \\ \hline 56 \end{array} \qquad \begin{array}{r} 7 \\ \times\,2 \\ \hline 14 \end{array}$$

3.

$$\begin{array}{r} 7 \\ \times\,9 \\ \hline 63 \end{array} \qquad \begin{array}{r} 3 \\ \times\,7 \\ \hline 21 \end{array} \qquad \begin{array}{r} 7 \\ \times\,7 \\ \hline 49 \end{array} \qquad \begin{array}{r} 7 \\ \times\,5 \\ \hline 35 \end{array} \qquad \begin{array}{r} 9 \\ \times\,1 \\ \hline 9 \end{array} \qquad \begin{array}{r} 4 \\ \times\,7 \\ \hline 28 \end{array} \qquad \begin{array}{r} 8 \\ \times\,5 \\ \hline 40 \end{array}$$

E Complete the division table.

7)	1	2	3	4	5	6	7	8	9
7	7	14	21	28	35	42	49	56	63

F Write the quotients.

1. $7\overline{)28}\!=\!4 \qquad 7\overline{)63}\!=\!9 \qquad 5\overline{)35}\!=\!7 \qquad 3\overline{)21}\!=\!7 \qquad 2\overline{)18}\!=\!9$

2. $4\overline{)20}\!=\!5 \qquad 7\overline{)7}\!=\!1 \qquad 7\overline{)21}\!=\!3 \qquad 4\overline{)28}\!=\!7 \qquad 7\overline{)49}\!=\!7$

3. $7\overline{)35}\!=\!5 \qquad 2\overline{)14}\!=\!7 \qquad 7\overline{)56}\!=\!8 \qquad 7\overline{)42}\!=\!6 \qquad 3\overline{)18}\!=\!6$

4. $5\overline{)25}\!=\!5 \qquad 7\overline{)14}\!=\!2 \qquad 3\overline{)27}\!=\!9 \qquad 2\overline{)16}\!=\!8 \qquad 4\overline{)32}\!=\!8$

MULTIPLICATION AND DIVISION BY 8

 Complete each sentence. Look for a pattern.

1. 8 + 8 = __16__   2 × 8 = __16__

2. 8 + 8 + 8 = __24__   3 × 8 = __24__

3. 8 + 8 + 8 + 8 = __32__   4 × 8 = __32__

4. 8 + 8 + 8 + 8 + 8 = __40__   5 × 8 = __40__

5. 8 + 8 + 8 + 8 + 8 + 8 = __48__   6 × 8 = __48__

6. 8 + 8 + 8 + 8 + 8 + 8 + 8 = __56__   7 × 8 = __56__

7. 8 + 8 + 8 + 8 + 8 + 8 + 8 + 8 = __64__   8 × 8 = __64__

8. 8 + 8 + 8 + 8 + 8 + 8 + 8 + 8 + 8 = __72__   9 × 8 = __72__

 Complete the table.

	Multiplication Facts		Division Facts	
1.	4 × 8 = 32	8 × 4 = 32	32 ÷ 8 = 4	32 ÷ 4 = 8
2.	1 × 8 = 8	8 × 1 = 8	8 ÷ 8 = 1	8 ÷ 1 = 8
3.	6 × 8 = 48	8 × 6 = 48	48 ÷ 8 = 6	48 ÷ 6 = 8
4.	9 × 8 = 72	8 × 9 = 72	72 ÷ 8 = 9	72 ÷ 9 = 8
5.	3 × 8 = 24	8 × 3 = 24	24 ÷ 8 = 3	24 ÷ 3 = 8
6.	7 × 8 = 56	8 × 7 = 56	56 ÷ 8 = 7	56 ÷ 7 = 8
7.	5 × 8 = 40	8 × 5 = 40	40 ÷ 8 = 5	40 ÷ 5 = 8
8.	2 × 8 = 16	8 × 2 = 16	16 ÷ 8 = 2	16 ÷ 2 = 8
9.	8 × 8 = 64		64 ÷ 8 = 8	

Complete the table.

X	0	1	2	3	4	5	6	7	8	9
8	0	8	16	24	32	40	48	56	64	72

 Write the products.

1.

$$\begin{array}{r} 8 \\ \times\ 3 \\ \hline 24 \end{array} \quad \begin{array}{r} 6 \\ \times\ 8 \\ \hline 48 \end{array} \quad \begin{array}{r} 4 \\ \times\ 4 \\ \hline 16 \end{array} \quad \begin{array}{r} 5 \\ \times\ 8 \\ \hline 40 \end{array} \quad \begin{array}{r} 8 \\ \times\ 9 \\ \hline 72 \end{array} \quad \begin{array}{r} 6 \\ \times\ 7 \\ \hline 42 \end{array} \quad \begin{array}{r} 0 \\ \times\ 8 \\ \hline 0 \end{array}$$

2.

$$\begin{array}{r} 9 \\ \times\ 7 \\ \hline 63 \end{array} \quad \begin{array}{r} 8 \\ \times\ 4 \\ \hline 32 \end{array} \quad \begin{array}{r} 8 \\ \times\ 8 \\ \hline 64 \end{array} \quad \begin{array}{r} 4 \\ \times\ 5 \\ \hline 20 \end{array} \quad \begin{array}{r} 2 \\ \times\ 8 \\ \hline 16 \end{array} \quad \begin{array}{r} 7 \\ \times\ 8 \\ \hline 56 \end{array} \quad \begin{array}{r} 6 \\ \times\ 6 \\ \hline 36 \end{array}$$

3.

$$\begin{array}{r} 1 \\ \times\ 8 \\ \hline 8 \end{array} \quad \begin{array}{r} 9 \\ \times\ 8 \\ \hline 72 \end{array} \quad \begin{array}{r} 8 \\ \times\ 6 \\ \hline 48 \end{array} \quad \begin{array}{r} 7 \\ \times\ 4 \\ \hline 28 \end{array} \quad \begin{array}{r} 8 \\ \times\ 5 \\ \hline 40 \end{array} \quad \begin{array}{r} 9 \\ \times\ 3 \\ \hline 27 \end{array} \quad \begin{array}{r} 8 \\ \times\ 7 \\ \hline 56 \end{array}$$

 Complete the division table.

	1	2	3	4	5	6	7	8	9
8)	8	16	24	32	40	48	56	64	72

F Write the quotients.

1. $8\overline{)16}\ ^{2} \qquad 7\overline{)28}\ ^{4} \qquad 8\overline{)48}\ ^{6} \qquad 6\overline{)42}\ ^{7} \qquad 8\overline{)72}\ ^{9}$

2. $2\overline{)18}\ ^{9} \qquad 8\overline{)8}\ ^{1} \qquad 4\overline{)24}\ ^{6} \qquad 8\overline{)32}\ ^{4} \qquad 5\overline{)45}\ ^{9}$

3. $8\overline{)24}\ ^{3} \qquad 3\overline{)21}\ ^{7} \qquad 6\overline{)54}\ ^{9} \qquad 7\overline{)35}\ ^{5} \qquad 8\overline{)40}\ ^{5}$

4. $6\overline{)48}\ ^{8} \qquad 8\overline{)64}\ ^{8} \qquad 2\overline{)14}\ ^{7} \qquad 8\overline{)56}\ ^{7} \qquad 7\overline{)56}\ ^{8}$

Pupils having difficulty with any of the facts involving 8 should have repeated experiences with the initial teaching activities. Students having difficulty with other facts should complete the additional activity.

MULTIPLICATION AND DIVISION BY 9

 Complete each sentence. Look for a pattern.

1. $9 + 9 =$ _18_ $2 \times 9 =$ _18_

2. $9 + 9 + 9 =$ _27_ $3 \times 9 =$ _27_

3. $9 + 9 + 9 + 9 =$ _36_ $4 \times 9 =$ _36_

4. $9 + 9 + 9 + 9 + 9 =$ _45_ $5 \times 9 =$ _45_

5. $9 + 9 + 9 + 9 + 9 + 9 =$ _54_ $6 \times 9 =$ _54_

6. $9 + 9 + 9 + 9 + 9 + 9 + 9 =$ _63_ $7 \times 9 =$ _63_

7. $9 + 9 + 9 + 9 + 9 + 9 + 9 + 9 =$ _72_ $8 \times 9 =$ _72_

8. $9 + 9 + 9 + 9 + 9 + 9 + 9 + 9 + 9 =$ _81_ $9 \times 9 =$ _81_

 Complete the table.

	Multiplication Facts		Division Facts	
1.	$6 \times 9 = 54$	$9 \times 6 = 54$	$54 \div 9 = 6$	$54 \div 6 = 9$
2.	$3 \times 9 = 27$	$9 \times 3 = 27$	$27 \div 9 = 3$	$27 \div 3 = 9$
3.	$8 \times 9 = 72$	$9 \times 8 = 72$	$72 \div 9 = 8$	$72 \div 8 = 9$
4.	$4 \times 9 = 36$	$9 \times 4 = 36$	$36 \div 9 = 4$	$36 \div 4 = 9$
5.	$7 \times 9 = 63$	$9 \times 7 = 63$	$63 \div 9 = 7$	$63 \div 7 = 9$
6.	$1 \times 9 = 9$	$9 \times 1 = 9$	$9 \div 9 = 1$	$9 \div 1 = 9$
7.	$5 \times 9 = 45$	$9 \times 5 = 45$	$45 \div 9 = 5$	$45 \div 5 = 9$
8.	$2 \times 9 = 18$	$9 \times 2 = 18$	$18 \div 9 = 2$	$18 \div 2 = 9$
9.	$9 \times 9 = 81$		$81 \div 9 = 9$	

Have students cover the products and quotients in the table with a clean piece of paper and respond to each exercise again.

 Complete the table.

X	0	1	2	3	4	5	6	7	8	9
9	0	9	18	27	36	45	54	63	72	81

D Write the products.

1.
$$\begin{array}{r} 9 \\ \times 5 \\ \hline 45 \end{array}$$
$$\begin{array}{r} 9 \\ \times 8 \\ \hline 72 \end{array}$$
$$\begin{array}{r} 6 \\ \times 9 \\ \hline 54 \end{array}$$
$$\begin{array}{r} 4 \\ \times 8 \\ \hline 32 \end{array}$$
$$\begin{array}{r} 3 \\ \times 9 \\ \hline 27 \end{array}$$
$$\begin{array}{r} 5 \\ \times 7 \\ \hline 35 \end{array}$$
$$\begin{array}{r} 0 \\ \times 9 \\ \hline 0 \end{array}$$

2.
$$\begin{array}{r} 7 \\ \times 7 \\ \hline 49 \end{array}$$
$$\begin{array}{r} 4 \\ \times 9 \\ \hline 36 \end{array}$$
$$\begin{array}{r} 8 \\ \times 3 \\ \hline 24 \end{array}$$
$$\begin{array}{r} 9 \\ \times 2 \\ \hline 18 \end{array}$$
$$\begin{array}{r} 9 \\ \times 7 \\ \hline 63 \end{array}$$
$$\begin{array}{r} 9 \\ \times 9 \\ \hline 81 \end{array}$$
$$\begin{array}{r} 6 \\ \times 8 \\ \hline 48 \end{array}$$

3.
$$\begin{array}{r} 1 \\ \times 9 \\ \hline 9 \end{array}$$
$$\begin{array}{r} 9 \\ \times 6 \\ \hline 54 \end{array}$$
$$\begin{array}{r} 7 \\ \times 9 \\ \hline 63 \end{array}$$
$$\begin{array}{r} 9 \\ \times 4 \\ \hline 36 \end{array}$$
$$\begin{array}{r} 8 \\ \times 7 \\ \hline 56 \end{array}$$
$$\begin{array}{r} 6 \\ \times 5 \\ \hline 30 \end{array}$$
$$\begin{array}{r} 8 \\ \times 9 \\ \hline 72 \end{array}$$

E Complete the division table.

	1	2	3	4	5	6	7	8	9
9)	9	18	27	36	45	54	63	72	81

F Write the quotients.

1. $9\overline{)36}$ → 4 $5\overline{)45}$ → 9 $9\overline{)18}$ → 2 $7\overline{)35}$ → 5 $9\overline{)72}$ → 8

2. $2\overline{)14}$ → 7 $9\overline{)9}$ → 1 $7\overline{)49}$ → 7 $9\overline{)63}$ → 7 $3\overline{)24}$ → 8

3. $9\overline{)54}$ → 6 $4\overline{)36}$ → 9 $9\overline{)81}$ → 9 $8\overline{)64}$ → 8 $7\overline{)63}$ → 9

At this point, students should know all of the basic multiplication and division facts. Students who do not should complete the additional activity.

RECOGNIZING MULTIPLICATION AND DIVISION

 A Write *M* or *D* to tell if multiplication or division is used to solve the problem. Then write the multiplication or division sentence.

	M or D	**Sentence**
1. How many are 7 threes?	M	$7 \times 3 = 21$
2. 2 eights are how many?	M	$2 \times 8 = 16$
3. 30 equals how many sixes?	D	$30 \div 6 = 5$
4. How many are 5 nines?	M	$5 \times 9 = 45$
5. How many nines equal 27?	D	$27 \div 9 = 3$
6. 32 equals how many eights?	D	$32 \div 8 = 4$
7. 5 sets of 5 each are how many?	M	$5 \times 5 = 25$
8. 14 equals 7 sets of how many?	D	$14 \div 7 = 2$

B Complete the chart.

		Number of Equal Sets	**Number in Each Set**	**Total Number**	**Number Sentence**
1.	24 bottles in 4 cartons	4	6	24	$24 \div 4 = 6$
2.	2 teams of 5 children each	2	5	10	$2 \times 5 = 10$
3.	28 chairs in rows of 4 each	7	4	28	$28 \div 4 = 7$
4.	18 flowers in 3 vases	3	6	18	$18 \div 3 = 6$
5.	6 bunches of 8 carrots	6	8	48	$6 \times 8 = 48$
6.	9 rows of 6 glasses each	9	6	54	$9 \times 6 = 54$
7.	32 rabbits, 4 in each hutch	8	4	32	$32 \div 4 = 8$
8.	36 cupcakes in 9 rows	9	4	36	$36 \div 9 = 4$
9.	4 cars, 4 tires on each car	4	4	16	$4 \times 4 = 16$
10.	5 rows of chairs, 35 chairs	5	7	35	$35 \div 5 = 7$

MULTIPLICATION FACTS

 Complete the multiplication facts table.

✕	0	1	2	3	4	5	6	7	8	9
0	0	0	0	0	0	0	0	0	0	0
1	0	1	2	3	4	5	6	7	8	9
2	0	2	4	6	8	10	12	14	16	18
3	0	3	6	9	12	15	18	21	24	27
4	0	4	8	12	16	20	24	28	32	36
5	0	5	10	15	20	25	30	35	40	45
6	0	6	12	18	24	30	36	42	48	54
7	0	7	14	21	28	35	42	49	56	63
8	0	8	16	24	32	40	48	56	64	72
9	0	9	18	27	36	45	54	63	72	81

 Find the products.   Use the multiplication facts table if you need it.

1.

$$\begin{array}{r} 6 \\ \times 3 \\ \hline 18 \end{array} \qquad \begin{array}{r} 2 \\ \times 2 \\ \hline 4 \end{array} \qquad \begin{array}{r} 8 \\ \times 1 \\ \hline 8 \end{array} \qquad \begin{array}{r} 7 \\ \times 8 \\ \hline 56 \end{array} \qquad \begin{array}{r} 5 \\ \times 3 \\ \hline 15 \end{array} \qquad \begin{array}{r} 2 \\ \times 7 \\ \hline 14 \end{array} \qquad \begin{array}{r} 9 \\ \times 5 \\ \hline 45 \end{array}$$

2.

$$\begin{array}{r} 8 \\ \times 4 \\ \hline 32 \end{array} \qquad \begin{array}{r} 5 \\ \times 9 \\ \hline 45 \end{array} \qquad \begin{array}{r} 2 \\ \times 4 \\ \hline 8 \end{array} \qquad \begin{array}{r} 3 \\ \times 7 \\ \hline 21 \end{array} \qquad \begin{array}{r} 0 \\ \times 5 \\ \hline 0 \end{array} \qquad \begin{array}{r} 9 \\ \times 1 \\ \hline 9 \end{array} \qquad \begin{array}{r} 6 \\ \times 2 \\ \hline 12 \end{array}$$

3.

$$\begin{array}{r} 9 \\ \times 9 \\ \hline 81 \end{array} \qquad \begin{array}{r} 1 \\ \times 6 \\ \hline 6 \end{array} \qquad \begin{array}{r} 7 \\ \times 5 \\ \hline 35 \end{array} \qquad \begin{array}{r} 4 \\ \times 3 \\ \hline 12 \end{array} \qquad \begin{array}{r} 5 \\ \times 8 \\ \hline 40 \end{array} \qquad \begin{array}{r} 2 \\ \times 3 \\ \hline 6 \end{array} \qquad \begin{array}{r} 6 \\ \times 9 \\ \hline 54 \end{array}$$

DIVISION FACTS

 A Complete the division facts charts.

1.		**2.**		**3.**		**4.**		**5.**		**6.**		**7.**		**8.**	
÷	9	÷	8	÷	7	÷	6	÷	5	÷	4	÷	3	÷	2
9	1	8	1	7	1	6	1	5	1	4	1	3	1	2	1
18	2	16	2	14	2	12	2	10	2	8	2	6	2	4	2
27	3	24	3	21	3	18	3	15	3	12	3	9	3	6	3
36	4	32	4	28	4	24	4	20	4	16	4	12	4	8	4
45	5	40	5	35	5	30	5	25	5	20	5	15	5	10	5
54	6	48	6	42	6	36	6	30	6	24	6	18	6	12	6
63	7	56	7	49	7	42	7	35	7	28	7	21	7	14	7
72	8	64	8	56	8	48	8	40	8	32	8	24	8	16	8
81	9	72	9	63	9	45	9	45	9	36	9	27	9	18	9

B Find the quotients. Use the division facts charts if you need them.

1. $5\overline{)40}$ = 8 $3\overline{)12}$ = 4 $2\overline{)14}$ = 7 $4\overline{)24}$ = 6 $9\overline{)36}$ = 4

2. $8\overline{)16}$ = 2 $4\overline{)8}$ = 2 $7\overline{)49}$ = 7 $3\overline{)18}$ = 6 $6\overline{)6}$ = 1

3. $7\overline{)21}$ = 3 $2\overline{)18}$ = 9 $5\overline{)15}$ = 3 $9\overline{)81}$ = 9 $8\overline{)56}$ = 7

4. $3\overline{)27}$ = 9 $8\overline{)32}$ = 4 $6\overline{)24}$ = 4 $7\overline{)35}$ = 5 $2\overline{)6}$ = 3

5. $9\overline{)72}$ = 8 $5\overline{)45}$ = 9 $4\overline{)28}$ = 7 $2\overline{)10}$ = 5 $8\overline{)72}$ = 9

6. $6\overline{)42}$ = 7 $9\overline{)54}$ = 6 $4\overline{)32}$ = 8 $5\overline{)35}$ = 7 $3\overline{)21}$ = 7

USING MULTIPLICATION AND DIVISION

1. Bob stacked bags of flour on a shelf. He had 5 stacks of 7 bags each. How many bags of flour did he stack?

   _____35_____ bags

2. Bob put carrots in plastic bags. There were 72 carrots, and he put 8 carrots in each bag. How many bags did he fill? _____9_____ bags

3. Bob filled 6 sacks with 6 apples each. How many apples did he use? _____36_____ apples

4. Bob used 12 kilograms of birdseed to fill 6 sacks. How many kilograms of seed did he put into each sack? _____2_____ kilograms

5. Bob unpacked a carton of cereal. There were 24 cereal boxes in the carton. These boxes were in 4 equal rows. How many boxes were in each row? _____6_____ boxes

6. Bob sold 7 carrots costing 8¢ each to a friend. How much did Bob charge his friend? _____56_____ cents

7. Bob worked 3 hours a day for 6 days a week. How many hours did Bob work each week? _____18_____ hours

8. Bob's mother worked 54 hours each week at the store. Each day she worked 9 hours. How many days each week did Bob's mother work? _____6_____ days

MEASURING TEMPERATURE

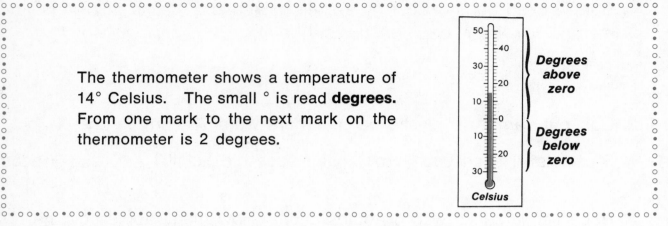

The thermometer shows a temperature of 14° Celsius. The small ° is read **degrees**. From one mark to the next mark on the thermometer is 2 degrees.

Degrees above zero

Degrees below zero

Celsius

A Find the temperature in each picture.

1.

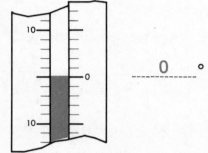

_____0_____ °

2.

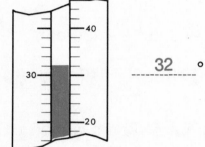

_____32_____ °

3.

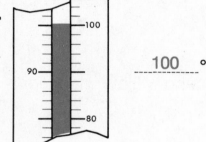

_____100_____ °

4.

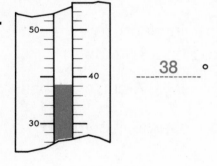

_____38_____ °

B Find 0° on each thermometer. Put an X on those which show temperatures **below** 0°.

1.
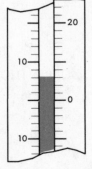

2.
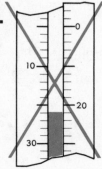

3.
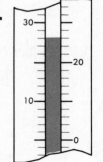

4.
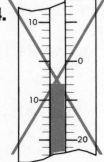

5.
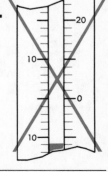

C For each sentence, show the temperature on a thermometer below.

1. A comfortable temperature for school is 22° above zero.

2. Ice skating is good when the temperature is 8° below zero.

3. The oven temperature was 246° above zero.

4. Wear your coat. The temperature is 4° above zero.

5. In summer, the temperature on a hot day might be 38° above zero.

1. 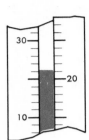 **2.** 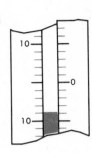 **3.** 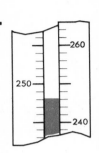 **4.** 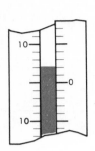 **5.**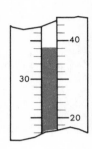

D Sally was writing a weather report. She recorded the temperatures 4 times a day. The pictures show the temperatures for one day. Answer the questions about these temperatures.

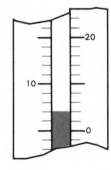 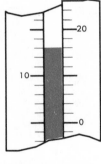 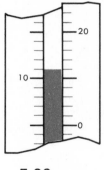 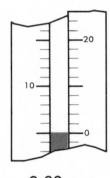

7:00 A.M.   12:00 Noon   5:00 P.M.   9:00 P.M.

1. What were the four temperatures Sally recorded? _4°_ _16°_ _12°_ _0°_

2. Did Sally write her report in the summer or winter? _____winter_____

3. At what time of the day was it warmest? _____12 noon_____

4. At what time of the day was it coldest? _____9:00 P.M._____

5. Was it colder at 7:00 A.M. or 5:00 P.M. ? _____7:00 A.M._____

6. What was the difference in the 7:00 A.M. and 5:00 P.M. temperatures?

_____8°_____

CHAPTER REVIEW

A For each dot picture, write two multiplication and two division sentences.

1.
$2 \times 6 = 12$
$6 \times 2 = 12$
$12 \div 6 = 2$
$12 \div 2 = 6$

2.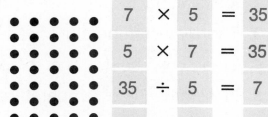
$7 \times 5 = 35$
$5 \times 7 = 35$
$35 \div 5 = 7$
$35 \div 7 = 5$

B Use the number line to help you find the quotients.

$32 \div 4 = \underline{8}$ $\qquad$ $16 \div 4 = \underline{4}$ $\qquad$ $36 \div 4 = \underline{9}$ $\qquad$ $24 \div 4 = \underline{6}$

C Find the products.

8	7	9	8	5	3	9
$\times 4$	$\times 6$	$\times 3$	$\times 8$	$\times 9$	$\times 7$	$\times 9$
32	42	27	64	45	21	81

D Find the quotients.

1. $4\overline{)16}$ → 4 $\qquad$ $3\overline{)21}$ → 7 $\qquad$ $2\overline{)10}$ → 5 $\qquad$ $5\overline{)30}$ → 6 $\qquad$ $3\overline{)12}$ → 4 $\qquad$ $2\overline{)18}$ → 9

2. $8\overline{)24}$ → 3 $\qquad$ $6\overline{)42}$ → 7 $\qquad$ $9\overline{)36}$ → 4 $\qquad$ $7\overline{)49}$ → 7 $\qquad$ $6\overline{)54}$ → 9 $\qquad$ $8\overline{)72}$ → 9

E Solve each of these word problems.

1. Amy collected empty soda bottles to return to the store. She had 24 bottles and was putting them in cartons of 6. How many cartons will she need? __4__ cartons

2. James was putting books on shelves. He put 7 books on each of 4 shelves. How many books did James put on the shelves?

__28__ books

114

CHECK-UP

 For each fact, write the related multiplication and division facts.

1. $3 \times 7 = 21$ | 7 | × | 3 | = | 21 | | 21 | ÷ | 7 | = | 3 | | 21 | ÷ | 3 | = | 7 |

2. $36 \div 9 = 4$ | 36 | ÷ | 4 | = | 9 | | 4 | × | 9 | = | 36 | | 9 | × | 4 | = | 36 |

3. $8 \times 5 = 40$ | 5 | × | 8 | = | 40 | | 40 | ÷ | 5 | = | 8 | | 40 | ÷ | 8 | = | 5 |

 Use the number line to help you find the quotients.

1. $45 \div 5 = \underline{\ 9\ }$ $24 \div 6 = \underline{\ 4\ }$ $32 \div 8 = \underline{\ 4\ }$ $30 \div 6 = \underline{\ 5\ }$

2. $16 \div 2 = \underline{\ 8\ }$ $27 \div 9 = \underline{\ 3\ }$ $36 \div 4 = \underline{\ 9\ }$ $20 \div 5 = \underline{\ 4\ }$

3. $49 \div 7 = \underline{\ 7\ }$ $18 \div 3 = \underline{\ 6\ }$ $56 \div 8 = \underline{\ 7\ }$ $35 \div 7 = \underline{\ 5\ }$

 Find the products.

9	7	8	3	9	5	7
$\times 5$	$\times 6$	$\times 4$	$\times 7$	$\times 9$	$\times 8$	$\times 9$
45	42	32	21	81	40	63

D Find the quotients.

1. $7\overline{)35}$ gives 5 $8\overline{)48}$ gives 6 $4\overline{)24}$ gives 6 $5\overline{)30}$ gives 6 $2\overline{)18}$ gives 9

2. $6\overline{)12}$ gives 2 $1\overline{)8}$ gives 8 $3\overline{)21}$ gives 7 $9\overline{)54}$ gives 6 $6\overline{)42}$ gives 7

E Solve each of these word problems.

1. There were 7 layers of 5 bricks each. How many bricks were there?

   $\underline{\ 35\ }$ bricks

2. Bill arranged 36 plates in 4 equal stacks. How many plates were in each stack? $\underline{\ 9\ }$ plates

6 • GEOMETRY AND MEASUREMENT

LINES, RAYS, AND LINE SEGMENTS

This is a picture of a **line**. The arrows show the line goes on in both directions. Lines are straight.

 Draw rings around the pictures of lines.

1.   **2.**  **3.**  **4.**  **5.**

This is a picture of **part** of a line. It is called a **ray**. The point shows where the ray starts. The arrow at one end shows the ray goes on in one direction. Rays are straight.

 Draw rings around the pictures of rays.

1.   **2.**   **3.**  **4.**  **5.**

This is a picture of **part** of a line. It is called a **line segment**. It starts at the point named B and stops at the point named C. Line segments are straight.

 Draw rings around the pictures of line segments.

1.   **2.**   **3.**   **4.**   **5.**

D In each set of pictures, put an X on the figure that does not belong.

1.

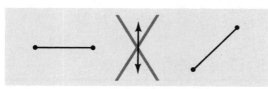

line

2.

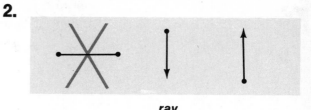

ray

3.

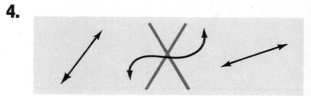

line segment

4.

line

Have students complete exercises E and F independently. Check their work using chalkboard drawings. Discuss the fact that there is only one straight path which connects two points.

E Use a ruler and draw a picture of each figure.

1. A line segment with end points A and B.

2. A ray that starts at C and passes through D.

3. A ray that starts at F and passes through E.

4. A line passing through points G and H.

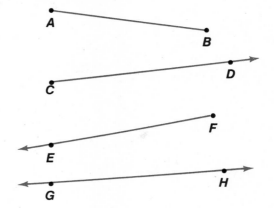

F Use points M and N to complete these.

1. Draw a line segment from M to N.

2. Draw two other paths from M to N.

3. Are these last two paths straight? ___no___

4. How many straight paths connect two points? ___one___

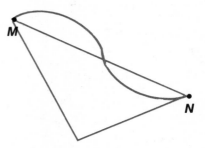

COMPARING LINE SEGMENTS

 Place an *X* on the shorter line segment in each pair.

1.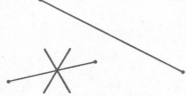

2.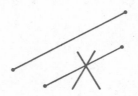

3.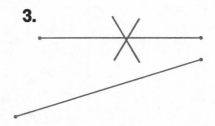

Comparing Lengths of Line Segments

Step 1	Step 2	Step 3
Place an edge of a piece of paper along one of the segments.	Make a copy of the segment on the paper.	Move the paper to the other segment and match an end point. Compare the lengths.

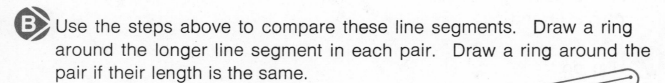

 Use the steps above to compare these line segments. Draw a ring around the longer line segment in each pair. Draw a ring around the pair if their length is the same.

1.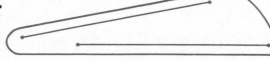

2.

3.

4.

5.

6.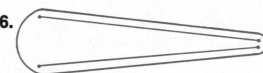

MEASURING LENGTHS

A Carol laid paper clips end-to-end to measure a piece of yarn. The paper clip is a unit of measure. Study Carol's work.

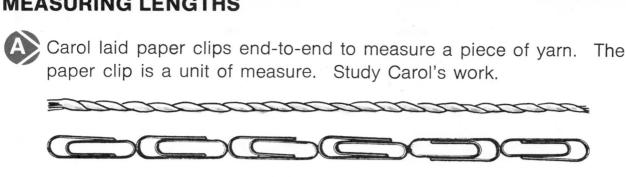

1. Do the paper clips form a segment as long as the yarn? __yes__

2. How many paper clips did Carol use? __6__ paper clips

3. The length of the yarn is __6__ paper clips.

Discuss the illustration in exercise B. Then have students complete the exercises on pages 119—20.

B Tom had a problem when measuring his yarn. Study Tom's work.

The segment Tom formed was **not** just as long as the yarn.

1. 4 paper clips form a segment that is too __short__.

2. 5 paper clips form a segment that is too __long__.

3. Is the length of the yarn closer to 4 paper clips or to 5 paper clips?

__5__ paper clips

4. The length of Tom's yarn is about __5__ paper clips.

C Use paper clips to find the length of the object. First, use big paper clips like ⬭; then use little paper clips like ⬭.

about __4__ big paper clips   about __5__ little paper clips

119

D Find the length of each object using big and little paper clips.

1.

about __2__ big paper clips   about __3__ little paper clips

2.

about __3__ big paper clips   about __4__ little paper clips

3.

about __3__ big paper clips   about __4__ little paper clips

4.

about __1__ big paper clips   about __2__ little paper clips

5.

about __4__ big paper clips   about __6__ little paper clips

E Use the lengths you found in exercise D to answer these questions.

1. Which objects have the same lengths? _____crayon_____ and

_____scissors_____

2. Which objects are longer than 3 big paper clips?

_____crayon, scissors, saw blade_____

3. Which object is shorter than 3 little paper clips? _____feather_____

MILLIMETERS, CENTIMETERS, DECIMETERS

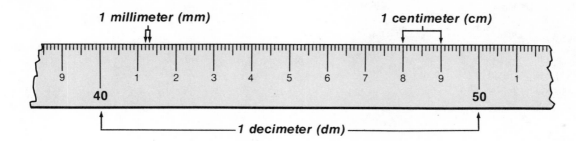

1 millimeter (mm)   1 centimeter (cm)

1 decimeter (dm)

A **millimeter** is about the thickness of a dime.
A **centimeter** is about the thickness of your little finger.
A **decimeter** is about one-half the length of a new pencil.

A Without measuring, tell if the length is closer to 1 millimeter (mm), 1 centimeter (cm), or 1 decimeter (dm) by writing mm, cm, or dm in the blank.

1. the width of the palm of your hand ___dm___

2. the width of a big paper clip ___cm___

3. the thickness of the lead in your pencil ___mm___

4. the length of your index finger ___dm___

B Use a centimeter ruler to find each length.

1.

___3___ cm

2.

___9___ cm

3.

___2___ cm

4.
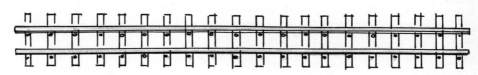
___12___ cm

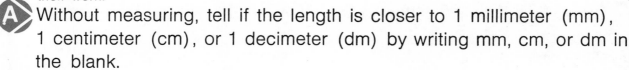

Find the widths of these coins in millimeters. Then answer the questions.

50¢   25¢   10¢   5¢   1¢

___31___ mm   ___24___ mm   ___18___ mm   ___21___ mm   ___19___ mm

1. Which coins have widths less than 20 mm? ___dime___, ___penny___

2. Which coins have widths less than 2 cm? ___dime___, ___penny___

3. Which coin has the smallest width? ___dime___

D Use your ruler to draw line segments with these lengths.

1. 10 cm

2. 4 cm

3. 5½ cm

E How long are the segments you drew in exercise D in millimeters?

1. ___100___ mm   **2.** ___40___ mm   **3.** ___55___ mm

F Use your ruler to draw line segments with these lengths.

1. 17 mm   **2.** 32 mm   **3.** 26 mm

4. 22 mm   **5.** 12 mm   **6.** 19 mm

G How long are the segments you drew in exercise F to the nearest centimeter?

1. ___2___ cm   **2.** ___3___ cm   **3.** ___3___ cm

4. ___2___ cm   **5.** ___1___ cm   **6.** ___2___ cm

RELATIVE LENGTHS OF MILLIMETERS, CENTIMETERS, DECIMETERS, AND METERS

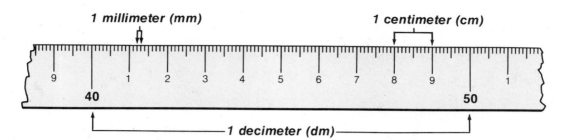

A Use the picture to help you answer these questions.

1. How many millimeters are in 1 centimeter? ___10___

2. How many centimeters are in 1 decimeter? ___10___

3. How many millimeters are in 1 decimeter? ___100___

> A **meter** is 10 decimeters or 100 centimeters long.

B Draw a ring around the longer length.

1. 10 cm (10 dm)   **2.** (12 cm) 100 mm   **3.** (1 m) 100 mm

4. 20 cm (1 m)   **5.** 5 dm (100 cm)   **6.** (12 mm) 1 cm

C Fill the blank to make each sentence true.

1. 2 m = ___200___ cm   5 m = ___500___ cm   1 m = ___100___ cm

2. 1 m = ___1,000___ mm   3 m = ___3,000___ mm   7 m = ___7,000___ mm

D Complete the chart.

	Millimeters	Meters	Decimeters	Centimeters	Millimeters
1.	1,603	1	6	0	3
2.	5,924	5	9	2	4
3.	6,005	6	0	0	5

ANGLES AND RIGHT ANGLES

A Use a ruler to draw a picture of each ray.

1. The ray that starts at A and passes through B.

2. The ray that starts at A and passes through C.

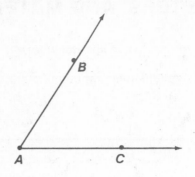

You have drawn a picture of an **angle.** An angle has 2 sides that come together in a point.

B Draw a ring around the pictures that make you think of an angle.

1.

2.

3.

4.
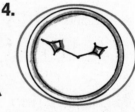

A **right angle** makes a square corner. Right angles can be tested by using a corner of a page and fitting it inside the angle.

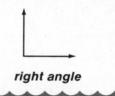

right angle

C Draw a ring around the pictures that make you think of a right angle.

1.

2.
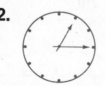

3.
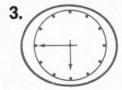

4.
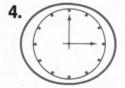

5.
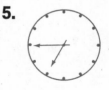

D Draw each of these pictures.

1. Draw a picture of an angle.

2. Draw a picture of a right angle.

PARALLEL LINE SEGMENTS

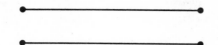

Lay a straightedge on each line segment. Use your pencil to extend each segment as far as you can. Do these lines cross?

___no___ Do they get closer together? ___no___

> These line segments are said to be **parallel** because the lines which contain them never cross.

 A Draw a ring around the pictures that make you think of parallel lines.

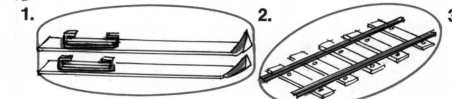

1.   2.   3.

B Draw a ring around the pictures that look like parallel line segments.

    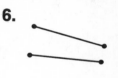

1.   2.   3.   4.   5.   6.

C Use the figure at right to answer these questions. [ ]

1. Extend the colored line segments in the figure. Are they parallel? ___yes___

2. Extend the black line segments in the figure. Are they parallel? ___yes___

3. Are opposite sides of the figure parallel? ___yes___

D In each figure, mark the parallel line segments by writing an *X* on both segments.

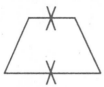 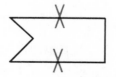

1.   2.   3.   4.

TRIANGLES, SQUARES, RECTANGLES, AND PARALLELOGRAMS

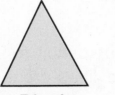
Triangle

Parallelogram

Rectangle

Square

Study the pictures above to help you do exercises A through D.

A Use your ruler to connect points A to B, B to C, and A to C.

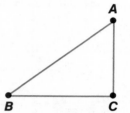

1. How many sides does this figure have? ___3___

2. How many angles does this figure have? ___3___

3. This figure is called a ___triangle___.

4. The lengths in millimeters of the sides are

___35___ mm, ___20___ mm, and ___28___ mm.

B Use your ruler to connect points D to E, E to F, F to G, and G to D.

1. How many sides does this figure have? ___4___

2. How many angles does this figure have? ___4___

3. Are opposite sides parallel? ___yes___

4. Are the angles right angles? ___yes___

5. Are the lengths of all sides equal? ___no___

6. This figure is called a ___rectangle___.

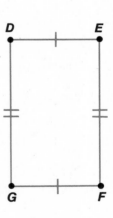

7. The lengths in millimeters of the sides are

___40___ mm, ___40___ mm, ___24___ mm, and

___24___ mm.

8. Mark the sides that have the same length. We say **opposite sides have the same length.**

126   Each child should have a ruler marked in millimeters. Treat exercise A as a class exercise. Have students discuss the figures at the top of the page. Tell them that the exercises explore the properties of these figures. Have students complete pages 126—27.

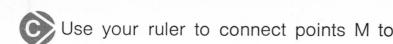 Use your ruler to connect points M to N, N to L, L to P, and P to M.

1. How many sides does this figure have? ____4____

2. How many angles does this figure have? ____4____

3. Are opposite sides parallel? ____yes____

4. Are the angles right angles? ____yes____

5. Are the lengths of all sides equal? ____yes____

6. This figure is called a ____square____.

7. The lengths in millimeters of the sides are

____30____ mm, ____30____ mm, ____30____ mm, and ____30____ mm.

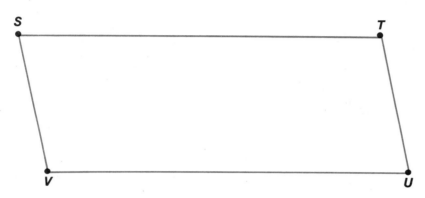

 Use your ruler to connect points S to T, T to U, U to V, and V to S.

1. How many sides does this figure have? ____4____

2. How many angles does this figure have? ____4____

3. Are opposite sides parallel? ____yes____

4. Are the angles right angles? ____no____

5. Are the lengths of all sides equal? ____no____

6. Do opposite sides have the same length? ____yes____

7. This shape is called a ____parallelogram____.

8. The lengths in millimeters of the sides are

____96____ mm, ____96____ mm, ____38____ mm, and ____38____ mm.

MAKING GEOMETRIC SHAPES

A Cut 3 strips of poster board of lengths 10 cm, 15 cm, and 20 cm. Fasten the strips together with paper fasteners to form a triangle. Can you change the shape of the triangle? __no__

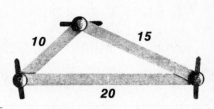

B Cut 3 strips of poster board of lengths 20 cm, 8 cm, and 10 cm.

Can these strips be put together to form a triangle? __no__

Why not? __two sides have total length shorter than the third side__

C Cut 4 strips of poster board of lengths 10 cm, 12 cm, 15 cm, and 8 cm. Fasten the strips together to form a 4-sided figure. Can you change the shape of this figure? __yes__ Can you make it into a square? __no__ a rectangle? __no__ a parallelogram? __no__. Why not?

__opposite sides do not have equal length__

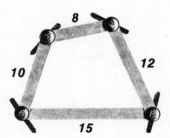

D Cut 4 strips of poster board of lengths 10 cm, 10 cm, 15 cm, and 15 cm. Fasten the strips together to form a 4-sided figure with opposite sides equal. Can you change the shape of this figure? __yes__ As the shape changes, are opposite sides always parallel? __yes__ This is a model of a parallelogram. Can it be changed into a rectangle? __yes__

E Cut 4 strips of poster board, each of length 15 cm. Fasten the strips together to form a square. Can it be changed to form a different parallelogram? __yes__

Emphasize that a triangle is a rigid figure whose shape cannot be changed, whereas a four-sided figure is not rigid. Encourage students to make more figures and investigate their properties.

CIRCLES

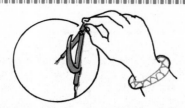 Elaine is drawing a picture of a **circle.** Every point on a circle is the same distance from a point called its **center.**

A Put an *X* on or near the center point of each picture that makes you think of a circle.

1.    **2.**    **3.**   **4.**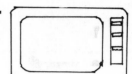

Two line segments are drawn inside this circle. A **diameter** of a circle is any line segment which passes through the center and has end points on the circle.   A **radius** of a circle is any line segment with one end point the center and the other a point on the circle.

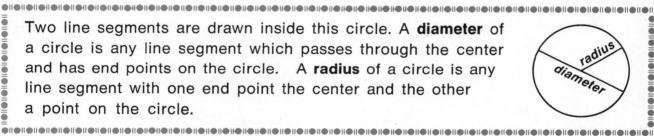

Discuss the terms *diameter* and *radius.* Have students study the diagram. Then have them complete exercises B and C.

B Draw a diameter and a radius in each circle.

1.    **2.**   **3.**   **4.**

C Find the length in millimeters of each diameter and each radius.

1.    **2.**   **3.**

_24_ mm diameter   _16_ mm diameter   _20_ mm diameter

_12_ mm radius   _8_ mm radius   _10_ mm radius

INCHES, FEET, AND YARDS

> An **inch** is a unit of length.
> This line segment is one inch.

 This ruler shows inches placed end-to-end. Write the length of each object to the nearest inch.

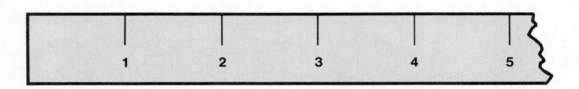

1.

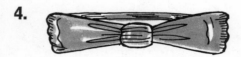

_____3_____ inches

2.

_____5_____ inches

3.

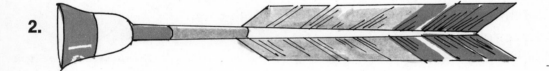

_____5_____ inches

4.

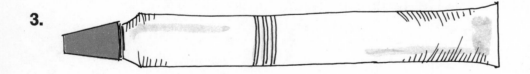

_____2_____ inches

B Use a ruler to draw line segments with these lengths.

1. 4 inches ●———————————————●

2. 1 inch ●————————●

3. 2 inches ●———————————●

4. $3\frac{1}{2}$ inches ●—————————————————●

130

C Study the picture of a yardstick. Then answer the questions.

1. How many inches are in 1 foot? ____12____ inches

2. How many feet are in 1 yard? ____3____ feet

3. How many inches are in 1 yard? ____36____ inches

about 1 yard

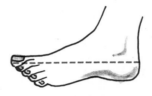

about 1 foot

about 1 inch

Discuss the ancient practice of using parts of the body as units of measure. Have students measure other parts of the body about equal in length to 1 inch, 1 foot, and 1 yard.

D Without measuring, tell if the length is closer to 1 inch (in.), 1 foot (ft.), or 1 yard (yd.) by writing *in., ft.,* or *yd.* in the blank.

1. edge of this book ____ft.____   2. paper clip ____in.____

3. baseball bat ____yd.____   4. diameter of a quarter ____in.____

5. new pencil ____ft.____   6. width of a window ____yd.____

> 12 inches = 1 foot   3 feet = 1 yard   36 inches = 1 yard

E Write >, <, or = in each ● to make the sentence true.

1. 1 yard > 1 foot   2. 12 inches = 1 foot

3. 2 feet < 1 yard   4. 4 feet > 1 yard

5. 36 inches = 3 feet   6. 30 inches < 1 yard

7. 13 inches > 1 foot   8. 6 feet = 2 yards

9. 40 inches > 1 yard   10. 1 inch < 1 foot

Students having difficulty with exercise E should have additional experiences with activity 3. **131**

PERIMETER

The distance around a shape is called its **perimeter**. To find the perimeter of a triangle, we add the lengths of its sides.

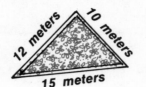

10 m
15 m
+ 12 m
perimeter = 37 m

 A Add to find the perimeters.

1.

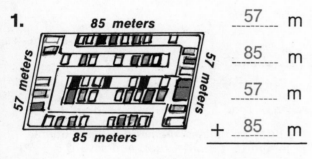

85 meters
57 meters
57 meters
85 meters

_57_ m
_85_ m
_57_ m
+ _85_ m

perimeter = _284_ m

2.

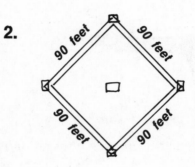

90 feet
90 feet
90 feet
90 feet

_90_ ft.
_90_ ft.
_90_ ft.
+ _90_ ft.

perimeter = _360_ ft.

B Measure the length of each side in millimeters. Find each perimeter.

1.

_46_ mm
_40_ mm
+ _45_ mm

perimeter = _131_ mm

2.

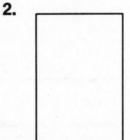

_23_ mm
_37_ mm
_23_ mm
+ _37_ mm

perimeter = _120_ mm

3.

_18_ mm
_40_ mm
_27_ mm
+ _40_ mm

perimeter = _125_ mm

4.

_26_ mm
_26_ mm
_26_ mm
+ _26_ mm

perimeter = _104_ mm

MEASURING LONG DISTANCES

Rosa and her family went on a vacation. To measure the distance she traveled, Rosa used **kilometers**. One kilometer equals 1,000 meters. Rosa drew this map.

Salt Lake City   Denver   Kansas City   St. Louis

Day 3   Day 2   Day 1
811 km   1,030 km   410 km

A Use Rosa's map to solve these problems.

1. On which day did Rosa travel the longest distance? ___day 2___

2. How far did Rosa travel on day 1 and day 3? ___1,221___ kilometers

3. How much farther did Rosa travel on day 2 than she did on day 3?

___219___ kilometers

4. What is the difference between the distance traveled on day 2

and that traveled on day 1? ___620___ kilometers

5. How far did Rosa travel altogether? ___2,251___ kilometers

Guillermo, Rosa's brother, kept his map in **miles**. One mile equals 5,280 feet. He drew this map.

Salt Lake City   Denver   Kansas City   St. Louis

Day 3   Day 2   Day 1
507 miles   644 miles   256 miles

B Use Guillermo's map to solve these problems.

1. On which day did Guillermo travel the shortest distance? ___day 1___

2. How far did Guillermo travel on day 1 and day 2? ___900___ miles

3. How much farther did Guillermo travel on day 2 than on day 3?

___137___ miles

4. How far did Guillermo travel altogether? ___1,407___ miles

COMPARING REGIONS

A figure together with its inside is called a **region**.

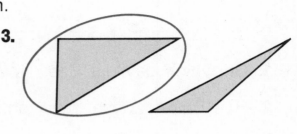

square   square region

A Draw a ring around the larger region.

1. 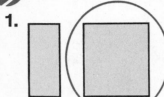   **2.** 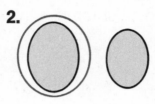   **3.**

B Count the number of square regions like ▨ in each region.   Then answer the questions.

1. ___7___   **2.** ___12___   **3.** ___6___

4. ___12___   **5.** ___14___

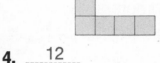

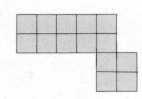

a. Which region has the most square regions? ___5___

b. Which region is largest? ___5___

c. Which region has the least square regions? ___3___

d. Which region is smallest? ___3___

e. Which regions have the same number of square regions?

___2___, ___4___

f. Which regions have the same size? ___2___, ___4___

AREA

To measure regions, we choose a **square region** as a unit.
The number of square regions in a region is called its **area**.

 Find the areas of these regions by counting.

1.

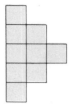

area =

___9___ square units

2.

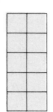

area =

___10___ square units

3.

area =

___12___ square units

A standard unit of area is a **square
centimeter**. It is a square region
one centimeter on each side.

 Use the marks to draw square centimeters in each region. Then
find the area of the region.

1.

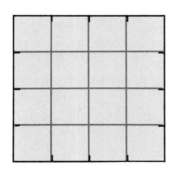

area = ___16___
square centimeters

2.

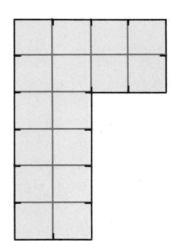

area = ___16___
square centimeters

3.

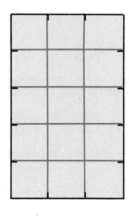

area = ___15___
square centimeters

Complete the sentences below each region.

1.

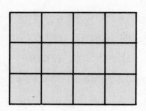

2.

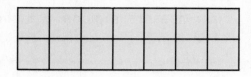

number of rows ___3___

squares in each row ___4___

area = 3 × 4 = 12 square units

number of rows ___2___

squares in each row ___7___

area = ___2___ × ___7___ = ___14___ square units

> The area of a rectangular region can be found by multiplying the number of rows of squares times the number of squares in each row.

 Find the area by multiplying. Check by counting.

1.

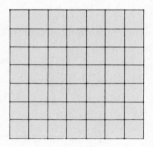

7 × 7 = ___49___

area = ___49___ square units

2.

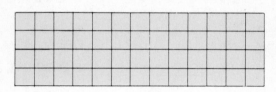

area = ___52___ square units

3.

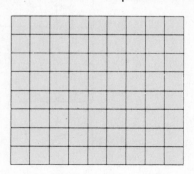

area = ___72___ square units

4.

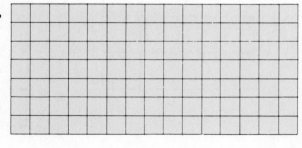

area = ___105___ square units

CHAPTER REVIEW

 A Match names with pictures. Write the number of the word next to the picture it best describes.

1. parallel lines

2. triangle

3. diameter of circle

4. ray

5. rectangle

6. line

7. parallelogram

8. right angle

a. __3__ 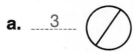 **b.** __8__

c. __5__ **d.** __2__

e. __6__ **f.** __7__

g. __4__ **h.** __1__

B Measure each side in millimeters and add the lengths to find the perimeter of each shape.

1.

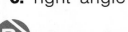

$$\begin{aligned} &\underline{40} \text{ mm}\\ &\underline{25} \text{ mm}\\ &\underline{40} \text{ mm}\\ +&\underline{25} \text{ mm}\\ \hline \end{aligned}$$

perimeter = __130__ mm

2.

$$\begin{aligned} &\underline{43} \text{ mm}\\ &\underline{45} \text{ mm}\\ +&\underline{28} \text{ mm}\\ \hline \end{aligned}$$

perimeter = __116__ mm

 C Count the number of squares to find the area of each region.

1.

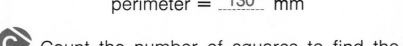

area = __44__ square units

2.

area = __28__ square units

137

CHECK-UP

 A Use a ruler and a square corner to draw pictures.

1. right angle

2. rectangle

3. parallelogram

B Find the length of each segment in millimeters and inches.

1. •———•   **2.** •——————————————•

___25___ millimeters

___1___ inch

___102___ millimeters

___4___ inches

C Use the given lengths to find the perimeter of each shape. Add the lengths to find the perimeter.

1.

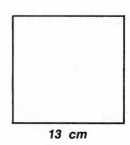

13 cm

___13___ cm

___13___ cm

___13___ cm

+ ___13___ cm

perimeter = ___52___ cm

2.

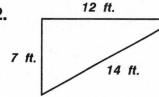

12 ft.

7 ft.

14 ft.

___7___ ft.

___14___ ft.

+ ___12___ ft.

perimeter = ___33___ ft.

D Find the area of each region.

1.

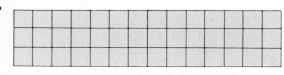

area = ___42___ square units

2.

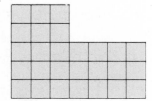

area = ___27___ square units

7 • FRACTIONS

PARTS OF A WHOLE

A Use the pictures above to help you answer the questions.

1. The square is divided into how many parts of the same size?

___2___ How many parts are shaded? ___1___

$\frac{1}{2}$ (one-half) names the part of the square that is shaded.

2. The triangle is divided into how many parts of the same size?

___4___ How many parts are shaded? ___3___

$\frac{3}{4}$ (three-fourths) names the part of the triangle that is shaded.

3. The circle is divided into how many parts of the same size?

___3___ How many parts are shaded? ___1___

$\frac{1}{3}$ (one-third) names the part of the circle that is shaded.

4. The pentagon is divided into how many parts of the same size?

___5___ How many parts are shaded? ___2___

$\frac{2}{5}$ (two-fifths) names the part of the pentagon that is shaded.

> $\frac{1}{2}$, $\frac{3}{4}$, $\frac{1}{3}$, and $\frac{2}{5}$ are called fractions. Fractions tell us about parts of a whole or parts of a set.

B Put an X on those pictures which show $\frac{1}{2}$.

1. 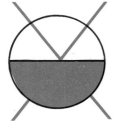 **2.** 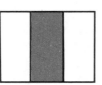 **3.** 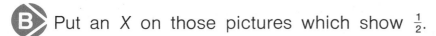 **4.**

Put an *X* on those pictures which show $\frac{2}{3}$.

1. 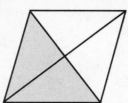 **2.** 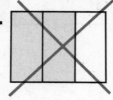 **3.** 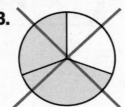 **4.**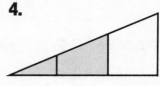

 Use the pictures in exercise C to complete the sentences.

1. Picture 1 does not show $\frac{2}{3}$ since there are ___4___ parts of the same size.

2. Picture 1 shows the fraction $\frac{2}{4}$.

3. Picture 4 does not show $\frac{2}{3}$ since the 3 parts are not ___equal___ .

 Look at this picture.

1. Color with your pencil 3 of the 4 equal parts in the picture. You have colored $\frac{3}{4}$ (three-fourths) of the rectangle.

2. $\frac{3}{4}$ means 3 of ___4___ equal parts.

Have students complete exercise F independently.

 What part of each picture is shaded?

1. ___$\frac{2}{4}$___   **2.** ___$\frac{4}{5}$___   **3.** ___$\frac{1}{3}$___

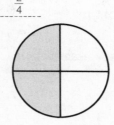   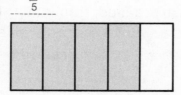   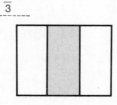

4. ___$\frac{3}{5}$___   **5.** ___$\frac{1}{5}$___   **6.** ___$\frac{1}{4}$___

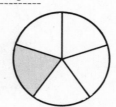   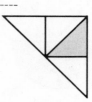

Review each exercise by asking students to identify the whole, the number of pieces into which it is divided, and the fraction which shows the part of the whole.

READING FRACTIONS

Look at the picture. How many parts of the same size are there? ____8____ How many of these parts are shaded?

____3____

The fraction which names this part is $\frac{3}{8}$. It is read "three-eighths."

$\frac{3}{8}$ Number of parts that are shaded—numerator

     Total number of equal parts—denominator

 Complete the table.

		Number of Parts Shaded (numerator)	Total Number of Parts (denominator)	Fraction	Word Name
1.		1	4	$\frac{1}{4}$	one-fourth
2.		5	6	$\frac{5}{6}$	five-sixths
3.		2	3	$\frac{2}{3}$	two-thirds
4.		3	10	$\frac{3}{10}$	three-tenths
5.		4	5	$\frac{4}{5}$	four-fifths
6.		6	8	$\frac{6}{8}$	six-eighths

141

B Name the numerator, the denominator, and the fraction for each picture.

1.

$\frac{5}{8}$ numerator
        denominator

$\frac{5}{8}$ fraction

2.

$\frac{1}{4}$

$\frac{1}{4}$

3.

$\frac{3}{10}$

$\frac{3}{10}$

4.

$\frac{7}{12}$

$\frac{7}{12}$

5.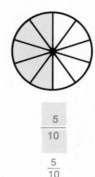

$\frac{5}{10}$

$\frac{5}{10}$

6.

$\frac{7}{8}$

$\frac{7}{8}$

C For each fraction, name the numerator and the denominator.

	$\frac{3}{4}$	$\frac{7}{8}$	$\frac{9}{12}$	$\frac{5}{9}$	$\frac{3}{5}$	$\frac{6}{10}$	$\frac{4}{6}$
Numerator	3	7	9	5	3	6	4
Denominator	4	8	12	9	5	10	6

D Write the fraction.

1. seven-tenths $\frac{7}{10}$ one-eighth $\frac{1}{8}$ two-thirds $\frac{2}{3}$

2. one-half $\frac{1}{2}$ three-fifths $\frac{3}{5}$ four-ninths $\frac{4}{9}$

3. five-twelfths $\frac{5}{12}$ four-sixths $\frac{4}{6}$ one-fourth $\frac{1}{4}$

E Complete each sentence.

1. $\frac{6}{12}$ is _____six_____ -twelfths.   **2.** $\frac{5}{9}$ is _____five_____ -ninths.

3. $\frac{4}{10}$ is _____four_____ -tenths.   **4.** $\frac{2}{5}$ is _____two_____ -fifths.

Treat exercise A orally. Remind students of the meanings of *numerator* and *denominator*.
Point out that *denominator* and *down* both begin with *d*, and this can be used to remember
which number in a fraction is the denominator.

PARTS OF SETS

 Use the picture to help you fill the

blanks. ___4___ bells ___3___ blue bells

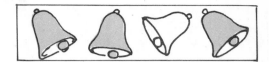

$\frac{3}{4}$	Number of colored objects in the set—numerator
	Total number of objects in the set—denominator

Point out that objects in a set need not be the same size or shape for part of the set to be
named by a fraction. Then have students complete pages 143—44.

B Write the fraction that tells the part of the set that is in blue.

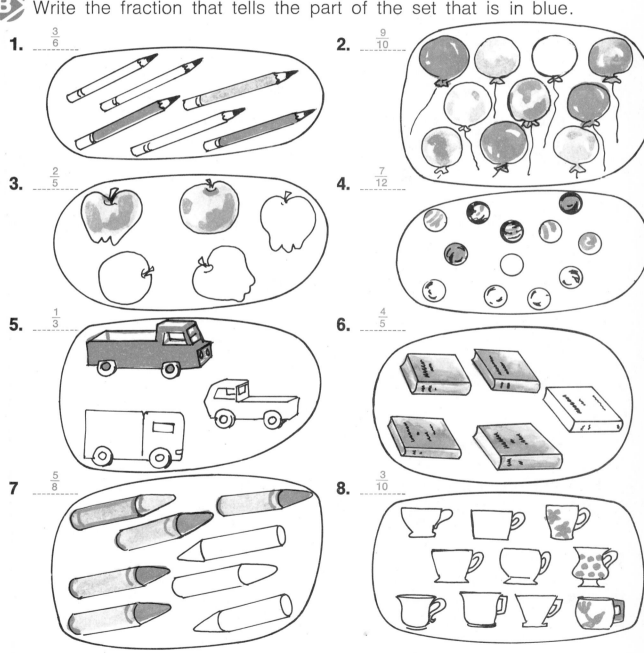

1. $\frac{3}{6}$

2. $\frac{9}{10}$

3. $\frac{2}{5}$

4. $\frac{7}{12}$

5. $\frac{1}{3}$

6. $\frac{4}{5}$

7. $\frac{5}{8}$

8. $\frac{3}{10}$

Shade the part of each set named by the fraction.

1. $\frac{5}{6}$

2. $\frac{2}{3}$

3. $\frac{3}{8}$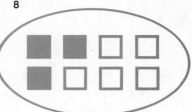

4. $\frac{2}{6}$

5. $\frac{1}{3}$

6. $\frac{7}{8}$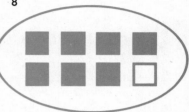

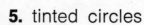 For each fraction, draw a set of small circles. Then shade the part of the circles shown by the fraction.

1. $\frac{1}{2}$

2. $\frac{1}{5}$

3. $\frac{3}{4}$

4. $\frac{2}{3}$

5. $\frac{4}{6}$

6. $\frac{2}{4}$

 Use the picture. Write a fraction to name each part of the set.

1. triangles $\frac{5}{12}$

2. black triangles $\frac{2}{12}$

3. tinted triangles $\frac{3}{12}$

4. circles $\frac{7}{12}$

5. tinted circles $\frac{5}{12}$

6. black circles $\frac{2}{12}$

7. tinted shapes $\frac{8}{12}$

8. black shapes $\frac{4}{12}$

NAMES FOR A WHOLE

The fraction $\frac{2}{2}$ means that a whole has been broken into 2 equal pieces. The fraction $\frac{2}{2}$ is another name for a whole, or 1.

 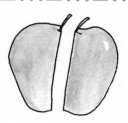

 What fraction names the shaded part of each picture?

1. $\frac{4}{4}$

2. $\frac{3}{3}$

3. $\frac{5}{5}$

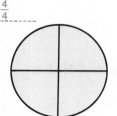 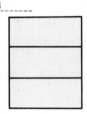

 Divide each whole into the correct number of pieces. Then shade the number of pieces named in the numerator.

1. $\frac{2}{2}$

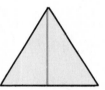

2. $\frac{4}{4}$

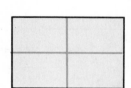

3. $\frac{3}{3}$

4. $\frac{6}{6}$

5. $\frac{8}{8}$

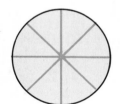

6. $\frac{5}{5}$

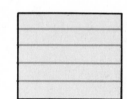

When the numerator and the denominator are equal, the fraction names a whole, or the number 1.

C Draw a ring around each fraction which names the number 1.

1. $\frac{2}{3}$ $\boxed{\frac{5}{5}}$ $\frac{1}{2}$

2. $\frac{5}{10}$ $\frac{6}{8}$ $\boxed{\frac{10}{10}}$

3. $\boxed{\frac{8}{8}}$ $\frac{1}{6}$ $\frac{3}{5}$

4. $\frac{1}{3}$ $\boxed{\frac{1}{1}}$ $\frac{1}{2}$

145

REVIEWING WHOLE NUMBERS

A Complete the number lines.

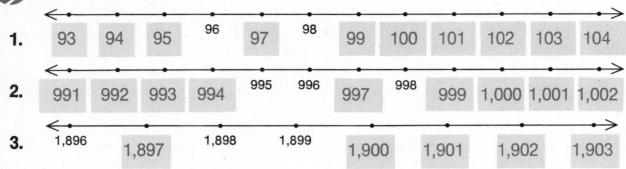

1. | 93 | 94 | 95 | 96 | 97 | 98 | 99 | 100 | 101 | 102 | 103 | 104 |

2. | 991 | 992 | 993 | 994 | 995 | 996 | 997 | 998 | 999 | 1,000 | 1,001 | 1,002 |

3. | 1,896 | 1,897 | 1,898 | 1,899 | 1,900 | 1,901 | 1,902 | 1,903 |

B Numbers have many different names. Complete the chart.

	Standard Name	Expanded Name	Word Name
1.	3,742	3,000 + 700 + 40 + 2	three thousand, seven hundred forty-two
2.	68	60 + 8	sixty-eight
3.	594	500 + 90 + 4	five hundred ninety-four
4.	807	800 + 7	eight hundred seven
5.	1,015	1,000 + 10 + 5	one thousand, fifteen

C Write <, >, or = in each 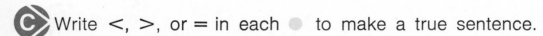 to make a true sentence.

1. 79 > 69

2. 584 = 500 + 80 + 4

3. 4,762 < 4,860

4. 8,604 > 8,000 + 60 + 4

5. 7,541 < 8,541

6. 6,900 = 6,000 + 900

D Complete the number patterns.

1. 87 88 89 __90__

2. 970 980 990 __1,000__

3. 143 142 141 __140__

4. 1,687 1,688 1,689 __1,690__

5. 520 510 500 __490__

6. 1,970 1,980 1,990 __2,000__

COMPARING PARTS OF A WHOLE

 Shade the part of each picture named by the fraction.

1.

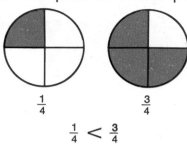

$\frac{1}{4}$ $\frac{3}{4}$

$\frac{1}{4} < \frac{3}{4}$

2.

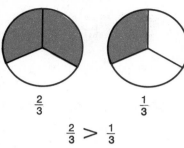

$\frac{2}{3}$ $\frac{1}{3}$

$\frac{2}{3} > \frac{1}{3}$

B Write the fraction for the part of each picture that is shaded.

$\frac{1}{5}$ _____ $\frac{2}{5}$ _____ $\frac{3}{5}$ _____ $\frac{4}{5}$ _____ $\frac{5}{5}$ _____

C Study the pictures in exercise B. Draw a ring around the fraction which names the greater part.

1. $\frac{1}{5}$ ⟨$\frac{3}{5}$⟩   ⟨$\frac{4}{5}$⟩ $\frac{2}{5}$ ⟨$\frac{5}{5}$⟩ $\frac{4}{5}$ $\frac{3}{5}$ ⟨$\frac{5}{5}$⟩

2. ⟨$\frac{4}{5}$⟩ $\frac{3}{5}$ ⟨$\frac{5}{5}$⟩ $\frac{1}{5}$ $\frac{1}{5}$ ⟨$\frac{2}{5}$⟩   ⟨$\frac{3}{5}$⟩ $\frac{1}{5}$

D Write < or > in each ● to make the sentence true.

1. $\frac{1}{5} < \frac{3}{5}$ $\frac{4}{5} > \frac{2}{5}$ $\frac{5}{5} > \frac{4}{5}$ $\frac{3}{5} < \frac{5}{5}$

2. $\frac{4}{5} > \frac{3}{5}$ $\frac{5}{5} > \frac{1}{5}$ $\frac{1}{5} < \frac{2}{5}$ $\frac{3}{5} > \frac{1}{5}$

E Write < or > in each ●. Shade the picture to help you.

1. $\frac{1}{2} < \frac{2}{2}$

2. $\frac{3}{6} < \frac{5}{6}$

3. $\frac{3}{4} > \frac{2}{4}$

4. $\frac{4}{4} > \frac{3}{4}$

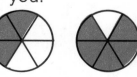

The additional activity may be completed by pairs of students or by the more capable students working alone.   **147**

COMPARING PARTS OF A SET

A Use the set of hearts to help you answer the questions.

1. How many hearts are in $\frac{3}{8}$ of the set? ____3____

2. How many hearts are in $\frac{5}{8}$ of the set? ____5____

3. Which part has more hearts, $\frac{3}{8}$ or $\frac{5}{8}$? ____$\frac{5}{8}$____ $\frac{3}{8} < \frac{5}{8}$

4. How many hearts are in $\frac{6}{8}$ of the set? ____6____

5. How many hearts are in $\frac{2}{8}$ of the set? ____2____

6. Which part has more hearts, $\frac{6}{8}$ or $\frac{2}{8}$? ____$\frac{6}{8}$____ $\frac{6}{8} > \frac{2}{8}$

7. Draw a ring around the part of the set that has more hearts.

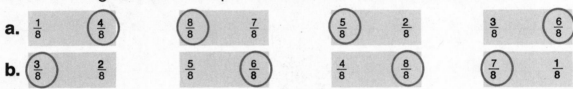

a. $\frac{1}{8}$ ⬭$\frac{4}{8}$ ⬭$\frac{8}{8}$ $\frac{7}{8}$ ⬭$\frac{5}{8}$ $\frac{2}{8}$ $\frac{3}{8}$ ⬭$\frac{6}{8}$

b. ⬭$\frac{3}{8}$ $\frac{2}{8}$ $\frac{5}{8}$ ⬭$\frac{6}{8}$ $\frac{4}{8}$ ⬭$\frac{8}{8}$ ⬭$\frac{7}{8}$ $\frac{1}{8}$

8. Write < or > in each ⚪ to make the sentence true.

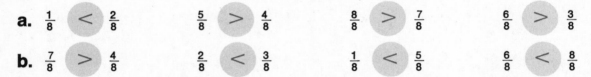

a. $\frac{1}{8}$ < $\frac{2}{8}$ $\frac{5}{8}$ > $\frac{4}{8}$ $\frac{8}{8}$ > $\frac{7}{8}$ $\frac{6}{8}$ > $\frac{3}{8}$

b. $\frac{7}{8}$ > $\frac{4}{8}$ $\frac{2}{8}$ < $\frac{3}{8}$ $\frac{1}{8}$ < $\frac{5}{8}$ $\frac{6}{8}$ < $\frac{8}{8}$

B Use the set of triangles to help you answer the questions.

1. Write the number of triangles in each part.

a. $\frac{3}{6}$ ___3___ $\frac{5}{6}$ ___5___ $\frac{2}{6}$ ___2___

b. $\frac{6}{6}$ ___6___ $\frac{1}{6}$ ___1___ $\frac{4}{6}$ ___4___

2. Draw a ring around the part of the set that has more triangles.

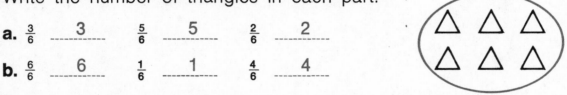

$\frac{3}{6}$ ⬭$\frac{6}{6}$ ⬭$\frac{5}{6}$ $\frac{1}{6}$ $\frac{2}{6}$ ⬭$\frac{4}{6}$ $\frac{1}{6}$ ⬭$\frac{3}{6}$

3. Write < or > in each ⚪ to make the sentence true.

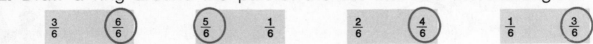

$\frac{3}{6}$ < $\frac{6}{6}$ $\frac{4}{6}$ > $\frac{2}{6}$ $\frac{5}{6}$ < $\frac{6}{6}$ $\frac{1}{6}$ < $\frac{4}{6}$

Students having difficulty with exercise B should have more experiences with the initial teaching activity for this lesson.

FRACTIONS ON THE NUMBER LINE

 Write the fraction which names the part of the bar to the left of the blue line.

1. 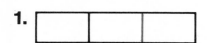 $\frac{2}{3}$ ----------

2.  $\frac{2}{2}$ ----------

3.  $\frac{3}{5}$ ----------

4.  $\frac{1}{6}$ ----------

5. 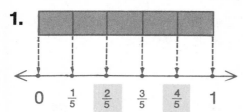 $\frac{7}{10}$ ----------

6. 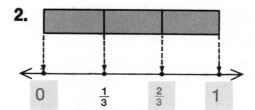 $\frac{5}{8}$ ----------

B Each fraction names the part of the bar to the left of it. Fill the blanks below the arrows to complete the number lines.

1.

$0 \quad \frac{1}{5} \quad \frac{2}{5} \quad \frac{3}{5} \quad \frac{4}{5} \quad 1$

2.

$0 \quad \frac{1}{3} \quad \frac{2}{3} \quad 1$

3.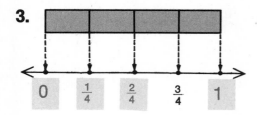

$0 \quad \frac{1}{4} \quad \frac{2}{4} \quad \frac{3}{4} \quad 1$

4.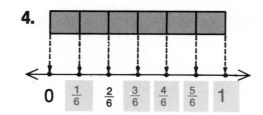

$0 \quad \frac{1}{6} \quad \frac{2}{6} \quad \frac{3}{6} \quad \frac{4}{6} \quad \frac{5}{6} \quad 1$

5.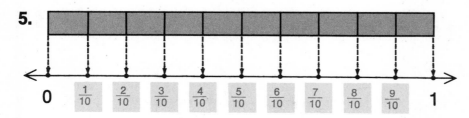

$0 \quad \frac{1}{10} \quad \frac{2}{10} \quad \frac{3}{10} \quad \frac{4}{10} \quad \frac{5}{10} \quad \frac{6}{10} \quad \frac{7}{10} \quad \frac{8}{10} \quad \frac{9}{10} \quad 1$

C Remember: Smaller numbers are to the left of larger numbers on a number line. Write < or > in each ⬤ to make the sentence true.

1. $\frac{1}{10}$ < $\frac{5}{10}$ $\frac{3}{6}$ < $\frac{6}{6}$ $\frac{1}{3}$ < $\frac{2}{3}$ 1 > $\frac{3}{10}$

2. 0 < $\frac{2}{4}$ $\frac{4}{5}$ > $\frac{3}{5}$ $\frac{7}{10}$ < $\frac{9}{10}$ $\frac{4}{6}$ > $\frac{2}{6}$

149

Review the concept of a fraction and the names for the parts of a fraction. Then have students complete exercise A.

WORKING WITH FRACTIONS

 A Complete each sentence so that it tells the meaning of the fraction.

Fraction	Meaning
1. $\frac{3}{4}$ of the apple	The whole apple is divided into 4 equal pieces and the part has 3 of these.
2. $\frac{4}{8}$ of the apple	The whole apple is divided into __8__ equal pieces and the part has __4__ of these.
3. $\frac{5}{6}$ of the apple	The whole apple is divided into __6__ equal pieces and the part has __5__ of these.

Provide several examples similar to the exercises in B. Then have students complete the page.

B Answer the questions for each of these word problems.

1. Scott baked a pizza which he cut into 6 equal pieces.

   a. Scott ate 1 piece. What part of the pizza did he eat? __$\frac{1}{6}$__

   b. Scott's **sister** ate 2 pieces. What part did she eat? __$\frac{2}{6}$__

   c. The rest of the pizza was put into the refrigerator. What part of the **pizza** was this? __$\frac{3}{6}$__

2. Holli's reading group had eight children in it.

   a. $\frac{5}{8}$ of these children were girls. How many girls were there? __5__

   b. What fraction names the part of the group that was boys? __$\frac{3}{8}$__

   c. What fraction names the whole group of children? __$\frac{8}{8}$__

3. Hua had an **apple** which he cut into 5 equal pieces. He gave 2 of these pieces to Kevin and kept 3 for himself.

   a. What part of the **apple** did Hua keep? __$\frac{3}{5}$__

   b. What part of the **apple** did he give to Kevin? __$\frac{2}{5}$__

   c. Who got the bigger part? __Hua__

Students who have difficulty with these exercises due to reading difficulties should be grouped so the exercises can be treated orally.

REVIEWING MULTIPLICATION AND DIVISION FACTS

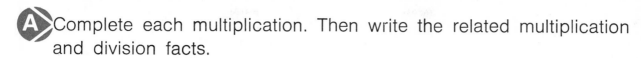 Complete each multiplication. Then write the related multiplication and division facts.

1.	$4 \times 8 = 32$	$8 \times 4 = 32$	$32 \div 4 = 8$	$32 \div 8 = 4$
2.	$3 \times 7 = 21$	$7 \times 3 = 21$	$21 \div 3 = 7$	$21 \div 7 = 3$
3.	$9 \times 5 = 45$	$5 \times 9 = 45$	$45 \div 9 = 5$	$45 \div 5 = 9$
4.	$8 \times 7 = 56$	$7 \times 8 = 56$	$56 \div 8 = 7$	$56 \div 7 = 8$

B Use the number line to help you find the quotients.

1. $18 \div 9 = \underline{2}$ $21 \div 3 = \underline{7}$ $14 \div 2 = \underline{7}$ $24 \div 8 = \underline{3}$

2. $40 \div 5 = \underline{8}$ $28 \div 7 = \underline{4}$ $18 \div 6 = \underline{3}$ $32 \div 4 = \underline{8}$

3. $18 \div 2 = \underline{9}$ $15 \div 3 = \underline{5}$ $35 \div 5 = \underline{7}$ $24 \div 6 = \underline{4}$

C Find these products.

1.
$$\begin{array}{r} 9 \\ \times 7 \\ \hline 63 \end{array} \quad \begin{array}{r} 4 \\ \times 6 \\ \hline 24 \end{array} \quad \begin{array}{r} 8 \\ \times 8 \\ \hline 64 \end{array} \quad \begin{array}{r} 7 \\ \times 5 \\ \hline 35 \end{array} \quad \begin{array}{r} 6 \\ \times 9 \\ \hline 54 \end{array} \quad \begin{array}{r} 5 \\ \times 3 \\ \hline 15 \end{array} \quad \begin{array}{r} 9 \\ \times 3 \\ \hline 27 \end{array} \quad \begin{array}{r} 6 \\ \times 7 \\ \hline 42 \end{array}$$

2.
$$\begin{array}{r} 2 \\ \times 8 \\ \hline 16 \end{array} \quad \begin{array}{r} 8 \\ \times 9 \\ \hline 72 \end{array} \quad \begin{array}{r} 5 \\ \times 6 \\ \hline 30 \end{array} \quad \begin{array}{r} 9 \\ \times 9 \\ \hline 81 \end{array} \quad \begin{array}{r} 4 \\ \times 8 \\ \hline 32 \end{array} \quad \begin{array}{r} 3 \\ \times 7 \\ \hline 21 \end{array} \quad \begin{array}{r} 8 \\ \times 7 \\ \hline 56 \end{array} \quad \begin{array}{r} 5 \\ \times 9 \\ \hline 45 \end{array}$$

D Find these quotients.

1. $9 \overline{)36}^{\;4} \qquad 8 \overline{)48}^{\;6} \qquad 3 \overline{)27}^{\;9} \qquad 7 \overline{)35}^{\;5} \qquad 6 \overline{)30}^{\;5}$

2. $7 \overline{)56}^{\;8} \qquad 9 \overline{)63}^{\;7} \qquad 8 \overline{)64}^{\;8} \qquad 6 \overline{)54}^{\;9} \qquad 9 \overline{)45}^{\;5}$

ONE-HALF OR ONE-THIRD OF A SET

Jerry has a set of 8 dolls. The set is divided into two parts, each with the same number of dolls. Each part is $\frac{1}{2}$ of the set. $\frac{1}{2}$ of 8 is 4.

A Put an *X* on the set which is divided into halves by the line.

1. 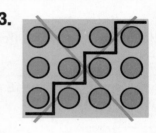   **2.** 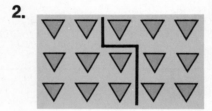   **3.**

B Divide each set into halves and complete the sentence.

1.    **2.** 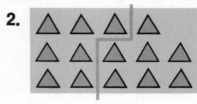   **3.**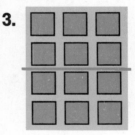

$\frac{1}{2}$ of 6 is ___3___. $\frac{1}{2}$ of __14__ is ___7___. $\frac{1}{2}$ of __12__ is ___6___.

C Follow these steps to find $\frac{1}{2}$ of 10.

1. Draw a set of 10 objects.

2. Divide the set into 2 parts, each with the same number of objects.

3. Find the number of objects in each part.

4. $\frac{1}{2}$ of 10 is ___5___.

D Use the steps in exercise C to help you complete each sentence.

1. $\frac{1}{2}$ of 4 is ___2___.   **2.** $\frac{1}{2}$ of 16 is ___8___.   **3.** $\frac{1}{2}$ of 18 is ___9___.

To divide a set into thirds, divide it into 3 parts, each with the same number of objects.

E Follow these steps to find $\frac{1}{3}$ of 12.

1. Divide the set into 3 parts, each with the same number of circles.

2. How many circles are in each part? ___4___

3. $\frac{1}{3}$ of 12 is ___4___.

Have students complete the page.

F Put an X on the set which is divided into thirds by the lines.

1.

2.

3.

G Divide each set into thirds and complete the sentence.

1.

2.

3.

$\frac{1}{3}$ of __18__ is __6__. $\frac{1}{3}$ of __9__ is __3__. $\frac{1}{3}$ of __15__ is __5__.

H Write $\frac{1}{2}$ or $\frac{1}{3}$ in the blank to name the shaded part of each set.

1. __$\frac{1}{2}$__

2. __$\frac{1}{3}$__

3. __$\frac{1}{2}$__

4. __$\frac{1}{3}$__

5. __$\frac{1}{3}$__

6. __$\frac{1}{2}$__

Students having difficulty should have repeated experiences with concrete objects and pictures of objects.

153

ONE-FOURTH OR ONE-FIFTH OF A SET

To divide a set into fourths, divide it into 4 equal parts.
To divide a set into fifths, divide it into 5 equal parts.

 A Answer the questions about each picture.

1.
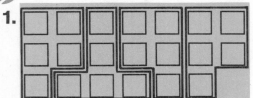

a. How many squares? ___20___

b. How many sets? ___4___

c. How many in each set? ___5___

d. $\frac{1}{4}$ of 20 is 5.

2.
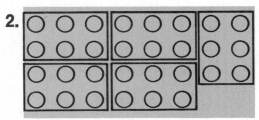

a. How many circles? ___30___

b. How many sets? ___5___

c. How many in each set? ___6___

d. $\frac{1}{5}$ of 30 is 6.

Have students complete the exercises on pages 154—55.

B Put an X on the sets which are divided into fourths by the lines.

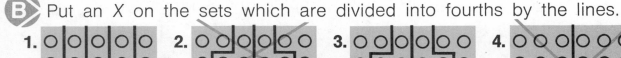

C Put an X on the sets which are divided into fifths by the lines.

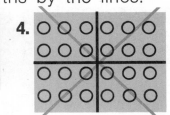

D Divide each set into fourths and complete the sentence.

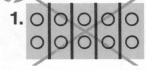 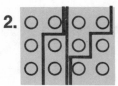 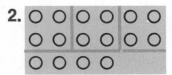 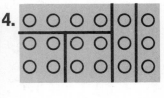 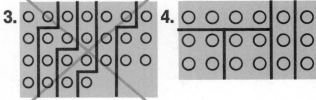 

$\frac{1}{4}$ of ___8___ is ___2___. $\frac{1}{4}$ of ___16___ is ___4___. $\frac{1}{4}$ of ___24___ is ___6___.

154

E Divide each set into fifths and complete the sentence.

1.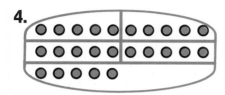

2.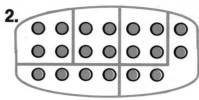

3.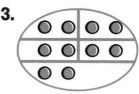

$\frac{1}{5}$ of __5__ is __1__. $\frac{1}{5}$ of __20__ is __4__. $\frac{1}{5}$ of __10__ is __2__.

4.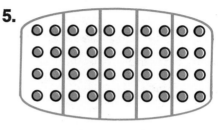

5.

$\frac{1}{5}$ of __25__ is __5__. $\frac{1}{5}$ of __40__ is __8__.

F Complete each sentence. Draw a picture to help you.

1. $\frac{1}{5}$ of 15 is __3__.   **2.** $\frac{1}{4}$ of 4 is __1__.   **3.** $\frac{1}{4}$ of 12 is __3__.

   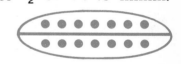

4. $\frac{1}{5}$ of 35 is __7__.   **5.** $\frac{1}{3}$ of 18 is __6__.   **6.** $\frac{1}{2}$ of 14 is __7__.

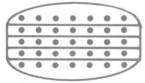   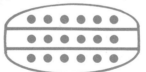   

G Solve each of these word problems.

1. Mark's book has 21 pages. He has read $\frac{1}{3}$ of them. How many

pages has Mark read? __7__

2. Rita used $\frac{1}{4}$ dozen eggs when baking. How many eggs did Rita

use? __3__

3. Sara went to the store and bought $\frac{1}{2}$ dozen eggs. How many eggs

did Sara buy? __6__

PARTS OF A METER

 A Use a meter stick to help you answer these questions.

1. How many decimeters are in one meter? ___10___

2. How many centimeters are in one meter? ___100___

> Each decimeter is one-tenth of a meter. One-tenth = $\frac{1}{10}$.
> Each centimeter is one-hundredth of a meter. One-hundredth = $\frac{1}{100}$.

Have students work the rest of the page.

B Write a fraction to show the part of a meter (m). Each fraction will be in tenths or hundredths.

1. 5 decimeters = $\frac{5}{10}$ m   9 decimeters = $\frac{9}{10}$ m

2. 8 decimeters = $\frac{8}{10}$ m   4 decimeters = $\frac{4}{10}$ m

3. 25 centimeters = $\frac{25}{100}$ m   16 centimeters = $\frac{16}{100}$ m

4. 40 centimeters = $\frac{40}{100}$ m   75 centimeters = $\frac{75}{100}$ m

5. 5 centimeters = $\frac{5}{100}$ m   68 centimeters = $\frac{68}{100}$ m

6. 6 decimeters = $\frac{6}{10}$ m   24 centimeters = $\frac{24}{100}$ m

C How many centimeters (cm) are in each of these parts of a meter?

1. $\frac{30}{100}$ m = ___30___ cm $\frac{50}{100}$ m = ___50___ cm $\frac{7}{100}$ m = ___7___ cm

2. $\frac{19}{100}$ m = ___19___ cm $\frac{2}{100}$ m = ___2___ cm $\frac{34}{100}$ m = ___34___ cm

3. $\frac{95}{100}$ m = ___95___ cm $\frac{11}{100}$ m = ___11___ cm $\frac{100}{100}$ m = ___100___ cm

D Answer each of these questions.

1. Max measured his pencil. Its length was 19 centimeters. What fractional part of a meter was this? $\frac{19}{100}$

2. Measure your pencil. Its length is _____ centimeters. What fractional part of a meter is this? _____

PARTS OF A DOLLAR

Half-dollar

Quarter

Dime

Penny

A Answer each of these questions.

1. How many half-dollars are in a dollar? — 2

2. A half-dollar is what part of a dollar? — $\frac{1}{2}$

3. How many quarters are in a dollar? — 4

4. A quarter is what part of a dollar? — $\frac{1}{4}$

5. How many dimes are in a dollar? — 10

6. A dime is what part of a dollar? — $\frac{1}{10}$

7. How many pennies are in a dollar? — 100

8. A penny is what part of a dollar? — $\frac{1}{100}$

B Complete the tables.

1.

	Money	Part of a Dollar	Number of Cents
a.	2 quarters	$\frac{2}{4}$	50
b.	7 dimes	$\frac{7}{10}$	70
c.	15 pennies	$\frac{15}{100}$	15
d.	3 quarters	$\frac{3}{4}$	75
e.	4 dimes	$\frac{4}{10}$	40
f.	80 pennies	$\frac{80}{100}$	80
g.	8 dimes	$\frac{8}{10}$	80

2.

	Money	Part of a Dollar	Number of Cents
a.	1 half-dollar	$\frac{1}{2}$	50
b.	5 dimes	$\frac{5}{10}$	50
c.	50 pennies	$\frac{50}{100}$	50
d.	2 half-dollars	$\frac{2}{2}$	100
e.	4 quarters	$\frac{4}{4}$	100
f.	10 dimes	$\frac{10}{10}$	100
g.	100 pennies	$\frac{100}{100}$	100

NAMES FOR MONEY

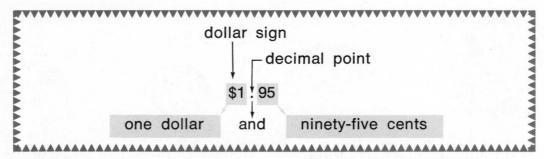

A Read each name for an amount of money.

1. $.75 $1.80 $5.52 $.05 $1.00

2. $9.43 $6.05 $.17 $5.00 $10.00

B Complete the chart.

	Amount of Money	Number of Dollars	Number of Cents	Name Using $ and .
1.	three dollars and seven cents	3	7	$3.07
2.	six dollars and thirty-seven cents	6	37	$6.37
3.	four dollars and five cents	4	5	$4.05
4.	forty cents	0	40	$.40

C Draw a ring around the larger amount of money.

1. (($.10)) $.01   2. $1.00 (($1.01))   3. (($3.30)) $3.03

4. $.75 (($7.50))   5. (($2.00)) $1.95   6. $.65 (($.70))

D Write each amount of money two ways.

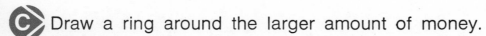

1. 1 half-dollar and 1 quarter   75¢ $.75 or $0.75

2. 2 dollars and 3 nickels   215¢ $2.15

3. 5 dimes and 7 pennies   57¢ $.57 or $0.57

4. 1 quarter and 2 dimes   45¢ $.45 or $0.45

UNDERSTANDING PICTURE GRAPHS

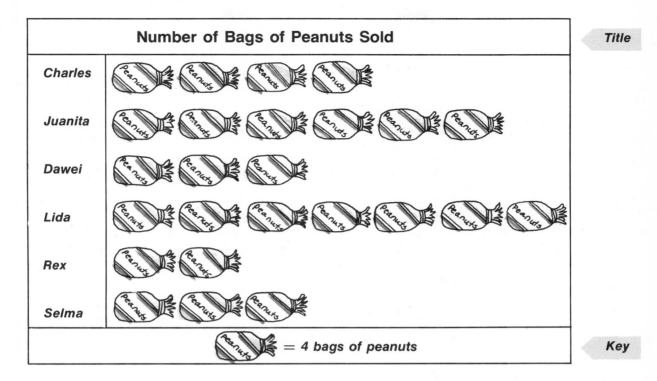

Number of Bags of Peanuts Sold ◄ Title

= 4 bags of peanuts ◄ Key

A **picture graph** tells a number story using **pictures**. The **title** tells us what the graph is about. The **key** tells us what each picture represents.

A Study the picture graph and answer these questions.

1. How many pictures are next to Juanita's name? __6__

2. How many bags of peanuts does each 🥜 equal? __4__

3. How many bags of peanuts did Juanita sell? __24__ bags

4. Find the number of bags of peanuts sold by each child.

Charles	__16__ bags		Lida	__28__ bags
Juanita	__24__ bags		Rex	__8__ bags
Dawei	__12__ bags		Selma	__12__ bags

5. Who sold the most bags of peanuts? __Lida__

6. Who sold the fewest bags of peanuts? __Rex__

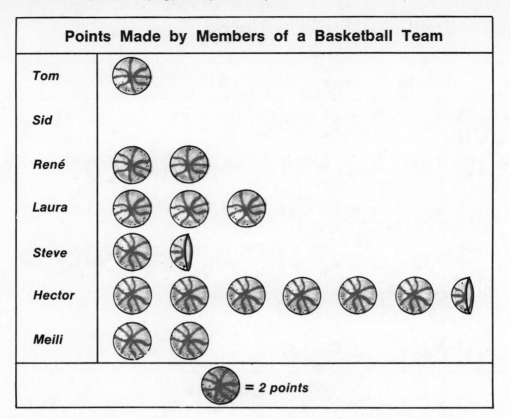

Points Made by Members of a Basketball Team

Tom	
Sid	
René	
Laura	
Steve	
Hector	
Meili	

= 2 points

B Study the picture graph and answer these questions.

1. Find the key. How many points does each ⊛ equal? __2__ points

2. How many points does each ◖ equal? __1__ point

3. Who scored the most points? _____ Hector _____

4. What player did not score? _____ Sid _____

5. Which players made fewer points than Meili? ___ Steve, Tom, Sid ___

6. Which players made more points than Meili? ___ Laura, Hector ___

7. How many points did each player make?

Tom __2__ points   Laura __6__ points   Hector __13__ points

Sid __0__ points   Steve __3__ points   Meili __4__ points

René __4__ points

8. How many points did the whole team make? ___ 32 ___ points

CHAPTER REVIEW

 A Write the fraction that names the shaded part of the whole.

1. $\frac{1}{4}$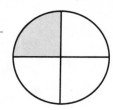

2. $\frac{3}{8}$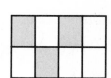

3. $\frac{1}{3}$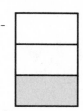

B Write the fraction that names the shaded part of the set.

1. $\frac{2}{3}$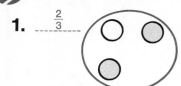

2. $\frac{5}{6}$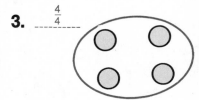

3. $\frac{4}{4}$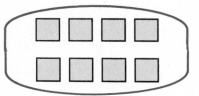

C Look at the set of squares.

1. Write the number of squares in each part.

a. $\frac{3}{8}$ ___3___ $\frac{6}{8}$ ___6___ $\frac{1}{8}$ ___1___

b. $\frac{7}{8}$ ___7___ $\frac{2}{8}$ ___2___ $\frac{8}{8}$ ___8___

2. Draw a ring around the part of the set that has more squares.

$\boxed{\frac{3}{8}}$ $\frac{2}{8}$ $\boxed{\frac{6}{8}}$ $\frac{1}{8}$ $\boxed{\frac{8}{8}}$ $\frac{7}{8}$ $\frac{1}{8}$ $\boxed{\frac{3}{8}}$

3. Write < or > in each ⬤ to make the sentence true.

$\frac{3}{8}$ **>** $\frac{2}{8}$ $\frac{6}{8}$ **>** $\frac{1}{8}$ $\frac{7}{8}$ **<** $\frac{8}{8}$ $\frac{3}{8}$ **>** $\frac{2}{8}$

 D Divide each set into fourths and complete the sentence.

1.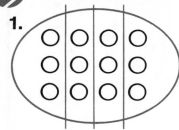

2.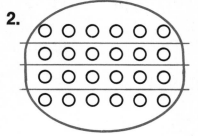

3.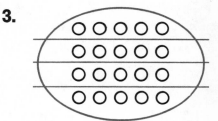

$\frac{1}{4}$ of 12 is ___3___. $\frac{1}{4}$ of ___24___ is ___6___. $\frac{1}{4}$ of ___20___ is ___5___.

CHECK-UP

 A Write the fraction that names the shaded part.

1. $\frac{3}{4}$

2. $\frac{2}{5}$
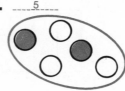

3. $\frac{1}{2}$

4. $\frac{4}{10}$

5. $\frac{6}{6}$
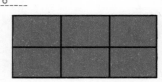

B Show the part named by each fraction by shading.

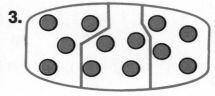

$\frac{1}{6}$ $\frac{2}{6}$ $\frac{3}{6}$ $\frac{4}{6}$ $\frac{5}{6}$ $\frac{6}{6}$

C Use exercise B. Write $<$ or $>$ in each ⬤ to make the sentence true.

$\frac{1}{6}$ $<$ $\frac{5}{6}$ $\frac{3}{6}$ $<$ $\frac{4}{6}$ $\frac{6}{6}$ $>$ $\frac{2}{6}$ $\frac{3}{6}$ $>$ $\frac{2}{6}$

D Divide each set into thirds and complete the sentence.

1.    **2.**   **3.**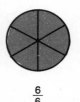

$\frac{1}{3}$ of __6__ is __2__. $\frac{1}{3}$ of __18__ is __6__. $\frac{1}{3}$ of __12__ is __4__.

E Answer these questions by writing a fraction.

1. What part of the set is made up of triangles? $\frac{4}{9}$

2. What part of the set is in blue? $\frac{3}{9}$

3. What part of the set is the square? $\frac{1}{9}$

4. $\frac{1}{3}$ of 9 is __3__.

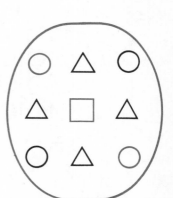

162

8 • ADDITION AND SUBTRACTION

REVIEWING ADDITION

Herman's Addition

Gwen's Addition

A Answer the questions about Herman's addition and Gwen's addition.

1. Who had to rename 10 ones as 1 ten? _____Gwen_____

2. Who had to rename 10 tens as 1 hundred? ___Gwen, Herman___

3. Who had to rename twice? _____Gwen_____

4. Did both students add correctly? _____yes_____

Have students complete exercises B and C.

B Find the sums.

1.
```
  65       84       25       78       59       96
+ 23     + 32     + 69     + 48     + 27     + 45
----     ----     ----     ----     ----     ----
  88      116       94      126       86      141
```

2.
```
  131      638      718      267      575
+ 724    + 540    + 169    + 182    + 297
-----    -----    -----    -----    -----
  855    1,178      887      449      872
```

C Solve each of these word problems.

1. Mr. Esposito filled the gasoline tank of his truck with 78 liters of gasoline. At his next gas stop he put in 49 liters. How much gasoline did he put in his truck? ___127___ liters

2. On a deer hunt, 2 deer were killed. One weighed 155 pounds and the other weighed 169 pounds. How much was the combined weight? ___324___ pounds

ADDING MONEY

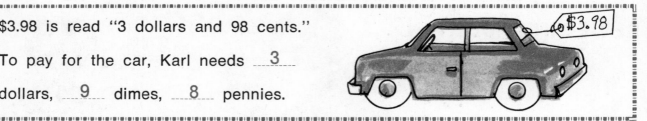

$3.98 is read "3 dollars and 98 cents."

To pay for the car, Karl needs __3__ dollars, __9__ dimes, __8__ pennies.

A Match an amount of money in column A with an equal amount of money in column B. Do the same in columns C and D.

Column A	Column B	Column C	Column D
$1.00	five pennies	$.01	2 dimes and 1 nickel
$.05	seventy-five cents	$5.04	1¢
$2.50	ten dimes	$.25	2 dollars and 65 cents
$.75	two dollars and fifty cents	$2.65	five dollars and four cents

B Study the example. Answer the questions.

1. Are the decimal points in a column? __yes__

2. What is the sum of the pennies? __8__

3. What is the sum of the dimes? __8__

4. What is the sum of the dollars? __6__

Dollars	Cents
$2 .	63
+ 4 .	25
$6 .	88

C Add the pennies first, the dimes second, and the dollars last. Be sure to put the dollar sign ($) and decimal point (.) in the sum.

1.
$1.62	$.32	$6.24	$5.09	$2.41	$8.13
+ 3.05	+ .17	+ .51	+ 1.70	+ 4.56	+ .75
$4.67	$.49	$6.75	$6.79	$6.97	$8.88

2.
$3.29	$ .62	$2.53	$1.80	$6.81	$2.39
+ 4.60	+ 1.34	+ 5.42	+ .07	+ 1.05	+ 4.60
$7.89	$1.96	$7.95	$1.87	$7.86	$6.99

On the chalkboard, work several problems involving addition of amounts of money with renaming. Stress the renaming process; through questioning have students perform the additions step by step.

D Study the example.   Answer the questions.

1. What is the sum of the pennies? __12__

2. 12 pennies = __1__ dime, __2__ pennies

3. What is the sum of the dimes? __14__

4. 14 dimes = __1__ dollar, __4__ dimes

5. What is the sum of the dollars? __8__

Dollars	Cents
$\overset{1}{\$4}$.	$\overset{1}{83}$
+ 3 .	59
$8 .	42

E Add.   Exchange 10 pennies for 1 dime.

$3.17	$4.05	$7.48	$5.57	$6.39	$4.26
+ 2.59	+ 1.86	+ 2.24	+ 3.15	+ 2.52	+ 1.68
$5.76	$5.91	$9.72	$8.72	$8.91	$5.94

F Add.   Exchange 10 dimes for 1 dollar.

$1.85	$3.74	$4.61	$1.52	$3.47	$7.24
+ .90	+ 1.53	+ 3.65	+ 1.83	+ 5.90	+ 1.84
$2.75	$5.27	$8.26	$3.35	$9.37	$9.08

G Add.   Exchange 10 pennies for 1 dime and 10 dimes for 1 dollar.

$1.69	$3.85	$4.53	$ .94	$6.24	$2.76
+ 2.46	+ 1.69	+ .87	+ 1.38	+ 2.76	+ 4.55
$4.15	$5.54	$5.40	$2.32	$9.00	$7.31

H Copy each of these, keeping the decimal points in a column.   Find the sums.

1. $4.82 and $.58 $5.40

2. $1.65 and $3.93 $5.58

3. $.97 and $1.97 $2.94

4. $6.84 and $2.16 $9.00

5. $4.47 and $1.69 $6.16

REVIEWING SUBTRACTION

$$\begin{array}{r} 365 \\ -187 \\ \hline 178 \end{array}$$

Kim's Subtraction

$$\begin{array}{r} 539 \\ -157 \\ \hline 482 \end{array}$$

Fred's Subtraction

A Answer the questions about Fred's subtraction and Kim's subtraction.

1. Who had to rename 1 ten as 10 ones? _____Kim_____

2. Who had to rename twice? _____Kim_____

3. Which student subtracted incorrectly? _____Fred_____

4. What is the correct difference for Fred's subtraction? _____382_____

Have students complete exercises B and C independently.

B Find the differences.

1.

| $\begin{array}{r} 17 \\ -9 \\ \hline 8 \end{array}$ | $\begin{array}{r} 48 \\ -15 \\ \hline 33 \end{array}$ | $\begin{array}{r} 52 \\ -26 \\ \hline 26 \end{array}$ | $\begin{array}{r} 41 \\ -4 \\ \hline 37 \end{array}$ | $\begin{array}{r} 84 \\ -47 \\ \hline 37 \end{array}$ | $\begin{array}{r} 73 \\ -38 \\ \hline 35 \end{array}$ | $\begin{array}{r} 90 \\ -53 \\ \hline 37 \end{array}$ |

2.

| $\begin{array}{r} 407 \\ -132 \\ \hline 275 \end{array}$ | $\begin{array}{r} 536 \\ -278 \\ \hline 258 \end{array}$ | $\begin{array}{r} 840 \\ -365 \\ \hline 475 \end{array}$ | $\begin{array}{r} 695 \\ -488 \\ \hline 207 \end{array}$ | $\begin{array}{r} 923 \\ -246 \\ \hline 677 \end{array}$ | $\begin{array}{r} 572 \\ -98 \\ \hline 474 \end{array}$ |

C Solve each of these word problems.

1. Two scout troops collected trash from along the highway. The first troop collected 59 bags. The second troop collected 88 bags. How many more bags did the second troop collect? __29__ bags

2. On Monday night the odometer on Billie's bike showed 784 kilometers. On Tuesday night it showed 812 kilometers. How many kilometers did Billie ride on Tuesday? __28__ kilometers

SUBTRACTING MONEY

 Mr. Tonemah bought a sweater for his niece Joni. The sweater cost $8.12. He gave the clerk $8.25. Answer the questions below to find out how much money Mr. Tonemah should get back from the clerk.

1. Are the decimal points in a column? __Yes__

2. What is the difference of the pennies? __3__

3. What is the difference of the dimes? __1__

4. What is the difference of the dollars? __0__

Dollars	Cents
$8 .	25
− 8 .	12
$0 .	13

5. How much change should Mr. Tonemah receive?

__13__ cents

Have students complete exercises B and C independently.

 Subtract the pennies first, the dimes second, and the dollars last.

Be sure to put the dollar sign ($) and decimal point (.) in the difference.

$5.98	$4.73	$8.65	$5.46	$7.92
− 1.25	− .41	− 4.62	− 2.34	− 3.42
$4.73	$4.32	$4.03	$3.12	$4.50

C Subtract. Check by addition.

1.
```
        Check
$7.58   $2.13
−2.13  +5.45
$5.45   $7.58
```

2.
```
        Check
$5.37   $1.15
−1.15  +4.22
$4.22   $5.37
```

3.
```
        Check
$6.38   $5.02
−5.02  +1.36
$1.36   $6.38
```

4.
```
        Check
$4.59   $2.24
−2.24  +2.35
$2.35   $4.59
```

5.
```
        Check
$8.96   $1.32
−1.32  +7.64
$7.64   $8.96
```

6.
```
        Check
$3.82   $3.00
−3.00  +0.82
$0.82   $3.82
```

7.
```
        Check
$8.54   $1.40
−1.40  +7.14
$7.14   $8.54
```

8.
```
        Check
$5.93   $2.71
−2.71  +3.22
$3.22   $5.93
```

9.
```
        Check
$8.79   $5.67
−5.67  +3.12
$3.12   $8.79
```

Study the example.   Answer the questions.

Dollars	Cents
$5 . $ $\overset{4}{\cancel{5}}$. $\overset{12}{\cancel{3}}\overset{10}{0}$	
$-1 . 59$	
$3 . 71$	

1. Are there enough pennies to subtract from? __no__
Exchange 1 dime for 10 pennies in $5.30.

2. How many dimes? __2__   How many pennies? __10__

3. The difference of the pennies is __1__.

4. Are there enough dimes to subtract from? __no__
Exchange 1 dollar for 10 dimes.

5. How many dimes? __12__   How many dollars? __4__

6. The difference of the dimes is __7__.

7. The difference of the dollars is __3__.

 Subtract.   Exchange 1 dime for 10 pennies.

$4.65	$9.80	$3.52	$5.73	$2.41
-1.47	-3.14	$-.25$	-2.68	-1.19
$3.18	$6.66	$3.27	$3.05	$1.22

F Subtract.   Exchange 1 dollar for 10 dimes.

$2.28	$7.45	$6.17	$4.39	$9.05
-1.65	-3.50	-2.31	$-.92$	-2.84
$0.63	$3.95	$3.86	$3.47	$6.21

G Subtract.   Exchange 1 dime for 10 pennies and 1 dollar for 10 dimes.

$4.13	$6.15	$4.42	$8.70	$5.31
-1.68	-5.97	-2.65	-5.84	-3.72
$2.45	$0.18	$1.77	$2.86	$1.59

H Copy each of these, keeping the decimal points in a column. Find the differences.

1. $4.03 less $1.53 $2.50

2. $6.42 less $3.19 $3.23

3. $1.84 less $.95 $0.89

Exercise D requires students to rename to subtract amounts of money. Treat this exercise orally, emphasizing the renaming process, the correct placement of the decimal point, and the use of the dollar sign.

PROBLEMS INVOLVING MONEY

 Solve these problems by adding or subtracting.

1. Jane bought one record album for $4.65 and another for $4.98.   How much did she spend for both albums? __$9.63__

2. Mr. Wakole bought a pipe for $4.85.   He gave the clerk $5.00.   How much money should he receive in change? __$ .15__

3. Ginny was saving money to buy a baseball glove.   The glove cost $9.50, and she had saved $7.34.   How much more money did Ginny need? __$2.16__

4. Tyler had $5.00.   He wanted to buy a wallet for his mother and a key case for his father.   The wallet cost $2.95 and the key case cost $2.50.   Did Tyler have enough money? __no__

5. Daniel has $5.45 and Sylvia has $4.43.   If they put their money together, how much can they spend for their father's birthday present? __$9.88__

6. Fran and Henry baby-sit.   Last week Fran earned $5.75 and Henry earned $6.25.   How much more did Henry earn than Fran? __$0.50__

7. Mrs. Green bought two lamps at a sale.   She paid $4.60 for one lamp and $3.85 for the other.   How much did she spend for both? __$8.45__ How much change did she get from $10.00? __$1.55__

8. Sandy's mother gave her $4.50 to pay for a bike repair charge of $2.92.   How much change should she get? __$1.58__

9. Jerry bought 40 marbles for $.75 and David bought 80 marbles for $1.45.   How much did all the marbles cost? __$2.20__

ZEROS IN SUBTRACTION

 Complete the chart.

	Standard Name	Rename 1 Hundred as 10 Tens	Rename 1 Ten as 10 Ones
1.	300 →	300 = 200 + 100 + 0 →	300 = 200 + 90 + 10
2.	500 →	500 = 400 + 100 + 0 →	500 = 400 + 90 + 10
3.	405 →	405 = 300 + 100 + 5 →	405 = 300 + 90 + 15

Review renaming using the subtractions in exercise B. Remind students that the short form of renaming is shown below.

B Study steps A, B, and C. Subtract in step C.

	Step A	Step B	Step C

1.   300   300 + 0 + 0   200 + 100 + 0   200 + 90 + 10
   − 168   − 100 + 60 + 8   − 100 + 60 + 8   − 100 + 60 + 8

                                                            100 + 30 + 2 = 132

2.   503   500 + 0 + 3   400 + 100 + 3   400 + 90 + 13
   − 156   − 100 + 50 + 6   − 100 + 50 + 6   − 100 + 50 + 6

                                                            300 + 40 + 7 = 347

Discuss the example. Emphasize that the renaming process is the same but the expanded names are written in a different form.

How To Subtract 405 − 287

Step 1	405 − 287	Are there enough ones to subtract from? __no__
		Are there any tens to rename as 10 ones? __no__
Step 2	3 10 / 4̸0̸5 − 287	Rename 1 hundred as 10 tens.
Step 3	9 / 3 10 15 / 4̸0̸5̸ − 287	Rename 1 ten as 10 ones.
Step 4	9 / 3 10 15 / 4̸0̸5̸ − 287 / 118	Subtract.

Subtract.

1.

307	$4.00	905	200	600
− 189	− 2.04	− 468	− 85	− 199
118	$1.96	437	115	401

2.

$1.00	802	$6.08	$7.00	505
− .75	− 208	− 3.29	− 1.36	− 227
$0.25	594	$2.79	$5.64	278

 Subtract.   Check by addition.

1.
$$\begin{array}{r} \overset{14}{\overset{7\cancel{4}12}{\cancel{8}\cancel{5}\cancel{2}}} \\ -169 \\ \hline 683 \end{array} \quad \begin{array}{r} 169 \\ +683 \\ \hline 852 \end{array}$$

2.
$$\begin{array}{r} 703 \\ -458 \\ \hline 245 \end{array} + \begin{array}{r} 458 \\ 245 \\ \hline 703 \end{array}$$

3.
$$\begin{array}{r} \$5.82 \\ -1.47 \\ \hline \$4.35 \end{array} + \begin{array}{r} \$1.47 \\ 4.35 \\ \hline \$5.82 \end{array}$$

4.
$$\begin{array}{r} \$4.00 \\ -1.63 \\ \hline \$2.37 \end{array} \quad \begin{array}{r} \$1.63 \\ +2.37 \\ \hline \$4.00 \end{array}$$

5.
$$\begin{array}{r} 296 \\ -188 \\ \hline 108 \end{array} \quad \begin{array}{r} 188 \\ +108 \\ \hline 296 \end{array}$$

6.
$$\begin{array}{r} 403 \\ -275 \\ \hline 128 \end{array} \quad \begin{array}{r} 275 \\ +128 \\ \hline 403 \end{array}$$

7.
$$\begin{array}{r} 301 \\ -47 \\ \hline 254 \end{array} \quad \begin{array}{r} 47 \\ +254 \\ \hline 301 \end{array}$$

8.
$$\begin{array}{r} \$6.00 \\ -1.98 \\ \hline \$4.02 \end{array} \quad \begin{array}{r} \$1.98 \\ +4.02 \\ \hline \$6.00 \end{array}$$

9.
$$\begin{array}{r} \$5.71 \\ -4.67 \\ \hline \$1.04 \end{array} \quad \begin{array}{r} \$4.67 \\ +1.04 \\ \hline \$5.71 \end{array}$$

 Find each sum or difference.

1.

823	477	527	$2.25	203
+ 169	+ 386	− 184	+ 4.95	− 169
992	863	343	$7.20	34

2.

$4.00	$1.95	475	500	$4.52
− 2.65	+ 3.99	+ 253	− 192	− 1.85
$1.35	$5.94	728	308	$2.67

3.

107	$ .84	$2.05	$4.03	162
+ 95	+ .67	− .97	− .79	+ 488
202	$1.51	$1.08	$3.24	650

4.

826	$.95	$2.93	$5.84	620
− 179	− .88	+ 1.69	− 1.35	− 82
647	$.07	$4.62	$4.49	538

Student answers to exercise D should include the check.

REVIEWING 4-DIGIT NUMBERS

 Bob guessed there were one thousand, six hundred fifty-seven beans in a jar. He wrote 1,657 on his card. Jane guessed there were two thousand, one hundred thirty-five beans. Answer these questions.

1. What number should Jane write? ___2,135___

2. Who guessed the larger number of beans? ___Jane___

3. What does the 1 in Bob's number mean? ___one thousand___

4. What does the 1 in Jane's number mean? ___one hundred___

5. Does the 1 in Bob's number mean the same as the 1 in Jane's number? ___no___

 Complete the chart.

	Standard Name	Thousands	Hundreds	Tens	Ones	Expanded Name
1.	4,635	4	6	3	5	4,000 + 600 + 30 + 5
2.	2,840	2	8	4	0	2,000 + 800 + 40
3.	6,921	6	9	2	1	6,000 + 900 + 20 + 1
4.	7,059	7	0	5	9	7,000 + 50 + 9
5.	4,427	4	4	2	7	4,000 + 400 + 20 + 7

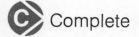 Complete the number patterns.

1. 3,007 3,008 3,009 ___3,010___   **2.** 5,697 5,698 5,699 ___5,700___

3. 1,997 1,998 1,999 ___2,000___   **4.** 8,970 8,980 8,990 ___9,000___

5. 6,070 6,080 6,090 ___6,100___   **6.** 7,700 7,800 7,900 ___8,000___

7. 5,100 5,200 5,300 ___5,400___   **8.** 1,400 1,500 1,600 ___1,700___

If students do not have an intuitive grasp of large numbers, have them complete the additional activity.

ADDING 4-DIGIT NUMBERS—NO RENAMING

 Find the sums.   Look for a pattern.

1.
5 tens	5 hundreds	5 thousands
+4 tens	+4 hundreds	+4 thousands
_9_ tens	_9_ hundreds	_9_ thousands

2.
30	300	3,000
+ 30	+ 300	+ 3,000
60	600	6,000

3.
6 tens	6 hundreds	6 thousands
+7 tens	+7 hundreds	+7 thousands
_13_ tens	_13_ hundreds	_13_ thousands

4.
80	800	8,000
+ 80	+ 800	+ 8,000
160	1,600	16,000

Discuss the example below. Then have students complete exercises B and C independently. Stress adding beginning with the ones.

Two Ways To Add 6,537 + 2,421

Expanded Form

$$6,537 = 6,000 + 500 + 30 + 7$$
$$+ 2,421 = 2,000 + 400 + 20 + 1$$
$$8,000 + 900 + 50 + 8 = 8,958$$

Short Form

6,537	Add the ones, tens,
+ 2,421	hundreds, and
8,958	thousands.

 Find the sums.

1.
$$4,784 = 4,000 + 700 + 80 + 4$$
$$+ 1,213 = 1,000 + 200 + 10 + 3$$
$$\underline{5,000} + \underline{900} + \underline{90} + \underline{7} = \underline{5,997}$$

2.
$$2,354 = 2,000 + 300 + 50 + 4$$
$$+ 3,435 = 3,000 + 400 + 30 + 5$$
$$\underline{5,000} + \underline{700} + \underline{80} + \underline{9} = \underline{5,789}$$

Remind students to be careful of the dollar sign and the decimal point in their answers in row 2.

C Use the short form to find the sums.   Remember: Add the ones first, the tens second, the hundreds third, and the thousands last.

1.

4,816	1,215	7,206	6,203	1,448
+ 1,052	+ 3,643	+ 1,192	+ 2,583	+ 4,250
5,868	4,858	8,398	8,786	5,698

2.

$17.50	$43.75	$61.03	$32.41	$29.53
+ 10.35	+ 20.23	+ 28.54	+ 14.37	+ 60.15
$27.85	$63.98	$89.57	$46.78	$89.68

ADDING 4-DIGIT NUMBERS—WITH RENAMING

 Complete the charts.

1. Rename 10 hundreds as 1 thousand.

	Thousands	Hundreds	Thousands	Hundreds	Standard Name
a.	3	15 →	4	5	4,500
b.	6	11 →	7	1	7,100
c.	5	17 →	6	7	6,700
d.	4	10 →	5	0	5,000
e.	1	12 →	2	2	2,200

2. Rename 10 ones as 1 ten, 10 tens as 1 hundred, and 10 hundreds as 1 thousand.

	Thousands	Hundreds	Tens	Ones	Thousands	Hundreds	Tens	Ones	Standard Name
a.	1	14	11	15 →	2	5	2	5	2,525
b.	3	12	17	16 →	4	3	8	6	4,386
c.	5	10	13	12 →	6	1	4	2	6,142
d.	3	9	15	10 →	4	0	6	0	4,060
e.	6	18	11	17 →	7	9	2	7	7,927

B Find the sums.

1.

$$4,376 = 4,000 + 300 + 70 + 6$$
$$+ 2,914 = 2,000 + 900 + 10 + 4$$
$$6,000 + 1,200 + 80 + 10 = 7,290$$

2.

$$1,643 = 1,000 + 600 + 40 + 3$$
$$+ 4,772 = 4,000 + 700 + 70 + 2$$
$$5,000 + 1,300 + 110 + 5 = 6,415$$

174

Exercise C is developmental and should be completed under teacher guidance. Each step in the algorithm for adding two 4-digit numbers is shown. Students should refer to the addition as they complete the sentences. Board work with more additions should follow.

Complete the sentences as you study the example.

```
  1
 2,398
+1,876
─────
     4
```

First: Add ones. 6 + 8 = __14__.

Rename 14 ones as __1__ ten, __4__ ones.
Write 4 in the ones' column in the sum.
Write the 1 in the tens' column above the 9.

```
 1 1
 2,395
+1,876
─────
    74
```

Second: Add tens. 1 + 9 + 7 = __17__.

Rename 17 tens as __1__ hundred, __7__ tens.
Write 7 in the tens' column in the sum.
Write the 1 in the hundreds' column above the 3.

```
 1 11
 2,398
+1,876
─────
   274
```

Third: Add hundreds. 1 + 3 + 8 = __12__.

Rename 12 hundreds as __1__ thousand, __2__ hundreds.
Write 2 in the hundreds' column in the sum.
Write the 1 in the thousands' column above the 2.

```
 1 11
 2,398
+1,876
─────
 4,274
```

Fourth: Add thousands. 1 + 2 + 1 = __4__.
Write 4 in the thousands' column in the sum.

Have students complete the additions in exercise D independently. These additions provide an opportunity to assess student capability for adding 4-digit numbers.

Find the sums.

1.

1,295	3,760	6,517	5,773	4,583
+ 2,847	+ 1,584	+ 2,839	+ 1,718	+ 2,974
4,142	5,344	9,356	7,491	7,557

2.

1,345	7,698	2,784	7,572	4,342
+ 5,827	+ 1,324	+ 3,926	+ 1,098	+ 2,688
7,172	9,022	6,710	8,670	7,030

3.

$15.69	$11.38	$17.19	$32.84	$54.95
+ 21.15	+ 56.43	+ 17.19	+ 19.27	+ 17.85
$36.84	$67.81	$34.38	$52.11	$72.80

4.

7	4	45	14	36
140	20	350	490	480
+ 2,800	+ 280	+ 2,500	+ 5,600	+ 1,800
2,947	304	2,895	6,104	2,316

Row 4 asks students to find sums of three numbers which could be partial products in a multiplication. These exercises anticipate multiplication of a 1-digit number times a 3-digit number, which will be developed in the next chapter.

REVIEWING FRACTIONS

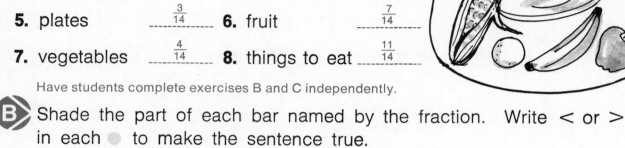

A Use the picture of the set. Write a fraction to name each part of the set.

1. apples ___ $\frac{2}{14}$ ___   **2.** oranges ___ $\frac{3}{14}$ ___

3. ears of corn ___ $\frac{4}{14}$ ___   **4.** bananas ___ $\frac{2}{14}$ ___

5. plates ___ $\frac{3}{14}$ ___   **6.** fruit ___ $\frac{7}{14}$ ___

7. vegetables ___ $\frac{4}{14}$ ___   **8.** things to eat ___ $\frac{11}{14}$ ___

Have students complete exercises B and C independently.

B Shade the part of each bar named by the fraction. Write < or > in each ● to make the sentence true.

1. $\frac{0}{5}$ $\frac{0}{5}$ < $\frac{5}{5}$

2. $\frac{1}{5}$ $\frac{0}{5}$ < $\frac{1}{5}$

3. $\frac{2}{5}$ $\frac{2}{5}$ > $\frac{1}{5}$

4. $\frac{3}{5}$ $\frac{3}{5}$ < $\frac{5}{5}$

5. $\frac{4}{5}$ $\frac{4}{5}$ > $\frac{2}{5}$

6. $\frac{5}{5}$ $\frac{0}{5}$ < $\frac{5}{5}$

C Divide each set into fourths and complete the sentence.

1. 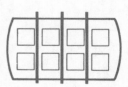   **2.** 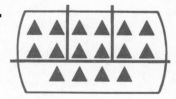   **3.**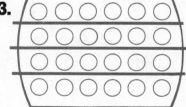

$\frac{1}{4}$ of ___8___ is ___2___. $\frac{1}{4}$ of ___16___ is ___4___. $\frac{1}{4}$ of ___24___ is ___6___.

Exercise A is developmental. The subtraction algorithm is broken down into steps. Treat exercise A orally. Have students do more subtractions on the chalkboard. Develop the idea of checking these subtractions by addition.

SUBTRACTING 4-DIGIT NUMBERS—NO RENAMING

 A Subtract using the short form. Follow the steps and fill each ▪.

Subtraction	Step 1 Ones	Step 2 Tens	Step 3 Hundreds	Step 4 Thousands
4,795 − 1,324	4,795 − 1,324 1	4,795 − 1,324 71	4,795 − 1,324 471	4,795 − 1,324 3,471

Have students complete the page independently.

 B Subtract using the short form.

1.

7,842 − 1,612 6,230	4,956 − 2,513 2,443	8,437 − 3,105 5,332	7,796 − 4,781 3,015	9,872 − 1,602 8,270

2.

4,537 − 1,132 3,405	7,825 − 621 7,204	5,375 − 1,223 4,152	9,848 − 7,512 2,336	6,287 − 1,243 5,044

C 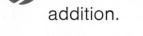 Write the subtraction in column form. Subtract and check by addition.

1. 7,835 − 4,712

Subtraction	Check
7,835 − 4,712 3,123	4,712 + 3,123 7,835

2. 8,496 − 1,422

Subtraction　Check
7,074

3. 4,787 − 2,513
2,274

4. 6,439 − 5,031
1,408

5. 9,387 − 164
9,223

6. 7,283 − 5,032
2,251

Student answers to exercise C should be in the form shown in item 1.

SUBTRACTING 4-DIGIT NUMBERS—WITH RENAMING

 Complete the table.

Rename 1 thousand as 10 hundreds *or* 1 hundred as 10 tens *or* 1 ten as 10 ones.

	Standard Name	Thousands	Hundreds	Tens	Ones	Thousands	Hundreds	Tens	Ones
1.	3,241	3	2	4	1 →	2	12	3	11
2.	4,073	4	0	7	3 →	3	9	16	13
3.	2,514	2	5	1	4 →	2	4	10	14
4.	6,000	6	0	0	0 →	5	9	9	10
5.	2,374	2	3	7	4 →	1	13	6	14

 Fill the blanks and boxes.

$$6,381 = 6,000 + 300 + 80 + 1$$
$$-\,1,795 = 1,000 + 700 + 90 + 5$$

Are there enough ones to subtract from? __no__

$$6,381 = 6,000 + 300 + 70 + \boxed{11}$$
$$-\,1,795 = 1,000 + 700 + 90 + 5$$

Rename 1 ten as 10 ones. Subtract the ones.

$$ \underline{6}$$

Are there enough tens to subtract from? __no__

$$6,381 = 6,000 + 200 + \boxed{170} + 11$$
$$-\,1,795 = 1,000 + 700 + 90 + 5$$

Rename 1 hundred as 10 tens. Subtract the tens.

$$ \underline{80} + 6$$

Are there enough hundreds to subtract from? __no__

$$6,381 = 5,000 + \boxed{1,200} + 170 + 11$$
$$-\,1,795 = 1,000 + 700 + 90 + 5$$

Rename 1 thousand as 10 hundreds.

$$\underline{4,000} + \underline{500} + 80 + 6$$

Subtract the hundreds.
Subtract the thousands.

$$6,381 - 1,795 = \underline{4,586}$$

C Subtract using the short form. Follow the steps and fill each ▮ .

Subtraction	Step 1	Step 2	Step 3	Step 4
1. 3,641 − 1,985	³¹¹ 3,641 − 1,985 ___ 6	¹³ ⁵ ∕³11 3,641 − 1,985 ___ 56	¹⁵ ¹³ ² ∕⁵ ∕³11 3,641 − 1,985 ___ 6 56	¹⁵¹³ 2 ⁵ ∕³11 3,641 − 1,985 ___ 1,656
2. 4,000 − 1,652	³ 9 9 10 4,000 − 1,652 ___ 8	3 9 9 10 4,000 − 1,652 ___ 48	3 9 9 10 4,000 − 1,652 ___ 3 48	3 9 9 10 4,000 − 1,652 ___ 2,348

Have students complete exercises D and E independently.

D Find the differences.

1. 7,562 − 1,847 ___ 5,715	2,743 − 1,995 ___ 748	3,654 − 687 ___ 2,967	8,402 − 1,625 ___ 6,777	4,473 − 2,595 ___ 1,878
2. $45.92 − 17.66 ___ $28.26	$39.75 − 12.99 ___ $26.76	$40.00 − 25.63 ___ $14.37	2,563 − 1,747 ___ 816	6,327 − 2,859 ___ 3,468
3. $22.00 − 8.95 ___ $13.05	$71.48 − 15.62 ___ $55.86	2,751 − 1,985 ___ 766	1,980 − 493 ___ 1,487	2,073 − 1,483 ___ 590

E Subtract. Check by addition.

1.
⁶ ⁹10
4,700
− 2,635
___
2,065

→ 2,635
+ 2,065
___
4,700

2.
8,442
− 3,975
___
4,467

3,975
+4,467
___
8,442

3.
4,359
− 1,792
___
2,567

1,792
+2,567
___
4,359

4.
5,000
− 1,728
___
3,272

1,728
+3,272
___
5,000

Student answers to exercise E should be in the form shown in item 1.

179

PROBLEM SOLVING

The children in the fourth grade classes counted ducks migrating south for the winter. The table shows how many ducks each class counted.

Class	Number of Ducks
Mrs. Green's	1,318
Miss Watson's	2,504
Mrs. Pérez's	2,540
Mr. Holmes's	1,895

Answer these questions.

1. Whose class counted the most ducks? _____ Mrs. Pérez's _____

2. Whose class counted the fewest ducks? _____ Mrs. Green's _____

3. How many ducks were counted by the children in Miss Watson's and Mr. Holmes's classes? _____ 4,399 _____ ducks

4. How many more ducks were counted by the children in Miss Watson's class than were counted by the children in Mrs. Green's class? _____ 1,186 _____ ducks

5. How many more ducks were counted by Mrs. Pérez's class than by Mr. Holmes's class? _____ 645 _____ ducks

6. How many ducks were counted by Mrs. Green's and Mr. Holmes's classes? _____ 3,213 _____ ducks

7. Who counted more ducks, the children in Mrs. Green's and Mrs. Pérez's classes, or the children in Miss Watson's and Mr. Holmes's classes? _____ Miss Watson's and Mr. Holmes's _____

8. How many ducks were counted by Mrs. Green's, Miss Watson's, and Mrs. Pérez's classes? _____ 6,362 _____ ducks

9. How many ducks were counted by all four classes? _____ 8,257 _____ ducks

UNDERSTANDING BAR GRAPHS

Diane sold tickets to the school carnival. This **bar graph** shows the number of tickets Diane sold each day.

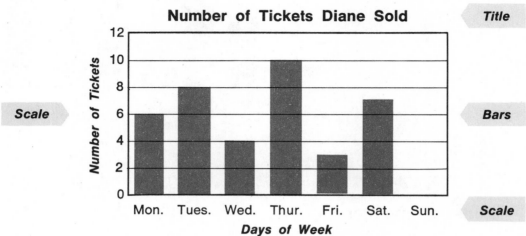

Number of Tickets Diane Sold — Title

Scale

Bars

Scale

Number of Tickets

Days of Week

A Study the bar graph and answer these questions.

1. The bar for Monday ends on the line marked 6. How many tickets did Diane sell on Monday? __6__ tickets

2. The bar for Friday ends halfway between the lines marked 2 and 4. What number is halfway between 2 and 4? __3__

3. How many tickets did Diane sell on Friday? __3__ tickets

4. Find the number of tickets sold on each day.

Monday	__6__ tickets	Tuesday	__8__ tickets
Wednesday	__4__ tickets	Thursday	__10__ tickets
Saturday	__7__ tickets	Sunday	__0__ tickets

5. On which day did Diane sell the most tickets? __Thursday__

6. On which day did Diane sell the fewest tickets? __Sunday__

7. How many more tickets did Diane sell on Thursday than on Saturday? __3__ tickets

8. How many tickets did Diane sell in all? __38__ tickets

181

Roger took piano lessons. He recorded his practice time on a bar graph.

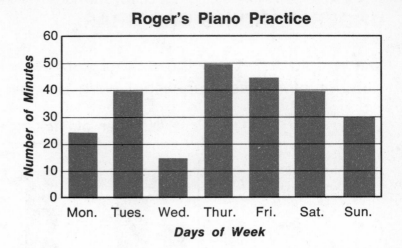

Roger's Piano Practice

B Answer these questions.

1. What does the scale at the left of the bar graph tell us?

   _____ number of minutes played _____

2. What does the scale at the bottom of the bar graph tell us?

   _____ days of week _____

3. On which day did Roger practice most? _____ Thursday _____

4. Of the days practiced, on which day did Roger practice least?

   _____ Wednesday _____

5. How many minutes are in $\frac{1}{2}$ hour? __30__ minutes

6. On which days did Roger practice less than $\frac{1}{2}$ hour?

   _____ Monday, Wednesday _____

7. The bar for Monday ends halfway between the lines marked 20 and

   30. How many minutes did Roger practice on Monday? __25__ minutes

8. How many more minutes did Roger practice on Thursday than on

   Wednesday? __35__ minutes

9. How many minutes in all did Roger practice on Friday and on

   Saturday? __85__ minutes

10. Suppose Roger practiced 30 minutes on Sunday. Show that on the bar graph.

CHAPTER REVIEW

 Find the sums.

1.

205	693	574	358	463
+ 179	+ 186	+ 269	+ 563	+ 239
384	879	843	921	702

2.

$3.52	$4.37	$1.89	$2.66	$7.53
+ 1.45	+ 3.57	+ 4.78	+ 5.49	+ 5.86
$4.97	$7.94	$6.67	$8.15	$13.39

3.

2,357	4,758	6,536	7,958	1,479
+ 1,632	+ 2,037	+ 2,849	+ 1,673	+ 5,845
3,989	6,795	9,385	9,631	7,324

 Find the differences.

1.

679	758	432	920	854
− 152	− 264	− 185	− 475	− 198
527	494	247	445	656

2.

$2.35	$5.46	$3.28	$7.52	$9.30
− 1.08	− 1.73	− 2.69	− 4.57	− 3.78
$1.27	$3.73	$0.59	$2.95	$5.52

3.

6 9 10				
7̸0̸0̸	500	603	208	900
− 165	− 284	− 156	− 189	− 396
535	216	447	19	504

4.

2,758	4,823	9,304	7,523	8,416
− 1,695	− 1,568	− 1,682	− 3,885	− 2,798
1,063	3,255	7,622	3,638	5,618

 Solve these word problems.

1. Bob saved $8.43 during the month of May. His sister saved $6.87.

How much did both children save? __$15.30__

2. Mr. López spent $21.87 at the supermarket. He gave the cashier

$25.00. How much change did he receive? __$3.13__

CHECK-UP

 A Find the sums.

357	782	2,987	$ 6.43	2,807
+ 165	+ 954	+ 6,169	+ 4.58	+ 4,965
522	1,736	9,156	$11.01	7,772

B Find the differences.

593	400	$8.25	4,652	7,240
− 267	− 175	− 3.98	− 1,388	− 3,657
326	225	$4.27	3,264	3,583

C Find the sum or the difference.

1.

426	285	$4.42	1,835	5,332
− 146	+ 397	+ 1.78	− 1,646	+ 1,728
280	682	$6.20	189	7,060

2.

4,427	$42.75	604	300	2,498
+ 3,894	− 15.35	− 128	− 172	+ 3,736
8,321	$27.40	476	128	6,234

D Solve these problems.

1. Mary has 379 bottle caps, and Peter has 783 bottle caps. How many bottle caps do the two have? ___1,162___ bottle caps

2. Two championship Little League games were played. On Saturday, there were 1,847 people at the game. On Sunday, there were 2,154 people at the game. How many more people were at the game on Sunday than on Saturday? ___307___ people

3. Inez had $4.00 and spent $1.25. How much money did she have left? ___$2.75___

9 • MULTIPLICATION

MULTIPLICATION FACTS

 Write the answer to each fact as soon as you read it.

1.

4	5	1	8	3	9	6
× 3	× 7	× 5	× 2	× 3	× 4	× 7
12	35	5	16	9	36	42

2.

3	7	4	8	5	6	2
× 9	× 0	× 6	× 5	× 8	× 6	× 7
27	0	24	40	40	36	14

3.

8	4	3	6	9	5	7
× 9	× 4	× 7	× 4	× 6	× 4	× 7
72	16	21	24	54	20	49

4.

2	7	9	4	6	8	5
× 3	× 4	× 9	× 8	× 3	× 4	× 6
6	28	81	32	18	32	30

B Check the answers to exercise A. Use the multiplication table on the inside back cover of this book. Be sure all products are correct. Read the correct multiplication facts to yourself several times. Then place a piece of paper over your answers. Find the products for all of the facts in exercise A again.

C Complete the multiplication charts.

1.

×	4	9	6	2	7	5
7	28	63	42	14	49	35

2.

×	4	5	3	8	9	7
9	36	45	27	72	81	63

3.

×	3	6	8	5	7	9
4	12	24	32	20	28	36

4.

×	7	4	8	6	5	9
6	42	24	48	36	30	54

5.

×	9	5	8	6	7	3
8	72	40	64	48	56	24

6.

×	3	7	9	5	8	4
5	15	35	45	25	40	20

MULTIPLYING BY 10 AND 100

 Fill the blanks.

1. How many tens? ___4___

2. How many sticks? ___40___

3. 4 tens = ___40___. 4 × 10 = ___40___.

4. How many hundreds? ___2___

5. How many sticks? ___200___

6. 2 hundreds = ___200___. 2 × 100 = ___200___.

B **Multiply by 10. Look for a pattern.**

1. 3 tens = ___30___   3 × 10 = ___30___   **2.** 5 tens = ___50___   5 × 10 = ___50___

3. 7 tens = ___70___   7 × 10 = ___70___   **4.** 10 tens = ___100___   10 × 10 = ___100___

5. 12 tens = ___120___   12 × 10 = ___120___   **6.** 18 tens = ___180___   18 × 10 = ___180___

C **Multiply by 100. Look for a pattern.**

1. 6 hundreds = ___600___   6 × 100 = ___600___

2. 9 hundreds = ___900___   9 × 100 = ___900___

3. 10 hundreds = ___1,000___   10 × 100 = ___1,000___

4. 15 hundreds = ___1,500___   15 × 100 = ___1,500___

D **Find the products.**

1.

10	100		10	100		10	100
× 8	× 8		× 2	× 2		× 9	× 9
80	800		20	200		90	900

2.

10	100		10	100		10	100
× 5	× 5		× 4	× 4		× 10	× 10
50	500		40	400		100	1,000

MULTIPLYING MULTIPLES OF 10 OR 100

 A Complete each sentence. Look for a pattern.

1. $2 + 2 + 2 + 2 =$ _____8_____ $4 \times 2 =$ _____8_____

2. $20 + 20 + 20 + 20 =$ _____80_____ $4 \times 20 =$ _____80_____

3. $200 + 200 + 200 + 200 =$ _____800_____ $4 \times 200 =$ _____800_____

4. $7 + 7 + 7 =$ _____21_____ $3 \times 7 =$ _____21_____

5. $70 + 70 + 70 =$ _____210_____ $3 \times 70 =$ _____210_____

6. $700 + 700 + 700 =$ _____2,100_____ $3 \times 700 =$ _____2,100_____

B Study the example below. Find the products.

1.
$$\begin{array}{c} 3 \\ \times\,8 \\ \hline 24 \end{array} \quad \begin{array}{c} 30 \\ \times\,8 \\ \hline 240 \end{array} \quad \begin{array}{c} 300 \\ \times\,8 \\ \hline 2,400 \end{array}$$

2.
$$\begin{array}{c} 9 \\ \times\,4 \\ \hline 36 \end{array} \quad \begin{array}{c} 90 \\ \times\,4 \\ \hline 360 \end{array} \quad \begin{array}{c} 900 \\ \times\,4 \\ \hline 3,600 \end{array}$$

3.
$$\begin{array}{c} 7 \\ \times\,7 \\ \hline 49 \end{array} \quad \begin{array}{c} 70 \\ \times\,7 \\ \hline 490 \end{array} \quad \begin{array}{c} 700 \\ \times\,7 \\ \hline 4,900 \end{array}$$

4.
$$\begin{array}{c} 8 \\ \times\,5 \\ \hline 40 \end{array} \quad \begin{array}{c} 80 \\ \times\,5 \\ \hline 400 \end{array} \quad \begin{array}{c} 800 \\ \times\,5 \\ \hline 4,000 \end{array}$$

C Complete the charts.

1.

$\times$	4	40	400	6	60	600	9	90	900
3	12	120	1,200	18	180	1,800	27	270	2,700

2.

$\times$	1	4	7	10	40	70	100	400	700
5	5	20	35	50	200	350	500	2,000	3,500

3.

$\times$	700	70	7	800	80	8	500	50	5
6	4,200	420	42	4,800	480	48	3,000	300	30

4.

$\times$	300	500	900	30	50	90	3	5	9
9	2,700	4,500	8,100	270	450	810	27	45	81

FINDING NEW PRODUCTS

 Write the expanded name.

1. 37 = 30 + __7__   **2.** 235 = 200 + __30__ + __5__   **3.** 82 = __80__ + __2__

4. 53 = __50__ + __3__   **5.** 167 = __100__ + __60__ + __7__

Treat exercise B orally. Have students study the pictures. Then explain each sentence used to help find the products.

 Study each picture.

1. Find the number of eggs using these steps.

$$3 \times 12 = 3 \times (10 + 2)$$
$$= (3 \times 10) + (3 \times 2)$$
$$= 30 + 6 = \underline{36}$$

__36__ eggs

2. Find the number of crayons using these steps.

$$2 \times 24 = 2 \times (20 + 4)$$
$$= (2 \times \underline{20}) + (2 \times \underline{4})$$
$$= 40 + 8 = \underline{48}$$

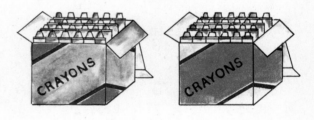

__48__ crayons

Have students complete exercise C independently.

 Study the example below. Find the products.

1.
$$5 \times 67 = 5 \times (60 + 7)$$
$$= (5 \times 60) + (5 \times 7)$$
$$= 300 + 35$$
$$= 335$$

2.
$$7 \times 83 = 7 \times (\underline{80} + \underline{3})$$
$$= (7 \times \underline{80}) + (7 \times \underline{3})$$
$$= \underline{560} + \underline{21}$$
$$= \underline{581}$$

3.
$$9 \times 42 = \underline{9} \times (40 + 2)$$
$$= (\underline{9} \times \underline{40}) + (\underline{9} \times \underline{2})$$
$$= \underline{360} + \underline{18}$$
$$= \underline{378}$$

MULTIPLYING A 2-DIGIT NUMBER BY A 1-DIGIT NUMBER

How To Multiply Using the Long Form

Step 1	Step 2	Step 3
Multiply the ones.	Multiply the tens.	Add.

Step 1
Multiply the ones.

```
  56
×  7
─────
  42   (7 × 6)
```

Step 2
Multiply the tens.

```
  56
×  7
─────
  42
 350   (7 × 50)
```

Step 3
Add.

```
  56
×  7
─────
  42
+350
─────
 392
```

 A Copy the exercise. Fill each ▓ to find the products.

```
   35
 ×  4
 ─────
   20    (4 × 5)
 + 120   (4 × 30)
 ─────
   140
```

```
   62
 ×  9
 ─────
   18    (9 × 2)
 + 540   (9 × 60)
 ─────
   558
```

```
   51
 ×  3
 ─────
    3    (3 × 1)
 + 150   (3 × 50)
 ─────
   153
```

 B Name the missing factors for each step.

```
   65
 ×  7
 ─────
   35    (7 ×  5 )
 + 420   (7 × 60 )
 ─────
   455
```

```
   29
 ×  5
 ─────
   45    ( 5  × 9)
 + 100   ( 5  × 20)
 ─────
   145
```

```
   97
 ×  4
 ─────
   28    ( 4  ×  7 )
 + 360   ( 4  × 90 )
 ─────
   388
```

 C Find the products using the long form.

```
   56      80      73      24      68      91
 ×  6    ×  5    ×  9    ×  7    ×  4    ×  4
 ─────   ─────   ─────   ─────   ─────   ─────
  336     400     657     168     272     364
```

Student answers to exercise C should show partial products.

MULTIPLYING USING THE SHORT FORM—NO RENAMING

How To Multiply Using the Short Form—No Renaming

Step 1 Multiply the ones.	Step 2 Multiply the tens.
82 × 3 ――― 6	82 × 3 ――― 246

Work through the first two items in exercise A with students. Then have them complete the page.

 A Complete these multiplications.

32	13	64	51	73	71
× 4	× 3	× 2	× 5	× 2	× 8
128	39	128	255	146	568

B Multiply using the short form.

1.
23	62	21	13	11	74
× 3	× 4	× 5	× 2	× 7	× 2
69	248	105	26	77	148

2.
61	53	22	84	31	43
× 9	× 3	× 4	× 2	× 6	× 2
549	159	88	168	186	86

3.
70	51	33	82	74	41
× 6	× 8	× 3	× 4	× 2	× 7
420	408	99	328	148	287

C Solve each of these word problems.

1. Miyo bought 2 sacks of apples. There were 13 apples in each sack. How many apples did she buy? __26__ apples

2. Luke bought 4 boxes of 12 pencils each. How many pencils did he buy? __48__ pencils

RENAMING ONES AS TENS

 Complete each sentence.

1. $3 \times 8 =$ ___24___ $24 =$ ___2___ tens, ___4___ ones

2. $5 \times 9 =$ ___45___ $45 =$ ___4___ tens, ___5___ ones

3. $6 \times 3 =$ ___18___ $18 =$ ___1___ ten, ___8___ ones

4. $7 \times 9 =$ ___63___ $63 =$ ___6___ tens, ___3___ ones

How To Multiply Using the Short Form—Renaming Ones as Tens

$$\begin{array}{r} \overset{2}{4}6 \\ \times\ 4 \\ \hline 4 \end{array}$$

First: Multiply the ones. $4 \times 6 = 24$.
    Rename 24 as 2 tens, 4 ones.
    Write 4 in the ones' column.
    Write 2 in the tens' column above the 4.

$$\begin{array}{r} \overset{2}{4}6 \\ \times\ 4 \\ \hline 184 \end{array}$$

Second: Multiply the tens. 4×4 tens $= 16$ tens.
    Add tens. 16 tens $+$ 2 tens $= 18$ tens.
    Write 18 tens.

 Copy the exercise. Complete the multiplications.

1.
$$\begin{array}{r} \overset{1}{3}8 \\ \times\ 2 \\ \hline 76 \end{array} \qquad \begin{array}{r} \overset{2}{2}7 \\ \times\ 3 \\ \hline 81 \end{array} \qquad \begin{array}{r} \overset{2}{4}5 \\ \times\ 4 \\ \hline 180 \end{array} \qquad \begin{array}{r} \overset{1}{2}6 \\ \times\ 3 \\ \hline 78 \end{array} \qquad \begin{array}{r} \overset{1}{5}6 \\ \times\ 2 \\ \hline 112 \end{array} \qquad \begin{array}{r} \overset{3}{3}8 \\ \times\ 4 \\ \hline 152 \end{array}$$

2.
$$\begin{array}{r} \overset{1}{6}3 \\ \times\ 5 \\ \hline 315 \end{array} \qquad \begin{array}{r} \overset{5}{4}9 \\ \times\ 6 \\ \hline 294 \end{array} \qquad \begin{array}{r} \overset{4}{2}5 \\ \times\ 9 \\ \hline 225 \end{array} \qquad \begin{array}{r} \overset{2}{7}8 \\ \times\ 3 \\ \hline 234 \end{array} \qquad \begin{array}{r} \overset{1}{6}2 \\ \times\ 8 \\ \hline 496 \end{array} \qquad \begin{array}{r} \overset{2}{5}4 \\ \times\ 7 \\ \hline 378 \end{array}$$

3.
$$\begin{array}{r} \overset{2}{3}5 \\ \times\ 4 \\ \hline 140 \end{array} \qquad \begin{array}{r} \overset{3}{6}5 \\ \times\ 7 \\ \hline 455 \end{array} \qquad \begin{array}{r} \overset{1}{8}2 \\ \times\ 8 \\ \hline 656 \end{array} \qquad \begin{array}{r} \overset{4}{3}7 \\ \times\ 6 \\ \hline 222 \end{array} \qquad \begin{array}{r} \overset{2}{5}3 \\ \times\ 9 \\ \hline 477 \end{array} \qquad \begin{array}{r} \overset{1}{7}4 \\ \times\ 3 \\ \hline 222 \end{array}$$

C Multiply using the short form.

1.	56 × 3 ── 168	27 × 4 ── 108	91 × 7 ── 637	63 × 4 ── 252	58 × 6 ── 348	74 × 8 ── 592
2.	38 × 4 ── 152	75 × 8 ── 600	69 × 9 ── 621	54 × 8 ── 432	46 × 7 ── 322	26 × 5 ── 130
3.	47 × 2 ── 94	84 × 4 ── 336	95 × 5 ── 475	78 × 6 ── 468	96 × 9 ── 864	65 × 8 ── 520

D Find the products. Look for a pattern.

1.
40	47	50
× 3	× 3	× 3
120	141	150

2.
20	24	30
× 7	× 7	× 7
140	168	210

3.
80	85	90
× 6	× 6	× 6
480	510	540

4.
60	63	70
× 9	× 9	× 9
540	567	630

5.
30	39	40
× 4	× 4	× 4
120	156	160

6.
70	72	80
× 5	× 5	× 5
350	360	400

7.
50	57	60
× 8	× 8	× 8
400	456	480

8.
10	19	20
× 7	× 7	× 7
70	133	140

E Write < or > in each ●. Remember: < means **is less than** and > means **is greater than.**

1. 5×34 **<** 5×40 7×60 **<** 7×68 4×52 **>** 4×50

2. 6×80 **<** 6×85 3×28 **>** 3×20 2×30 **>** 2×28

3. 9×50 **>** 9×45 4×70 **<** 4×73 8×60 **<** 8×65

ADDITION AND SUBTRACTION REVIEW

 Complete each number pattern.

1. 35 40 45 <u>50</u>   **2.** 30 28 26 <u>24</u>

3. 27 24 21 <u>18</u>   **4.** 170 180 190 <u>200</u>

5. 187 188 189 <u>190</u>   **6.** 700 600 500 <u>400</u>

7. 16 20 24 <u>28</u>   **8.** 81 72 63 <u>54</u>

 Find the sums by adding up the column.   Check by adding down.

26	27	65	18	20
39	37	48	300	300
+ 84	+ 47	+ 52	+ 1,200	+ 2,500
149	111	165	1,518	2,820

 Find the differences.   Check by adding.

84	168	151	846	352
− 29	− 94	− 63	− 166	− 284
	74	88	680	68
+ 55				
84				

Student answers to exercise C should be in the form shown in item 1.

 Do each exercise.   Be careful—sometimes you must add and sometimes you must subtract.

1.
328	153	54	179	73
− 9	+ 671	+ 83	− 84	+ 168
319	824	137	95	241

2.
459	432	314	421	146
− 168	+ 168	− 81	+ 193	− 98
291	600	233	614	48

3.
46	243	231	486	169
+ 87	− 184	+ 95	− 132	+ 74
133	59	326	354	243

FOLLOWING DIRECTIONS

1. Find the sum of 72 and 19. Multiply the sum by 4. The answer is

___364___.

2. Multiply 6 times 23. Add 286 to the product. The answer is

___424___.

3. Multiply 7 times 8. Multiply the product by 3. The answer is

___168___.

4. Subtract 352 from 407. Multiply the difference by 9. The answer is

___495___.

5. Multiply 9 times 84. Subtract the product from 963. The answer is

___207___.

6. Multiply 6 times 9. Multiply the product by 8. The answer is

___432___.

7. Subtract 643 from 729. Add the difference to 468. The answer is

___554___.

8. Find the sum of 16, 23, and 45. Multiply the sum by 3. The

answer is ___252___.

9. Find the product of 6 times 94. Subtract 428 from the product.

The answer is ___136___.

Students who have difficulty with these problems should work them in a manner similar to that suggested in the activity.

EXTENDING MULTIPLICATION

The students in Mrs. Blake's class were asked to multiply 3 × 123.

Tom's Method
$$\begin{array}{r} 123 \\ 123 \\ + 123 \\ \hline 369 \end{array}$$

Erica's Method
$$\begin{array}{r} 100 + 20 + 3 \\ \times\ 3 \\ \hline 300 + 60 + 9 = 369 \end{array}$$

Tom used repeated addition to find the sum. Erica wrote the expanded name and multiplied.

A Use Erica's method to find the product. Check your work using Tom's method.

1.
$$\begin{array}{r} 412 \\ \times 4 \end{array}$$

$$\begin{array}{r} 400\ +\ 10\ +\ 2 \\ \times\ 4 \\ \hline 1{,}600\ +\ 40\ +\ 8\ =\ 1{,}648 \end{array}$$

$$\begin{array}{r} 412 \\ 412 \\ 412 \\ + 412 \\ \hline 1{,}648 \end{array}$$

2.
$$\begin{array}{r} 232 \\ \times 3 \end{array}$$

$$\begin{array}{r} 200\ +\ 30\ +\ 2 \\ \times\ 3 \\ \hline 600\ +\ 90\ +\ 6\ =\ 696 \end{array}$$

$$\begin{array}{r} 232 \\ 232 \\ + 232 \\ \hline 696 \end{array}$$

3.
$$\begin{array}{r} 543 \\ \times 2 \end{array}$$

$$\begin{array}{r} 500\ +\ 40\ +\ 3 \\ \times\ 2 \\ \hline 1{,}000\ +\ 80\ +\ 6\ =\ 1{,}086 \end{array}$$

$$\begin{array}{r} 543 \\ + 543 \\ \hline 1{,}086 \end{array}$$

4.
$$\begin{array}{r} 311 \\ \times 5 \end{array}$$

$$\begin{array}{r} 300\ +\ 10\ +\ 1 \\ \times\ 5 \\ \hline 1{,}500\ +\ 50\ +\ 5\ =\ 1{,}555 \end{array}$$

$$\begin{array}{r} 311 \\ 311 \\ 311 \\ 311 \\ + 311 \\ \hline 1{,}555 \end{array}$$

Candy said she could find the product using an easier method.

Candy's Method

```
  123
  × 3
    9    (3 × 3)
   60    (3 × 20)
+ 300    (3 × 100)
  369
```

Study Candy's method. She multiplied the ones first, the tens second, and the hundreds third. To find the product, she added the partial products.

Have students complete the exercises on this page. These exercises are developmental. If a student has difficulty in exercise B, resolve the difficulty before the student goes on.

B Copy the exercise. Fill each ▉ to find the products.

```
    324                      562                      653
   × 3                      × 7                      × 5
    12    (3 × 4)            14    (7 × 2)            15    (5 × 3)
    60    (3 × 20)          420    (7 × 60)          250    (5 × 50)
+  900    (3 × 300)    +  3500    (7 × 500)    +  3000    (5 × 600)
   972                    3,934                    3,265
```

C Name the missing factors for each step.

```
    175                      835                      258
   × 8                      × 6                      × 9
     40    (8 × _5_ )         30    ( _6_ × 5)          72    ( _9_ × _8_ )
    560    (8 × _70_ )       180    ( _6_ × 30)        450    ( _9_ × _50_ )
+   800    (8 × _100_ )  +  4800    ( _6_ × 800)  +  1800    ( _9_ × _200_ )
  1,400                    5,010                    2,322
```

D Find the products using Candy's method.

```
    352          215          479          638
   × 3          × 8          × 2          × 5
  1,056        1,720          958        3,190
```

Student answers to exercise D should show partial products.

MULTIPLYING USING THE SHORT FORM

How To Multiply Using the Short Form—No Renaming

Step 1 Multiply the ones.	Step 2 Multiply the tens.	Step 3 Multiply the hundreds.
324 × 2 —— 8	324 × 2 —— 48	324 × 2 —— 648

 Complete each multiplication.

Multiply the ones. Multiply the tens. Multiply the hundreds.

1.
431
× 3
——
3

3 × 1 = 3

431
× 3
——
93

3 × 3 tens = 9 tens

431
× 3
——
1,293

3 × 4 hundreds = 12 hundreds

2.
543
× 2
——
6

2 × 3 = 6

543
× 2
——
86

2 × 4 tens = 8 tens

543
× 2
——
1,086

2 × 5 hundreds = 10 hundreds

B Complete these multiplications.

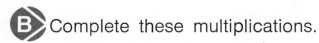

523 × 2 —— 1,046	432 × 3 —— 1,296	722 × 4 —— 2,888	614 × 2 —— 1,228	332 × 3 —— 996

C Multiply using the short form.

1.

311 × 6 —— 1,866	724 × 2 —— 1,448	620 × 4 —— 2,480	501 × 5 —— 2,505	912 × 3 —— 2,736

2.

834 × 2 —— 1,668	603 × 3 —— 1,809	510 × 8 —— 4,080	711 × 6 —— 4,266	432 × 3 —— 1,296

RENAMING TENS AS HUNDREDS

 Complete each sentence.

1. 4×6 tens = __24__ tens   24 tens = __2__ hundreds, __4__ tens

2. 5×9 tens = __45__ tens   45 tens = __4__ hundreds, __5__ tens

3. 7×3 tens = __21__ tens   21 tens = __2__ hundreds, __1__ ten

4. 5×8 tens = __40__ tens   40 tens = __4__ hundreds, __0__ tens

Treat exercise B orally.

 Complete this multiplication.

Multiply the ones.

$$
\begin{array}{r}
251 \\
\times\ 3 \\
\hline
3
\end{array}
$$

$3 \times 1 = $ **3**

Multiply the tens.

$$
\begin{array}{r}
{}^{1} \\
251 \\
\times\ 3 \\
\hline
53
\end{array}
$$

3×5 tens = **15** tens
tens = **1** hundred, **5** tens

Multiply the hundreds.

$$
\begin{array}{r}
{}^{1} \\
251 \\
\times\ 3 \\
\hline
753
\end{array}
$$

3×2 hundreds + 1 hundred = **7** hundreds

Have students complete exercise C independently.

 Complete these multiplications.

1.

¹	⁴	²	⁵	³
394	571	683	470	192
× 2	× 6	× 3	× 8	× 4
788	3,426	2,049	3,760	768

2.

³	²	¹	¹	²
251	630	162	531	373
× 7	× 9	× 3	× 5	× 3
1,757	5,670	486	2,655	1,119

Students having difficulty with any portion of this lesson should have repeated experiences with activity 2.

RENAMING ONES AS TENS AND TENS AS HUNDREDS

How To Multiply 6 × 257 Using the Short Form

⁴
257
× 6
———
2

First: Multiply the ones. 6 × 7 = 42.
   Rename 42 as 4 tens, 2 ones.
   Write 2 in the ones' column.
   Write 4 in the tens' column above the 5.

^{3 4}
257
× 6
———
42

Second: Multiply the tens.
   6 × (5 tens) + 4 tens = 30 tens + 4 tens = 34 tens.
   Rename 34 tens as 3 hundreds, 4 tens.
   Write 4 in the tens' column.
   Write 3 in the hundreds' column above the 2.

³
257
× 6
———
1,542

Third: Multiply the hundreds.
   6 × (2 hundreds) + 3 hundreds =
   12   hundreds + 3 hundreds = 15 hundreds.
   Write 15 hundreds.

Treat exercise A orally. Have students supply answers and reasons for answers.

A Complete each multiplication.

Multiply the ones.	Multiply the tens.	Multiply the hundreds.

1.

$\overset{1}{473}$ × 5 = 5

$\overset{3\ 1}{473}$ × 5 = 65

$\overset{3\ 1}{473}$ × 5 = 2,365

2.

$\overset{4}{586}$ × 7 = 2

$\overset{6\ 4}{586}$ × 7 = 02

$\overset{6\ 4}{586}$ × 7 = 4,102

3.

$\overset{3}{759}$ × 4 = 6

$\overset{2\ 3}{759}$ × 4 = 36

$\overset{2\ 3}{759}$ × 4 = 3,036

4.

$\overset{4}{286}$ × 8 = 8

$\overset{6\ 4}{286}$ × 8 = 88

$\overset{6\ 4}{286}$ × 8 = 2,288

Discuss the example. Ask students to explain what was done in each step. Emphasize the renaming process. Remind students that renaming in this way requires writing a result in the product *and* above a number in the multiplicand.

Complete each multiplication.

1.

$$\begin{array}{r} \overset{2\,3}{359} \\ \times\ 4 \\ \hline 1,436 \end{array}$$

$$\begin{array}{r} \overset{6\,3}{584} \\ \times\ 8 \\ \hline 4,672 \end{array}$$

$$\begin{array}{r} \overset{2\,1}{275} \\ \times\ 3 \\ \hline 825 \end{array}$$

$$\begin{array}{r} \overset{1\,4}{638} \\ \times\ 5 \\ \hline 3,190 \end{array}$$

$$\begin{array}{r} \overset{1\,3}{426} \\ \times\ 6 \\ \hline 2,556 \end{array}$$

2.

$$\begin{array}{r} \overset{2\,2}{187} \\ \times\ 3 \\ \hline 561 \end{array}$$

$$\begin{array}{r} \overset{2\,1}{432} \\ \times\ 9 \\ \hline 3,888 \end{array}$$

$$\begin{array}{r} \overset{3\,4}{657} \\ \times\ 7 \\ \hline 4,599 \end{array}$$

$$\begin{array}{r} \overset{2\,4}{526} \\ \times\ 8 \\ \hline 4,208 \end{array}$$

$$\begin{array}{r} \overset{1\,3}{248} \\ \times\ 4 \\ \hline 992 \end{array}$$

C Multiply using the short form.

1.

$$\begin{array}{r} 328 \\ \times\ 3 \\ \hline 984 \end{array}$$

$$\begin{array}{r} 695 \\ \times\ 2 \\ \hline 1,390 \end{array}$$

$$\begin{array}{r} 842 \\ \times\ 4 \\ \hline 3,368 \end{array}$$

$$\begin{array}{r} 916 \\ \times\ 9 \\ \hline 8,244 \end{array}$$

$$\begin{array}{r} 258 \\ \times\ 8 \\ \hline 2,064 \end{array}$$

2.

$$\begin{array}{r} 689 \\ \times\ 7 \\ \hline 4,823 \end{array}$$

$$\begin{array}{r} 694 \\ \times\ 6 \\ \hline 4,164 \end{array}$$

$$\begin{array}{r} 751 \\ \times\ 9 \\ \hline 6,759 \end{array}$$

$$\begin{array}{r} 275 \\ \times\ 3 \\ \hline 825 \end{array}$$

$$\begin{array}{r} 517 \\ \times\ 5 \\ \hline 2,585 \end{array}$$

3.

$$\begin{array}{r} 546 \\ \times\ 4 \\ \hline 2,184 \end{array}$$

$$\begin{array}{r} 898 \\ \times\ 2 \\ \hline 1,796 \end{array}$$

$$\begin{array}{r} 437 \\ \times\ 6 \\ \hline 2,622 \end{array}$$

$$\begin{array}{r} 208 \\ \times\ 7 \\ \hline 1,456 \end{array}$$

$$\begin{array}{r} 673 \\ \times\ 8 \\ \hline 5,384 \end{array}$$

D Find the products. Look for a pattern.

1.

$$\begin{array}{r} 140 \\ \times\ 3 \\ \hline 420 \end{array} \quad \begin{array}{r} 148 \\ \times\ 3 \\ \hline 444 \end{array} \quad \begin{array}{r} 150 \\ \times\ 3 \\ \hline 450 \end{array}$$

2.

$$\begin{array}{r} 280 \\ \times\ 4 \\ \hline 1,120 \end{array} \quad \begin{array}{r} 283 \\ \times\ 4 \\ \hline 1,132 \end{array} \quad \begin{array}{r} 290 \\ \times\ 4 \\ \hline 1,160 \end{array}$$

3.

$$\begin{array}{r} 690 \\ \times\ 2 \\ \hline 1,380 \end{array} \quad \begin{array}{r} 698 \\ \times\ 2 \\ \hline 1,396 \end{array} \quad \begin{array}{r} 700 \\ \times\ 2 \\ \hline 1,400 \end{array}$$

4.

$$\begin{array}{r} 360 \\ \times\ 6 \\ \hline 2,160 \end{array} \quad \begin{array}{r} 364 \\ \times\ 6 \\ \hline 2,184 \end{array} \quad \begin{array}{r} 370 \\ \times\ 6 \\ \hline 2,220 \end{array}$$

E Write < or > in each ● to make the sentence true.

1. $5 \times 430 \ < \ 5 \times 432$ $9 \times 167 \ > \ 9 \times 160$ $2 \times 187 \ < \ 2 \times 190$

2. $7 \times 390 \ > \ 7 \times 385$ $4 \times 460 \ < \ 4 \times 468$ $6 \times 632 \ > \ 6 \times 630$

PROBLEM SOLVING

1. There are 100 centimeters in a meter. How many centimeters are in 4 meters? ___400___ centimeters

2. There are 25 pennies in a quarter. How many pennies are in 7 quarters? ___175___ pennies

3. There are 16 ounces in a pound. How many ounces are in 9 pounds? ___144___ ounces

4. There are 4 cups in a quart. How many cups are in 40 quarts? ___160___ cups

5. There are 50 pennies in a half-dollar. How many pennies are in 8 half-dollars? ___400___ pennies

6. There are 7 days in a week. How many days are in 52 weeks? ___364___ days

7. There are 24 hours in a day. How many hours are in a week? ___168___ hours

8. There are 168 hours in one week. How many hours would be in 5 weeks? ___840___ hours

9. There are 60 minutes in an hour. How many minutes are in 6 hours? ___360___ minutes

10. There are 365 days in a year. How many days are in 3 years? ___1,095___ days

REVIEWING DIVISION FACTS

 A Use the number line to help you find the quotients.

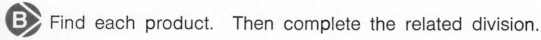

1. 14 ÷ 2 = 7	18 ÷ 6 = 3	24 ÷ 4 = 6
2. 45 ÷ 5 = 9	21 ÷ 3 = 7	27 ÷ 9 = 3
3. 42 ÷ 6 = 7	18 ÷ 2 = 9	48 ÷ 8 = 6
4. 15 ÷ 5 = 3	54 ÷ 9 = 6	32 ÷ 4 = 8

B Find each product. Then complete the related division.

1. 4
 × 9   9) 36
 ——   4
 36

2. 7
 × 8   7) 56
 ——   8
 56

3. 6
 × 5   5) 30
 ——   6
 30

4. 5
 × 7   7) 35
 ——   5
 35

5. 8
 × 6   8) 48
 ——   6
 48

6. 9
 × 9   9) 81
 ——   9
 81

C Complete these division charts.

1.

5) 20	35	10	40	5	25	45	30
4	7	2	8	1	5	9	6

2.

8) 16	40	64	32	72	48	8	24
2	5	8	4	9	6	1	3

3.

3) 21	3	15	27	9	18	24	12
7	1	5	9	3	6	8	4

4.

7) 7	35	49	14	42	63	28	56
1	5	7	2	6	9	4	8

MULTIPLICATION PRACTICE

 A Find the products.

1.

9	7	6	7	8	5
× 8	× 7	× 9	× 5	× 4	× 9
72	49	54	35	32	45

2.

6	7	9	8	6	7
× 6	× 3	× 7	× 8	× 7	× 8
36	21	63	64	42	56

B Find the products.

1.

70	30	50	80	20	40
× 4	× 6	× 5	× 9	× 7	× 8
280	180	250	720	140	320

2.

21	43	52	63	94	81
× 6	× 3	× 4	× 2	× 2	× 7
126	129	208	126	188	567

3.

59	64	34	48	96	68
× 3	× 5	× 7	× 9	× 6	× 8
177	320	238	432	576	544

C Multiply.

1.

400	800	700	900	600
× 6	× 5	× 7	× 6	× 8
2,400	4,000	4,900	5,400	4,800

2.

523	724	119	620	425
× 3	× 2	× 4	× 4	× 2
1,569	1,448	476	2,480	850

3.

496	755	791	398	967
× 4	× 5	× 7	× 8	× 6
1,984	3,775	5,537	3,184	5,802

NUMBER PUZZLES

A Operate these number machines.

1.

×8		
Push Button To Operate		
1	=	8
5	=	40
3	=	24
6	=	48
8	=	64
4	=	32

2.

−3		
Push Button To Operate		
6	=	3
10	=	7
4	=	1
17	=	14
9	=	6
12	=	9

3.

÷2		
Push Button To Operate		
4	=	2
10	=	5
16	=	8
6	=	3
2	=	1
18	=	9

B Find out how each machine works. Then operate the machines.

1.

+6		
Push Button To Operate		
5	=	11
9	=	15
11	=	17
4	=	10
7	=	13
14	=	20

2.

÷3		
Push Button To Operate		
18	=	6
30	=	10
12	=	4
27	=	9
21	=	7
15	=	5

3.

×5		
Push Button To Operate		
4	=	20
9	=	45
3	=	15
8	=	40
11	=	55
20	=	100

C Complete each pattern.

1. 17, 26, 35, 44, __53__, __62__, __71__

2. 1, 2, 4, 7, 11, __16__, __22__, __29__

3. 72, 65, 58, 51, __44__, __37__, __30__

4. 27, 26, 24, 21, __17__, __12__, __6__

5. 1, 2, 4, 8, __16__, __32__, __64__

6. 1, 9, 2, 10, __3__, __11__, __4__

7. 1, 3, 7, 15, 31, __63__, __127__

CHAPTER REVIEW

 Find the products.

1.
```
   9        90       900
  × 3      × 3      × 3
  ───      ───     ─────
  27       270     2,700
```

2.
```
   6        60       600
  × 5      × 5      × 5
  ───      ───     ─────
  30       300     3,000
```

3.
```
   7        70       700
  × 8      × 8      × 8
  ───      ───     ─────
  56       560     5,600
```

4.
```
   4        40       400
  × 7      × 7      × 7
  ───      ───     ─────
  28       280     2,800
```

B Complete each sentence to find the product.

1. 5 × 37 = 5 × (30 + 7)

= (5 × _30_) + (5 × _7_)

= _150_ + _35_

= _185_

2. 9 × 28 = 9 × (20 + _8_)

= (9 × _20_) + (9 × _8_)

= _180_ + _72_

= _252_

C Use the short form to find the products.

1.
```
   4
  27       65       34       79       53       86
  × 6      × 9      × 3      × 2      × 8      × 7
  ───      ───      ───      ───      ───      ───
  162      585      102      158      424      602
```

2.
```
  142      321      418      670      534
  × 2      × 4      × 5      × 7      × 8
  ───    ─────    ─────    ─────    ─────
  284    1,284    2,090    4,690    4,272
```

D Solve these problems.

1. Gus bought 6 packages of baseball cards. In each package there were 32 cards. How many cards did Gus get? __192__ cards

2. Find the sum of 27 and 36. Multiply this sum by 4. The answer is __252__.

CHECK-UP

 Find the products.

10	9	100	300	70	600
× 7	× 9	× 8	× 2	× 4	× 6
70	81	800	600	280	3,600

B Complete these multiplications.

1.

³ 45	⁵ 38	63	³ 27	³ 78
× 6	× 7	× 9	× 5	× 4
270	266	567	135	312

2.

¹ 384	¹² 137	³⁴ 469	³⁴ 256	²⁵ 527
× 2	× 3	× 5	× 7	× 8
768	411	2,345	1,792	4,216

C Multiply using the short form.

1.

51	37	49	62	86
× 8	× 3	× 7	× 9	× 4
408	111	343	558	344

2.

170	218	346	183	475
× 5	× 4	× 6	× 9	× 7
850	872	2,076	1,647	3,325

D Solve these problems.

1. Find the product of 6 and 8. Multiply this product by 4. The answer is __192__.

2. Mr. Pérez bought 6 cases of eggs from the OK Farm. Each case contained 288 eggs. How many eggs did he buy? __1,728__ eggs

10 • DIVISION

REVIEWING DIVISION

Three Methods for Finding the Quotient for 18 ÷ 6

Joan's Method	Tim's Method	Bob's Method
Form rows of 6.	$$\begin{array}{r} 18 \\ -6 \\ \hline 12 \\ -6 \\ \hline 6 \\ -6 \\ \hline 0 \end{array}$$ Subtract by 6. 6 can be subtracted 3 times.	Skip count by 6.

There are 3 rows of 6.

18 ÷ 6 = 3

18 ÷ 6 = 3

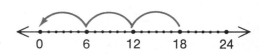

There are 3 jumps of 6.

18 ÷ 6 = 3

A Divide using Joan's method. Place the dots in the boxes.

12 ÷ 4 = _____3_____

18 ÷ 9 = _____2_____

24 ÷ 4 = _____6_____

B Divide using Tim's method.

$$\begin{array}{r} 4 \\ 7\overline{)28} \\ -7 \\ \hline 21 \\ -7 \\ \hline 14 \\ -7 \\ \hline 7 \\ -7 \\ \hline 0 \end{array} \qquad \begin{array}{r} 5 \\ 8\overline{)40} \\ -8 \\ \hline 32 \\ -8 \\ \hline 24 \\ -8 \\ \hline 16 \\ -8 \\ \hline 8 \\ -8 \\ \hline 0 \end{array} \qquad \begin{array}{r} 3 \\ 9\overline{)27} \\ -9 \\ \hline 18 \\ -9 \\ \hline 9 \\ -9 \\ \hline 0 \end{array}$$

C Divide using Bob's method.

16 ÷ 4 = _____4_____

25 ÷ 5 = _____5_____

20 ÷ 4 = _____5_____

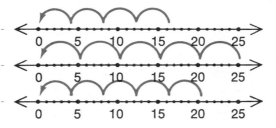

DIVISION FACTS

 Find each product. Then complete the related division.

1.
   7
 × 8
 ───
  56
     8) 56 (7)

2.
   5
 × 5
 ───
  25
     5) 25 (5)

3.
   9
 × 6
 ───
  54
     6) 54 (9)

4.
   4
 × 8
 ───
  32
     4) 32 (8)

5.
   8
 × 9
 ───
  72
     9) 72 (8)

6.
   7
 × 7
 ───
  49
     7) 49 (7)

B Complete the division charts.

1. 7) 42

	6	2	5	3	9	1	8	7	4
7)	42	14	35	21	63	7	56	49	28

2. 9) 36

	4	9	6	7	2	5	8	3	1
9)	36	81	54	63	18	45	72	27	9

3. 6) 48

	8	5	7	9	3	6	1	4	2
6)	48	30	42	54	18	36	6	24	12

4. 4) 12

	3	8	4	1	6	9	2	5	7
4)	12	32	16	4	24	36	8	20	28

5. 8) 32

	4	1	7	5	9	2	6	8	3
8)	32	8	56	40	72	16	48	64	24

6. 3) 3

	1	3	7	2	6	9	4	8	5
3)	3	9	21	6	18	27	12	24	15

7. 5) 25

	5	3	8	4	1	6	9	2	7
5)	25	15	40	20	5	30	45	10	35

8. 2) 12

	6	9	2	5	1	4	8	3	7
2)	12	18	4	10	2	8	16	6	14

The divisions in exercise B can be reused by having students place a clean sheet of paper over the quotients and rework the divisions.

Discuss the example. Treat exercise A orally. Use repeated subtraction to complete the division 7⟌84. Do similar divisions having students guess the largest multiple of the divisor that can be subtracted from the dividend.

DIVISION USING SUBTRACTIONS

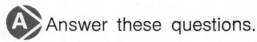

Rex	Pat	Carol
10	10	10
6)60	6)60	6)60
−30 5 sixes	−18 3 sixes	−60 10 sixes
30	42	0
−30 +5 sixes	−24 4 sixes	
0 10 sixes	18	
	−18 +3 sixes	
	0 10 sixes	

 A Answer these questions.

1. Did all three students get the correct quotient? __yes__

2. Whose method was shortest? __Carol's__

3. How many sixes did Rex subtract each time? __5__

4. If you subtract some sixes and the difference is still larger than 6,
   what do you do? __subtract more sixes__

Have students complete exercise B independently.

B Divide by subtracting.

      9   10   15   11

1. 7)63   9)90   2)30   8)88

      12   13   10   34

2. 6)72   4)52   3)30   2)68

Student answers to exercise B should be in one of the forms shown at the top of the page.

209

DIVISION WITH REMAINDERS

A Answer the questions for each picture.

1.

How many ✳s? __11__

How many rows of 4? __2__
For 11 ÷ 4, the **quotient** is

__2__; the **remainder** is __3__.

2.

How many ✪s? __13__

How many rows of 3? __4__
For 13 ÷ 3, the quotient is

__4__; the remainder is __1__.

3.
How many dots? __34__

How many rows of 7? __4__
For 34 ÷ 7, the quotient is

__4__; the remainder is __6__.

4.
How many dots? __31__

How many rows of 9? __3__
For 31 ÷ 9, the quotient is

__3__; the remainder is __4__.

Tell students they can draw dot pictures for each situation in exercise B if they need to.

B Complete the table. Imagine the rows of dots.

	Number of Dots	Dots per Row	Division	Quotient	Remainder
1.	17	5	17 ÷ 5	3	2
2.	10	3	10 ÷ 3	3	1
3.	19	6	19 ÷ 6	3	1
4.	20	3	20 ÷ 3	6	2

C Use the number line to find the quotient and the remainder.

1. $5\overline{)19}$ = 3 r 4

2. $7\overline{)30}$ = 4 r 2

3. $2\overline{)15}$ = 7 r 1

4. $4\overline{)27}$ = 6 r 3

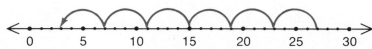

Go over the example in exercise D and have students fill the blanks. Have students complete similar exercises as board work. Then have them complete the page.

D Study the example and answer the questions.

$$\begin{array}{r} 5 \text{ r } 3 \\ 7\overline{)38} \\ -35 \qquad 5 \times 7 \\ \hline 3 \end{array}$$

1. How many sevens can be subtracted from 38?

_____5_____

2. $38 - 35 =$ ___3___

3. Is 3 less than 7? __yes__

5 is the **quotient**. 3 is the **remainder**.
7 is the **divisor**.
The remainder must be less than the divisor.

E Complete these divisions.

1.
$$\begin{array}{r} 3 \text{ r } 1 \\ 8\overline{)25} \\ -24 \qquad 3 \times 8 \\ \hline 1 \end{array}$$

$$\begin{array}{r} 6 \text{ r } 2 \\ 5\overline{)32} \\ -30 \qquad 6 \times 5 \\ \hline 2 \end{array}$$

$$\begin{array}{r} 3 \text{ r } 3 \\ 4\overline{)15} \\ -12 \qquad 3 \times 4 \\ \hline 3 \end{array}$$

2.
$$\begin{array}{r} 5 \text{ r } 1 \\ 2\overline{)11} \\ -10 \qquad 5 \times 2 \\ \hline 1 \end{array}$$

$$\begin{array}{r} 2 \text{ r } 1 \\ 3\overline{)7} \\ -6 \qquad 2 \times 3 \\ \hline 1 \end{array}$$

$$\begin{array}{r} 3 \text{ r } 2 \\ 6\overline{)20} \\ -18 \qquad 3 \times 6 \\ \hline 2 \end{array}$$

FINDING TRIAL QUOTIENTS

To complete the division $7\overline{)46}$, we guess how many 7s can be subtracted from 46. This guess is called the trial quotient.

How To Tell the Correct Quotient

Trial Quotient Too Small	Trial Quotient Correct	Trial Quotient Too Large
$$\begin{array}{r} 5 \\ 7\overline{)46} \\ -35 \\ \hline 11 \end{array}$$ (5 × 7)	$$\begin{array}{r} 6 \\ 7\overline{)46} \\ -42 \\ \hline 4 \end{array}$$ (6 × 7)	$$\begin{array}{r} 7 \\ 7\overline{)46} \\ -49 \end{array}$$ (7 × 7)
Remainder larger than or equal to the divisor.	Remainder smaller than the divisor.	Product to be subtracted is too large.

A In each division the trial quotient is either too large or too small. Write the correct quotient in the ■.

1.
$$\begin{array}{r} \boxed{3} \\ 4 \\ 8\overline{)30} \\ -32 \end{array}$$ (4 × 8)
$$\begin{array}{r} \boxed{8} \\ 7 \\ 5\overline{)43} \end{array}$$
$$\begin{array}{r} \boxed{9} \\ 8 \\ 2\overline{)19} \end{array}$$
$$\begin{array}{r} \boxed{8} \\ 7 \\ 4\overline{)32} \end{array}$$

2.
$$\begin{array}{r} \boxed{6} \\ 7 \\ 3\overline{)19} \end{array}$$
$$\begin{array}{r} \boxed{5} \\ 6 \\ 9\overline{)47} \end{array}$$
$$\begin{array}{r} \boxed{7} \\ 6 \\ 7\overline{)52} \end{array}$$
$$\begin{array}{r} \boxed{5} \\ 6 \\ 5\overline{)28} \end{array}$$

B Write the correct quotient in the ■ and the remainder in the ●.

1.
$$\begin{array}{r} \boxed{9}\ r\ 2 \\ 4\overline{)38} \end{array}$$
$$\begin{array}{r} \boxed{7}\ r\ 3 \\ 6\overline{)45} \end{array}$$
$$\begin{array}{r} \boxed{4}\ r\ 6 \\ 8\overline{)38} \end{array}$$
$$\begin{array}{r} \boxed{6}\ r\ 1 \\ 4\overline{)25} \end{array}$$

2.
$$\begin{array}{r} \boxed{8}\ r\ 4 \\ 7\overline{)60} \end{array}$$
$$\begin{array}{r} \boxed{5}\ r\ 5 \\ 9\overline{)50} \end{array}$$
$$\begin{array}{r} \boxed{7}\ r\ 2 \\ 5\overline{)37} \end{array}$$
$$\begin{array}{r} \boxed{9}\ r\ 1 \\ 3\overline{)28} \end{array}$$

Discuss the way to arrive at the correct quotient by using trial quotients. Illustrate the process on the chalkboard. Stress how to tell if a trial quotient is too small, too large, or correct. Have students complete the page.

CHECKING DIVISIONS WITH REMAINDERS

 Find the quotient and the remainder for each division. Remember the remainder must be less than the divisor.

1.
$$
\begin{array}{r}
3\,r\,5 \\
8\,)\overline{29} \\
-24 \quad (3 \times 8) \\
\hline
5
\end{array}
$$

$$
\begin{array}{r}
6\,r\,2 \\
5\,)\overline{32}
\end{array}
$$

$$
\begin{array}{r}
8\,r\,1 \\
2\,)\overline{17}
\end{array}
$$

$$
\begin{array}{r}
5\,r\,3 \\
4\,)\overline{23}
\end{array}
$$

2.
$$
\begin{array}{r}
6\,r\,1 \\
6\,)\overline{37}
\end{array}
$$

$$
\begin{array}{r}
5\,r\,2 \\
8\,)\overline{42}
\end{array}
$$

$$
\begin{array}{r}
4\,r\,6 \\
7\,)\overline{34}
\end{array}
$$

$$
\begin{array}{r}
3\,r\,7 \\
9\,)\overline{34}
\end{array}
$$

Division
$$
\begin{array}{r}
9\,r\,2 \\
3\,)\overline{29} \\
-27 \quad (9 \times 3) \\
\hline
2
\end{array}
$$

Check
$$
\begin{array}{r}
9 \\
\times\ 3 \\
\hline
27 \\
+\ 2 \\
\hline
29
\end{array}
$$
Multiply

Add

1. Multiply the quotient and the divisor.

2. Add the remainder to the product of the quotient and the divisor.

3. The sum should equal the dividend.

 Divide and check.

1.
$$
\begin{array}{r}
7\,r\,2 \\
4\,)\overline{30}
\end{array}
$$

Check
$$
\begin{array}{r}
7 \\
\times\ 4 \\
\hline
28 \\
+\ 2 \\
\hline
30
\end{array}
$$

2.
$$
\begin{array}{r}
7\,r\,3 \\
5\,)\overline{38}
\end{array}
$$

Check
$$
\begin{array}{r}
7 \\
\times\ 5 \\
\hline
35 \\
+\ 3 \\
\hline
38
\end{array}
$$

3.
$$
\begin{array}{r}
7\,r\,2 \\
9\,)\overline{65}
\end{array}
$$

$$
\begin{array}{r}
7 \\
\times\ 9 \\
\hline
63 \\
+\ 2 \\
\hline
65
\end{array}
$$

4.
$$
\begin{array}{r}
7\,r\,3 \\
7\,)\overline{52}
\end{array}
$$

$$
\begin{array}{r}
7 \\
\times\ 7 \\
\hline
49 \\
+\ 3 \\
\hline
52
\end{array}
$$

Have students complete exercise A. Then discuss the example showing how to check a division. Have students check several divisions in exercise A before going on to complete the page.

DIVIDING MULTIPLES OF 10

 Complete the multiplications to help you find the quotients.

1. 2 × 10 = __20__

2 × 20 = __40__ $\overset{20}{2\overline{)40}}$

2 × 30 = __60__

2. 4 × 40 = __160__

4 × 50 = __200__ $\overset{60}{4\overline{)240}}$

4 × 60 = __240__

3. 7 × 20 = __140__

7 × 30 = __210__ $\overset{20}{7\overline{)140}}$

7 × 40 = __280__

4. 8 × 40 = __320__

8 × 50 = __400__ $\overset{60}{8\overline{)480}}$

8 × 60 = __480__

5. 3 × 70 = __210__

3 × 80 = __240__ $\overset{70}{3\overline{)210}}$

3 × 90 = __270__

6. 5 × 50 = __250__

5 × 60 = __300__ $\overset{60}{5\overline{)300}}$

5 × 70 = __350__

B Complete these divisions. Look for a pattern.

1. $\overset{2}{5\overline{)10}}$ $\overset{20}{5\overline{)100}}$

2. $\overset{4}{7\overline{)28}}$ $\overset{40}{7\overline{)280}}$

3. $\overset{3}{6\overline{)18}}$ $\overset{30}{6\overline{)180}}$

4. $\overset{5}{9\overline{)45}}$ $\overset{50}{9\overline{)450}}$

5. $\overset{8}{2\overline{)16}}$ $\overset{80}{2\overline{)160}}$

6. $\overset{7}{8\overline{)56}}$ $\overset{70}{8\overline{)560}}$

7. $\overset{4}{3\overline{)12}}$ $\overset{40}{3\overline{)120}}$

8. $\overset{7}{5\overline{)35}}$ $\overset{70}{5\overline{)350}}$

9. $\overset{9}{4\overline{)36}}$ $\overset{90}{4\overline{)360}}$

C Complete each division. Check by multiplying the quotient times the divisor.

1. $\overset{40}{5\overline{)200}}$ $\overset{50}{2\overline{)100}}$ $\overset{90}{7\overline{)630}}$ $\overset{70}{4\overline{)280}}$ $\overset{40}{8\overline{)320}}$

2. $\overset{30}{9\overline{)270}}$ $\overset{80}{6\overline{)480}}$ $\overset{50}{3\overline{)150}}$ $\overset{90}{9\overline{)810}}$ $\overset{70}{7\overline{)490}}$

NUMBER OF DIGITS IN QUOTIENT

Sue said she could tell if a quotient had 1 or 2 digits. Study the examples which show Sue's method.

Trial Quotient			Quotient Between	Digits in Quotient
1	**10**	**100**		
$\begin{array}{r} 1 \\ 4\,)\overline{148} \\ -4 \\ \hline 144 \end{array}$	$\begin{array}{r} 10 \\ 4\,)\overline{148} \\ -40 \\ \hline 108 \end{array}$	$\begin{array}{r} 100 \\ 4\,)\overline{148} \\ -400 \\ \hline \textit{Too large} \end{array}$	10 and 100	2
$\begin{array}{r} 1 \\ 7\,)\overline{65} \\ -7 \\ \hline 58 \end{array}$	$\begin{array}{r} 10 \\ 7\,)\overline{65} \\ -70 \\ \hline \textit{Too large} \end{array}$	$\begin{array}{r} 100 \\ 7\,)\overline{65} \\ -700 \\ \hline \textit{Too large} \end{array}$	1 and 10	1

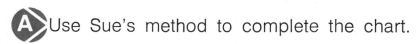 **A** Use Sue's method to complete the chart.

Trial Quotient			Quotient Between	Digits in Quotient
1	**10**	**100**		
$\begin{array}{r} 1 \\ 8\,)\overline{47} \\ -8 \\ \hline 39 \end{array}$	$\begin{array}{r} 10 \\ 8\,)\overline{47} \\ -80 \\ \hline \end{array}$	$\begin{array}{r} 100 \\ 8\,)\overline{47} \\ -800 \\ \hline \end{array}$	__1__ and __10__	1
$\begin{array}{r} 1 \\ 9\,)\overline{380} \\ -9 \\ \hline 371 \end{array}$	$\begin{array}{r} 10 \\ 9\,)\overline{380} \\ -90 \\ \hline 290 \end{array}$	$\begin{array}{r} 100 \\ 9\,)\overline{380} \\ -900 \\ \hline \end{array}$	__10__ and __100__	2
$\begin{array}{r} 1 \\ 5\,)\overline{475} \\ -5 \\ \hline 470 \end{array}$	$\begin{array}{r} 10 \\ 5\,)\overline{475} \\ -50 \\ \hline 425 \end{array}$	$\begin{array}{r} 100 \\ 5\,)\overline{475} \\ -500 \\ \hline \end{array}$	__10__ and __100__	2
$\begin{array}{r} 1 \\ 6\,)\overline{58} \\ -6 \\ \hline 52 \end{array}$	$\begin{array}{r} 10 \\ 6\,)\overline{58} \\ -60 \\ \hline \end{array}$	$\begin{array}{r} 100 \\ 6\,)\overline{58} \\ -600 \\ \hline \end{array}$	__1__ and __10__	1

Tell how many digits each quotient has.

1. $4\overline{)18}$ ___1___ $6\overline{)60}$ ___2___ $7\overline{)89}$ ___2___ $8\overline{)75}$ ___1___

2. $3\overline{)124}$ ___2___ $7\overline{)45}$ ___1___ $9\overline{)238}$ ___2___ $4\overline{)180}$ ___2___

3. $5\overline{)30}$ ___1___ $3\overline{)66}$ ___2___ $6\overline{)57}$ ___1___ $9\overline{)235}$ ___2___

Exercise C provides practice in completing divisions in which the quotients are a 1-digit number or a multiple of 10. Have students complete these exercises independently.

 Complete these divisions. Write the digits in the quotients in the correct columns. Hint: **T** stands for tens' column; **O** stands for ones' column. Check each division by multiplying.

1.

	T	O		Check
		9		9
4 $)$	3	6		× 4
− 3	6			36

	T	O		Check
	5	0		50
7 $)$	35	0		× 7
− 35	0			350

	T	O		Check
	4	0		
8 $)$	32	0		

2.

T O
6 0
5 $)$ 3 0 0

T O
  8
9 $)$ 7 2

T O
  7
4 $)$ 2 8

3.

T O
  7
8 $)$ 5 6

T O
6 0
6 $)$ 3 6 0

T O
  9
7 $)$ 6 3

4.

T O
6 0
2 $)$ 1 2 0

T O
  9
5 $)$ 4 5

T O
9 0
9 $)$ 8 1 0

5.

T O
5 0
7 $)$ 3 5 0

T O
  7
9 $)$ 6 3

T O
8 0
4 $)$ 3 2 0

2-DIGIT QUOTIENTS—NO REMAINDERS

A Draw rings around the divisions which have 2-digit quotients.

1. (5)‾75‾)   4)‾38‾   (7)‾133‾)   (9)‾720‾)   8)‾67‾

2. (2)‾84‾)   6)‾56‾   5)‾43‾   (8)‾232‾)   2)‾19‾

Discuss the example. The steps show what the students should think, find, and write.

How To Find the 2-Digit Quotient for 7)‾196‾

1. Set up the division. $\quad$ 7)‾196‾	**2.** Find the tens' digit. $\quad\quad$ 2 $\quad$ 7)‾196‾ $\quad\quad$ − 14 $\quad$ (2 × 7) $\quad\quad\quad$ 5
3. Write zero in the ones' place in the quotient. $\quad\quad$ 20 $\quad$ 7)‾196‾ $\quad$ − 140 $\quad$ (20 × 7) $\quad\quad$ 56	**4.** Find the ones' digit. $\quad\quad$ 20 $\quad\quad\quad$ 8 $\quad$ 7)‾196‾ $\quad$ 7)‾56‾ $\quad$ − 140 $\quad\quad$ − 56 $\quad$ (8 × 7) $\quad\quad$ 56
5. Write the ones' digit. $\quad\quad$ 8 $\quad\quad$ 20 $\quad\quad\quad$ 8 $\quad$ 7)‾196‾ $\quad$ 7)‾56‾ $\quad$ − 140 $\quad\quad$ − 56 $\quad$ (8 × 7) $\quad\quad$ 56 $\quad$ − 56	**6.** Write the quotient. $\quad\quad$ 8 $\quad\quad$ 20 → 28 $\quad$ 7)‾196‾ $\quad$ − 140 $\quad\quad$ 56 $\quad$ − 56

B Use the first division to help you find the tens in the quotient of the second division.

1.
$\quad$ 3 $\quad\quad\quad\quad$ 30
$\quad$ 5)‾16‾ $\quad\quad$ 5)‾165‾
$\quad$ − 15 $\quad$ (3 × 5) $\quad$ − 150 $\quad$ (30 × 5)
$\quad\quad$ 1 $\quad\quad\quad\quad$ 15

2.
$\quad$ 4 $\quad\quad\quad\quad$ 40
$\quad$ 6)‾24‾ $\quad\quad$ 6)‾246‾
$\quad$ − 24 $\quad\quad\quad$ − 240
$\quad\quad\quad\quad\quad\quad\quad$ 6

3.
$\quad$ 3 $\quad\quad\quad\quad$ 30
$\quad$ 8)‾30‾ $\quad\quad$ 8)‾308‾
$\quad$ − 24 $\quad\quad\quad$ − 240
$\quad\quad$ 6 $\quad\quad\quad\quad$ 68

4.
$\quad$ 8 $\quad\quad\quad\quad$ 80
$\quad$ 9)‾75‾ $\quad\quad$ 9)‾756‾
$\quad$ − 72 $\quad\quad\quad$ − 720
$\quad\quad$ 3 $\quad\quad\quad\quad$ 36

C Use the first division to help you find the ones in the quotient of the second division. Write the quotient in the ▪.

1.

$$7\overline{)28}$$
$$\underline{-28}\ (4 \times 7)$$
quotient: 4

$$7\overline{)378}$$
$$\underline{-350}\ (50 \times 7)$$
$$28$$
$$\underline{-28}\ (4 \times 7)$$
quotient: 50 4 | 54

2.

$$4\overline{)36}$$
quotient: 9

$$4\overline{)116}$$
$$\underline{-80}\ (20 \times 4)$$
$$36$$
$$\underline{-36}\ (9 \times 4)$$
quotient: 20 9 | 29

3.

$$8\overline{)32}$$
quotient: 4

$$8\overline{)272}$$
$$\underline{-240}\ (30 \times 8)$$
$$32$$
$$\underline{-32}\ (4 \times 8)$$
quotient: 30 4 | 34

4.

$$5\overline{)45}$$
quotient: 9

$$5\overline{)445}$$
$$\underline{-400}\ (80 \times 5)$$
$$45$$
$$\underline{-45}\ (9 \times 5)$$
quotient: 80 9 | 89

Treat exercise D orally.

D Complete each division. Write the quotient in the ▪.

1.

$$5\overline{)115}$$
$$\underline{-100}\ (20 \times 5)$$
$$15$$
$$\underline{-15}\ (3 \times 5)$$
quotient: 20 3 | 23

2.

$$2\overline{)74}$$
$$\underline{-60}\ (30 \times 2)$$
$$14$$
$$\underline{-14}\ (7 \times 2)$$
quotient: 30 7 | 37

3.

$$7\overline{)301}$$
$$\underline{-280}\ (40 \times 7)$$
$$21$$
$$\underline{-21}\ (3 \times 7)$$
quotient: 40 3 | 43

4.

$$9\overline{)486}$$
$$\underline{-450}\ (50 \times 9)$$
$$36$$
$$\underline{-36}\ (4 \times 9)$$
quotient: 50 4 | 54

5.

$$4\overline{)312}$$
$$\underline{-280}\ (70 \times 4)$$
$$32$$
$$\underline{-32}\ (8 \times 4)$$
quotient: 70 8 | 78

6.

$$3\overline{)198}$$
$$\underline{-180}\ (60 \times 3)$$
$$18$$
$$\underline{-18}\ (6 \times 3)$$
quotient: 60 6 | 66

7.

$$6\overline{)252}$$
$$\underline{-240}\ (40 \times 6)$$
$$12$$
$$\underline{-12}\ (2 \times 6)$$
quotient: 40 2 | 42

8.

$$8\overline{)432}$$
$$\underline{-400}\ (50 \times 8)$$
$$32$$
$$\underline{-32}\ (4 \times 8)$$
quotient: 50 4 | 54

9.

$$5\overline{)290}$$
$$\underline{-250}\ (50 \times 5)$$
$$40$$
$$\underline{-40}\ (8 \times 5)$$
quotient: 50 8 | 58

Remind students that the way to check divisions is by multiplying the divisor times the quotient. Tell them to study the example in exercise E and complete the page.

 E Divide. Check by multiplying.

Check

1.
```
        3
       50    53
   8 ) 424
     − 400   (50 × 8)
        24
     −  24   ( 3 × 8)
```
Check
```
    53
   ×  8
   424
```

2.
```
        2
       70    72
   4 ) 288
     − 280   (70 × 4)
         8
     −   8   ( 2 × 4)
```
Check
```
    72
   ×  4
   288
```

3.
```
        7
       30    37
   7 ) 259
     − 210   (30 × 7)
        49
     −  49   ( 7 × 7)
```
```
    37
   ×  7
   259
```

4.
```
        2
       40    42
   9 ) 378
     − 360   (40 × 9)
        18
     −  18   ( 2 × 9)
```
```
    42
   ×  9
   378
```

5.
```
        7
       80    87
   5 ) 435
     − 400   (80 × 5)
        35
     −  35   ( 7 × 5)
```
```
    87
   ×  5
   435
```

6.
```
        9
       90    99
   3 ) 297
     − 270   (90 × 3)
        27
     −  27   ( 9 × 3)
```
```
    99
   ×  3
   297
```

7.
```
        2
       50    52
   7 ) 364
     − 350   (50 × 7)
        14
     −  14   ( 2 × 7)
```
```
    52
   ×  7
   364
```

8.
```
        7
       80    87
   6 ) 522
     − 480   (80 × 6)
        42
     −  42   ( 7 × 6)
```
```
    87
   ×  6
   522
```

9.
```
        9
       80    89
   2 ) 178
     − 160   (80 × 2)
        18
     −  18   ( 9 × 2)
```
```
    89
   ×  2
   178
```

10.
```
        4
       30    34
   8 ) 272
     − 240   (30 × 8)
        32
     −  32   ( 4 × 8)
```
```
    34
   ×  8
   272
```

If students have difficulty finding these quotients, identify the step that is causing difficulty and provide additional instruction from that point in the division algorithm to its completion.

2-DIGIT QUOTIENTS—WITH REMAINDERS

A Find the quotient and the remainder. Each quotient has 1 digit. The remainder must be less than the divisor.

1.
```
      6 r 2
  5 ) 32
  − 30   (6 × 5)
      2
```

2.
```
      7 r 2
  4 ) 30
```

3.
```
      6 r 5
  7 ) 47
```

4.
```
      5 r 1
  3 ) 16
```

Have students study the example in exercise B and answer the questions orally. Emphasize that the remainder must be less than the divisor. Then have them complete exercise C and check their work.

B Study the example and answer the questions.

```
       4
      90      94 r 2
  3 ) 284
  − 270   (90 × 3)
     14
   − 12   (4 × 3)
      2
```

1. What is the tens' digit in the quotient? __9__

2. What is the ones' digit in the quotient? __4__

3. 14 − 12 = __2__

4. Is 2 less than 3? __yes__

5. What is the quotient? __94__

6. What is the remainder? __2__

C Complete each division. Write the quotient in the ▨ and the remainder in each ●

1.
```
       1
      70   71 r 1
  4 ) 285
  − 280   (70 × 4)
      5
    − 4   (1 × 4)
      1
```
```
       7
      80   87 r 4
  6 ) 526
  − 480   (80 × 6)
     46
   − 42   (7 × 6)
      4
```
```
       4
      70   74 r 1
  3 ) 223
  − 210   (70 × 3)
     13
   − 12   (4 × 3)
      1
```

2.
```
       8
      10   18 r 1
  2 ) 37
  − 20   (10 × 2)
     17
   − 16   (8 × 2)
      1
```
```
       6
      40   46 r 4
  5 ) 234
  − 200   (40 × 5)
     34
   − 30   (6 × 5)
      4
```
```
       5
      10   15 r 3
  7 ) 108
  − 70   (10 × 7)
     33
   − 35   (5 × 7)
      3
```

220

Checking Division

Division	Check
4	1
80 84 r 1	84 quotient } Multiply
4) 337	× 4 divisor
− 320 (80 × 4)	336
17	+ 1 remainder } Add
− 16 (4 × 4)	337 dividend
1	

D Complete each division and check.

1.
```
        6
       20    26 r 1          Check
   3)79                        26
     − 60   (20 × 3)          × 3
       19                      78
     − 18   (6 × 3)           + 1
        1                      79
```

2.
```
        9
       50    59 r 6          Check
   7)419                       59
     − 350   (50 × 7)         × 7
        69                    413
     − 63   (9 × 7)           + 6
         6                    419
```

3.
```
        7
       40    47 r 3           47
   5)238                      × 5
     − 200   (40 × 5)         235
        38                    + 3
     − 35   (7 × 5)           238
         3
```

4.
```
        1
       30    31 r 4           31
   9)283                      × 9
     − 270   (30 × 9)         279
        13                    + 4
     − 9   (1 × 9)            283
         4
```

5.
```
        2
       20    22 r 3           22
   8)179                      × 8
     − 160   (20 × 8)         176
        19                    + 3
     − 16   (2 × 8)           179
         3
```

6.
```
        6
       10    16 r 2           16
   4)66                       × 4
     − 40   (10 × 4)          64
        26                    + 2
     − 24   (6 × 4)           66
         2
```

SOLVING DIVISION PROBLEMS

1. There were 16 children at Isabel's party. To play one game they had to form 2 equal teams. How many children were on each team?

   _____8_____ children

2. A train traveled 350 kilometers in 5 hours. How many kilometers did it travel each hour? _____70_____ kilometers

3. A peach orchard has 64 trees in 4 equal rows. How many trees are in each row? _____16_____ trees

4. Betty Wahnee bought a book case. The book case has 8 shelves. Each shelf holds 9 books. Betty has 68 books of the same size that she wants to put in the book case.

   a. How many shelves will be full? _____7_____ shelves

   b. Will there be a shelf that will not be full? _____yes_____

   c. How many books will be on that shelf? _____5_____ books

5. Fernando collected 118 bottles to return to the store.

   a. How many full cartons of 6 bottles did Fernando have?

   _____19_____ full cartons

   b. How many bottles were in the carton that was not full?

   _____4_____ bottles

6. Cindy wants to change quarters for dollar bills. She has 27 quarters.

   a. How many dollar bills can she get for these quarters?

   _____6_____ dollar bills

   b. How many quarters will she have left? _____3_____ quarters

DIVIDING BY MULTIPLES OF TEN

 Complete the multiplications to help you find the quotients.

1. $3 \times 10 = \underline{30}$

$4 \times 10 = \underline{40}$ $10\overline{)40}$ — quotient 4

$5 \times 10 = \underline{50}$

2. $7 \times 30 = \underline{210}$

$8 \times 30 = \underline{240}$ $30\overline{)270}$ — quotient 9

$9 \times 30 = \underline{270}$

3. $2 \times 80 = \underline{160}$

$3 \times 80 = \underline{240}$ $80\overline{)160}$ — quotient 2

$4 \times 80 = \underline{320}$

4. $6 \times 40 = \underline{240}$

$7 \times 40 = \underline{280}$ $40\overline{)320}$ — quotient 8

$8 \times 40 = \underline{320}$

5. $1 \times 90 = \underline{90}$

$2 \times 90 = \underline{180}$ $90\overline{)180}$ — quotient 2

$3 \times 90 = \underline{270}$

6. $5 \times 70 = \underline{350}$

$6 \times 70 = \underline{420}$ $70\overline{)490}$ — quotient 7

$7 \times 70 = \underline{490}$

Discuss the example in exercise B. Emphasize that both divisions have the same quotient. Show that instead of thinking of the division $50\overline{)250}$, we can think of $5\overline{)25}$ and arrive at the correct quotient.

 Complete these divisions. Look for a pattern.

1. $5\overline{)35}$ = 7 $50\overline{)350}$ = 7 **2.** $7\overline{)28}$ = 4 $70\overline{)280}$ = 4 **3.** $4\overline{)36}$ = 9 $40\overline{)360}$ = 9

4. $2\overline{)16}$ = 8 $20\overline{)160}$ = 8 **5.** $8\overline{)64}$ = 8 $80\overline{)640}$ = 8 **6.** $6\overline{)18}$ = 3 $60\overline{)180}$ = 3

Have students look at the first item in exercise C. Tell them to look at the shaded digits to find the trial quotient.

C Use the numerals in the shaded boxes to help you find trial quotients.

1. $20\overline{)40}$ = 2 $40\overline{)120}$ = 3 $70\overline{)350}$ = 5 $30\overline{)30}$ = 1

2. $60\overline{)360}$ = 6 $20\overline{)80}$ = 4 $50\overline{)300}$ = 6 $90\overline{)270}$ = 3

3. $50\overline{)100}$ = 2 $80\overline{)400}$ = 5 $10\overline{)90}$ = 9 $60\overline{)480}$ = 8

Discuss the example in exercise A. Show how the products can be used to find the quotient. Point out that the first numbers in each set of multiplications can be used as trial quotients. Work several more examples and then have students complete exercise A.

Stress the statement at the top of the page. Then have students complete exercise D.

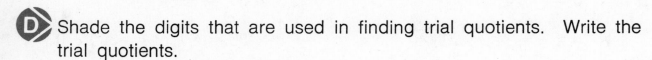

To find the trial quotient, look at the first digit in the
divisor and the first one or two digits of the dividend.

D Shade the digits that are used in finding trial quotients. Write the
trial quotients.

1. $\overset{7}{40\,)\,280}$ $\overset{2}{70\,)\,140}$ $\overset{3}{20\,)\,60}$ $\overset{5}{70\,)\,350}$

2. $\overset{3}{30\,)\,90}$ $\overset{9}{60\,)\,540}$ $\overset{4}{80\,)\,320}$ $\overset{2}{90\,)\,180}$

3. $\overset{5}{50\,)\,250}$ $\overset{5}{20\,)\,100}$ $\overset{2}{30\,)\,60}$ $\overset{7}{60\,)\,420}$

Exercises E and F are practice exercises which should be completed after students can
complete exercise D.

E Find the quotients. Check each division by multiplication.

1. $\overset{7}{30\,)\,210}$ Check
          30
        $\times\ 7$
        $\overline{210}$ $\overset{9}{40\,)\,360}$ Check $\overset{4}{50\,)\,200}$ Check

2. $\overset{7}{70\,)\,490}$ $\overset{5}{60\,)\,300}$ $\overset{6}{90\,)\,540}$

3. $\overset{1}{40\,)\,40}$ $\overset{4}{20\,)\,80}$ $\overset{9}{80\,)\,720}$

Student answers to exercise E should include the check.

F Solve these problems.

1. Sam put his 80 baseball cards in stacks of 20. How many stacks

    did he have? __4__ stacks

2. Mary stacked 90 pennies in stacks of 10. How many stacks did

    she have? __9__ stacks

DIVISION PRACTICE

 Find each quotient and remainder.

1.

$$\begin{array}{r} 6\ r\ 3 \\ 7\overline{)45} \\ -42 \quad (6\times7) \\ \hline 3 \end{array}$$

$$\begin{array}{r} 7\ r\ 5 \\ 9\overline{)68} \\ -63 \quad (7\times9) \\ \hline 5 \end{array}$$

$$\begin{array}{r} 8\ r\ 2 \\ 6\overline{)50} \\ -48 \quad (8\times6) \\ \hline 2 \end{array}$$

$$\begin{array}{r} 6\ r\ 3 \\ 4\overline{)27} \\ -24 \quad (6\times4) \\ \hline 3 \end{array}$$

2.

$$\begin{array}{r} 8\ r\ 1 \\ 2\overline{)17} \\ -16 \quad (8\times2) \\ \hline 1 \end{array}$$

$$\begin{array}{r} 7\ r\ 4 \\ 5\overline{)39} \\ -35 \quad (7\times5) \\ \hline 4 \end{array}$$

$$\begin{array}{r} 9\ r\ 1 \\ 3\overline{)28} \\ -27 \quad (9\times3) \\ \hline 1 \end{array}$$

$$\begin{array}{r} 7\ r\ 4 \\ 8\overline{)60} \\ -56 \quad (7\times8) \\ \hline 4 \end{array}$$

3.

$$\begin{array}{r} 3 \\ 40 \\ 4\overline{)175} \\ -160 \quad (40\times4) \\ \hline 15 \\ -12 \quad (3\times4) \\ \hline 3 \end{array}$$ **43 r 3**

$$\begin{array}{r} 5 \\ 30 \\ 8\overline{)281} \\ -240 \quad (30\times8) \\ \hline 41 \\ -40 \quad (5\times8) \\ \hline 1 \end{array}$$ **35 r 1**

$$\begin{array}{r} 7 \\ 50 \\ 7\overline{)400} \\ -350 \quad (50\times7) \\ \hline 50 \\ -49 \quad (7\times7) \\ \hline 1 \end{array}$$ **57 r 1**

4.

$$\begin{array}{r} 80 \\ 5\overline{)402} \\ -400 \quad (80\times5) \\ \hline 2 \end{array}$$ **80 r 2**

$$\begin{array}{r} 9 \\ 90 \\ 2\overline{)199} \\ -180 \quad (90\times2) \\ \hline 19 \\ -18 \quad (9\times2) \\ \hline 1 \end{array}$$ **99 r 1**

$$\begin{array}{r} 5 \\ 50 \\ 6\overline{)334} \\ -300 \quad (50\times6) \\ \hline 34 \\ -30 \quad (5\times6) \\ \hline 4 \end{array}$$ **55 r 4**

5.

$$\begin{array}{r} 8 \\ 80 \\ 3\overline{)265} \\ -240 \quad (80\times3) \\ \hline 25 \\ -24 \quad (8\times3) \\ \hline 1 \end{array}$$ **88 r 1**

$$\begin{array}{r} 4 \\ 40 \\ 9\overline{)398} \\ -360 \quad (40\times9) \\ \hline 38 \\ -36 \quad (4\times9) \\ \hline 2 \end{array}$$ **44 r 2**

$$\begin{array}{r} 50 \\ 4\overline{)203} \\ -200 \\ \hline 3 \end{array}$$ **50 r 3**

If students have difficulty with any type of exercise on this page, refer them to pages in the chapter dealing with that type of division. Page references are given in the manual portion of this Teacher's Edition.

225

PROBLEM SOLVING

 Write *add, subtract, multiply,* or *divide* to show what to do to solve each problem. Solve each problem mentally and write just the answer.

1. How many nickels can Boyd get for 40 pennies?

2. Tom is 9 years old. His big sister is 15 years old. What is the difference in their ages?

3. Angie paid 15¢ for an apple and 20¢ for milk. How much did she spend?

4. How many 10¢ stamps can you buy for 70¢?

5. Sarah bought 8 pencils for 9¢ each. How much did she spend?

6. For Easter, Gloria dyed 8 eggs red and 9 eggs green. How many eggs did she dye?

7. There were 20 marbles to be shared equally by 4 children. How many marbles did each child get?

8. Rafael spent $.95 and gave the clerk $1.00. How much change should he get back?

9. Alice rode her bike 21 miles in 3 hours. How far did she ride in 1 hour?

10. David bought 3 model airplanes for 50¢ each. How much did he spend?

11. Bill Acoya has 18¢. How much more money does he need to buy a toy that costs 29¢?

1. divide	8 nickels
2. subtract	6 years
3. add	35¢
4. divide	7 stamps
5. multiply	72¢
6. add	17 eggs
7. divide	5 marbles
8. subtract	$0.05
9. divide	7 miles
10. multiply	150¢
11. subtract	11¢

Go over the directions for the page. Have a student read the first problem. Through questioning, bring out what must be done to solve the problem, what the division is, and what the answer is. Have students complete the page in the same way.

MEASURING TEMPERATURE IN DEGREES FAHRENHEIT

Sometimes temperature is measured using a thermometer and degrees Fahrenheit. The temperature shown on the thermometer is 54° Fahrenheit. 54° is read "54 degrees."

A Use the thermometer to answer these questions.

1. At what Fahrenheit temperature does water freeze? ___32°___

2. Could children go ice skating if the temperature is 54°F? ___no___

3. Could children go swimming if the temperature is 32°F? ___no___

4. Is it warmer at 32°F or 54°F?

   ___54°F___

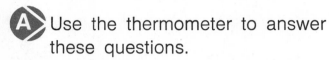

Fahrenheit (F)

freezing point of water

Have students complete exercises B and C independently.

B Mark these temperatures on the thermometer.

1. 10 degrees above zero
2. 62°
3. 20 degrees below zero
4. 80°
5. 48°
6. 106°

C Find the temperature in each picture.

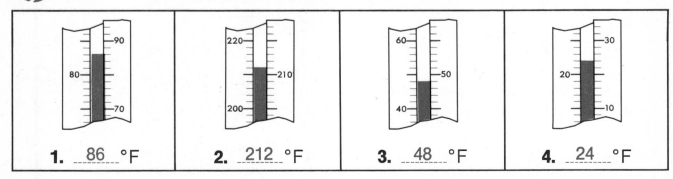

1. ___86___ °F
2. ___212___ °F
3. ___48___ °F
4. ___24___ °F

CHAPTER REVIEW

 A Complete these division facts.

$$8\overline{)56}^{\,7} \qquad 5\overline{)45}^{\,9} \qquad 2\overline{)18}^{\,9} \qquad 6\overline{)48}^{\,8} \qquad 9\overline{)54}^{\,6}$$

B Determine if each trial quotient is too large or too small. Then write the correct quotient in the ■.

$$
\begin{array}{r}
6 \quad \boxed{5} \\
8\overline{)45} \\
-48
\end{array}
\qquad
\begin{array}{r}
7 \quad \boxed{8} \\
4\overline{)35}
\end{array}
\qquad
\begin{array}{r}
6 \quad \boxed{5} \\
9\overline{)52}
\end{array}
\qquad
\begin{array}{r}
6 \quad \boxed{7} \\
6\overline{)43}
\end{array}
$$

C Tell how many digits are in the quotient by writing *1* or *2* in the ■.

$$4\overline{)63} \;\boxed{2} \qquad 7\overline{)65} \;\boxed{1} \qquad 9\overline{)185} \;\boxed{2} \qquad 6\overline{)50} \;\boxed{1}$$

D Complete these divisions.

$$
\begin{array}{r}
3 \\
40 \quad \boxed{43} \; r \; \boxed{2}\\
4\overline{)174} \\
-160 \quad (40 \times 4)\\
\hline
14 \\
-12 \quad (3 \times 4)\\
\hline
2
\end{array}
\qquad
\begin{array}{r}
7 \; r \; 5 \\
9\overline{)68} \\
-63 \quad (7 \times 9)\\
\hline
5
\end{array}
\qquad
\begin{array}{r}
9 \\
60 \quad \boxed{69} \; r \; \boxed{5}\\
7\overline{)488} \\
-420 \quad (\underline{60} \times 7)\\
\hline
68 \\
-63 \quad (9 \times 7)\\
\hline
5
\end{array}
$$

E Complete these divisions and check.

1.
$$
\begin{array}{r}
2 \\
90 \quad \boxed{92} \; r \; \boxed{2}\\
3\overline{)278} \\
-270 \quad (90 \times 3)\\
\hline
8 \\
-6 \quad (2 \times 3)\\
\hline
2
\end{array}
\qquad
\begin{array}{r}
\textbf{Check} \\
92 \\
\times 3 \\
\hline
276 \\
+ 2 \\
\hline
278
\end{array}
$$

2.
$$
\begin{array}{r}
4 \\
20 \quad \boxed{24} \; r \; \boxed{3}\\
8\overline{)195} \\
-160 \quad (20 \times 8)\\
\hline
35 \\
-32 \quad (4 \times 8)\\
\hline
3
\end{array}
\qquad
\begin{array}{r}
\textbf{Check} \\
24 \\
\times 8 \\
\hline
192 \\
+ 3 \\
\hline
195
\end{array}
$$

228

CHECK-UP

A Complete these division facts.

1.
$$5\overline{)40}^{\,8} \qquad 9\overline{)63}^{\,7} \qquad 8\overline{)32}^{\,4} \qquad 6\overline{)36}^{\,6} \qquad 7\overline{)56}^{\,8}$$

2.
$$7\overline{)35}^{\,5} \qquad 4\overline{)24}^{\,6} \qquad 5\overline{)25}^{\,5} \qquad 8\overline{)40}^{\,5} \qquad 3\overline{)21}^{\,7}$$

B Complete these divisions.

```
     8 r 3              7 r 4               9 r 3
7 ) 59             5 ) 39              8 ) 75
 − 56  ( 8 × 7)     − 35  (7 × 5)       − 72  (9 × 8)
    3                  4                   3
```

C Complete each division. Write the quotient in the ▪.

```
     2                   3                    5
    10  | 12 |          80  | 83 |           50  | 55 |
 4 ) 48              6 ) 498              7 ) 385
  − 40  (10 × 4)      − 480  (80 × 6)      − 350  (50 × 7)
     8                  18                   35
   − 8  (2 × 4)       − 18  (3 × 6)        − 35  (5 × 7)
```

D Complete each division. Write the quotient in the ▪ and the remainder in the ●.

```
      4                    9                     4
     40  | 44 | r ( 4)    90  | 99 | r ( 2)     30  | 34 | r ( 3)
 9 ) 400              3 ) 299               5 ) 173
  − 360  (40 × 9)      − 270  (90 × 3)       − 150  (30 × 5)
     40                  29                    23
   − 36  (4 × 9)       − 27  (9 × 3)         − 20  (4 × 5)
      4                   2                     3
```

229

11 • GEOMETRY AND MEASUREMENT

PLANES AND PLANE FIGURES

Any flat surface represents a **plane**. The pictures of the desk top and the parallelogram make us think of a plane.

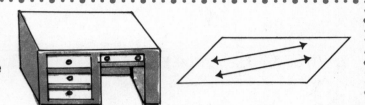

A Draw a ring around each picture that makes you think of a plane.

1.  2.  3. 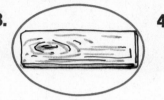 4.

B Draw rings around the words that make you think of a plane.

tin can   (wall)   (windowpane)   basketball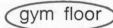

(chalkboard)   steeple   (gym floor)   pencil sharpener

Figures that have all their points in a plane are called **plane figures.**

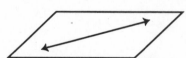 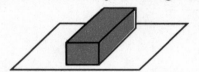

A line is a plane figure.   A box is **not** a plane figure.

C Draw rings around the pictures that show plane figures.

1. 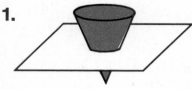 2. 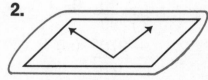 3.

4. 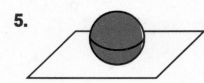 5. 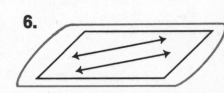 6.

SPACE FIGURES

Figures that do not have all of their points in a plane are called **space figures**.

 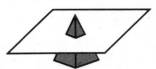

 A Draw a ring around each picture that makes you think of a space figure.

1.  **2.**   **3.**   **4.**

 B Draw rings around the words that make you think of a space figure.

box   room   square region   line

circle   ceiling   ice-cream cone   desk

 C Write *plane* or *space* in the blank to tell if the figure is a plane figure or a space figure.

1.

plane

2.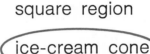

space

3.

space

4.

space

5.

plane

6.

space

7.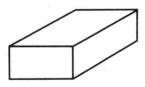

space

8.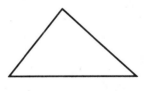

plane

9.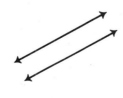

plane

RECTANGULAR BOXES AND CUBES

Here is a picture of a **rectangular box.** It is made of rectangular regions. Each region is called a **face** of the box. Each side of a face is called an **edge.** Each corner of a face is called a **vertex** of the box.

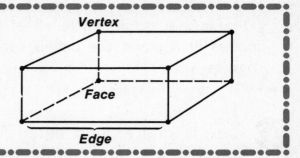

Vertex

Face

Edge

Have students complete the exercises on this page.

 Use the picture of the rectangular box to find the number of

1. faces _____6_____

2. edges _____12_____

3. vertices _____8_____

B Follow these steps to draw a rectangular box. Use your ruler.

1. Draw rectangle ABCD.

2. Draw parallel line segments DE, CF, and BH each with the same length.

3. Draw line segments EF and FH.

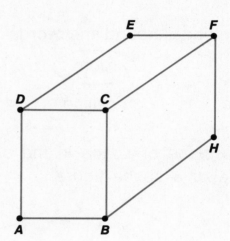

C Complete each box started below. Then draw 4 boxes on a piece of paper.

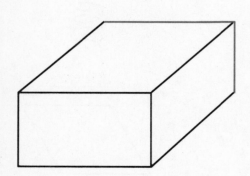

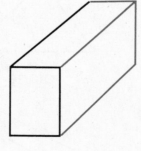

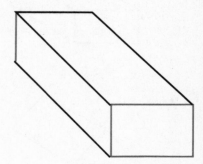

Discuss the picture and description of a rectangular box. Have students tell what the dotted lines represent and why it is hard to draw a box on a piece of paper. Identify and count the faces, edges, and vertices of the box.

If all faces of a box are square regions, it is called a **cube**.

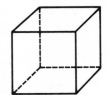

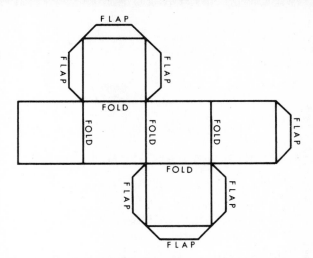

D Copy the pattern for making a cube. Cut out the copied pattern. Fold it on the line segments marked **fold**. Paste the flaps.

Have students complete exercise E. Treat exercise F as a class exercise. Discuss each object before students fill the blanks.

E Use your model to help you answer these questions.

1. How many square regions were used to form the cube? ___6___

2. Were all these square regions the same size? ___yes___

3. How many faces are in a cube? ___6___

4. How many edges are in a cube? ___12___

5. What is the length of each edge of your cube? ___17___mm

6. Are the lengths of the edges of a cube equal? ___yes___

7. How many vertices does a cube have? ___8___

8. What is the shape of each face of a cube? ___square___

F Fill the blank to tell if the object is a cube or a box.

1. your classroom ___box___   **2.** alphabet block ___cube___

3. aquarium ___box___   **4.** file cabinet ___box___

5. box with square faces ___cube___   **6.** book ___box___

CYLINDERS, CONES, AND SPHERES

Cylinder

Cone

Sphere

A Study the pictures of a cylinder, cone, and sphere to help you answer these questions.

1. How many flat parts does a cylinder have? ___2___

2. What shape are the flat parts of a cylinder? ___circles___

3. How many flat parts does a cone have? ___1___

4. What shape is the flat part of a cone? ___circle___

5. How many flat parts does a sphere have? ___0___

B Fill the blank to tell if the figure is a cylinder, cone, or sphere.

1.
cylinder

2.
cylinder

3.
cone

4.
sphere

5.
cylinder

6.
sphere

C Write the name for each shape below the picture. Tell whether it is a cylinder, cone, sphere, box, or cube.

1.
cube

2.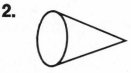
cone

3.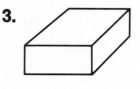
box

4.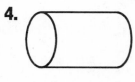
cylinder

Discuss the answers given by students. Have them tell why a certain figure is a cylinder, a cone, or a sphere.

COMPARING SOLID REGIONS

A space figure together with its inside is called a **solid region**. The space figure is the boundary of the solid region.

cylinder   **solid region**

A Put an *X* on those pictures which show solid regions. Name the boundary on the blank.

1.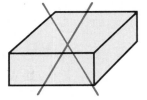

box

2.

cone

3.

sphere

4.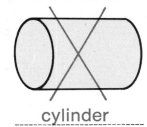

cylinder

5.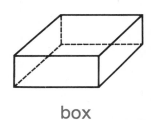

box

6.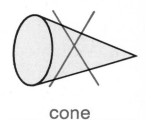

cone

B Draw a ring around the picture of the larger solid region in each pair.

1.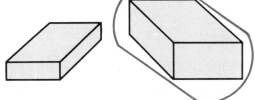

2.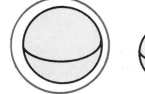

3.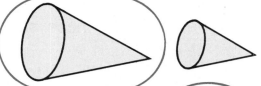

4.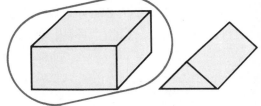

5.

6.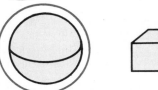

Discuss the description of a solid region. By questioning, bring out the features that are common to space figures and solid regions and those that are not. Stress that a space figure which is shaded indicates a solid region. Have students complete the page.

235

VOLUME

 A Count the number of cubes like this 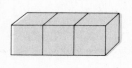 needed to build each shape. Then answer the questions.

1.

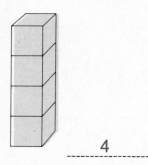

_____3_____

2.

_____4_____

3.

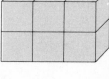

_____6_____

4.

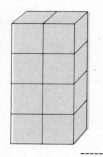

_____4_____

5.

_____8_____

6.

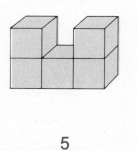

_____5_____

a. Which solid region has the most cubes? ___5___

b. Which solid region is largest? ___5___

c. Which solid region has the fewest cubes? ___1___

d. Which solid region is smallest? ___1___

e. Which solid regions have the same number of cubes?

___2___, ___4___

f. Which solid regions have the same size? ___2___, ___4___

B In each shape some of the cubes needed to build a solid region are hidden. Count all of the cubes needed to build these shapes.

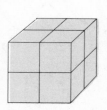

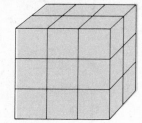

1. _____8_____

2. _____18_____

Stress that the volume of a region is the number of cubic regions in the shape. Use counting blocks to build shapes and have students find the volumes by counting. For each region, complete the sentence "volume = _____ cubic units" on the chalkboard.

A cube that is one centimeter on each side is called a **cubic centimeter**. A cubic centimeter is sometimes written as cm³.

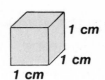

1 cm
1 cm
1 cm

C Find the volume of these solid regions in cubic centimeters by counting. Remember some of the cubic regions may be hidden.

1.

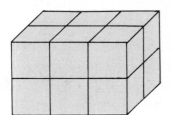

volume = ___12___ cubic cm

2.

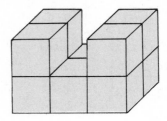

volume = ___10___ cubic cm

D How many cubic centimeters (cm³) will each box hold?

1.

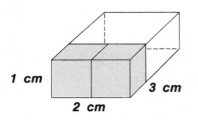

1 cm
2 cm
3 cm

volume = ___6___ cubic cm (cm³)

2.

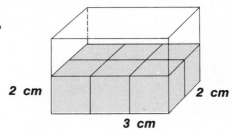

2 cm
2 cm
3 cm

volume = ___12___ cubic cm (cm³)

3.

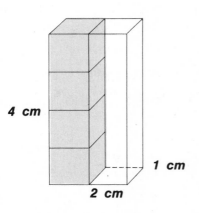

4 cm
1 cm
2 cm

volume = ___8___ cubic cm (cm³)

4.

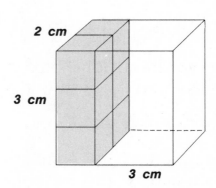

2 cm
3 cm
3 cm

volume = ___18___ cubic cm (cm³)

237

ADDITION—SUBTRACTION REVIEW

 Find the sums by adding up the columns. Check by adding down the columns.

17	39	76	283	323	186
35	27	51	165	708	599
+ 24	+ 32	+ 42	+ 477	+ 452	+ 374
76	98	169	925	1,483	1,159

 Find the differences. Check by adding.

295	480	804	1,263	2,774	3,027
− 163	− 247	− 158	− 955	− 1,099	− 1,643
132	233	646	308	1,675	1,384

 Add or subtract.

1.

268	488	365	403	1,765	$2.00
+ 175	+ 109	− 174	+ 496	− 486	− 1.36
443	597	191	899	1,279	$0.64

2.

7,569	2,744	8,560	$14.28	1,000	257
+ 1,438	− 1,378	− 2,793	+ 47.95	− 463	+ 839
9,007	1,366	5,767	$62.23	537	1,096

D Solve each problem.

1. Sam had $8.00. He spent $3.95 for a model ship. How much money does he have left? ___$4.05___

2. The volume of one box is 1,350 cubic centimeters. The volume of another box is 2,336 cubic centimeters. What is the total volume?

___3,686___ cm³

3. Eva recorded the number of kilometers she rode on her bicycle. The numbers she recorded for four weeks were 17 km, 15 km, 27 km, and 9 km. How far did she ride? ___68___ km

Remember that a common error is adding in a subtraction or subtracting in an addition. If this occurs, remind students to check the operation sign.

Go over the introductory material with the class. Work exercise A as a class exercise.
Have students explain how they were able to tell which container in each group holds
the most.

MEASURING LIQUID CAPACITY

We measure liquid in containers such as spoons, cups, eyedroppers, and buckets.

 Draw a ring around the container that holds the most liquid.

1.

2.

3.

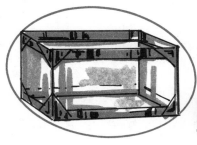

To measure liquid we use a standard-sized container
called a **liter.** It is a cubic container that measures 1
decimeter on each side. A **milliliter** is a cubic container
that measures 1 centimeter on each side. There are
1,000 milliliters (ml) in 1 liter (l).

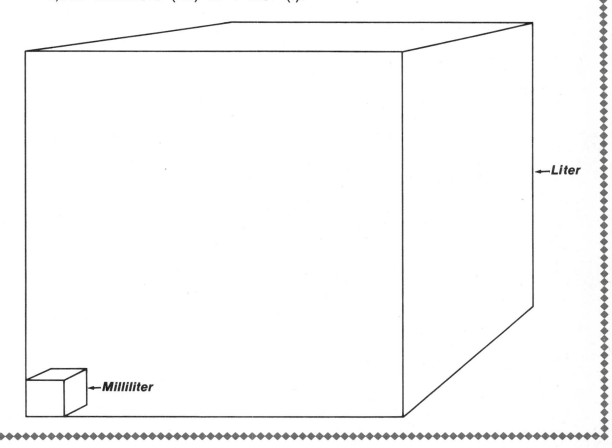

←*Liter*

←*Milliliter*

Discuss the illustrations of an eyedropper, a glass, and a milk carton. Actual objects could be helpful. Discuss the amount of liquid held in each container.

about 1 milliliter   *about 250 milliliters*   *about 1 liter*

Have students complete exercise B. Discuss the reasonableness of each answer by comparing each item to the quantities shown as examples.

B Study the pictures above which represent amounts of liquid. Then draw a ring around the most reasonable answer in each sentence.

1. A cup of coffee is about

2 milliliters   20 milliliters   (200 milliliters)   2 liters

2. A teaspoonful of medicine is about

(5 milliliters)   50 milliliters $\frac{1}{2}$ liter   1 liter

A can of oil is about

1 milliliter   10 milliliters   100 milliliters   (1 liter)

4. A gasoline can holds about

4 milliliters   40 milliliters   400 milliliters   (4 liters)

Write 1 liter = 1,000 milliliters on the chalkboard. Have students tell how many milliliters are in so many liters and vice versa. Have students complete the page.

C Write the correct number of milliliters.

1. 4 liters = ___4,000___ milliliters   **2.** 7 liters = ___7,000___ milliliters

3. 2 liters = ___2,000___ milliliters   **4.** $\frac{1}{2}$ liter = ___500___ milliliters

D Use the pictures at the top of this page to help you answer these questions.

1. Carlos took 4 eyedroppers of medicine. How many milliliters of medicine did he take? ___4___ milliliters

2. Mrs. Scott bought 5 cartons of milk. How many milliliters of milk did she buy? ___5,000___ milliliters

PARTS OF A GALLON

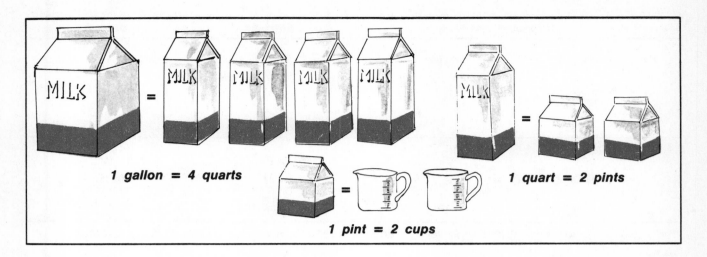

1 gallon = 4 quarts

1 quart = 2 pints

1 pint = 2 cups

A Study the pictures above. Draw a ring around the greater amount of liquid in each pair below.

1. 1 cup   (1 pint)   **2.** (1 gallon)   1 cup   **3.** (1 quart)   1 pint

4. 1 quart   (1 gallon)   **5.** 1 cup   (1 quart)   **6.** 1 pint   (1 gallon)

B Draw a ring around the most reasonable answer.

1. A large glass of milk is about

    1 cup   (1 pint)   1 quart   1 gallon

2. A gasoline can holds about

    1 cup   1 pint   1 quart   (1 gallon)

3. A can of soup holds about

    1 cup   (1 pint)   1 quart   1 gallon

4. A large can of juice holds about

    1 cup   1 pint   (1 quart)   1 gallon

C Complete each sentence.

1. 1 gallon = __8__ pints   **2.** 2 pints = __1__ quart

3. 1 gallon = __16__ cups   **4.** 1 quart = __4__ cups

Review exercise B. Discuss why the correct response is the most reasonable in each case. Then have students name other common containers and the approximate amounts of liquid they would hold.

241

MULTIPLYING THREE FACTORS

Multiplication	Step 1	Step 2
$3 \times (8 \times 7) = $ __168__	$\begin{array}{r} 7 \\ \times\ 8 \\ \hline 56 \end{array}$	$\begin{array}{r} {\scriptstyle 1} \\ 56 \\ \times\ 3 \\ \hline 168 \end{array}$
$(9 \times 5) \times 6 = $ __270__	$\begin{array}{r} 5 \\ \times\ 9 \\ \hline 45 \end{array}$	$\begin{array}{r} 45 \\ \times\ 6 \\ \hline 270 \end{array}$

Have students complete exercises A and B independently. Have them look for a pattern in exercise B.

 A Write the multiplications to find each product.

1. $7 \times (8 \times 8) = $ __448__ $\quad \begin{array}{r} 8 \\ \times\ 8 \\ \hline 64 \end{array} \quad \begin{array}{r} 64 \\ \times\ 7 \\ \hline 448 \end{array}$

2. $(7 \times 8) \times 8 = $ __448__ $\quad \begin{array}{r} 7 \\ \times\ 8 \\ \hline 56 \end{array} \quad \begin{array}{r} 56 \\ \times\ 8 \\ \hline 448 \end{array}$

3. $6 \times (4 \times 13) = $ __312__ $\quad \begin{array}{r} 13 \\ \times\ 4 \\ \hline 52 \end{array} \quad \begin{array}{r} 52 \\ \times\ 6 \\ \hline 312 \end{array}$

4. $(9 \times 7) \times 4 = $ __252__ $\quad \begin{array}{r} 9 \\ \times\ 7 \\ \hline 63 \end{array} \quad \begin{array}{r} 63 \\ \times\ 4 \\ \hline 252 \end{array}$

5. $3 \times (5 \times 20) = $ __300__ $\quad \begin{array}{r} 20 \\ \times\ 5 \\ \hline 100 \end{array} \quad \begin{array}{r} 100 \\ \times\ 3 \\ \hline 300 \end{array}$

6. $9 \times (7 \times 4) = $ __252__ $\quad \begin{array}{r} 4 \\ \times\ 7 \\ \hline 28 \end{array} \quad \begin{array}{r} 28 \\ \times\ 9 \\ \hline 252 \end{array}$

B Find each product without writing the multiplications.

1. $3 \times (5 \times 2) = $ __30__

2. $(3 \times 5) \times 2 = $ __30__

3. $7 \times (3 \times 3) = $ __63__

4. $(7 \times 3) \times 3 = $ __63__

5. $5 \times (2 \times 4) = $ __40__

6. $(5 \times 2) \times 4 = $ __40__

Students should see that pairs of sentences in exercise B have the same products and the same factors, with different factors grouped together. Have them complete exercise C.

C Look for a pattern between pairs of sentences in exercise B. Use that pattern to complete these sentences.

1. If $3 \times (7 \times 5) = 105$, then $(3 \times 7) \times 5 = $ __105__.

2. If $(4 \times 9) \times 6 = 216$, then $4 \times (9 \times 6) = $ __216__.

3. If $9 \times (5 \times 26) = 1{,}170$, then $(9 \times 5) \times 26 = $ __1,170__.

MEASURING WEIGHTS

 A seesaw, which is a balance, can be used to compare weights. Put an X on the heavier person in the picture.

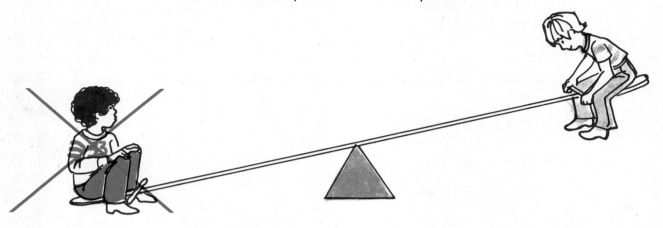

A balance can also be used to measure weights. The picture shows that 2 pencils balance 1 pen. The weight of the pen is about 2 pencils.

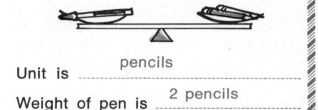

Unit is _____ pencils _____

Weight of pen is _____ 2 pencils _____

After students understand the use of nonstandard units of weight, have them complete exercise B.

 For each picture, write the unit of measure and the weight.

1.

unit is _____ blocks _____

weight of stone is _____ 5 blocks _____

2.

unit is _____ eraser _____

weight of pencil is _____ 1 eraser _____

3.

unit is _____ rings _____

weight of eraser is _____ 3 rings _____

4.

unit is _____ blocks _____

weight of cup is _____ 3 blocks _____

GRAMS AND KILOGRAMS

A **gram** (g) is a standard unit of weight.
A paper clip this size weighs about
1 gram.

 A Write the weight of each object in grams.

1.

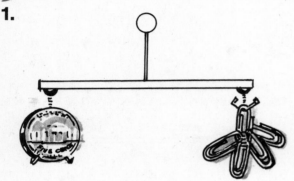

2.

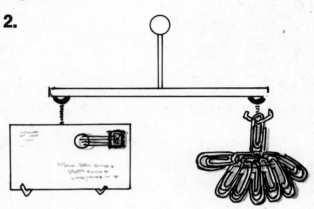

A nickel weighs ___5___ grams.   A letter weighs ___9___ grams.

A **kilogram** (kg) is another standard unit of weight.
A liter of water weighs about 1 kilogram.
1 kilogram (kg) = 1,000 grams (g)

B Write the weight of each object in kilograms.

1.

2.

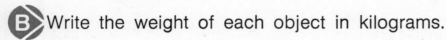

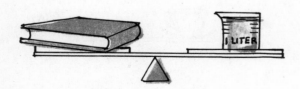

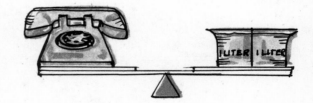

A book weighs ___1___ kilogram.   A telephone weighs ___2___ kilograms.

A paper clip weighs about 1 gram.　　　　**A stapler weighs about 400 grams.**　　　　**A brick weighs about 2 kilograms.**

C Study the pictures above which represent weights. Then draw a ring around the most reasonable answer in each sentence below.

1. A dime weighs about

　(3 grams)　　　　30 grams　　　　300 grams　　　　3 kilograms

2. A child weighs about

　30 grams　　　　300 grams　　　　3 kilograms　　　(30 kilograms)

3. A radio weighs about

　1 gram　　　　100 grams　　　(1 kilogram)　　　　10 kilograms

4. A book weighs about

　8 grams　　　　80 grams　　　(800 grams)　　　　8 kilograms

5. A basketball weighs about

　70 grams　　　(700 grams)　　　　7 kilograms　　　　70 kilograms

D Write the correct number of grams.

1. 3 kilograms = __3,000__ grams　　　　**2.** 8 kilograms = __8,000__ grams

3. $\frac{1}{2}$ kilogram = __500__ grams　　　　**4.** 2 kilograms = __2,000__ grams

E Complete each sentence.

1. 3,500 g = __3__ kg + __500__ g　　　　**2.** 1,750 g = __1__ kg + __750__ g

3. 7,000 g = __7__ kg + __0__ g　　　　**4.** 5,025 g = __5__ kg + __25__ g

POUNDS AND OUNCES

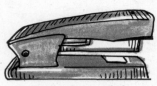

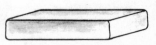

Pounds (lb.) and ounces (oz.) are also used to measure weight. 1 pound = 16 ounces.

A stapler weighs about 1 pound.

An eraser weighs about 1 ounce.

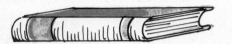

100 paper clips weigh about 4 ounces.

A book weighs about 1 pound 6 ounces or 22 ounces.

A brick weighs about 5 pounds.

A Study the pictures above which represent weights. Then draw a ring around the most reasonable answer in each sentence below.

1. A child weighs about

6 ounces   6 pounds   (60 pounds)   600 pounds

2. A radio weighs about

2 ounces   (2 pounds)   20 pounds   200 pounds

3. A spoon weighs about

(1 ounce)   1 pound   10 pounds   100 pounds

4. A bucket of water weighs about

2 ounces   20 ounces   (20 pounds)   200 pounds

5. An adult weighs about

2 ounces   2 pounds   20 pounds   (160 pounds)

B Multiply to find the number of ounces.

1. 7 pounds = __112__ ounces   **2.** 4 pounds = __64__ ounces

3. 9 pounds = __144__ ounces   **4.** 6 pounds = __96__ ounces

246

REVIEWING DIVISION

 A Complete these division facts.

1.
$$9\overline{)36}^{\,4} \qquad 5\overline{)40}^{\,8} \qquad 3\overline{)21}^{\,7} \qquad 4\overline{)16}^{\,4} \qquad 8\overline{)64}^{\,8}$$

2.
$$7\overline{)63}^{\,9} \qquad 2\overline{)12}^{\,6} \qquad 6\overline{)48}^{\,8} \qquad 9\overline{)54}^{\,6} \qquad 7\overline{)28}^{\,4}$$

B Draw a ring around those divisions which have 2-digit quotients.

1. $7\overline{)58}$ ⟨$5\overline{)80}$⟩ $6\overline{)54}$ ⟨$8\overline{)350}$⟩ ⟨$2\overline{)45}$⟩

2. ⟨$9\overline{)400}$⟩ ⟨$3\overline{)96}$⟩ $4\overline{)38}$ $2\overline{)10}$ $7\overline{)60}$

C Find the quotients and remainders.

1.
$$
\begin{array}{r}
7\ r\ 4 \\
7\overline{)53} \\
-49 \quad (7 \times 7)\\
\hline
4
\end{array}
\qquad
\begin{array}{r}
6\ r\ 1 \\
5\overline{)31} \\
-30 \quad (6 \times 5)\\
\hline
1
\end{array}
\qquad
\begin{array}{r}
6\ r\ 2 \\
8\overline{)50} \\
-48 \quad (6 \times 8)\\
\hline
2
\end{array}
\qquad
\begin{array}{r}
9\ r\ 2 \\
6\overline{)56} \\
-54 \quad (9 \times 6)\\
\hline
2
\end{array}
$$

2.
$$
\begin{array}{r}
6 \\
70 \quad \boxed{76}\ r\ 1 \\
4\overline{)305} \\
-280 \quad (70 \times 4)\\
\hline
25 \\
-24 \quad (6 \times 4)\\
\hline
1
\end{array}
\qquad
\begin{array}{r}
8 \\
20 \quad \boxed{28}\ r\ 2 \\
8\overline{)226} \\
-160 \quad (20 \times 8)\\
\hline
66 \\
-64 \quad (8 \times 8)\\
\hline
2
\end{array}
\qquad
\begin{array}{r}
6 \\
20 \quad \boxed{26}\ r\ 2 \\
3\overline{)80} \\
-60 \quad (20 \times 3)\\
\hline
20 \\
-18 \quad (6 \times 3)\\
\hline
2
\end{array}
$$

3.
$$
\begin{array}{r}
5 \\
70 \quad \boxed{75}\ r\ 1 \\
2\overline{)151} \\
-140 \quad (70 \times 2)\\
\hline
11 \\
-10 \quad (5 \times 2)\\
\hline
1
\end{array}
\qquad
\begin{array}{r}
1 \\
50 \quad \boxed{51}\ r\ 3 \\
7\overline{)360} \\
-350 \quad (50 \times 7)\\
\hline
10 \\
-7 \quad (1 \times 7)\\
\hline
3
\end{array}
\qquad
\begin{array}{r}
30 \quad \boxed{30}\ r\ 5 \\
6\overline{)185} \\
-180 \quad (30 \times 6)\\
\hline
5
\end{array}
$$

SOLVING PROBLEMS

A Fill each blank. Write *degrees, grams, liters,* or *meters* in the blanks.

1. The length of a fence is measured in _____ meters _____.

2. The weight of a book is measured in _____ grams _____.

3. An amount of lemonade is measured in _____ liters _____.

4. The temperature of an oven is measured in _____ degrees _____.

Read and discuss each problem in exercise B. Ask students to identify the operation that must be performed to solve each problem and tell why. Have them solve the problems.

B Solve these problems about Tim's garden.

1. Tim measured the sides of his garden. The lengths were 17 meters, 10 meters, 17 meters, and 10 meters. What is the perimeter of the garden? _____ 54 _____ meters

2. Tim planted 24 tomato plants in 4 rows. How many tomato plants are in each row? _____ 6 _____ plants

3. Tim weighed two tomatoes he grew. One weighed 342 grams; the other weighed 278 grams. What is the difference in the weights of the tomatoes? _____ 64 _____ grams

4. Tim planted 17 bean seeds in each of 6 rows. How many bean seeds did he plant? _____ 102 _____ seeds

5. Tim kept a record of the number of cucumbers he picked. On Monday he picked 14, on Tuesday he picked 9, and on Wednesday he picked 18. How many cucumbers did he pick?

   _____ 41 _____ cucumbers

6. Tim worked in his garden 45 minutes each day. How long would he work in one week? _____ 315 _____ minutes

CHAPTER REVIEW

 A Match names with pictures. Write the number of the word below the correct picture.

1. cone
2. plane
3. cube
4. rectangular box
5. sphere
6. cylinder

a.

_____6_____

b.

_____4_____

c.

_____2_____

d.

_____3_____

e.

_____5_____

f.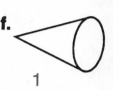

_____1_____

B Count the number of cubes to find the volume of each space figure.

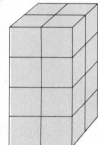

volume =

_____16_____ cubic units

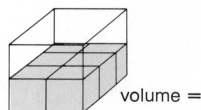

volume =

_____12_____ cubic centimeters

| 1 liter = 1,000 milliliters | 2 pints = 1 quart |
| 2 cups = 1 pint | 4 quarts = 1 gallon |

C Use the information in the box above to complete the sentences.

1. 7,000 milliliters = _____7_____ liters

2. 500 milliliters = _____$\frac{1}{2}$_____ liter

3. 4 cups = _____1_____ quart

4. 3 quarts = _____$\frac{3}{4}$_____ gallon

| 1,000 grams = 1 kilogram | 16 ounces = 1 pound |

D Use the information in the box above to complete the sentences.

1. 3 kilograms = _____3,000_____ grams

2. $\frac{1}{2}$ kilogram = _____500_____ grams

3. 32 ounces = _____2_____ pounds

4. 4 pounds = _____64_____ ounces

CHECK-UP

 A Write *sphere, cone, cube,* or *cylinder* under each picture.

1. 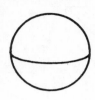   **2.**   **3.**    **4.**

<u>sphere</u>   <u>cube</u>   <u>cone</u>   <u>cylinder</u>

B Draw lines to match the unit of measure that would be used to measure each object.

1. the volume of a box   grams

2. the water in a bucket   cubic centimeters

3. the weight of a book   liters

C Find the volume of each solid figure.

   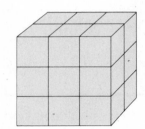

volume = __4__ cubic units   volume = __18__ cubic units

D Complete these sentences.

1. 3,000 grams = __3__ kilograms   **2.** 7 liters = __7,000__ milliliters

3. 16 ounces = __1__ pound   **4.** 4 cups = __1__ quart

E Draw a ring around the most reasonable answer.

1. A paper clip weighs about

   (1 gram)   10 grams   100 grams   1 kilogram

2. A bicycle weighs about

   2 ounces   2 pounds   (20 pounds)   200 pounds

12 • FRACTIONS

REVIEWING FRACTIONS

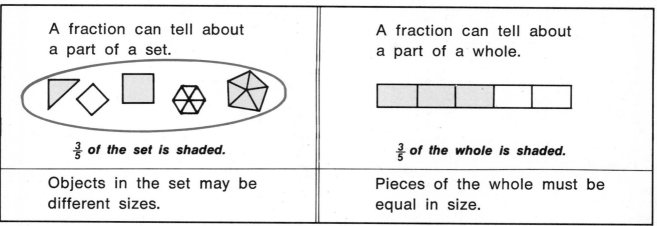

A fraction can tell about a part of a set.	A fraction can tell about a part of a whole.
$\frac{3}{5}$ **of the set is shaded.**	$\frac{3}{5}$ **of the whole is shaded.**
Objects in the set may be different sizes.	Pieces of the whole must be equal in size.

Have students complete exercises A and B.

 Write a fraction to name the part that is shaded.

1. $\frac{3}{6}$ _____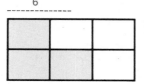

2. $\frac{2}{8}$ _____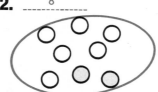

3. $\frac{1}{4}$ _____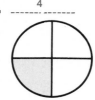

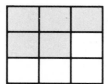 Answer each question.

1. Is $\frac{1}{2}$ of the whole shaded?

no

2. 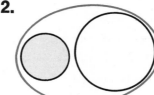 Is $\frac{1}{2}$ of the set shaded?

yes

3. Is $\frac{5}{9}$ of the whole shaded?

yes

4. 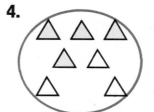 Is $\frac{4}{8}$ of the set shaded?

no

5. Is $\frac{3}{4}$ of the whole shaded?

no

6. 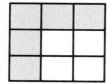 Is $\frac{7}{10}$ of the set shaded?

yes

If students have difficulty with these exercises, it may be necessary to reteach some of the concepts pertaining to fractions using physical objects.

251

$\dfrac{3}{5}$ 　number of pieces that are shaded (numerator)
number of pieces in all (denominator)

C Complete each sentence.

1. $\frac{5}{9}$ of a whole means __5__ of __9__ equal pieces.

2. $\frac{3}{6}$ of a set means __3__ of __6__ objects in the set.

3. $\frac{2}{4}$ of a whole means __2__ of __4__ equal pieces.

4. $\frac{9}{10}$ of a set means __9__ of __10__ objects in the set.

5. $\frac{3}{3}$ of a whole means __3__ of __3__ equal pieces.

D Complete the table.

		Numerator	Denominator	Fraction
1.		2	4	$\frac{2}{4}$
2.		1	2	$\frac{1}{2}$
3.		5	8	$\frac{5}{8}$
4.		3	3	$\frac{3}{3}$
5.		1	5	$\frac{1}{5}$
6.		3	8	$\frac{3}{8}$

Discuss the set in exercise E. Have students identify the number of elements in various subsets of the set. Have students complete exercise E.

E Use the picture. Write a fraction to name each part of the set.

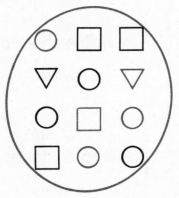

1. squares ___$\frac{4}{12}$___

2. triangles ___$\frac{2}{12}$___

3. circles ___$\frac{6}{12}$___

4. tinted shapes ___$\frac{5}{12}$___

5. tinted circles ___$\frac{3}{12}$___

EQUAL PARTS OF A WHOLE

 Write the fraction for the part of each picture that is shaded.

1. 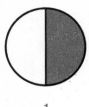 **2.** 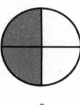 **3.**  **4.**

$\frac{1}{2}$ $\frac{2}{4}$ $\frac{3}{6}$ $\frac{4}{8}$

Is the same amount of each picture shaded? _____ yes _____

> The fraction $\frac{1}{2}$ names the same amount of the picture as $\frac{2}{4}$, $\frac{3}{6}$, or $\frac{4}{8}$. We write $\frac{1}{2} = \frac{2}{4}$, or $\frac{1}{2} = \frac{3}{6}$, or $\frac{1}{2} = \frac{4}{8}$.

Have students complete exercises B and C.

 Write the fraction for the part of each picture that is shaded.

1.    **2.**

$\frac{3}{4} = \frac{3}{4}$ $\frac{1}{3} = \frac{2}{6}$

3.   **4.**

$\frac{2}{3} = \frac{4}{6}$ $\frac{1}{4} = \frac{2}{8}$

 Use the pictures to help complete the sentences.

1.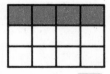

$\frac{1}{2} = \frac{2}{4}$ $\frac{2}{5} = \frac{4}{10}$ $\frac{4}{4} = \frac{8}{8}$ $\frac{1}{3} = \frac{4}{12}$

2.

$\frac{1}{2} = \frac{4}{8}$ $\frac{1}{3} = \frac{2}{6}$ $\frac{3}{5} = \frac{6}{10}$ $\frac{3}{4} = \frac{6}{8}$

If students have difficulty, repeat the initial teaching activity for this lesson.

253

Work exercise A orally. Discuss the statement about $\frac{1}{2}$ and $\frac{3}{6}$.

EQUAL PARTS OF SETS

 A Look at the set of 6 rectangles.
Answer the questions.

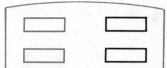

1. How many rectangles are in $\frac{3}{6}$ of the set? ___3___

2. How many rectangles are in $\frac{1}{2}$ of the set? ___3___

There are the same number of rectangles in $\frac{3}{6}$ of the set and in $\frac{1}{2}$ of the set. We write $\frac{1}{2} = \frac{3}{6}$.

Have students complete exercises B and C.

B Write two fractions for the part of each set that is tinted.

1. 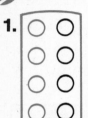 $\frac{4}{8}$ $\frac{1}{2}$

2. $\frac{2}{4}$ $\frac{1}{2}$

3. 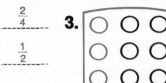 $\frac{3}{9}$ $\frac{1}{3}$

4. $\frac{4}{12}$ $\frac{1}{3}$

5. $\frac{5}{10}$ $\frac{1}{2}$

6. 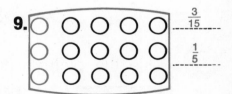 $\frac{3}{12}$ $\frac{1}{4}$

7. $\frac{2}{6}$ $\frac{1}{3}$

8. 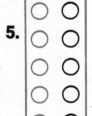 $\frac{2}{8}$ $\frac{1}{4}$

9. $\frac{3}{15}$ $\frac{1}{5}$

C Use the pictures to complete the sentences.

1. 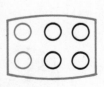 $\frac{2}{6} = \frac{1}{3}$

2. 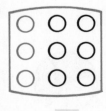 $\frac{1}{3} = \frac{3}{9}$

3. $\frac{1}{2} = \frac{4}{8}$

4. 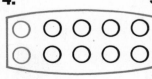 $\frac{2}{10} = \frac{1}{5}$

5. 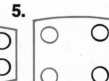 $\frac{1}{2} = \frac{2}{4}$

254 Students having difficulty should complete the additional activity.

COMPARING FRACTIONS

 A **1.** Write the fraction for the part of each picture that is shaded.

a. ___ $\frac{1}{6}$

b. ___ $\frac{2}{6}$

c. ___ $\frac{3}{6}$

d. ___ $\frac{4}{6}$

e. ___ $\frac{5}{6}$

f. ___ $\frac{6}{6}$

2. Study the pictures at left. Draw rings around the greater parts.

a. $\frac{1}{6}$ or $\left(\frac{3}{6}\right)$

b. $\left(\frac{6}{6}\right)$ or $\frac{5}{6}$

c. $\left(\frac{4}{6}\right)$ or $\frac{2}{6}$

d. $\frac{3}{6}$ or $\left(\frac{4}{6}\right)$

e. $\left(\frac{5}{6}\right)$ or $\frac{2}{6}$

f. $\frac{4}{6}$ or $\left(\frac{6}{6}\right)$

3. Write < or > in each ⬤ to make the sentence true.

a. $\frac{1}{6}$ < $\frac{3}{6}$ $\frac{6}{6}$ > $\frac{5}{6}$ $\frac{4}{6}$ > $\frac{2}{6}$ $\frac{3}{6}$ < $\frac{4}{6}$

b. $\frac{5}{6}$ > $\frac{2}{6}$ $\frac{4}{6}$ < $\frac{6}{6}$ $\frac{6}{6}$ > $\frac{1}{6}$ $\frac{1}{6}$ < $\frac{2}{6}$

Have students complete the page. Check their work.

B **1.** Write the fraction for the part of each picture that is shaded.

a. ___ $\frac{1}{2}$

b. ___ $\frac{1}{3}$

c. ___ $\frac{1}{4}$

d. ___ $\frac{1}{5}$

e. ___ $\frac{1}{6}$

f. ___ $\frac{1}{8}$

2. Study the pictures at left. Draw rings around the greater parts.

a. $\left(\frac{1}{2}\right)$ or $\frac{1}{3}$

b. $\frac{1}{8}$ or $\left(\frac{1}{4}\right)$

c. $\left(\frac{1}{5}\right)$ or $\frac{1}{6}$

d. $\left(\frac{1}{2}\right)$ or $\frac{1}{5}$

e. $\left(\frac{1}{3}\right)$ or $\frac{1}{6}$

f. $\left(\frac{1}{4}\right)$ or $\frac{1}{5}$

3. Write < or > in each ⬤ to make the sentence true.

a. $\frac{1}{2}$ > $\frac{1}{3}$ $\frac{1}{6}$ < $\frac{1}{3}$ $\frac{1}{4}$ < $\frac{1}{2}$ $\frac{1}{5}$ < $\frac{1}{4}$

b. $\frac{1}{4}$ > $\frac{1}{8}$ $\frac{1}{6}$ > $\frac{1}{8}$ $\frac{1}{8}$ < $\frac{1}{2}$ $\frac{1}{2}$ > $\frac{1}{6}$

Have students complete the first part of exercise A. Point out that since all the pictures are the same length, the shaded parts can be compared to see which is greater. Have students do this to complete the rest of exercise A.

C Complete the table.

			Fractions		Larger Part	Number Sentence
1.			$\frac{1}{2}$	$\frac{1}{4}$	$\frac{1}{2}$	$\frac{1}{2} > \frac{1}{4}$
2.			$\frac{1}{3}$	$\frac{1}{4}$	$\frac{1}{3}$	$\frac{1}{3} > \frac{1}{4}$
3.			$\frac{1}{2}$	$\frac{3}{4}$	$\frac{3}{4}$	$\frac{1}{2} < \frac{3}{4}$
4.			$\frac{2}{3}$	$\frac{3}{8}$	$\frac{2}{3}$	$\frac{2}{3} > \frac{3}{8}$
5.			$\frac{1}{4}$	$\frac{1}{6}$	$\frac{1}{4}$	$\frac{1}{4} > \frac{1}{6}$

D Shade the part of each set named by the fraction. Then complete the number sentence by writing > or < in each ●.

1.	$\frac{1}{2}$ of 6 is ___3___.	$\frac{1}{3}$ of 6 is ___2___.	$\frac{1}{2}$ ⬤> $\frac{1}{3}$
2.	$\frac{1}{3}$ of 12 is ___4___.	$\frac{1}{4}$ of 12 is ___3___.	$\frac{1}{3}$ ⬤> $\frac{1}{4}$
3.	$\frac{3}{4}$ of 8 is ___6___.	$\frac{3}{8}$ of 8 is ___3___.	$\frac{3}{4}$ ⬤> $\frac{3}{8}$

If students have difficulty with exercise D, they should complete similar exercises using concrete objects. You may wish to make a worksheet similar to exercise C using sets of objects rather than whole objects divided into parts.

REVIEWING NUMBERS

 A Numbers have many different names. Complete the chart.

	Word Name	Expanded Name	Standard Name
1.	seventy-nine	70 + 9	79
2.	three hundred twelve	300 + 10 + 2	312
3.	two thousand, forty-five	2,000 + 40 + 5	2,045
4.	six thousand, nine hundred twenty-eight	6,000 + 900 + 20 + 8	6,928

B Complete the number lines.

1. 88 89 **90** **91** 92 **93**

2. 1,997 1,998 **1,999** **2,000** **2,001**

3. **5,998** **5,999** 6,000 6,001 6,002

4. **487** 488 489 **490** **491**

C Complete the number patterns.

1. 150   160   170   __180__   **2.** 95   90   85   __80__

3. 700   800   900   __1,000__   **4.** 1,464   1,466   1,468   __1,470__

5. 2,000   3,000   4,000   __5,000__   **6.** 784   782   780   __778__

D In the blank after each word name, write the standard name for the number. Then answer the questions.

Bob saved four hundred eighty __480__ baseball cards. Lupe saved four hundred eight __408__ cards. Sheila saved three hundred ninety-seven __397__ cards.

1. Who saved the most cards? __Bob__

2. Who saved the fewest cards? __Sheila__

Students who have difficulty may need small group instruction using activity 1 or 2.

257

FRACTIONS AND MIXED NUMERALS

 A Complete the chart.

	Picture	Number of Wholes	Part of Whole	Sum
1.		4	$\frac{3}{4}$	$4 + \frac{3}{4}$
2.		1	$\frac{1}{2}$	$1 + \frac{1}{2}$
3.		3	$\frac{2}{3}$	$3 + \frac{2}{3}$
4.		2	$\frac{1}{5}$	$2 + \frac{1}{5}$
5.		1	$\frac{5}{6}$	$1 + \frac{5}{6}$

Mixed Numeral

$2\frac{3}{4}$

means the sum $2 + \frac{3}{4}$ is read "two and three-fourths"

B In each set, draw a ring around the mixed numeral.

1. $\frac{5}{8}$ 3 $\left(3\frac{5}{8}\right)$ 2. $\left(1\frac{2}{3}\right)$ $3 + \frac{1}{4}$ $\frac{7}{10}$

3. $6 + 1$ $\left(4\frac{1}{2}\right)$ $2 + \frac{3}{4}$ 4. $\frac{1}{2} + 3$ $\frac{4}{9}$ $\left(2\frac{3}{10}\right)$

C Write the meaning of each mixed numeral.

1. $1\frac{2}{3}$ $\underline{1 + \frac{2}{3}}$ $2\frac{5}{8}$ $\underline{2 + \frac{5}{8}}$ $4\frac{1}{2}$ $\underline{4 + \frac{1}{2}}$

2. $3\frac{6}{10}$ $\underline{3 + \frac{6}{10}}$ $1\frac{3}{4}$ $\underline{1 + \frac{3}{4}}$ $5\frac{2}{5}$ $\underline{5 + \frac{2}{5}}$

D Write the mixed numeral for each picture.

1. $2\frac{1}{2}$

2. $1\frac{3}{4}$

3. $1\frac{2}{6}$

4. $2\frac{2}{3}$

5. $3\frac{3}{5}$

6. $1\frac{5}{8}$

If students have difficulty with exercise D, you might use questioning to help them see how many wholes and parts of wholes are shaded and what the addition and mixed

E Match each numeral to the picture it names. numeral are.

1. $2\frac{3}{4}$

2. $1\frac{5}{8}$

3. $\frac{3}{5}$

4. $2\frac{4}{6}$

5. 3

6. $2\frac{1}{2}$

7. $1\frac{2}{3}$

8. $2\frac{1}{3}$

9. $\frac{5}{6}$

10. $1\frac{1}{4}$

In exercise E, some students may need to write the correct mixed numeral beside each picture and then match the mixed numerals.

MIXED NUMERALS AND FRACTIONS

A Look at the picture and complete the sentences.

1. Each bar has been divided into ___halves___.

2. The number of halves that are shaded is ___5___.

3. A mixed numeral that names the shaded part

   is ___$2\frac{1}{2}$___.

   A fraction that names the shaded part is $\frac{5}{2}$.

Work the sample exercise in B with the class. Have students complete the chart.

B Complete the chart.

		Mixed Numeral	Portions Shaded	Portions in One Whole	Fraction
1.		$1\frac{2}{4}$	6	4	$\frac{6}{4}$
2.		$1\frac{1}{3}$	4	3	$\frac{4}{3}$
3.		$1\frac{3}{4}$	7	4	$\frac{7}{4}$
4.		$2\frac{3}{6}$	15	6	$\frac{15}{6}$
5.		$1\frac{7}{10}$	17	10	$\frac{17}{10}$

Treat exercise A orally. Have students answer each question and read the statement describing the fraction $\frac{5}{2}$. Do additional exercises on the chalkboard. Emphasize that the fraction is the number of equal pieces that are shaded written over the number of equal pieces in one whole.

C Name the shaded part in two ways.

1. $1\frac{1}{2}$ $\frac{3}{2}$

2. $1\frac{1}{4}$ $\frac{5}{4}$

3. $2\frac{1}{3}$ $\frac{7}{3}$

4. $2\frac{3}{4}$ $\frac{11}{4}$

5. $1\frac{3}{5}$ $\frac{8}{5}$

6. $1\frac{2}{3}$ $\frac{5}{3}$

D Shade the boxes to show the mixed numeral. Name the shaded part using a fraction.

1. $1\frac{1}{5}$ $\frac{6}{5}$

2. $3\frac{1}{2}$ $\frac{7}{2}$

3. $2\frac{4}{6}$ $\frac{16}{6}$

4. $1\frac{3}{8}$ $\frac{11}{8}$

E Shade the boxes to show the fraction. Name the shaded part using a mixed or whole numeral.

1. $\frac{9}{5}$ $1\frac{4}{5}$

2. $\frac{6}{3}$ 2

3. $\frac{10}{4}$ $2\frac{2}{4}$

Have students complete this page independently. Some students may need assistance; use questioning to guide them through the first part of each exercise and have them complete the last one or two items independently.

261

FRACTIONS ON THE NUMBER LINE

Study the number line. Each whole has been divided into 3 equal parts. Some points are named two ways.
$1 = \frac{3}{3}$, and $2 = \frac{6}{3}$.

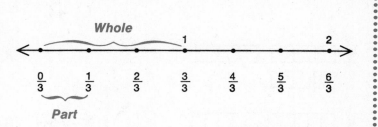

Whole

$\frac{0}{3}$ $\frac{1}{3}$ $\frac{2}{3}$ $\frac{3}{3}$ $\frac{4}{3}$ $\frac{5}{3}$ $\frac{6}{3}$

Part

Complete the first number line in exercise A as a class exercise. Have students complete the rest of the page independently.

 A Name the points on these number lines with fractions.

1.

$\frac{0}{4}$ $\frac{1}{4}$ $\frac{2}{4}$ $\frac{3}{4}$ $\frac{4}{4}$ $\frac{5}{4}$ $\frac{6}{4}$ $\frac{7}{4}$ $\frac{8}{4}$ $\frac{9}{4}$ $\frac{10}{4}$ $\frac{11}{4}$ $\frac{12}{4}$

2.

$\frac{0}{5}$ $\frac{1}{5}$ $\frac{2}{5}$ $\frac{3}{5}$ $\frac{4}{5}$ $\frac{5}{5}$ $\frac{6}{5}$ $\frac{7}{5}$ $\frac{8}{5}$ $\frac{9}{5}$ $\frac{10}{5}$ $\frac{11}{5}$ $\frac{12}{5}$ $\frac{13}{5}$ $\frac{14}{5}$ $\frac{15}{5}$

B Use the number line to help you fill the blanks.

A   B   C   D   E   F   G

1. Write a fraction equal to each of these whole numbers.

$0 = \frac{0}{2}$ $1 = \frac{2}{2}$ $2 = \frac{4}{2}$ $4 = \frac{8}{2}$

2. Write a fraction for each of these letters.

A $\frac{1}{2}$ B $\frac{3}{2}$ D $\frac{5}{2}$ E $\frac{6}{2}$

3. Write a mixed numeral for each of these letters.

B $1\frac{1}{2}$ D $2\frac{1}{2}$ F $3\frac{1}{2}$ G $4\frac{1}{2}$

C Use the number line and write a fraction that tells the length of each line segment.

1.   0 $\frac{2}{2}$ $\frac{8}{2}$

2.   0 $\frac{3}{3}$ $\frac{5}{3}$

Discuss the pictures showing parts of an inch. Explain how we can tell half inches, fourth inches, and eighth inches on a ruler by the lengths of the marks.

PARTS OF AN INCH

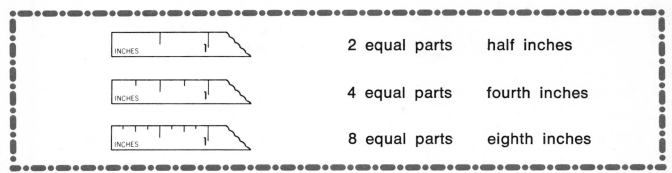

2 equal parts   half inches

4 equal parts   fourth inches

8 equal parts   eighth inches

Have students complete these exercises independently.

A Use a ruler marked in eighth inches to find each length.

1. $1\frac{5}{8}$ inches

2. $\frac{7}{8}$ inch

3. $2\frac{1}{8}$ inches

B Draw line segments for each of these lengths.

1. $\frac{5}{8}$ inch   **2.** $1\frac{3}{8}$ inches   **3.** $2\frac{2}{8}$ inches

C Study the picture. Then answer the questions.

1. Is the top segment nearer to $\frac{5}{8}$ inch or $\frac{6}{8}$ inch? $\frac{5}{8}$ inch

2. Is the bottom segment nearer to $\frac{4}{8}$ inch or $\frac{5}{8}$ inch? $\frac{5}{8}$ inch

We say that both segments measure $\frac{5}{8}$ inch to the nearest eighth inch.

D Find the length of each segment to the nearest eighth inch.

1. $1\frac{6}{8}$ inches

2. $1\frac{1}{8}$ inches

Have students use their rulers to draw line segments with lengths such as $2\frac{3}{4}$ and $1\frac{5}{8}$ inches.

ADDITION AND SUBTRACTION REVIEW

 A The addition 7 + 5 is shown on the number line. Use the number line to help you find the sums.

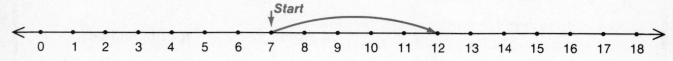

1. 7 + 5 = __12__   5 + 3 = __8__   9 + 6 = __15__   8 + 4 = __12__

2. 9 + 8 = __17__   7 + 7 = __14__   8 + 3 = __11__   6 + 5 = __11__

B The subtraction 15 − 7 is shown on the number line. Use the number line to help you find the differences.

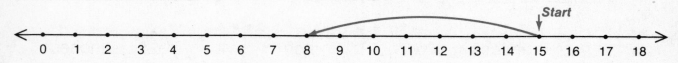

1. 15 − 7 = __8__   10 − 4 = __6__   18 − 9 = __9__   11 − 8 = __3__

2. 12 − 5 = __7__   9 − 8 = __1__   13 − 4 = __9__   16 − 9 = __7__

C Find the sums or differences.

1.
$$
\begin{array}{r} 43 \\ + 65 \\ \hline 108 \end{array}
\qquad
\begin{array}{r} 87 \\ - 62 \\ \hline 25 \end{array}
\qquad
\begin{array}{r} 184 \\ - 67 \\ \hline 117 \end{array}
\qquad
\begin{array}{r} 64 \\ + 79 \\ \hline 143 \end{array}
\qquad
\begin{array}{r} 168 \\ + 329 \\ \hline 497 \end{array}
\qquad
\begin{array}{r} 475 \\ - 198 \\ \hline 277 \end{array}
$$

2.
$$
\begin{array}{r} 4{,}816 \\ + 1{,}378 \\ \hline 6{,}194 \end{array}
\qquad
\begin{array}{r} 1{,}695 \\ - 831 \\ \hline 864 \end{array}
\qquad
\begin{array}{r} 4{,}739 \\ + 2{,}684 \\ \hline 7{,}423 \end{array}
\qquad
\begin{array}{r} 3{,}672 \\ - 3{,}328 \\ \hline 344 \end{array}
\qquad
\begin{array}{r} 1{,}704 \\ - 386 \\ \hline 1{,}318 \end{array}
$$

D Solve these word problems.

1. Pauline saved $8.45 to buy a transistor radio. The radio cost $14.95.

How much more money does Pauline need? __$6.50__

2. On their vacation, the Myers traveled 234 kilometers the first day, 497 kilometers the second day, and 385 kilometers the third day.

How far did the Myers travel? __1,116__ kilometers

ADDING FRACTIONS WITH COMMON DENOMINATORS

 A Answer the questions.

1. Mr. Cooper ate $\frac{2}{6}$ of the pizza. Shade $\frac{2}{6}$ of the pizza with your pencil.

2. Al ate $\frac{1}{6}$ of the pizza. Shade $\frac{1}{6}$ of the pizza with your pencil.

3. What fraction tells the part of the pizza that Mr. Cooper and Al ate? $\frac{3}{6}$

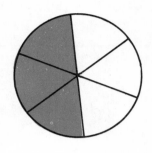

We write $\frac{2}{6} + \frac{1}{6} = \frac{2+1}{6} = \frac{3}{6}$.

Explain the example in exercise B. Tell students that in each remaining item they should shade the fractions to be added in the circle; the total part shaded is the sum.

 B Use the circles to help you find the sums.

1.
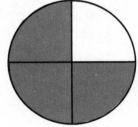
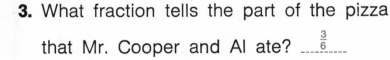

$\frac{1}{6} + \frac{1}{6} = \frac{2}{6}$ $\qquad$ $\frac{1}{6} + \frac{3}{6} = \frac{4}{6}$ $\qquad$ $\frac{2}{6} + \frac{2}{6} = \frac{4}{6}$ $\qquad$ $\frac{2}{6} + \frac{3}{6} = \frac{5}{6}$

2.
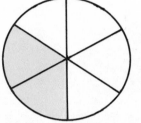
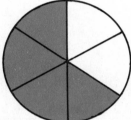
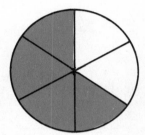
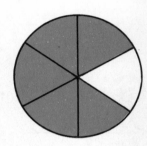

$\frac{1}{4} + \frac{2}{4} = \frac{3}{4}$ $\qquad$ $\frac{1}{4} + \frac{1}{4} = \frac{2}{4}$ $\qquad$ $\frac{1}{3} + \frac{1}{3} = \frac{2}{3}$ $\qquad$ $\frac{2}{3} + \frac{1}{3} = \frac{3}{3}$

3.
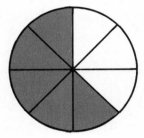
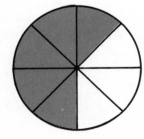
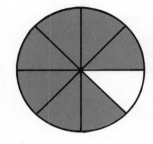
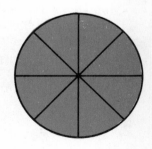

$\frac{3}{8} + \frac{2}{8} = \frac{5}{8}$ $\qquad$ $\frac{4}{8} + \frac{1}{8} = \frac{5}{8}$ $\qquad$ $\frac{5}{8} + \frac{2}{8} = \frac{7}{8}$ $\qquad$ $\frac{4}{8} + \frac{4}{8} = \frac{8}{8}$

Through discussion, bring out the rule that to add fractions with a common denominator, add the numerators and write this sum over the common denominator.

265

ADDING FRACTIONS ON THE NUMBER LINE

 A Use the number lines to help you complete the sentences.

1.

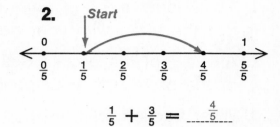

$\frac{3}{6} + \frac{1}{6} = \underline{\frac{4}{6}}$

2. *Start*

$\frac{1}{5} + \frac{3}{5} = \underline{\frac{4}{5}}$

3. *Start*

$\frac{2}{8} + \frac{4}{8} = \underline{\frac{6}{8}}$

4. *Start*

$\frac{1}{3} + \frac{1}{3} = \underline{\frac{2}{3}}$

B Use the number line to help you find the sums.

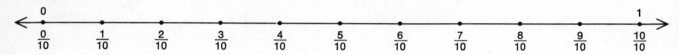

1. $\frac{3}{10} + \frac{4}{10} = \underline{\frac{7}{10}}$ $\frac{1}{10} + \frac{8}{10} = \underline{\frac{9}{10}}$ $\frac{4}{10} + \frac{4}{10} = \underline{\frac{8}{10}}$

2. $\frac{2}{10} + \frac{3}{10} = \underline{\frac{5}{10}}$ $\frac{7}{10} + \frac{1}{10} = \underline{\frac{8}{10}}$ $\frac{8}{10} + \frac{2}{10} = \underline{\frac{10}{10}}$

> **Rule:** To add two fractions with a common denominator, add the numerators and place the sum over the common denominator. $\frac{4}{10} + \frac{3}{10} = \frac{4+3}{10} = \frac{7}{10}$

C Find the sums.

1. $\frac{1}{5} + \frac{3}{5} = \underline{\frac{4}{5}}$ $\frac{3}{8} + \frac{4}{8} = \underline{\frac{7}{8}}$ $\frac{1}{5} + \frac{1}{5} = \underline{\frac{2}{5}}$

2. $\frac{3}{4} + \frac{1}{4} = \underline{\frac{4}{4}}$ $\frac{7}{10} + \frac{2}{10} = \underline{\frac{9}{10}}$ $\frac{1}{3} + \frac{2}{3} = \underline{\frac{3}{3}}$

3. $\frac{4}{8} + \frac{1}{8} = \underline{\frac{5}{8}}$ $\frac{3}{6} + \frac{2}{6} = \underline{\frac{5}{6}}$ $\frac{4}{12} + \frac{7}{12} = \underline{\frac{11}{12}}$

SUBTRACTING FRACTIONS WITH COMMON DENOMINATORS

 $\frac{5}{6}$ of a box is filled with sandwiches.   Ruth eats two of the sandwiches.

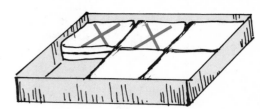

1. Put an X on two sandwiches to show Ruth ate these.

2. How many sandwiches are left?   _____3_____

3. What fraction tells us the part of the box that still has sandwiches? _____$\frac{3}{6}$_____
We write $\frac{5}{6} - \frac{2}{6} = \frac{5-2}{6} = \frac{3}{6}$.

Explain the example in exercise B. The minuend, $\frac{3}{6}$, has been shown by shading. An X shows the shaded piece taken away. The difference is the shaded part without an X.

B Use the rectangles to help you find the differences.

1.

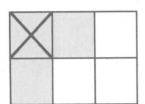

$\frac{3}{6} - \frac{1}{6} = $ _____$\frac{2}{6}$_____

2.

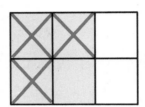

$\frac{4}{6} - \frac{3}{6} = $ _____$\frac{1}{6}$_____

3.

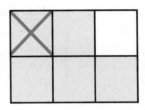

$\frac{5}{6} - \frac{1}{6} = $ _____$\frac{4}{6}$_____

4.

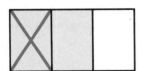

$\frac{2}{3} - \frac{1}{3} = $ _____$\frac{1}{3}$_____

5.

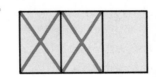

$\frac{3}{3} - \frac{2}{3} = $ _____$\frac{1}{3}$_____

6.

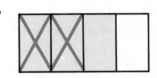

$\frac{3}{4} - \frac{2}{4} = $ _____$\frac{1}{4}$_____

7.

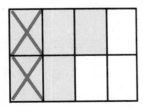

$\frac{5}{8} - \frac{2}{8} = $ _____$\frac{3}{8}$_____

8.

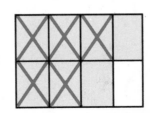

$\frac{7}{8} - \frac{5}{8} = $ _____$\frac{2}{8}$_____

9.

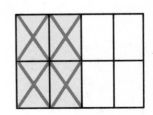

$\frac{4}{8} - \frac{4}{8} = $ _____$\frac{0}{8}$_____

Discuss the rule that to subtract two fractions with a common denominator, subtract **267** the numerators and place this difference over the common denominator.

SUBTRACTING FRACTIONS ON THE NUMBER LINE

 Use the number lines to help you complete the sentences.

1.

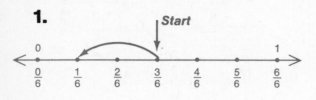

$$\frac{3}{6} - \frac{2}{6} = \underline{\frac{1}{6}}$$

2.

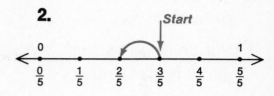

$$\frac{3}{5} - \frac{1}{5} = \underline{\frac{2}{5}}$$

3.

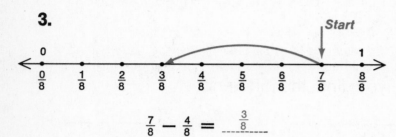

$$\frac{7}{8} - \frac{4}{8} = \underline{\frac{3}{8}}$$

4.

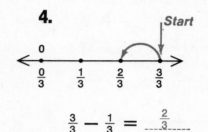

$$\frac{3}{3} - \frac{1}{3} = \underline{\frac{2}{3}}$$

B Use the number line to help you find the differences.

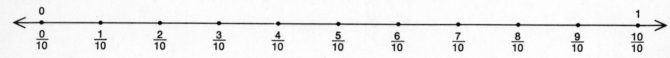

1. $\frac{7}{10} - \frac{2}{10} = \underline{\frac{5}{10}}$ $\frac{5}{10} - \frac{1}{10} = \underline{\frac{4}{10}}$ $\frac{6}{10} - \frac{4}{10} = \underline{\frac{2}{10}}$

2. $\frac{3}{10} - \frac{3}{10} = \underline{\frac{0}{10}}$ $\frac{10}{10} - \frac{7}{10} = \underline{\frac{3}{10}}$ $\frac{9}{10} - \frac{5}{10} = \underline{\frac{4}{10}}$

Rule: To subtract fractions with a common denominator, subtract the numerators and place this difference over the common denominator.

$$\frac{6}{10} - \frac{3}{10} = \frac{6-3}{10} = \frac{3}{10}$$

C Find the differences.

1. $\frac{3}{5} - \frac{2}{5} = \underline{\frac{1}{5}}$ $\frac{4}{6} - \frac{1}{6} = \underline{\frac{3}{6}}$ $\frac{5}{10} - \frac{3}{10} = \underline{\frac{2}{10}}$

2. $\frac{6}{8} - \frac{6}{8} = \underline{\frac{0}{8}}$ $\frac{2}{4} - \frac{1}{4} = \underline{\frac{1}{4}}$ $\frac{3}{3} - \frac{2}{3} = \underline{\frac{1}{3}}$

3. $\frac{4}{10} - \frac{3}{10} = \underline{\frac{1}{10}}$ $\frac{9}{12} - \frac{9}{12} = \underline{\frac{0}{12}}$ $\frac{11}{12} - \frac{3}{12} = \underline{\frac{8}{12}}$

4. $\frac{7}{8} - \frac{2}{8} = \underline{\frac{5}{8}}$ $\frac{11}{12} - \frac{7}{12} = \underline{\frac{4}{12}}$ $\frac{5}{5} - \frac{2}{5} = \underline{\frac{3}{5}}$

MULTIPLICATION AND DIVISION REVIEW

 A Complete these multiplication and division facts.

1.

8	5	9	7	4	6	7
× 7	× 9	× 9	× 6	× 8	× 3	× 4
56	45	81	42	32	18	28

2. $8\overline{)56}$ = 7 $9\overline{)45}$ = 5 $9\overline{)81}$ = 9 $6\overline{)42}$ = 7 $4\overline{)32}$ = 8 $6\overline{)18}$ = 3

B Find the products.

1.

23	31	24	47	89	68
× 3	× 6	× 4	× 2	× 7	× 5
69	186	96	94	623	340

2.

642	323	184	369	243	176
× 2	× 3	× 6	× 8	× 9	× 7
1,284	969	1,104	2,952	2,187	1,232

C Find the quotients and the remainders.

1. $5\overline{)38}$ = 7 r 3 $7\overline{)46}$ = 6 r 4 $4\overline{)22}$ = 5 r 2 $9\overline{)58}$ = 6 r 4 $6\overline{)50}$ = 8 r 2

2. $3\overline{)69}$ = 23 $2\overline{)96}$ = 48 $5\overline{)165}$ = 33 $8\overline{)304}$ = 38 $7\overline{)98}$ = 14

3. $40\overline{)80}$ = 2 $10\overline{)90}$ = 9 $20\overline{)160}$ = 8 $60\overline{)300}$ = 5 $30\overline{)60}$ = 2

WORKING WITH FRACTIONS

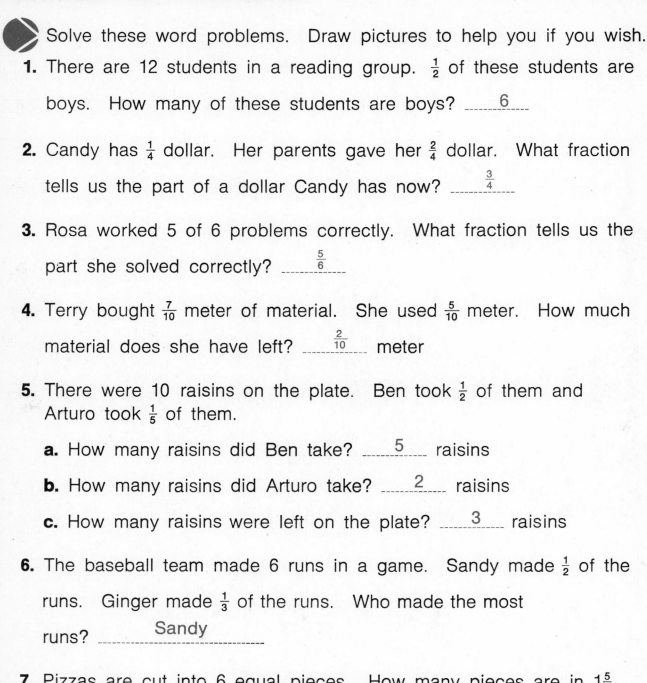

Solve these word problems. Draw pictures to help you if you wish.

1. There are 12 students in a reading group. $\frac{1}{2}$ of these students are boys. How many of these students are boys? ____6____

2. Candy has $\frac{1}{4}$ dollar. Her parents gave her $\frac{2}{4}$ dollar. What fraction tells us the part of a dollar Candy has now? ____$\frac{3}{4}$____

3. Rosa worked 5 of 6 problems correctly. What fraction tells us the part she solved correctly? ____$\frac{5}{6}$____

4. Terry bought $\frac{7}{10}$ meter of material. She used $\frac{5}{10}$ meter. How much material does she have left? ____$\frac{2}{10}$____ meter

5. There were 10 raisins on the plate. Ben took $\frac{1}{2}$ of them and Arturo took $\frac{1}{5}$ of them.

   a. How many raisins did Ben take? ____5____ raisins

   b. How many raisins did Arturo take? ____2____ raisins

   c. How many raisins were left on the plate? ____3____ raisins

6. The baseball team made 6 runs in a game. Sandy made $\frac{1}{2}$ of the runs. Ginger made $\frac{1}{3}$ of the runs. Who made the most runs? ____Sandy____

7. Pizzas are cut into 6 equal pieces. How many pieces are in $1\frac{5}{6}$ pizzas? ____11____

8. There are 9 books on the shelf. Mary says she has read $\frac{1}{3}$ of the books, and June says she has read $\frac{3}{9}$ of the books. Have Mary and June read the same number of books? ____yes____

270

MAGIC SQUARES

4	14	15	1
9	7	6	12
5	11	10	8
16	2	3	13

A square of numbers in which the sums of the rows, the sums of the columns, and the sums of the diagonals are all equal is called a **magic square**.

 A Find these sums.

Rows			
4	9	5	16
14	7	11	2
15	6	10	3
+ 1	+ 12	+ 8	+ 13
34	34	34	34

Columns			
4	14	15	1
9	7	6	12
5	11	10	8
+ 16	+ 2	+ 3	+ 13
34	34	34	34

Diagonals	
4	16
7	11
10	6
+ 13	+ 1
34	34

Are all of the sums equal? ___yes___

Have students complete exercises B and C independently.

B Complete this square of numbers by multiplying 6 times each of the numbers in the square above.

24	84	90	6
54	42	36	72
30	66	60	48
96	12	18	78

1. Add the numbers in each row.

2. Add the numbers in each column.

3. Add the numbers in each diagonal.

4. Is this new square a magic square? ___yes___

C Make up a magic square using the numbers 1, 2, 3, 4, 5, 6, 7, 8, 9. Some of these numbers are already in the square. The magic sum is 15.

2	7	6
9	5	1
4	3	8

CHAPTER REVIEW

 A Different fractions often name the same part of a whole or the same part of a set. Use the pictures to help you complete the sentences.

1.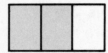

$$\frac{2}{3} = \underline{\frac{4}{6}}$$

2.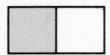

$$\underline{\frac{1}{2}} = \underline{\frac{2}{4}}$$

3.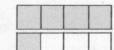

$$\frac{1}{4} = \underline{\frac{2}{8}}$$

4.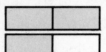

$$\frac{3}{9} = \underline{\frac{1}{3}}$$

5.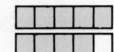

$$\underline{\frac{1}{2}} = \frac{5}{10}$$

B Write < or > in each ● to make the sentence true. Use the pictures to help you.

1. 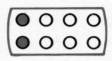 $\quad \frac{1}{2} \;\text{>}\; \frac{1}{4}$ **2.** 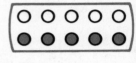 $\quad \frac{1}{2} \;\text{>}\; \frac{1}{3}$

3.  $\quad \frac{2}{3} \;\text{>}\; \frac{1}{2}$ **4.**  $\quad \frac{1}{4} \;\text{>}\; \frac{1}{5}$

C Write the mixed numeral and a fraction for each picture.

1. 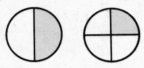 $\quad 1\frac{1}{4} \quad \frac{5}{4}$ **2.** 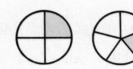 $\quad 1\frac{1}{2} \quad \frac{3}{2}$

3. 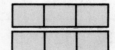 $\quad 2\frac{2}{3} \quad \frac{8}{3}$ **4.** $\quad 1\frac{4}{5} \quad \frac{9}{5}$

D Use the number lines to help you add and subtract.

1.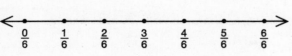

$$\frac{3}{6} + \frac{2}{6} = \underline{\frac{5}{6}}$$

$$\frac{1}{6} + \frac{3}{6} = \underline{\frac{4}{6}}$$

2.

$$\frac{4}{5} - \frac{2}{5} = \underline{\frac{2}{5}}$$

$$\frac{5}{5} - \frac{4}{5} = \underline{\frac{1}{5}}$$

CHECK-UP

 A Write the fraction that tells the part that is shaded.

1.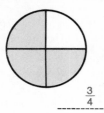

$\frac{3}{4}$

2.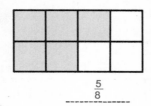

$\frac{5}{8}$

3.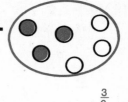

$\frac{3}{6}$

 **B** Use the pictures to help you complete the sentences.

1.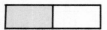

$\frac{1}{2} = \frac{3}{6}$

2.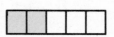

$\frac{2}{5} = \frac{4}{10}$

3.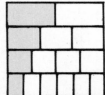

$\frac{4}{8} = \frac{1}{2}$

4.

$\frac{2}{3} = \frac{4}{6}$

C Shade the boxes to show the fraction. Name the shaded part using a mixed numeral.

1. $\frac{9}{5}$

$1\frac{4}{5}$

2. $\frac{5}{2}$

$2\frac{1}{2}$

D Write < or > in each ●. Use the pictures to help you.

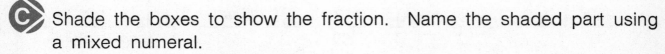

1. $\frac{1}{2}$ ⬤> $\frac{1}{3}$ **2.** $\frac{1}{6}$ ⬤< $\frac{1}{4}$

3. $\frac{1}{6}$ ⬤< $\frac{1}{3}$ **4.** $\frac{1}{3}$ ⬤> $\frac{1}{4}$

E Use the number line to help you complete the sentences.

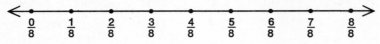

1. $\frac{1}{8} + \frac{2}{8} = \frac{3}{8}$ $\frac{4}{8} + \frac{4}{8} = \frac{8}{8}$ $\frac{3}{8} + \frac{4}{8} = \frac{7}{8}$

2. $\frac{7}{8} - \frac{1}{8} = \frac{6}{8}$ $\frac{5}{8} - \frac{3}{8} = \frac{2}{8}$ $\frac{2}{8} - \frac{2}{8} = \frac{0}{8}$

ADDITION FACTS

1.
  7   4   3   6   1   5   0   4   2   8
+3 +2 +8 +0 +7 +5 +9 +1 +4 +6
10   6   11   6   8   10   9   5   6   14

2.
  5   8   8   3   7   2   1   9   6   4
+3 +2 +8 +0 +7 +5 +9 +1 +4 +6
  8   10 16   3   14   7   10   10   10   10

3.
  2   0   1   5   6   7   3   3   8   9
+3 +2 +8 +0 +7 +5 +9 +1 +4 +6
  5   2   9   5   13   12   12   4   12   15

4.
  8   5   2   0   5   9   2   8   3   1
+3 +2 +8 +0 +7 +5 +9 +1 +4 +6
11   7   10   0   12   14   11   9   7   7

5.
  1   7   0   9   2   3   4   1   5   6
+3 +2 +8 +0 +7 +5 +9 +1 +4 +6
  4   9   8   9   9   8   13   2   9   12

6.
  3   6   5   2   8   4   8   7   0   2
+3 +2 +8 +0 +7 +5 +9 +1 +4 +6
  6   8   13   2   15   9   17   8   4   8

7.
  0   1   4   8   0   6   6   5   7   3
+3 +2 +8 +0 +7 +5 +9 +1 +4 +6
  3   3   12   8   7   11   15   6   11   9

8.
  4   9   9   1   3   0   7   6   4   5
+3 +2 +8 +0 +7 +5 +9 +1 +4 +6
  7   11   17   1   10   5   16   7   8   11

ADDITION PRACTICE

1.
18	70	21	35	71	13	53	12	34
+ 51	+ 25	+ 46	+ 32	+ 16	+ 14	+ 26	+ 30	+ 24
69	95	67	67	87	27	79	42	58

2.
73	81	24	67	92	50	33	48	53
+ 52	+ 95	+ 80	+ 61	+ 95	+ 78	+ 81	+ 60	+ 85
125	176	104	128	187	128	114	108	138

3.
19	58	15	69	47	26	48	57	48
+ 27	+ 29	+ 65	+ 24	+ 28	+ 34	+ 36	+ 19	+ 27
46	87	80	93	75	60	84	76	75

4.
7	6	3	9	8	1	7	6	3
3	9	8	9	6	9	7	7	7
+ 4	+ 4	+ 8	+ 5	+ 5	+ 8	+ 2	+ 6	+ 8
14	19	19	23	19	18	16	19	18

5.
73	35	26	53	30	17	9	52	48
21	17	35	78	95	45	13	40	9
+ 15	+ 64	+ 42	+ 14	+ 6	+ 18	+ 7	+ 18	+ 12
109	116	103	145	131	80	29	110	69

6.
831	527	637	592	637	738	395	408
+ 265	+ 145	+ 180	+ 224	+ 501	+ 247	+ 172	+ 185
1,096	672	817	816	1,138	985	567	593

7.
237	196	804	673	578	294	759	995
+ 385	+ 597	+ 359	+ 354	+ 166	+ 830	+ 324	+ 233
622	793	1,163	1,027	744	1,124	1,083	1,228

8.
635	557	796	848	378	659	372	740
+ 297	+ 843	+ 324	+ 596	+ 227	+ 984	+ 859	+ 395
932	1,400	1,120	1,444	605	1,643	1,231	1,135

9.
273	495	632	708	438	787	269	556
+ 727	+ 885	+ 194	+ 196	+ 683	+ 395	+ 843	+ 478
1,000	1,380	826	904	1,121	1,182	1,112	1,034

ADDITION PRACTICE

1.

$7.53	$5.23	$.65	$.88	$8.90	$4.32	$4.79
+ 1.69	+ .47	+ 1.75	+ .57	+ .75	+ .99	+ 3.59
$9.22	$5.70	$2.40	$1.45	$9.65	$5.31	$8.38

2.

$.88	$7.95	$2.84	$7.60	$.34	$.75	$5.60
+ .88	+ 1.68	+ .59	+ 1.80	+ .89	+ 3.97	+ 2.99
$1.76	$9.63	$3.43	$9.40	$1.23	$4.72	$8.59

3.

2,569	3,429	5,967	3,645	1,936	3,695	6,466
+ 4,754	+ 2,176	+ 2,049	+ 2,649	+ 2,377	+ 2,729	+ 2,487
7,323	5,605	8,016	6,294	4,313	6,424	8,953

4.

4,583	6,345	7,698	5,418	7,923	2,784	7,572
+ 2,974	+ 1,857	+ 1,395	+ 1,683	+ 1,278	+ 3,926	+ 1,098
7,557	8,202	9,093	7,101	9,201	6,710	8,670

5.

1,157	6,071	5,945	1,709	2,668	8,197	3,958
+ 2,967	+ 3,092	+ 2,886	+ 4,493	+ 1,275	+ 1,654	+ 3,768
4,124	9,163	8,831	6,202	3,943	9,851	7,726

6.

$11.38	$15.69	$21.15	$35.65	$62.80	$53.79	$17.18
+ 56.41	+ 13.75	+ 37.95	+ 29.79	+ 17.78	+ 28.32	+ 49.54
$67.79	$29.44	$59.10	$65.44	$80.58	$82.11	$66.72

7.

27	45	64	75	19	83	44	24	38
56	45	32	38	31	72	68	30	38
28	45	70	21	52	35	57	97	38
+ 41	+ 45	+ 53	+ 66	+ 78	+ 69	+ 91	+ 65	+ 38
152	180	219	200	180	259	260	216	152

8.

389	600	408	697	725	452	380	487	357
978	357	162	103	293	79	380	165	94
+ 204	+ 162	+ 873	+ 511	+ 388	+ 168	+ 380	+ 298	+ 88
1,571	1,119	1,443	1,311	1,406	699	1,140	950	539

SUBTRACTION FACTS

1.
$$\begin{array}{r} 5 \\ -4 \\ \hline 1 \end{array}$$
$$\begin{array}{r} 7 \\ -1 \\ \hline 6 \end{array}$$
$$\begin{array}{r} 6 \\ -0 \\ \hline 6 \end{array}$$
$$\begin{array}{r} 12 \\ -6 \\ \hline 6 \end{array}$$
$$\begin{array}{r} 15 \\ -9 \\ \hline 6 \end{array}$$
$$\begin{array}{r} 7 \\ -7 \\ \hline 0 \end{array}$$
$$\begin{array}{r} 14 \\ -7 \\ \hline 7 \end{array}$$
$$\begin{array}{r} 3 \\ -1 \\ \hline 2 \end{array}$$
$$\begin{array}{r} 0 \\ -0 \\ \hline 0 \end{array}$$
$$\begin{array}{r} 4 \\ -3 \\ \hline 1 \end{array}$$

2.
$$\begin{array}{r} 8 \\ -5 \\ \hline 3 \end{array}$$
$$\begin{array}{r} 11 \\ -9 \\ \hline 2 \end{array}$$
$$\begin{array}{r} 16 \\ -7 \\ \hline 9 \end{array}$$
$$\begin{array}{r} 2 \\ -2 \\ \hline 0 \end{array}$$
$$\begin{array}{r} 10 \\ -4 \\ \hline 6 \end{array}$$
$$\begin{array}{r} 6 \\ -3 \\ \hline 3 \end{array}$$
$$\begin{array}{r} 9 \\ -5 \\ \hline 4 \end{array}$$
$$\begin{array}{r} 13 \\ -4 \\ \hline 9 \end{array}$$
$$\begin{array}{r} 8 \\ -2 \\ \hline 6 \end{array}$$
$$\begin{array}{r} 6 \\ -6 \\ \hline 0 \end{array}$$

3.
$$\begin{array}{r} 1 \\ -0 \\ \hline 1 \end{array}$$
$$\begin{array}{r} 5 \\ -2 \\ \hline 3 \end{array}$$
$$\begin{array}{r} 8 \\ -7 \\ \hline 1 \end{array}$$
$$\begin{array}{r} 6 \\ -4 \\ \hline 2 \end{array}$$
$$\begin{array}{r} 10 \\ -3 \\ \hline 7 \end{array}$$
$$\begin{array}{r} 17 \\ -8 \\ \hline 9 \end{array}$$
$$\begin{array}{r} 9 \\ -2 \\ \hline 7 \end{array}$$
$$\begin{array}{r} 10 \\ -8 \\ \hline 2 \end{array}$$
$$\begin{array}{r} 7 \\ -5 \\ \hline 2 \end{array}$$
$$\begin{array}{r} 11 \\ -3 \\ \hline 8 \end{array}$$

4.
$$\begin{array}{r} 9 \\ -6 \\ \hline 3 \end{array}$$
$$\begin{array}{r} 7 \\ -2 \\ \hline 5 \end{array}$$
$$\begin{array}{r} 1 \\ -1 \\ \hline 0 \end{array}$$
$$\begin{array}{r} 9 \\ -9 \\ \hline 0 \end{array}$$
$$\begin{array}{r} 8 \\ -1 \\ \hline 7 \end{array}$$
$$\begin{array}{r} 12 \\ -4 \\ \hline 8 \end{array}$$
$$\begin{array}{r} 9 \\ -3 \\ \hline 6 \end{array}$$
$$\begin{array}{r} 2 \\ -0 \\ \hline 2 \end{array}$$
$$\begin{array}{r} 16 \\ -8 \\ \hline 8 \end{array}$$
$$\begin{array}{r} 3 \\ -3 \\ \hline 0 \end{array}$$

5.
$$\begin{array}{r} 10 \\ -2 \\ \hline 8 \end{array}$$
$$\begin{array}{r} 4 \\ -1 \\ \hline 3 \end{array}$$
$$\begin{array}{r} 8 \\ -8 \\ \hline 0 \end{array}$$
$$\begin{array}{r} 13 \\ -7 \\ \hline 6 \end{array}$$
$$\begin{array}{r} 18 \\ -9 \\ \hline 9 \end{array}$$
$$\begin{array}{r} 5 \\ -3 \\ \hline 2 \end{array}$$
$$\begin{array}{r} 9 \\ -0 \\ \hline 9 \end{array}$$
$$\begin{array}{r} 10 \\ -5 \\ \hline 5 \end{array}$$
$$\begin{array}{r} 13 \\ -9 \\ \hline 4 \end{array}$$
$$\begin{array}{r} 2 \\ -1 \\ \hline 1 \end{array}$$

6.
$$\begin{array}{r} 12 \\ -7 \\ \hline 5 \end{array}$$
$$\begin{array}{r} 15 \\ -8 \\ \hline 7 \end{array}$$
$$\begin{array}{r} 9 \\ -1 \\ \hline 8 \end{array}$$
$$\begin{array}{r} 7 \\ -6 \\ \hline 1 \end{array}$$
$$\begin{array}{r} 3 \\ -2 \\ \hline 1 \end{array}$$
$$\begin{array}{r} 5 \\ -5 \\ \hline 0 \end{array}$$
$$\begin{array}{r} 9 \\ -8 \\ \hline 1 \end{array}$$
$$\begin{array}{r} 11 \\ -2 \\ \hline 9 \end{array}$$
$$\begin{array}{r} 11 \\ -5 \\ \hline 6 \end{array}$$
$$\begin{array}{r} 17 \\ -9 \\ \hline 8 \end{array}$$

7.
$$\begin{array}{r} 4 \\ -4 \\ \hline 0 \end{array}$$
$$\begin{array}{r} 12 \\ -9 \\ \hline 3 \end{array}$$
$$\begin{array}{r} 10 \\ -6 \\ \hline 4 \end{array}$$
$$\begin{array}{r} 6 \\ -1 \\ \hline 5 \end{array}$$
$$\begin{array}{r} 16 \\ -9 \\ \hline 7 \end{array}$$
$$\begin{array}{r} 14 \\ -5 \\ \hline 9 \end{array}$$
$$\begin{array}{r} 11 \\ -8 \\ \hline 3 \end{array}$$
$$\begin{array}{r} 9 \\ -4 \\ \hline 5 \end{array}$$
$$\begin{array}{r} 7 \\ -0 \\ \hline 7 \end{array}$$
$$\begin{array}{r} 4 \\ -2 \\ \hline 2 \end{array}$$

8.
$$\begin{array}{r} 15 \\ -6 \\ \hline 9 \end{array}$$
$$\begin{array}{r} 12 \\ -5 \\ \hline 7 \end{array}$$
$$\begin{array}{r} 9 \\ -7 \\ \hline 2 \end{array}$$
$$\begin{array}{r} 3 \\ -0 \\ \hline 3 \end{array}$$
$$\begin{array}{r} 14 \\ -6 \\ \hline 8 \end{array}$$
$$\begin{array}{r} 7 \\ -3 \\ \hline 4 \end{array}$$
$$\begin{array}{r} 10 \\ -1 \\ \hline 9 \end{array}$$
$$\begin{array}{r} 15 \\ -7 \\ \hline 8 \end{array}$$
$$\begin{array}{r} 13 \\ -5 \\ \hline 8 \end{array}$$
$$\begin{array}{r} 8 \\ -0 \\ \hline 8 \end{array}$$

9.
$$\begin{array}{r} 10 \\ -9 \\ \hline 1 \end{array}$$
$$\begin{array}{r} 8 \\ -3 \\ \hline 5 \end{array}$$
$$\begin{array}{r} 12 \\ -3 \\ \hline 9 \end{array}$$
$$\begin{array}{r} 5 \\ -1 \\ \hline 4 \end{array}$$
$$\begin{array}{r} 7 \\ -4 \\ \hline 3 \end{array}$$
$$\begin{array}{r} 14 \\ -8 \\ \hline 6 \end{array}$$
$$\begin{array}{r} 11 \\ -4 \\ \hline 7 \end{array}$$
$$\begin{array}{r} 5 \\ -0 \\ \hline 5 \end{array}$$
$$\begin{array}{r} 10 \\ -7 \\ \hline 3 \end{array}$$
$$\begin{array}{r} 14 \\ -9 \\ \hline 5 \end{array}$$

SUBTRACTION PRACTICE

1.

43	78	85	47	54	98	69	57	89
−12	−24	−32	−34	−44	−65	−31	−12	−83
31	54	53	13	10	33	38	45	6

2.

86	92	41	54	47	73	21	92	50
−8	−6	−6	−9	−8	−7	−4	−7	−3
78	86	35	45	39	66	17	85	47

3.

94	60	53	77	93	71	85	56	92
−35	−27	−19	−48	−29	−38	−28	−27	−44
59	33	34	29	64	33	57	29	48

4.

135	169	107	321	278	456	304	283	148
−64	−92	−57	−80	−93	−73	−42	−91	−77
71	77	50	241	185	383	262	192	71

5.

413	324	963	254	150	315	630	846	521
−85	−95	−67	−76	−95	−39	−54	−88	−46
328	229	896	178	55	276	576	758	475

6.

983	460	746	739	673	815	872	985	649
−752	−150	−213	−514	−372	−414	−520	−131	−232
231	310	533	225	301	401	352	854	417

7.

784	642	831	395	290	876	581	931	894
−358	−316	−324	−146	−125	−549	−262	−217	−635
426	326	507	249	165	327	319	714	259

8.

419	809	576	628	765	337	643	715	974
−285	−419	−182	−383	−194	−263	−152	−482	−594
134	390	394	245	571	74	491	233	380

9.

832	576	457	985	642	841	627	710	613
−654	−197	−169	−896	−275	−542	−379	−542	−436
178	379	288	89	367	299	248	168	177

SUBTRACTION PRACTICE

1.

$.89	$.07	$.60	$.98	$.63	$.75	$.50
− .64	− .02	− .29	− .90	− .17	− .08	− .32
$.25	$.05	$.31	$.08	$.46	$.67	$.18

2.

$1.65	$7.49	$5.25	$2.38	$8.29	$1.25	$3.70
− .95	− 2.30	− 3.16	− 2.19	− 3.29	− .78	− 2.95
$0.70	$5.19	$2.09	$0.19	$5.00	$0.47	$0.75

3.

304	500	702	900	400	207	603
− 167	− 241	− 109	− 207	− 175	− 189	− 394
137	259	593	693	225	18	209

4.

6,738	5,392	8,654	9,285	7,186	5,489	6,379
− 1,502	− 2,162	− 4,351	− 7,053	− 1,124	− 3,425	− 1,342
5,236	3,230	4,303	2,232	6,062	2,064	5,037

5.

8,645	3,826	8,494	5,860	6,514	9,632	4,519
− 4,927	− 1,188	− 2,795	− 3,482	− 2,736	− 1,824	− 1,618
3,718	2,638	5,699	2,378	3,778	7,808	2,901

6.

8,852	7,685	9,148	9,572	3,685	8,746	5,041
− 1,647	− 2,997	− 3,568	− 5,285	− 2,596	− 3,784	− 1,928
7,205	4,688	5,580	4,287	1,089	4,962	3,113

7.

7,103	6,025	4,001	7,000	2,070	5,009	6,021
− 2,356	− 1,773	− 2,607	− 3,955	− 1,352	− 2,736	− 5,748
4,747	4,252	1,394	3,045	718	2,273	273

8.

4,087	2,756	1,004	3,674	5,023	2,903	9,030
− 953	− 899	− 227	− 887	− 364	− 459	− 487
3,134	1,857	777	2,787	4,659	2,444	8,543

9.

$72.40	$34.70	$17.43	$53.60	$50.00	$30.75	$8.73
− 31.70	− 6.85	− 10.95	− 37.84	− 17.98	− 15.91	− 1.79
$40.70	$27.85	$ 6.48	$15.76	$32.02	$14.84	$6.94

MULTIPLICATION FACTS

1.
4	5	0	6	2	9	4	6	9	0
×1	×3	×1	×3	×8	×9	×0	×9	×1	×4
4	15	0	18	16	81	0	54	9	0

2.
1	9	2	2	1	8	9	5	3	4
×6	×2	×3	×5	×3	×7	×3	×7	×5	×4
6	18	6	10	3	56	27	35	15	16

3.
0	7	7	1	8	1	6	7	3	6
×6	×9	×1	×0	×0	×8	×4	×2	×9	×7
0	63	7	0	0	8	24	14	27	42

4.
6	2	4	9	7	6	1	0	1	7
×6	×0	×2	×0	×6	×1	×5	×3	×4	×4
36	0	8	0	42	6	5	0	4	28

5.
9	4	3	1	7	2	9	6	4	5
×6	×6	×7	×7	×5	×1	×7	×8	×3	×1
54	24	21	7	35	2	63	48	12	5

6.
7	3	8	4	3	5	5	3	8	6
×0	×3	×9	×8	×2	×0	×9	×4	×6	×2
0	9	72	32	6	0	45	12	48	12

7.
7	5	2	3	0	8	8	1	4	6
×7	×4	×7	×6	×9	×1	×3	×9	×7	×5
49	20	14	18	0	8	24	9	28	30

8.
1	4	8	0	5	2	4	7	0	8
×2	×9	×2	×2	×5	×9	×5	×8	×5	×5
2	36	16	0	25	18	20	56	0	40

9.
0	2	5	8	9	5	0	5	7	2
×0	×6	×2	×8	×4	×6	×7	×8	×3	×4
0	12	10	64	36	30	0	40	21	8

MULTIPLICATION PRACTICE

1.
33	41	60	52	32	13	21	24	43
× 2	× 7	× 3	× 4	× 3	× 2	× 9	× 2	× 3
66	287	180	208	96	26	189	48	129

2.
23	34	42	61	84	40	22	31	54
× 3	× 2	× 4	× 6	× 2	× 5	× 3	× 8	× 2
69	68	168	366	168	200	66	248	108

3.
45	54	37	96	78	28	74	16	39
× 2	× 6	× 8	× 5	× 3	× 7	× 4	× 9	× 3
90	324	296	480	234	196	296	144	117

4.
62	47	35	72	98	55	83	47	53
× 8	× 3	× 9	× 6	× 2	× 4	× 5	× 7	× 9
496	141	315	432	196	220	415	329	477

5.
75	67	34	85	57	84	68	96	59
× 6	× 2	× 7	× 8	× 5	× 9	× 3	× 8	× 2
450	134	238	680	285	756	204	768	118

6.
700	610	400	320	501	930	702	423
× 5	× 7	× 8	× 4	× 5	× 3	× 4	× 3
3,500	4,270	3,200	1,280	2,505	2,790	2,808	1,269

7.
624	421	942	813	711	520	601	400
× 2	× 4	× 2	× 3	× 6	× 3	× 9	× 7
1,248	1,684	1,884	2,439	4,266	1,560	5,409	2,800

8.
328	235	119	237	318	726	419	513
× 3	× 2	× 4	× 2	× 5	× 3	× 4	× 7
984	470	476	474	1,590	2,178	1,676	3,591

9.
752	340	681	453	760	982	791	482
× 4	× 9	× 6	× 3	× 8	× 4	× 7	× 2
3,008	3,060	4,086	1,359	6,080	3,928	5,537	964

DIVISION FACTS

1. $3\overline{)18}$ = 6 $1\overline{)7}$ = 7 $5\overline{)10}$ = 2 $6\overline{)36}$ = 6 $2\overline{)10}$ = 5 $8\overline{)16}$ = 2

2. $5\overline{)5}$ = 1 $7\overline{)21}$ = 3 $1\overline{)9}$ = 9 $4\overline{)28}$ = 7 $9\overline{)27}$ = 3 $3\overline{)9}$ = 3

3. $2\overline{)16}$ = 8 $9\overline{)36}$ = 4 $6\overline{)6}$ = 1 $7\overline{)63}$ = 9 $5\overline{)25}$ = 5 $8\overline{)64}$ = 8

4. $5\overline{)35}$ = 7 $2\overline{)4}$ = 2 $7\overline{)28}$ = 4 $1\overline{)4}$ = 4 $4\overline{)32}$ = 8 $9\overline{)63}$ = 7

5. $7\overline{)42}$ = 6 $4\overline{)20}$ = 5 $5\overline{)20}$ = 4 $6\overline{)54}$ = 9 $2\overline{)14}$ = 7 $8\overline{)40}$ = 5

6. $3\overline{)3}$ = 1 $6\overline{)12}$ = 2 $4\overline{)12}$ = 3 $6\overline{)42}$ = 7 $3\overline{)24}$ = 8 $5\overline{)45}$ = 9

7. $6\overline{)24}$ = 4 $3\overline{)15}$ = 5 $8\overline{)56}$ = 7 $6\overline{)48}$ = 8 $7\overline{)35}$ = 5 $3\overline{)27}$ = 9

8. $2\overline{)8}$ = 4 $5\overline{)40}$ = 8 $8\overline{)32}$ = 4 $3\overline{)12}$ = 4 $1\overline{)6}$ = 6 $8\overline{)8}$ = 1

9. $5\overline{)30}$ = 6 $2\overline{)18}$ = 9 $9\overline{)9}$ = 1 $9\overline{)45}$ = 5 $4\overline{)16}$ = 4 $6\overline{)30}$ = 5

10. $7\overline{)7}$ = 1 $3\overline{)6}$ = 2 $7\overline{)49}$ = 7 $4\overline{)24}$ = 6 $9\overline{)72}$ = 8 $5\overline{)15}$ = 3

11. $9\overline{)54}$ = 6 $6\overline{)18}$ = 3 $3\overline{)21}$ = 7 $1\overline{)8}$ = 8 $4\overline{)8}$ = 2 $9\overline{)9}$ = 1

12. $7\overline{)56}$ = 8 $4\overline{)4}$ = 1 $8\overline{)24}$ = 3 $4\overline{)36}$ = 9 $1\overline{)3}$ = 3 $2\overline{)12}$ = 6

13. $8\overline{)72}$ = 9 $2\overline{)6}$ = 3 $9\overline{)18}$ = 2 $1\overline{)5}$ = 5 $8\overline{)48}$ = 6 $7\overline{)14}$ = 2

DIVISION PRACTICE

Find the quotients and remainders.

1.
$\overset{4\ r\ 1}{4\overline{)17}}$ $\overset{3\ r\ 2}{7\overline{)23}}$ $\overset{5\ r\ 5}{6\overline{)35}}$ $\overset{6\ r\ 1}{5\overline{)31}}$ $\overset{3\ r\ 3}{9\overline{)30}}$ $\overset{7\ r\ 1}{2\overline{)15}}$ $\overset{7\ r\ 1}{3\overline{)22}}$

2.
$\overset{4\ r\ 5}{8\overline{)37}}$ $\overset{9\ r\ 3}{5\overline{)48}}$ $\overset{4\ r\ 3}{9\overline{)39}}$ $\overset{7\ r\ 3}{7\overline{)52}}$ $\overset{2\ r\ 2}{4\overline{)10}}$ $\overset{7\ r\ 3}{4\overline{)31}}$ $\overset{4\ r\ 1}{2\overline{)9}}$

3.
$\overset{5\ r\ 2}{3\overline{)17}}$ $\overset{5\ r\ 5}{8\overline{)45}}$ $\overset{3\ r\ 2}{6\overline{)20}}$ $\overset{9\ r\ 2}{4\overline{)38}}$ $\overset{5\ r\ 7}{9\overline{)52}}$ $\overset{4\ r\ 4}{5\overline{)24}}$ $\overset{8\ r\ 4}{7\overline{)60}}$

4.
$\overset{22}{4\overline{)88}}$ $\overset{41}{6\overline{)246}}$ $\overset{53}{5\overline{)265}}$ $\overset{97}{3\overline{)291}}$ $\overset{59}{6\overline{)354}}$ $\overset{75}{4\overline{)300}}$ $\overset{64}{8\overline{)512}}$

5.
$\overset{35}{7\overline{)245}}$ $\overset{48}{2\overline{)96}}$ $\overset{25}{4\overline{)100}}$ $\overset{11}{7\overline{)77}}$ $\overset{21}{9\overline{)189}}$ $\overset{53}{6\overline{)318}}$ $\overset{94}{3\overline{)282}}$

6.
$\overset{86}{3\overline{)258}}$ $\overset{46}{7\overline{)322}}$ $\overset{42}{2\overline{)84}}$ $\overset{63}{3\overline{)189}}$ $\overset{77}{5\overline{)385}}$ $\overset{42}{9\overline{)378}}$ $\overset{77}{4\overline{)308}}$

7.
$\overset{11\ r\ 3}{5\overline{)58}}$ $\overset{16\ r\ 1}{4\overline{)65}}$ $\overset{13\ r\ 2}{6\overline{)80}}$ $\overset{18\ r\ 1}{2\overline{)37}}$ $\overset{21\ r\ 2}{3\overline{)65}}$ $\overset{13\ r\ 7}{9\overline{)124}}$ $\overset{12\ r\ 5}{7\overline{)89}}$

8.
$$\overset{34\ r\ 1}{7\overline{)239}}\quad \overset{52\ r\ 2}{3\overline{)158}}\quad \overset{52\ r\ 2}{9\overline{)470}}\quad \overset{81\ r\ 2}{5\overline{)407}}\quad \overset{49\ r\ 2}{8\overline{)394}}\quad \overset{92\ r\ 1}{2\overline{)185}}\quad \overset{23\ r\ 3}{4\overline{)95}}$$

9.
$$\overset{36\ r\ 2}{6\overline{)218}}\quad \overset{70\ r\ 3}{8\overline{)563}}\quad \overset{34\ r\ 1}{4\overline{)137}}\quad \overset{42\ r\ 2}{7\overline{)296}}\quad \overset{85\ r\ 3}{5\overline{)428}}\quad \overset{93\ r\ 7}{9\overline{)844}}\quad \overset{42\ r\ 1}{3\overline{)127}}$$

10.
$$\overset{8\ r\ 2}{5\overline{)42}}\quad \overset{12\ r\ 4}{7\overline{)88}}\quad \overset{89}{6\overline{)534}}\quad \overset{8\ r\ 8}{9\overline{)80}}\quad \overset{9}{7\overline{)63}}\quad \overset{16\ r\ 1}{4\overline{)65}}\quad \overset{31}{8\overline{)248}}$$

11.
$$\overset{21\ r\ 1}{4\overline{)85}}\quad \overset{32\ r\ 1}{9\overline{)289}}\quad \overset{67}{2\overline{)134}}\quad \overset{47\ r\ 1}{5\overline{)236}}\quad \overset{11\ r\ 7}{8\overline{)95}}\quad \overset{14}{6\overline{)84}}\quad \overset{9\ r\ 2}{3\overline{)29}}$$

12.
$$\overset{46\ r\ 7}{8\overline{)375}}\quad \overset{56}{3\overline{)168}}\quad \overset{36}{7\overline{)252}}\quad \overset{8}{4\overline{)32}}\quad \overset{78}{9\overline{)702}}\quad \overset{52\ r\ 1}{2\overline{)105}}\quad \overset{54\ r\ 2}{6\overline{)326}}$$

13.
$$\overset{7}{10\overline{)70}}\quad \overset{9}{40\overline{)360}}\quad \overset{3}{70\overline{)210}}\quad \overset{8}{80\overline{)640}}\quad \overset{9}{30\overline{)270}}\quad \overset{8}{60\overline{)480}}$$

14.
$$\overset{6}{50\overline{)300}}\quad \overset{7}{20\overline{)140}}\quad \overset{8}{90\overline{)720}}\quad \overset{6}{40\overline{)240}}\quad \overset{7}{70\overline{)490}}\quad \overset{7}{80\overline{)560}}$$